ĽUDOVÍT ŠTÚR
SLAVDOM

A Selection
of his Writings, in Prose
and Verse

This book was published with a financial support from SLOLIA,
Centre for Information on Literature in Bratislava

SLAVDOM

A Selection of his Writings, in Prose and Verse

by Ľudovít Štúr

Translated from the Slovak and introduced by
Charles S. Kraszewski

This book was published with a financial support from SLOLIA,
Centre for Information on Literature in Bratislava

Proofreading by Jonathan Campion

Publishers Maxim Hodak & Max Mendor

Book cover and interior design by Max Mendor

Cover image:
'Ľudovít Štúr' by Jozef Božetech Klemens (1872)

Introduction © 2021, Charles S. Kraszewski

© 2021, Glagoslav Publications

www.glagoslav.com

ISBN: 978-1-914337-01-7

First published in English
by Glagoslav Publications in March 2021

A catalogue record for this book is available from the British Library.

This book is in copyright. No part of this publication may be reproduced, stored in a retrieval system or transmitted in any form or by any means without the prior permission in writing of the publisher, nor be otherwise circulated in any form of binding or cover other than that in which it is published without a similar condition, including this condition, being imposed on the subsequent purchaser.

ĽUDOVIT ŠTÚR
SLAVDOM

A Selection of his Writings, in Prose and Verse

Translated from the Slovak and Introduced by
Charles S. Kraszewski

GLAGOSLAV PUBLICATIONS

Contents

INTRODUCTION:
No Justice, No Peace! Well, I Guess That Means No Peace.
Ľudovít Štúr and the Naïve Optimism
of the Innocent Nineteenth Century 7

SLOVAKIA 59
– A Journey Through the Region of the Váh 60
– The Slovaks, in Ancient Days and Now 65
– Svatoboj 124
– Matúš of Trenčín 141
– A Letter from a Hungarian Slav
  to the Editors of the *Literary Weekly* 185
– At Ján Hollý's Monument 188

PAN-SLAVISM 189
– A Journey to Lusatia 190
– Slavs, Brothers! 212
– *from* Štúr's Address to the Slavic Congress 213
– Speech at the Slavic Linden 217
– A Glance at Current Events in Slavdom, 1848 220
– The Contributions of the Slavs to European Civilisation . . 225
– Pan-Slavism and our Country 236

RUSSIA 247
– Pushkin. A Lament 248
– The Russians 250
– Slavdom and the World of the Future 252

GLOSSARY 325

BIBLIOGRAPHY 349

ABOUT THE AUTHOR 352

ABOUT THE TRANSLATOR 354

No Justice, No Peace! Well, I Guess That Means No Peace
Ľudovít Štúr and the Naïve Optimism of the Innocent Nineteenth Century

C.S. Kraszewski

I don't remember the first time I read the 'Journey through the Region of the Váh,' but it certainly was a long time ago. At any rate, when first I did, my eyes passed over the following sentence (in which Ľudovít Štúr records his first impressions of the poet Jan Hollý) without resting upon them for more than the time it took to scan them: 'The pleasant countenance and grey hair of this old man of fifty-six years lend him an especial charm that enchants the person who gazes upon him.' But now… those same eyes stopped dead in their tracks. 'Old man?!… fifty-six!?' For I passed that milestone two years ago and… Oh well. What's the use. I'm noting this down here not out of self-pity or vanity or anything of that sort. What really strikes me is how texts change over time, or at least the manner in which we read them does. We have a tendency to accept them, unthinkingly, like monuments carved in stone, as unchanging as the Discobolus, for example. After all, no one imagines that Myron's athlete will ever complete his motion, fling the discus, and reach for something else, like a javelin or a baseball bat. Literature is the same, in a manner of speaking, of course. The manner in which Dostoevsky spins out Raskolnikov's thoughts from the time we first meet him until he murders the old pawnbroker is so excruciatingly slow as we pass along Nevsky Prospekt with him — it takes a full 70 pages before the axe finally falls — that we're almost fooled into hoping that maybe 'this time' he'll turn away from the murder… But we know that this is impossible. *Crime and Punishment* does not change. But we do; the manner in which we read things changes as we change, due to our life experiences, due to the history that goes on around us, touching upon us, invading our consciousness, to a greater or lesser degree.

A better example of this can be found in the work of one of the great Slavic poets that Štúr mentions from time to time in his writings. In his narrative poem *Konrad Wallenrod*, which tells the story of a young Lithuanian lad who wishes to deliver his homeland from the invading German Knights of the Cross, the boy receives the following advice from an old bard (which determines his plan of action):

> 'Free knights,' he said, 'can choose which arms they please
> And on the open field fight man to man.
> You're a slave. Your only weapon's guile.
> Stay on and learn the German arts of war.
> First get their trust, then we'll see what comes next.'

'What comes next' is, Konrad passes himself off as one of them, with the premeditated plan of leading them to their destruction.

Konrad Wallenrod is one of the most important texts of Polish literature, one written by the greatest authority in nineteenth-century Polish life. Konrad may be a problematic character, but he has never been considered as anything less than a basically *positive* hero. Given the history of Mickiewicz's country, which has so often had to face overwhelming odds in its quest to survive, the no-holds-barred approach to national liberation outlined in the old man's advice — the 'strategy of the fox' as opposed to the 'strategy of the lion' — has generally been considered admissible given the extenuating circumstances. But now? Can we read these lines the same way after 11 September 2001, the nineteenth anniversary of which passed just six days previous to the date on which I'm writing this? Is it possible to see Konrad Wallenrod (whose name itself is a disguise; he was born Walter Alf) as anything but the violent terrorist of a sleeper cell, whose strings are pulled by a scheming imam? I may be exaggerating here, but it should be obvious, I reckon, that the matter is no longer as straightforward as it used to be. The text is the same, but we have changed.

My reception of the works included in this translation has changed too — and that over the course of just a few months. At least half of the translation, with which I am now busied, was completed in the United States, most recently, during the social unrest and 'calls for justice' that have roiled American streets during the summer of 2020. Watching the riots unfold, bombarded in a way that we never have been before, thanks to the never-ending 'news' programmes and ubiquitous cell-phone film-clips, it is impossible to read the bright shining lines, with which Štúr brings 'The Contribution of the

Slavs to European Civilisation' to a close without a jaded smirk. 'Humanity, in its progress, can simply never retrogress.' Really? Then why have we 'progressed' such a very little way in race relations since the 1960s, to say nothing of the 1860s? And on the other hand, is there not at least some naïveté in the convictions of the righteously angry marchers who seem to share Štúr's positive faith in actually getting something *done*?

Is not the promise of a great and better future nothing more than a political slogan, which reeks with added stench due to the corrupt lips that pronounce it, begging for our votes? If anything, the last four or five years seem to teach us that the idea of slow, but sure, and always incrementally further progress toward an ever better world is a myth. A myth no less fanciful and illusory than Marxist messianism, with its promise of the State eventually withering away as something unnecessary to a newer, progressively more angelic, I suppose, society. Human nature being what it is — and it's certainly not a very pretty little thing — humanity is not progressing along the straight upward line that optimists like Štúr have in mind, but rather is spinning in a vicious circle. The same old hatreds and problems, the same old brutal solutions in dealing with them, keep coming round and round again — whether it be 1848, 1948, or 2048, ad infinitum. To read Ľudovít Štúr, or any of the innocent nineteenth century nationalists, marching and protesting for justice for their own particular groups 'justly,' we must not forget that they were not destined to live through the bloody first half of the twentieth century, when their ontological definitions of nationhood, based on language and — as they would use the term — race, would lead, not to the

> …dawn of the long yearned-for, long demanded age of humanity [...] where] in place of the old congresses there shall be congresses of the nations, determining international affairs

as he puts it in 'The Russians,' but — the *Blitzkrieg* and the *Gulag* and the *Black Site*; the genocide of nations in Auschwitz, in the broad picture, and armed violence among neighbours who suddenly see one another as viscerally different, in the small. Is it imaginable that this basically decent man, a Lutheran pastor, with a heart big enough to think the best of the Magyar oppressors of his Slovak nation, trusting that one day 'they will shake off [their] bias and seek enlightenment and liberty not only for [themselves], but for others, especially the Slavs' ('Pan-Slavism and our Country'), would speak of the 'filthy clutches of the Jews' ('Slavdom and the World of the Future') if he knew what was awaiting them less than a century after he wrote that essay?

We have a broader perspective than Ľudovít Štúr, having recently marked the eightieth anniversary of the hell of World War II — something he surely could never have imagined happening in that bright future toward which humanity, he felt, was progressing. Now, if you're not going to say it, Sunshine, permit me to: there will be no justice, or peace, on this earth, ever. The closest we can get to optimism is that famous phrase that Štúr, if anyone, should know by rote: *inquietum est cor nostrum, donec requiescat in te;* 'our heart is restless, until it rest in Thee.'[1] Let's keep these things in mind, then, as we proceed to a consideration of the writings of Ľudovít Štúr, especially when we hear him say things like, 'First, the Magyar must be destroyed, and then, let the Danube unite our regions' ('Address to the Slavic Congress') or 'The Russian character is very attractive to all of our tribes who have not become alienated from their nature' ('Slavdom and the World of the Future'). Ľudovít Štúr must be read in the context of his times and his reality, times different from our own, the only reality he knew.

ĽUDOVÍT ŠTÚR, HUNGARIAN

The land into which Ľudovít Štúr (1815 - 1856) was born on 29 October of the year in which 'that colossus of a man' Napoléon[2] returned in triumph to France, only to arrive, at last, at Waterloo, was the multinational Kingdom of Hungary. Francis of Habsburg, the last of the Austrian Emperors to bear the title Holy Roman Emperor, was on the throne of what was later to become the Dual Monarchy of Austria-Hungary. When Štúr was thirty-three years old, in the tumultuous year of 1848, he was to witness the abdication of the beloved, ostensibly feeble-minded Ferdinand in favour of Franz Josef. This last-named, equally beloved of many, Emperor of Austria and King of Hungary, was to reign until his death in 1916 amid the catastrophe that would bring an end to the Austro-Hungarian Empire, and the establishment of the first Republic of Czechoslovakia — a fraternal unification of two closely-related Slavic 'tribes' such as Štúr longed for, and struggled for, all throughout his life.[3]

----

[1] St Augustine, *Confessions*, 1.1.2.
[2] Štúr, 'Pan-Slavism and our Country.'
[3] The last Habsburg Emperor was Franz Joseph's great-nephew, Bl. Karl I (1887 - 1922). Having inherited the misfortune of World War I, Karl worked behind the scenes to bring an end to the slaughter, and extricate his land from the conflict, whole. This was impossible, for many reasons, of course. Never abdicating the throne per se, he was exiled from the newly-proclaimed Republic of Austria. Attempts at reclaiming the throne of Hungary in 1921 were unsuccessful.

Like Austria itself, Hungary was home to many nationalities. The dominant ethnicity, the Magyars (the name of whom we conflate with 'Hungarian' today)[4] constituted some 50% of the population of the kingdom, which also contained sizeable numbers of Romanians, Germans, and of course Slavs — Slovaks, mainly in the mountainous north, bordering Polish, Moravian, and Austrian regions, and Croats to the south-west, along the Adriatic, with a good number of Serbs as well. It is for this reason that Štúr defines himself, interchangeably, as 'Slovak' and 'Hungarian Slav', using both terms, for example in his 1839 letter to the Polish-language *Tygodnik literacki* [Literary Weekly] in Poznań.[5] During Štúr's lifetime, the Magyars, a Finno-Ugric people who migrated into the Danube region in the late IX c., initiated a programme of successively greater linguistic and cultural repression of the ethnic minorities living in Hungary, replacing, for example, the lingua franca of Latin with Magyar as sole administrative language of the Kingdom, in 1840. This put an end to the idyllic period — if there ever was one — when in that 'one, Hungarian homeland, 'Magyar and Slovak lived proudly, [...] both being faithfully devoted to that common mother. [...] And they found it good to reside here, for the land waxed in prosperity and brotherhood.'[6]

It sounds so simplistic, but great matters sometimes are. Had the nations that made up Hungary respected each other's cultural autonomy, holding to Latin as the official, administrative tongue of all, while encouraging, or at least tolerating, the development of regional languages as far as literature and basic education were concerned, a lot of blood and tears might not have been shed, families not riven by disputes in which surface appearance (language) becomes more important than inner essence (humanity).[7] After all, Štúr, who

---

He was raised to the altar by St Pope John Paul II in 2004; the beatification process of his wife, Servant of God Zita, is ongoing as of 2020.

[4] According to Paul Robert Magocsi, the name itself is derived from 'Onogur,' which signified a 'loose federation of Finno-Ugric and Bulgar-Turkic tribes' of which the Magyars formed a part. See Magocsi, *With their Backs to the Mountains: A History of Carpathian Rus' and Carpatho-Rusyns* (Budapest and New York: Central European University Press, 2015), p. 41.

[5] 'List Słowaka Węgierskiego do redakcji *Tygodnika Literackiego* [The Letter of a Hungarian Slav to the Editors of the Literary Weekly], 21 January 1839. Collected in Ľudovít Štúr, *Wybór pism* [Selected Writings], ed. Halina Janaszek-Ivaničková (Wrocław: Ossolineum, 1983), pp. 406-412. Štúr wrote the letter originally in Polish.

[6] Štúr, 'The Slovaks, in Ancient Days and Now.'

[7] Hungarian history provides us with an eloquent example. Lajos Kossuth (1802 – 1894), father of the modern ethnic Hungarian state and determined magyariser, was of Slovak extraction; his uncle Juraj Košút (1776 – 1849), was just as strong a supporter of Slovak nationality.

gives as good as he gets in the rough polemical warfare between Magyar and Slav, was still able to write, in his 'Pan-Slavism and our Country:'

> In the end, our firm belief is that when the Magyars progress further in education and culture; when, as a consequence, they become more thoughtful and just, when they reflect more closely upon their state, their situation, and understand it better, more than one of them will shake off his bias and seek enlightenment and liberty not only for himself, but for others, especially the Slavs. What is more, not only will they wish it for the Slavs, they will actively engage in aiding them to its acquisition, [...] from good will, true conviction, and, let us still add — from prudence. We firmly believe that this will come to pass, we say, and, further, we believe also that we shall see the days when each oppression, indeed every incitement to oppression of the Slavs, will meet with round rejection and condemnation, while the more sublime amongst the Magyars will aid the Slavs to greater development and liberty, working toward these goals and publicly encouraging them.

Alas, we alone can look backwards with a perfect clarity. Generous statements like these are, as we are about to see, more than balanced in Štúr's writings with diatribes of an almost xenophobic character, and even here it is not difficult to sense a hint of 'or else' in his suggestion that, along with good will and conviction, the Magyars might be swayed 'by prudence.'

Again, we see things that happened almost two hundred years ago quite clearly. We cannot expect the same prescience from those involved in the heat of the moment, who — like ourselves now — cannot see the future. Unfortunately, Štúr's was an age of ethnonationalism, and it was the centripetal force of the fashionable concept of the *Volk* which was to lead to the premature dismemberment of Austria-Hungary, that European Union *avant le mot,* as Rio Preisner, a Czech devotee of *humanitas austriaca* notes:

> Throughout its entire existence the Austrian monarchy was bound to the preservation of the cultural and political integrity of Central Europe, in opposition to Germany and Russia. Its tragedy was that both the Germans and the Russians understood, and to a certain extent respected, this task of hers, whereas the nations that constituted Austria did not.[8]

---

[8] Rio Preisner, *Až na konec Česka* [To the Very End of Czechia] (London: Rozmluvy, 1987), p. 238.

For Austria-Hungary was evolving in a manner that might well have filled Štúr with hope, had he lived until the turn of the century. After the Meyerling tragedy, Franz Ferdinand, nephew of Franz Josef, became heir to the throne. Morganatically married to the Czech Žofie Chotková, he, if any, was the emperor to lift the Slavs — constituting a full 47% of the population — to fuller participation in the life of the state. As David Fromkin notes in his magisterial work on the First World War, *Europe's Last Summer*:

> According to [...] informants, it was the belief of the conspirators that Franz Ferdinand advocated 'trialism': he intended to make the Slavs full partners in government along with Austro-Germans and Hungarians [*i.e. Magyars*. ... And yet the Serb Gavrilo] Princip, who killed Franz Ferdinand, did so for a muddle of misinformed reasons. Although the Archduke was the most pro-Slav member of the Habsburg hierarchy, the youth believed that he was anti-Slav.[9]

The discouraging thing in the above citation is not Princip's mistaken belief in the heir's anti-Slavism, but the conspirators' motivation to do away with him *because* his pro-Slavic stance would defuse centripetal ethnonationalism among the Serbs, and preserve the multi-national monarchy, which they wanted to break apart. With the irony that only history — and stupid humanity — can provide, Franz Ferdinand, who was murdered by a Serb terrorist worried at Austrian designs upon his country, had recently told dinner guests 'that Austria had nothing to gain from conquering Serbia; going to war would be "a bit of nonsense."' So, Slavs killed a pro-Slav on behalf of the Slavs. Because the pro-Slavic policies of the pro-Slav 'might deprive them of their issue.'[10] And history shows us, unfortunately, how important 'issues' are to some people.

ĽUDOVÍT ŠTÚR'S ISSUE

The period in which Štúr was born is marked by a resurgence of ethnic consciousness among the constituent nations of Austria and Hungary — the Habsburg Empire. Following the defeat of the Hussite forces at the battle of Bílá Hora in 1620, which initiated a decades-long process of germanisation

---

[9] David Fromkin, *Europe's Last Summer: Who Started the Great War in 1917?* (New York: Vintage, 2007), pp 122, 261.
[10] Fromkin, pp. 100, 122.

amongst the Czechs of Bohemia and Moravia, the Czech language declined to such an extent that it had practically disappeared from all classes of society, save the peasantry. To get ahead in the new reality of Austrian Bohemia, one had to know German. Likewise, the ascendancy of Magyar in the Slovak lands was aided by its adoption among the noble families of the Slavic areas on the southern slopes of the Tatras — such as the Kossuths. Although the great swathes of the Slovak peasantry held to their tongue, here too it remained little more than an ethnolect, given the predominance of Latin in Catholic circles, and Czech among Protestant Slovaks. Neither the one language nor the other, Czech nor Slovak, offered much practical advantage, and even the young Štúr, at twelve, was sent by his parents over 100 miles south from his birth city of Uhrovec to a gymnasium in Ráb (now Győr, in Hungary) 'in order to deepen his knowledge of German and Magyar.'[11]

The mollifying of Counter-Reformative policies during the reign of the enlightened emperor Josef II (1780 – 1790) led not only to decrees of religious tolerance for the non-Catholic minorities of his realms, but also to the 1786 Civil Code, which, among other things, guaranteed national minorities the right to use their native languages. Although a germaniser himself, Josef made provision for the teaching of religion in elementary schools to be carried out in the native language of the pupils.[12]

Such tentative liberalisation — however gradual — was one factor among many others in the *národní obrození* or 'national revival' of the Czech areas, during which the native, Slavic tongue was resurrected as a language of cultural discourse by scholars and poets such as Josef Jungmann (1773 – 1847) and Antonín Jaroslav Puchmajer (1769 – 1820), and the first codification of Slovak as a literary language independent of Czech was carried out by Anton Bernolák (1762 – 1813). And while there still was a strong tendency toward amalgamating the two kindred dialects by important 'Czechoslovak' poets such as Ján Kollár (1793 – 1852), other Slovaks, like the great epic poet Ján Hollý (1785 – 1849), adopted the so-called *Bernoláčina* and through their works proved Slovak to be a literary language of great expressiveness. All of this activity, which pushed both deep — toward a reacquisition of Czech and Slovak by the cultured classes under the tutelage of the village, the collection of folk-songs and the scouring of libraries for ancient documents in the Slavic tongue[13] — and broad — the grafting of Polish and Russian terms

---

[11] Janaszek-Ivaničková, p. xvii.

[12] Janaszek-Ivaničková, p. viii.

[13] Such as we find described in 'A Journey through the Region of the Váh,' in which the

onto the native trunks (especially in the case of Czech), was to influence Štúr both as a Slovak 'son of the Tatras' and a Pan-Slav, addressing Russians and Croats and Lusatians as his brothers[14] — and this from his earliest years. According to Janaszek-Ivaničková:

> The education he commenced in Ráb blossomed in a way different from what had been expected. For here there occurred a precipitous process of national awakening in the young boy, who now realised that he was first a Slav and a Slovak, and only then a 'Hungarian,' that is, a citizen of the Hungarian portion of the Austro-Hungarian monarchy. This process took place in Štúr's consciousness under the influence of the teachings of the local gymnasium professor Leopold Petz — a German teacher of all things, a Slovak of German extraction, who having learned the 'hearth-speech of the Slovaks' only as an adult, became in his old age an ardent Slavophile in the spirit of... German ideas, that is, concepts chiefly derived from the German writer Johann Gottfried Herder, who idealised the Slavs. It is certainly to Petz as well that Štúr owed his familiarity with the selected writings of the great contemporary Czech and Slovak Slavophiles Šafárik and Kollár. Quite soon, Kollár's epic cycle *Slávy dcera* [The Daughter of Sláva] would become the Bible of Slavicism for Ľudovít Štúr, the alpha and the omega of his activity.[15]

ŠTÚR THE SLOVAK

Ľudovít Štúr's conception of, and attachment to, his particular homeland, that is, Slovakia, is threefold. First, he is firmly grounded in his Slovak nature, i.e. that of a person born of Slovak parents, as in the case of the 'young son' catechetically addressed by the pilgrim-poet of *The Slovaks, in Ancient Days and Now*:

> And who are your countrymen, young son?

---

discovery of a letter from King Matej Korvin 'proves that even the Kings of Hungary addressed their Slavic subjects in the Slavic tongue in matters of public importance, and it also testifies to the fact that the Czech tongue was familiar to, and favoured by, the courts of the Hungarian kings.'

[14] See 'Slavs, brothers!' and other of his writings from the time of the Slavic Congress in Prague, for example.

[15] Janaszek-Ivaničková, p. xvii. Pavel Josef Šafařík (Šáfarik in Slovak, 1795 – 1861) was a Slovak poet and writer, like Kollár, creative primarily in Czech.

> My parents are Slovak, and so my countrymen are also Slovak — it is to their benefit that I am preparing myself, my countryman!
>
> True are your words, young son.

While on his 'Journey through the Region of the Váh,' he makes something of a pilgrimage out of a visit to the first great poet of modern Slovak, Fr Ján Hollý, translator of Virgil and author of Slavic epics dealing with Svätopluk, SS Cyril and Methodius, and the Great Moravian Empire, topics which will also be of great import to Štúr's own literary compositions. Štúr speaks of Hollý's verse as arising 'from the most candid and cordial of hearts, and thus it is no surprise that it so moves the Slovaks.' We learn that, upon hearing that Hollý has set aside the composition of poetry, 'in the name of all sincere Slovaks [Štúr] begged him to take the lyre back down from the oak, once more to sing to us from the banks of the Váh' — a petition, which, considering the cultural struggle for the development of Slovak letters in which Štúr was already involved, is certainly more than mere courtesy. In the end, heartened by the news that a new collection of his work was currently in progress, the young poet joins the old in a cup of wine, toasting 'Slovakia, and ourselves.'

That Štúr is a Slovak by birth and language is an obvious thing, to us. Yet that was no sure matter in the times in which Štúr was fated to live, as we read from the continuation of his story of the Slovak boy, cited above:

> The mother gives birth to her child and presses the innocent infant to her bosom; the baby wails and the mother soothes him with the words of her mouth, which shall become the child's mother tongue.
>
> The child does not yet understand his mother's speech but his little eyes never leave her beloved countenance.
>
> The child is weaned and grows and the mother chirps and chatters about him; he begins to understand, and to imitate his mother's voice. And the mother kisses her child and plays with him.
>
> The child grows and speaks the words he has learnt from his mother's lips, and the mother's heart dances at the speech of her child.
>
> [...]
>
> And she rears him in fear of God, and he learns from his father, and his parents rejoice in their offspring.
>
> The little son has grown, learning from his parents and teachers to fear God; learning all things in his mother tongue.

Yet, it is not necessarily as obvious as it seems. For as his consideration of the Slovak child continues, we learn that 'they,' i.e. the Magyar-majority government, plan to

> ... tear your little son from your bosom and send him off to a settlement, where he shall have neither mother nor father, where he will have no one to talk with, and where he shall grow up without fear of God, deprived of all that is good.
>
> No one shall watch over your little son in that land, and the house in which he shall abide will remain foreign to him.
>
> They shall mock him there on account of his language, tormenting him, so that he will all the more willingly hold it in contempt himself.

Is this an expression of the twelve-year-old Štúr's anxiety when 'torn away' from his own home, he went off to Ráb for immersion in Magyar and German? Perhaps, but little did he suspect — or perhaps, after all, he did — that such violence would soon be written into law. Magyarising pressure on Slovak children was only to intensify. In 1874, some thirty years after this text was written, the government of Hungary enacted an official policy of forcibly relocating orphans and children deemed impoverished from their families to 'pure Magyar districts.'[16]

Who on earth would not be moved to anger at that? Thus, second, for Štúr, to be Slovak is *not* to be Magyar — as it was, it seems, for Fr Holly as well:

> When I remarked in response that indeed he was a hermit of sorts, secluded here in the pensive region of the Váh, he set to praising the peace he enjoys in Madunice and its groves, which he finds so pleasing. He had been offered a much more significant parish, but he turned it down, as he said, because of his great preference for the peace and quiet he enjoys here. It has been reported, nonetheless, that he would have allowed

---

[16] Gilbert L. Oddo, *Slovakia and its People* (New York: Robert Speller and Sons, 1960), p. 145. This is also the subject of Svetozar Hurban Vajanský's aptly-entitled narrative poem *Herodes* (1879). See Svetozar Hurban Vajanský, *Sobrané diela* [Collected Works] Vol. IV, *Tatry a more* [The Tatras and the Sea] (Trnava: G. Bežu, 1924), pp. 139 – 173. Of course, the Magyars weren't the only ones to do such a thing. The Nazis instituted the same policies in Poland and Eastern Europe in their *Lebensborn* programme, and the European Americans strove to assimilate Native American children through their boarding schools in which they described their aim to be 'saving the man by killing the Indian.'

himself to be transferred to a certain parish, but because the curate there was devoted to the Magyar cause, he elected to remain here, being as he is the confirmed enemy of all renegade attitudes.

The key word here is 'renegade,' in Slovak: *odrodilstvo*. This word has connotations of degeneracy, in the primary sense of the term, that is to say, a person unnaturally abandoning the identity into which he was born. The threat that should be underscored here then, is not that of Magyars per se, but rather of those Slovaks like the 'curate devoted to the Magyar cause,'[17] or the Slovak gentry, who defected from their natural ethnic identity for personal advantage. We will deal with this theme of Magyars and Magyarisation, as well as that of the responsibility of every Slovak, every Slav, in the upkeep of Slavic nationality, later.

Third, Štúr's understanding of Slovak identity is based on a somewhat mythologised conception of an enduring, ancient culture, which exists among the Tatra mountains and river valleys, in unbroken succession from the days of the Great Moravian Empire. In his aforementioned letter to the editors of the *Literary Weekly*, he defines himself, and his nation, in these terms:

> I am a Slovak. My home is in the inaccessible Carpathian mountains and their valleys, in which, as your author justly notes, ancient customs and mores, entertainments, legends, traditions, sayings and other dear treasures of our nationhood, most especially our songs, are preserved in all of their purity, untainted by any foreign influence. It is true: all of this can be found among us in profusion. The Slovak sings hymns to God, and raises his voice in songs of praise of the heroes of past ages; he expresses himself in gloomy meditations and thus lightens the oppression, which the long-vanished heroic ages of which he sings knew nothing.

This is not the last time that we will catch a hint of self-description in his image of a singer brooding on the heroic ages of the past. Is Štúr not thinking of himself when he introduces the character of the Bard in *Matúš of Trenčín*?

> In ancient songs and legends lies
>   The might of spells — a frightful force —
> For to him upon whom it alights

---

[17] Whom Štúr describes in but one strong word: *maďaroman*, i.e. Magyar-maniac.

> The gift brings misery, a curse;
> The fated man — 'tis not his choice —
>   Is emptied of himself, and all
> That was human within him falls
>   Away forever, except his voice.

For anyone remotely familiar with the writings of Ľudovít Štúr it is hard to think of anything else here. Few are those in history so consumed with an idea — in this case, the liberty and union of the Slavic tribes — as to be as steadily, and single-mindedly, devoted to one and one thing only. Goethe wrote scientific papers as well as *Faust*; Dante was a political theorist as well as the author of the *Divina Commedia*; Mickiewicz excelled in erotic verse and descriptive sonnets as well as his magnificent monumental drama; Ľudovít Štúr, it seems, never picked up a pen without a thought of somehow furthering the Slavic cause.

The two narrative poems included in this book, *Svatoboj* and *Matúš of Trenčín* are testimony enough to that. But his fascination with Great Moravia, his grounding of Slovak identity in that Slavic Empire of the early middle ages, is found again and again in his publicistic works. In the greatest of these, his quasi-biblical *The Slovaks, in Ancient Days and Now*, patterned after Adam Mickiewicz's *Books of the Polish Nation and Polish Pilgrimage* (1832), he encourages his fellow countrymen to patriotic activity in the present by reminding them of the glories of the past. Their land, he states, was grand indeed:

> From the river Torysa, there near the Tisa, it stretched toward the broad Danube, and from thence to the Tatras, and beyond the Tatras it stretched far and wide, with Poland and Bohemia and Silesia, toward the farthest bounds of land: a great country it was! Great, as is the Danube among the rivers of Europe, and the Tatras among the mountains!

This is not mere nostalgia. It is a patrimony. And in the face of what was presently going on in Hungary, with the progressive suppression of Slovak nationality in favour of the Magyar majority, it is a fulcrum against which to rest the lever; it is a call to effective, and justified action:

> Long ago it was, O long ago, a thousand years ago, when on this land, over which you now tread, and in the bosom of which, your hard labour done, you shall lay down your bones, adding them to the bones of your

fathers, that a great nation came to be — great and populous, rich and widely-famed. And the name they called it by was Great Moravia: and this was the land and patrimony of Your Fathers.

The patrimony, of which Štúr speaks here, might be pushed back in history to the first part of the VII century, when the Frankish merchant Samo established a Slavic realm consisting of Moravians, Czechs and Sorbs, which may have comprised the lands of western Slovakia as well. Štúr mentions Samo once, in the list of early Slavic rulers included in the opening paragraphs of his *Slavdom and the World of the Future*, but, whether because the realm was ephemeral, evaporating at Samo's death, or whether because it did not provide the sort of dramatic legendary material as the story of Svätopluk and his venally feuding sons, it is the Great Moravian Empire (833 – 907)[18] to which he appeals as a lost, golden land. 'Great' it certainly was, comprising most of the West, and some of the South, Slavic lands into one whole: spreading from the Sorbs in modern day Germany through the Czechs and Slovaks, north into Silesia and Southern Poland, to exert some influence upon the westernmost regions of today's Ukraine, and south again through modern-day Hungary toward Slovenia and Croatia in the Southwest and Serbia in the Southeast. Of course, for Štúr, the main attraction of the Great Moravian Empire is that very comprehensiveness. As much of a Slovak as he is, he is nonetheless a Pan-Slavic dreamer, and Great Moravia is bathed in the golden nimbus of a dream, a vanished reality, which brought into being the unity of the Slavic 'tribes' he longed for, with Slovakia as the central pivot around which everything spins:

> Who's never set foot on the Trenčín heights,
>   Or ranged along the Váh with happy tread
> Will find his soul incapable of flight,
>   Unable to lift high his sluggish head
> Where spirits, borne aloft on wing unfurled
>   Soar through the sky, and seem to rule the world,
>
> Over one hundred Mountains as they sweep
>   And tremble over myriad pied vales,
> Now over Poland to climb swift and steep,

---

[18] Anton Špiesz, *Ilustrované dejiny Slovenska: na ceste k sebauvedomiu* [Illustrated History of Slovakia: on the Path to Self-Consciousness] (Bratislava: Perfekt, 1992), pp. 17, 20.

> Above Moravian summits now to sail,
> Then down toward the Váh once more to swing
>   And, home on Nitra's aerie, fold the wing.
>   *Matúš of Trenčín*

It is the vanished glory of Great Moravia, of its capital, Slovak Nitra, that fires Matúš to his patriotic warring against the foreign usurper Robert, and it is no coincidence that Štúr describes his first triumphs thus:

> On daring wings the soul, emboldened, soars.
>   This is no time for luxury and rest:
> The Slovak regiments, refined in wars,
>   Now into neighbouring Moravia press,
> Where town and keep submit to Nitra's terms,
>   And daughter strayed to mother now returns.
>
> Now unto Danube gaily skips Morava,
>   A welcome friend, from infancy well-known;
> To Danube too, that summer, comes the Váh
>   To whisper, *No more shall you be alone!*
> While north to Wisła fleetly hastes Poprad
>   To bring her news of Matúš' daring thought.
>   *Matúš of Trenčín*

Slovakia, Moravia, the Danube (and thus the pre-Magyar Pannonia, Samo's realm), the Wisła (and thus southern Poland)… Matúš is doing nothing less than re-assembling the Pan-Slavic, or at least Austro-Slavic, Moravian Empire toward which Štúr himself is labouring. *This is no time for luxury and rest!* Štúr's narrator comments, and it is not hard to hear in this a direct address to his contemporaries. For if Great Moravia fell, she fell on the one hand because of the selfishness of individuals, who placed their own particular interest over the good of the whole,[19] and this ended in catastrophe:

> Those moans reach Slovak ears like peals of doom,
>   As tolling bells oppress the orphaned heart.
> Slovakia! They bear you to a tomb
>   Where you shall lie, benighted, set apart,

---

[19] A charge, in his Pan-Slavic writings, that he will constantly level at the Poles.

> Though lifeless, in the world for all to see —
> To toil, die, toil, and perish endlessly.
> *Svatoboj*

It is interesting how here, as elsewhere in *Svatoboj*, Štúr uses 'Slovakia' interchangeably with 'Moravia' as a shorthand for the Empire as a whole. It is a *pars pro toto* strategy, as it underscores a theme that runs throughout much of Štúr's thought: the Slavs, from the Russians in the east to the furthest settlements in Lusatia in the west, are one nation, made up of distinct, but closely related, tribes. It also serves to firmly set before the eyes of his readers — he is writing in Slovak, after all — the ontological continuum of their present being to that distant, glorious, idealised past. The message is a simple one: what a shame it was to see our nation destroyed before it had time enough to become firmly established! What a shame it would be, in this new age of opportunity, to waste our chances, and allow our nation to sink out of reach again! We must all put our shoulders to the wheel.

More than once, chiefly in *Slavdom and the World of the Future*, but elsewhere as well, Štúr bemoans the practice of dying kings dividing their kingdom up between their sons and hoping for the best. For the 'worst' is what always occurs — envy rears its ugly head and a war breaks out, which is to the advantage of no one but foreigners awaiting the proper time to leap into the fray and carry off the spoils. The theme is found at the very dawning of Slavic pre-history, in the legend of Lech, Czech and Rus — protoplasts of the Poles, Czechoslovaks and Eastern Slavs — who, when they were setting out from home, were warned against disunity by their father, in a graphic metaphor. Three staves bound together are hard to break. Separated, they can be snapped over one's knee with ease, one after the other. It is a warning that, later, Svätopluk's sons too chose not to heed, which led to whole ages of subjection for their descendants:

> Svätopluk's oldest son Mojmír, having obtained the greatest share of his father's divided state, assumed his father's throne. But his brothers envied him his place, and, rebelling against him, enkindled a civil war, the flames of which consumed the land at last. At this was Satan delighted, seeing that all was proceeding according to his intentions. So, swiftly he drove the pagan Magyars forth from the hills and against the Christian Slovaks, inciting also the Germans against them, to their destruction.[20]

---

[20] Štúr, *The Slovaks, in Ancient Days and Now*.

NOT TO BE A MAGYAR

Writing in *Archäologie in Deutschland*, the editors confirm the Magyar role in the downfall of the elder Svätopluk's empire, as the younger, known as Svätopluk II, rebelled against his brother, with their help, and that of the Bavarians[21] as well:

> [Svätopluk] allied himself with the Hungarians [*sic*] who had reappeared in the Carpathian Basin in 894 and were threatening Frankish Pannonia. This event triggered the Hungarian conquest, even if the Hungarian tribal association had not intended it.[22]

The role of Satan in all this must be listed under 'unconfirmed rumours,' or at best, as part of the quasi-biblical style adopted by Štúr for his *The Slovaks, in Ancient Days and Now*. It allows him to depict the Magyars more as a herd than a community, as they are 'driven' against the Christian Slovaks — which sidesteps the matter of the Christian Svätopluk's role in it all. At any rate, the emergence of the Magyars in Slovak history, at this crucial juncture at least, is described by Štúr as something diabolical. In writings such as these, which deal with the earliest interactions between the Magyars and the Slavs, Štúr rarely speaks of the former with anything less than unfeigned disgust. In *Svatoboj*, when the title character makes his long confession to the hermits he has taken up with, he speaks of the Magyars as 'savage pagan bands' and — with a deft shifting of the blame — suggests that they are 'allies of our allies,' i.e. not troops that we, good 'Christian Slovaks,' summoned forth, but 'savage pagan bands' called in by our allies, i.e. the Germans, who seem but little better than they:

> Our allies called up allies of their own
> — The savage pagan bands known as Magyars
> Who wander the wild steppes with no fixed home —
> Unto this weakened, squabbling land of ours.
> So Christians serve their brothers in the faith
> By urging pagans to put them to death!

---

[21] Špiesz, p. 24.

[22] 'Die Ungarn.' *Archäologie in Deutschland*, Sonderheft 2008: 75 – 108, p. 80a.

How much historical truth there is behind Štúr's literary handling of the ancient Magyars is, of course, beside the point. As we have mentioned, in a Hungary where magyarisation was the axe lain at the root of Slovak nationhood, one of the ways in which Slovak identity is confirmed is by underscoring the fact of one *not being a Magyar*. And if the nineteenth century Magyars were, on the whole, unkindly disposed to the Slovaks, Štúr takes the occasion to project the present situation of Magyar-Slav relations on the past. Once an oppressor, always an oppressor. The magyarising heavies of today are the direct, lineal descendants of the blood-quaffing savage hordes that laid waste to Great Moravia. They admit as much themselves, as the modern-day counsellors concocting plans to root out all ethnicity but their own are presented in *The Slovaks, in Ancient Days and Now*:

> And so they continued, saying: 'Because the Magyar nation is that which conquered this land and took unto itself the rule thereof, it is only right and just that their language should take precedence over all others and broaden its reach, while the languages of the subservient peoples should humble themselves before it. In time, they should be swept away, for good it is, and needful, that there be but one tongue in our motherland, and that one language that is to be spoken, that is to dominate all others, should be, by right, the tongue of the Magyar nation.'

It is a common thing to claim a moral victory when one cannot be expected on the field of battle. The Slovaks, although defeated by the superior might of the Magyars (and in the excerpt cited above, the entire Magyar argument is based on rights of conquest, brute force), are yet a higher culture, more refined. When they arrive at a *modus vivendi* with the invaders, who, it seems, are here to stay, the distinction between high and low culture, Christian and pagan, Slovak and Magyar, is brutal: 'The Slovaks agreed to the terms of this covenant and swore by their God to preserve the peace and not to take up arms against the Magyars. And these last, joyful at having achieved what they desired, quaffed blood to seal the agreement, for they were still pagans.'

A common, related theme of Štúr's writing in this vein is the ingratitude of the Magyars. They were a rough lot before they settled amongst the Slovaks, it seems, who introduced them not only to Christianity, but basic hygiene, as well. In this same work, he notes:

> Before this time, the Magyars had no permanent buildings or houses, for leading a nomadic life, they knew only quickly erected hovels and lean-

tos, in which filth reigned and no implements were to be found. It was the Slovaks who taught them how to construct clean, spacious dwellings and how to fashion various tools and implements for household use.

In 'Pan-Slavism and our Country,' Štúr's reasonable argument against a Magyar 'liberalism' that declares freedom of the press, on the one hand, while slurring over the fact that this is really all about freedom of the *Magyar* press, and suppression of all other types of free expression in the other languages of Hungary, leads to an extended excoriation of their ingratitude in the face of the benefits received at the hands of the Slovaks:

> And against whom did that Magyar liberalism come out so strongly? Against whom did it so fulminate? Whom did it wish to stifle, to destroy practically at one blow? Truly — one would hardly believe it — the Slavs!! The oldest, most ancient, most faithful companions of the Magyars. Their neighbours to the west and to the north, to the east and the south. The constant companions, surrounding neighbours, and friends of the Magyar nation from the very first days of their appearance in Europe, and throughout history. Those, who earnestly aided them to establish their commonwealth, who led them into the Christian Church, who taught them agriculture and the crafts; their instructors in the basics of education and enlightenment. This liberalism of theirs seeks the destruction of a good nation, an adventurous nation, a nation of comely men and women, full of ability; a nation upon whose wisdom and freedom, should they reflect a just a little, and weigh with honesty, certainly the Magyars, if anyone, should find that they infinitely depend.

All of this is part of Štúr's strategy of defining Slovak identity in contrast to all things Magyar, and is, as we have said, motivated by a perhaps understandable projection of the present difficulties of his nation upon the past. But Štúr does not always demonise the Magyars; here and there he extends an olive branch, seeking rapprochement — all would be well if *they* acted justly. Anyway, he takes pains, even in the polemical *The Slovaks, in Ancient Days and Now*, to refer to a better past, one in which, as he puts it above, 'Magyar and Slovak lived proudly, in one Hungarian homeland, both faithfully devoted to their common mother, in brotherhood.'

> Indeed, from time to time the motherland was threatened by various savage and murderous nations: Mongols, Tatars and Turks. But the con-

joined swords of her united sons swiftly vanquished all these hordes — all those who had come intending to pasture their steeds and herds on the fat meadows, on the fields covered with thick stalks of grain, and to spill the blood of the citizens of our land.

Likewise, in 'The Contribution of the Slavs to European Civilisation,' we read:

> And here we find that it was the Slavs indeed who, undaunted, set themselves in firm opposition to the fanatic hordes, risking their very existence in long years of war in defence of the freedom of Europe and Christendom. Many a blow did they exchange on behalf of their brothers in this so exhausting, and therefore all the more heroic service. Here we see that at different times, varied Slavic nations led the resistance against the arch-enemy. They were supported in this endeavour by the Magyars, who in this case can be termed their allies.

In these descriptions of a Hungary united, it is interesting to read how the Magyars, raised to a higher civilisation by the Slovaks, stand in defence of their land against new savage hordes, described in terms that used to be applicable to themselves. In other words, national identity, in the writings of Ľudovít Štúr, is something that is always defined in contrast to others, as it is always under attack. In his early journal of pilgrimage to the Lusatian Sorb communities in eastern Germany, which he describes as the 'westernmost outposts of Slavdom,' he notes this conversation with two 'brother Slavs' — a Lusatian and a Pole — met by chance in a train compartment:

> Thereupon we talked about the Sorbs of Lusatia and of the gradual disappearance of their native language, which the Lusatian there present confirmed with pain, bemoaning the fact of the various ways in which the national speech is being uprooted, i.e. by the forcible imposition of German upon all schools, even village schools; the inability to introduce legal actions in court in Lusatian Sorbian, and so forth. In conclusion, he added that they are unable to serve the Lord God properly in any language save their mother tongue, for which reason, it seems, he does not attend the German cathedral church, although the citizens of Budyšin customarily go there, preferring instead to remain true to divine services in Sorbian.

This is the same thing that has been going on in Hungary;[23] the Germans are oppressing the Sorbs in the same manner as the Magyars are oppressing the Slovaks. All of the Slavs are in the same boat: all of the Slavs are in a manner of speaking awakened to a deeper understanding of their identity by constant pressure of forces from without, seeking to make them over into something else than what they are.

In this way, Štúr progresses along a straight path leading from an awakened consciousness of himself as a Slovak, through a comparative realisation of the similar problems faced by all Slavs (save Russia, of which we will speak more later), to identification as a Slav by considerations of a shared past and present — to agitation for a better, shared, future for the most numerous 'nation' in Europe.

ŠTÚR THE PAN-SLAV: THE SON OF SLÁVA

In order to understand Štúr's concept of Slavic brotherhood, we must first get his terminology straight. We have grown used to conflating the term 'nation' with 'state,' using them interchangeably. In common parlance, the United States is a 'nation.' Take, for example, the common American credo known as the 'pledge of allegiance to the flag.' At one point, the saecular confessor professes his fidelity to 'the republic for which it stands, one nation, under God, indivisible.' This is not a reference to the Americans' ethnic identity, which of course is multifarious, but rather to the federal whole made up of the fifty individual states that constitute it — an allusion to the War between the States, the Civil War of the XIX century, and a pious statement of determination never to allow such a thing to happen again, by God... Curiously, we owe this conflation of terms to the Americans themselves, who carved up the map of Europe at Versailles. The determination to dismember the Habsburg and Hohenzollern empires was made at least a year previous to the conference at which the treaty bringing the Great War to a close was to take place. It created so-called 'rump states' of Austria and Hungary, re-establishing Poland, founding Czechoslovakia and other lands, the expanses of which were determined by (sometimes angrily) drawn ethnic borders. Thus, 'nation' and 'state' became more or less interchangeable ideas in the case of

---

[23] 'The Education Laws of 1879, 1833 and 1891 made the teaching of Hungarian compulsory in kindergartens and primary and secondary schools. Soon there were no Slovak secondary and higher elementary schools in [Slovak] Upper Hungary, and between 1880 and 1890 the number of church schools fell from 1,700 to 500.' Paul Lendvai, *Total Blindness: the Hungarian Sense of Mission and the Nationalities* (New Brunswick: Princeton University Press, 2003), p. 300.

newly-homogenised nations with only trace elements of ethnic minorities who could not, or would not, be transported from their natural homeland across the border to the one determined by Woodrow Wilson. After World War I, nearly all of the Hungarians truly are Magyars. 'Nation' now equals 'state,' and the term also began to be used in reference to those countries of immigrants, like the USA, Canada, Australia, where the population is nowhere near homogeneous.

For Štúr, the key terms are *národ* and *kmeň*. The first of these terms, signifying 'nation,' is a community bound by ties of blood, something that the term, found in all the Slavic languages, carries implicitly within it, as it springs from cognates such as *rod* [house, clan] *narodiť sa* [to be born], and so forth. It is this which prompts Štúr, in writings such as *Slavdom and the World of the Future*, to speak of Slavic nation-building as an extended family, rather than a political association of convenience.[24] The *kmeň*, or 'tribe,' is the particular, local manifestation of the nation: Poles, Czechs, Russians, Sorbs, etc. It is for this reason too, logically, that what we call the Slavic languages, Štúr speaks of as localised 'dialects' of the one Slavic tongue, rather than languages in their own right. Thus, according to Štúr's conception, there are as a result only a few large nations inhabiting Europe — the Latin, the Germanic, the Celtic and the Slav — although there are many states.

Of course, such groupings have more to do with linguistics than physical kinship. In the case of the Slavs, though, where all of the Slavic languages retain to this day a high degree of mutual intelligibility, it is easy to see how Štúr, and others, would arrive at such conclusions.[25] And thus, in the introductory paragraphs to his 'Journey to Lusatia,' he writes:

....

[24] Although, in the passage to which we refer, Štúr elaborates his statement using Poland as an example, this connection is even more apparent in the Russian term for 'homeland' — *rodina*. The same word in Slovak, Czech and Polish (*rodina, rodzina*) means 'family.' The Russian Slavophile Ivan Kireyevsky similarly theorised that whereas 'western states rest upon subjugation, the Russian state is founded upon familial peace' [*rodinný mir*] Cf. Samuel Štefan Osuský, *Šturova filozofia* [Štúr's Philosophy] (Bratislava: Slovenská liga, 1936), p. 33.

[25] I am always reminded here of the late, great Prof. William Schmalstieg, an authority on Lithuanian, Balto-Slavic, and linguistics in general, under whom I had the honour and great pleasure of studying Old Church Slavonic in the 1980s. Once, in response to a question concerning the difference between a 'language' and a 'dialect,' he responded: 'A language has an army.' Mutual intelligibility or not, the inroads that English has made all over the world since the Second World War seem destined to put an end to any Pan-Slavic dreams of a Slavic lingua franca. Quite recently, my wife and I were approached by a Ukrainian tourist in Kraków, who asked us to take his picture against the backdrop of the church of SS Peter and Paul on Ulica Grodzka. He made his request in English, and thanking us, complimented us on 'our beautiful city,' encouraging us to visit 'the beautiful cities of Kyiv and Lviv' — in English, despite our Slavic 'brotherhood.'

> The natural affection I have for my nation, which grew stronger immediately upon my acquisition of a clearer consciousness of my own self and my fellow-countrymen, augmented in good time through the lecture of the poetry of our priceless Kollár, swelled year by year, greater and greater in my breast, attracting me to everything that could help me to a better knowledge of our nation, as expressed in all of its tribes.

Quite clearly, the 'nation' he speaks of consists of the Slavs in general, of which his own Slovaks, and the Sorbs he is about to describe, are 'tribes,' the local expressions of the greater, organic whole. It is what allows him to speak of 'our' victory over the Turks at the lifting of the Siege of Vienna in 1683 by Polish King Jan III Sobieski,[26] 'our' cities, as in his complaint of their being overrun by a foreign (i.e. non-Slavic) element:

> So it goes for us Slavs, that we frequently find ourselves pushed out of our main cities by non-residents, not only in those regions close to foreign parts, and where foreign elements have widely spread, but also in purely Slavic regions. Examples of this are many and obvious: I might point out Trnava and Bystrica in Slovakia, Brno in Moravia and Kraków in Poland, etc.
>
> Journey to Lusatia

Likewise, 'our patriot' describes the perils faced by 'our language' although the tongue in question is the Lusatian Sorb, and the patriot, not a son of Slovakia, but rather Jan Hraběta, a Czech. Likewise, when in the essay 'Slavdom and the World of the Future,' he counts up '16 million speakers of the Slavic tongue in Austria,' he has in mind all the speakers of Czech, Slovak, Polish, Croatian, Serbian, and Ukrainian taken together, for all their tongues, to his way of thinking, are merely dialects of the one common Slavic language.

He is not alone in this. Before him, two Slovak pan-Slavs, Ján Kollár and Pavel Šafárik (or Šafařík, as he spelt it in Czech), spoke in similar fashion. In his influential essay *On Literary Reciprocity among the Slavic Tribes* (1836), the poet Kollár speaks of: 'the common participation of all parties and tribes in the spiritual and intellectual fruits of their nation through a reciprocal

---

[26] In his speech to the Slavic Congress in Prague: 'It was us that defeated the Turks, but the Germans ascribe that to themselves.'

purchase and lecture of books published in all the Slavic dialects.'[27] As for Šafárik, the author of the influential *Slovanské starožitnosti* [Slavic Antiquities] (1837), an eloquent testimony to his Pan-Slavic views is provided by Kollár in his sermon 'The Greatness of our Nation.' Upon visiting Šafárik in Prague and noticing the large map of Slavdom[28] hanging on the wall behind glass, he notes:

> When I asked him why he had hung it there, he told me of the national pride and joy it gives him to gaze upon the greatness of our nation, the many lands of which it is occupied, how broadly it spreads, how much it encompasses.[29]

'All of this is our homeland! Slávia, Omnislávia!' Kollár himself gushes, later in the sermon, going so far as to propose — it seems — a common name for the grand expanse of Slavdom — *Všeslávia*. Thus it is no surprise that Štúr, as admittedly under the spell of Kollár as he was in his youth, travelling through Upper and Lower Lusatia with the earlier poet's *Slávy dcera* in hand, should speak of his westernmost Slavic brethren[30] in such terms: 'the heart of each ardent Slav must glow with pride and esteem for them. For they, although few in number, have still remained true to their language and the traditions of their forefathers, in spite of all the fierce wars and catastrophes which have been inflicted upon our nation.' Again, *our* nation. The 'Journey to Lusatia' is interesting, not only as a discovery to his readers at home of the Slavic remnant in eastern Germany and their ancient past, but also an example of behaviour: like them, the Slavs of Hungary must also 'remain true to their language and traditions' in spite of all that may be inflicted upon them.

---

[27] Jan Kollár, *O literní vzájemnosti mezi rozličnými kmeny a nářečími slovanského národu* [On Literary Reciprocity among the Various Tribes and Dialects of the Slavic Nation] (Praha: Jan S. Tomíček, 1853), p. 3.

[28] Referred to as a *zeměvid slavjanský*, i.e. 'Slavic landimage' — a neologism intended to avoid borrowings from foreign languages. It didn't stick. In contemporary Czech, Slovak and Polish, one uses *mapa*. An even more frenetic example of linguistic Pan-Slavism is provided by Kollár's perhaps over-ebullient motto: *Slávme slávne slávu slávov slávnych* — 'Let us nobly celebrate the glory of famous Slavs.'

[29] Jan Kollár, *Prózy* [Prose Writings] (Prague: Knihovna Klasiků, 1956), p. 291.

[30] Or *Slavobratří*, to cite another of his charming neologisms.

ŠTÚR THE ROMANTIC IDEALIST

Following hard upon a sense of kinship with other Slavs, there arises in Štúr a sweet, romantic nostalgia for past ages, and an idealisation of the Slavic people of the present. As far as the first is concerned, along with his dusty labours, searching archive and library for old Slavic texts and his typical, given the time period, interest in the preservation of folksong, Štúr enthusiastically searches out the slightest archaeological evidences of pre-Christian life in the lands he visits. With what enthusiasm does he ascend Prašica (Frageberg), a mountain near the Lusatian city of Budyšin:

> That like the Greeks — those long-extinct brethren of ours — we Slavs also believed in auguries, cannot be doubted. The very name of this summit [...] offers ample proof, as do the legends that still live amongst the people. According to these, the priest would stand in the centre of this rock and emit utterances in answer to the questions posed by those enquiring of their future (hence the etymology of the name, Prašica, 'to enquire into'). To one side of the boulder there is a hole. According to folk belief, this was the ear of the god who concealed himself in the depths of the rock. These votives, these stones [...] justly might be named the obelisks and pyramids of far-distant Slavic antiquity.

Whether the 'legends that still live amongst the people' are of ancient date, or just wishful thinking, is better left to anthropologists to decide. Štúr himself, a product of the age that saw Madame de Staël develop her theories of a Northern antiquity to rival the Mediterranean past, who greeted the *Rukopisy královédvorský a zelenohorský*[31] as hard evidence of ancient poetry in Czech, dives in with both feet. His reference to 'our long-extinct brethren, the Greeks' is redolent of the North/South fad of the Romantic Age; the 'ear of the god' reference may well be something that he heard from the locals with whom he'd clambered up there, but his enthusiastic ascription to 'obelisks and pyramids of distant Slavic antiquity' is simply disarming in its naïveté. But after all, 'It is the most powerful feeling to gaze upon the splendid remains of the presence and glory of one's own people, for they best

---

[31] The 'Manuscripts of Králové Dvůr and Zelená hora,' were supposedly discovered by Václav Hanka circa 1817, but their authenticity was immediately questioned. Most scholars consider them forgeries, although even Goethe was enthused by them at the time.

direct our minds toward the happier past, contrasted with our present state of subjection, which latter they allow us to feel most sorely.'

That the ancient Slavs must have had some religious sense, not to say organisation, seems doubtless. They were, after all, as human as any. However, for whatever reason, be it the lack of a written language before the advent of SS Cyril and Methodius, or the swiftness, with which they accepted Christianity from both German and Thessalonian, except for a very few carvings in stone and wood[32] the ancient Slavs have left no record of their beliefs, to say nothing of the marbles left behind by 'our brethren the Greeks.' Mediaeval chroniclers conflated supposition with what they learned of the classical pantheon in their schools; this and the paucity of material artefacts leads the greatest of modern scholars of Slavic antiquity, Aleksander Brückner, to shrug with a sigh: 'After setting aside all the mythological inventions of old times, as well as the suppositions of more recent ones, the material that remains is so skimpy, that all conclusions to be arrived at concerning the essence of that mythology are, it seems, out of the question. Really, all we have are a few names which, to cap it all off, elude all analysis.'[33] Yet Štúr is undeterred. He is led to a dramatic cliff by his Lusatian hosts, and reports of it thus:

> In ancient pagan times, the steep, soaring cliffs doubtlessly served as a temple of sorts, since such were frequently located in such eerie, awe-inspiring locales. To this day people still point out the place where, in ancient times, according to popular legend, the idol of the god Flinc once stood, poured of pure gold. This Flinc was thought to be able to raise the dead back to life, but I doubt that he was a Slavic god, as his name has nothing Slavic about it; I reckon that later ages, rather, confused some original Slavic god with Flinc.

---

[32] The most famous of these is the stone idol of the four-faced god Światowid discovered in the River Zbrucz. See Henryk Łomiański, *Religia Słowian i jej upadek* [The Religion of the Slavs, and its Decline] (Warsaw: PWN, 1985), p. 158. This idol was discovered in 1848, and presented to the Archeological Museum in Kraków by Mieczysław Potocki on 13 May 1851, where it remains to this day. The donation was recorded in Josef Miloslav Hurban's *Slovenskje Pohladi* [Slovak Perspectives] 1851:I.5 (25 June), p. 198b., where in true Slavic antiquarian fervour, he notes that the idol is 'wearing a cap such as can be seen amongst the people still today.'

[33] Aleksander Brückner, *Mitologia słowiańska i polska* [Slavic and Polish Mythology] (Warsaw: PWN, 1985), p. 44.

Note that it is the name that he doubts here, not the existence of the Slavic idol...

Before he sets off on the final leg of his journey home, Štúr visits one more site, where the remnants of 'ancient Slavic altars' are to be found: a mound in Königshain, near Görlitz on the Polish border. In reading through Štúr's pilgrimages to what are — to him — obviously the remnants of Slavic temples, one begins to wonder if Brückner and his colleagues haven't been looking in the wrong places? In any event, a pilgrimage it is. For, as he gazes from this height toward the peaks in neighbouring Silesia and Moravia,

> sending off in their direction my most ardent words of greeting, one after another, I remained a long while amidst these ancient monuments. To these sacred altars I brought an offering of tears on behalf of our race such as, I reckon, had not been poured there for many a year. Over the fields that stretched out on all sides one could already sense delightful spring in the offing, the first stirrings of which I took for a benign response to the questions I posed to the deities hidden in the depths, which still watch over us.

Fairly bold that silent sacrifice to the deities in the depths, for a Lutheran minister, but this is the Romantic age, and Ľudovít Štúr is as romantic as any man.

Certainly, the reference to the yet-extant Slavic gods, still vibrant enough to respond to his questions, is a literary trope. However, it is a fact that Štúr idealises the Slavs of his own day and age in the same manner in which he idealises the Slavic past. The Slavs he comes among in Lusatia are model physical specimens:

> Since Sunday came round during the time I spent in Budyšin, I visited both the Evangelical and the Catholic churches in which the services were held in the Sorbian tongue. Both churches were packed, even though the weather was grim and rainy, and in both I saw much attention paid to the service, and much piety, which made me right glad as conclusive evidence of the godliness of our people. I also had occasion to cast my eyes about the congregations gathered there. The greater part of the men were of tall and robust posture, strong of limb; the women too were of comely form. Their eyes — as is common amongst the Slavs — are bright and piercing. They are fresh-faced, with round features. The fairer sex still mostly clad

themselves in their national dress, which does not differ much from the costume of our willowy Slovak women.

And they are models of moral excellence, too. On this same journey, he tells the story of requesting the aid of a chance Lusatian passer-by met on the road. It was a hot day, and he asked him to help carry his load of books some of the way along the road to his next stop:

> My companion kept me company all the way into Kamjenc, even though his own road would not have led him so far. We travelled together for several hours. When we reached the city at evening, I paid him a few coppers for his cheerful aid, but when he glanced at the money, he wanted to give me back half of the sum, with the words *jara wele ste mi dali*. Not only did I not take it back, but, moved by the man's disinterestedness and honesty, I wished to give him even more, which of course he stubbornly and absolutely refused. By his clothes I knew him for a poor man, and yet his poverty did not incite him to greed, or even to accepting recompense greater than what was just. Such virtues still find their homeland amongst us, where they abide almost as refugees, banished from elsewhere and serving as one more laughing stock for those who defame us. But come, take refuge here in the regions where our people live, you ornaments of humanity: amongst us, I reckon, you shall be preserved until better times come round!

The Slavs, it seems, are so pure, that they don't even need legislative institutions. Their 'tribal customs' and inherent morality are enough of a guide, as he reports in *Slavdom and the World of the Future*:

> It is not for the Slavs to plan, delineate and prescribe details in statal terms and legislation; let us leave such petty officialdom to the bureaucrats, so distasteful to our tribes. Amongst us is the fulness of our tribal customs, to which code and regulation are unnecessary. All of this flows directly from our moral state, and these are obvious to all of us at first glance. That which is the consequence of our moral nature is so much more valuable than all of your bylaws and regulations, paragraphs and measures, letters patent and resolutions of your bureaucrats, your Germans!

The only Slavs he does find blame with in his writings are: the Poles, for their arrogant particularisation,[34] those Serbs and Montenegrins who treated their rulers so poorly, and the Croatian Ban Josip Jelačić, for his supposed timidity in Slavic issues and servility to Vienna. However, it will be noted that these are political criticisms of political faults, not directed at any sort of inherent natural flaw.

Slavic idealisation serves an ideological aim in literary works such as *The Slovaks, in Ancient Days and Now*. Here we have a description of the ancient Slavic *polis*:

> Who might that be walking there, staff in hand, wrapped in a cloak tatty and worn; who climbs up on the rock that stands lonely in the empty field; and what host is that, which gathers round him, gazing with respect at his noble figure? The man on the rock is the chosen leader of the people who surround him, the leader who is to remember whence he came and whither he may descend, if he were not to rule his people with righteousness and justice.

The same trait he finds fault with — and not without reason — when speaking of the Poles, that is, elected kings subject to the consent of the governed, so to speak, he sets forth here as a praiseworthy characteristic of ancient Slavic commonwealths. Of course, the thrust is obvious to anyone steeped in the history of the Slavic people, especially Štúr's own Slovaks and Czechs: what we need, naturally, is a king from among us. Rulers imposed from without, like the Habsburgs — not the mention the Magyars — do not fit the bill.

The manner in which the idealisation of the Slavs is carried out in the narrative poem *Matúš of Trenčín* is quite interesting. During the decisive battle at Nitra, the walls are defended by a heroic captain of the Magyar Robert's troops, curiously named Roland. Štúr gives him his due — Roland is heroic, and the brave Slovak troops pay dearly for opposing him. He finally

---

[34] Polish Pan-Slavists are few and far between. Walerian Krasiński is one colourful exception to the rule; Alexander Maxwell provides an interesting introduction to this oddball in his article 'Walerian Krasiński's *Panslavism and Germanism* (1848): Polish Goals in a Pan-Slav Context,' in *The New Zealand Slavonic Journal*, 42 (2008):101-120. Although there were Polish delegates at the Slavic Congress in Prague, Georges Luciani points out that there were *none* at the follow-up Congress of Moscow in 1867 — no surprise considering the 'mutual hatred' between the two peoples and the January Insurrection of 1863 falling just four years previous. See Georges Luciani, 'Du Congrès de Prague (1848) au Congrès de Moscou (1867)' [From the Congress of Prague (1848) to the Congress of Moscow (1867)] in *Revue des études slaves* 47 (1968): 85-93.

falls when the second Slavic hero of the work, Boleslavín, finds a moment of advantage in their duel, raises his sword aloft, and:

> 'Die, foreigner! You must!' calls out,
> In raging wrath, Boleslavín.
> And from above, with one swift clout
> He splits Roland's helmet in twain.

Roland, like Robert, is not a Slav — not with a name like that. He is a foreigner, an invader of Slovakia, and falls, fighting for what is not his. It is perhaps no coincidence that it is not Matúš, but Boleslavín, who fells the enemy in an uprush of patriotic fervour. For Boleslavín is not a Slovak, but a Czech. And that is just the point: he is a Slav defending Slavdom; no Slavic tribesman is away from home, as long as he finds himself within the bounds of 'Všeslávia.'[35]

Now, every Troy has its Sinon, and Slavdom is no exception to the rule. Ctibor and Radmír, erstwhile comrades in arms of bold Boleslavín and Matúš, overcome by the lucre and promises of King Robert, connive to abandon Matúš at the very moment he needs them most. Wavering more out of fear than from pangs of conscience, they hold their troops back until, finally, when they're sure the battle is going against Matúš, they turn their men away, and the Slovak forces are routed, Matúš' great dream of resurrecting the Moravian Empire shattered. Previous to their final abandonment of the Slovaks, Ctibor and Radmír worked to undermine Matúš' confidence by spreading the disheartening rumour of Piotr Piotrovich, the count of Bretčan, breaking troth with Matúš and thus leaving his eastern flank unprotected. Still the doughty Matúš marched on, and we forget all about the traitorous count until, near the conclusion of the work, lo and behold:

> Even the Count of Bretčan (ever true,
>   Though slandered by the perjury of men),
> Hearing of Matúš' baneful fall, he too
>   Could not hold out long by himself, and when
> Dansa attacked in all his massive might,
>   Piotr fell — bravely — in the uneven fight.

---

[35] Part of the retouching of history in *Matúš of Trenčín* concerns the character of Matúš himself. Štúr deftly evades the question of his hero's ethnicity, which may well have been Magyar (Csák), by shrouding his genesis in a Byronic darkness. 'So, you know Skalka, the castle above Trenčín? / Monks brought him there, they say, when he was small. / Where he was born, who his folks might have been, / This no one knows, and no one ever shall.'

Roland, the foreigner, had to die. It could not be otherwise. Piotr Piotrovich, a Ruthene, and therefore a brother Slav, is proven as pure as snow. Might it have been otherwise? It's doubtful. Ctibor and Radmír are truly exceptions that prove the rule. And yet — is this not a lesson, too? The only way the Slavic troops could have been defeated is... by the Slavs themselves. And that for the second time, after all. For in the story of the fall of the Great Moravian Empire, told in the poem *Svatoboj*, and elsewhere, what initiated the process of disintegration in the grand, ancient Central European state of Svätopluk was neither Magyar invasion nor German pressure, but the traitorous falling out of his sons.

Let this be a lesson to the Slavs. Štúr certainly intends it to be. In *Svatoboj*, when the eponymous hero reveals to the hermits (who seem to live so deep in the wilds, that the rumours of the fall of the Moravian state did not reach them) his role in that affair, they seek to turn him from his intention to spend the rest of his life doing penitence, and return him to the battlefield. Svatoboj wavers, but then, with resignation, demurs:

'God will have none of such a sinner's aid.
    And I am steeped in sin, from heel to head.
Here shall I serve Him, in this quiet glade,
    To all the world's concerns I am quite dead.
But God the most merciful will never cease
    To pour on the repentant grace and peace.

'And our despoiled land lies like these wilds:
    Deserted; there's no man that I might bring
To war — here a woman, there an orphaned child...
    That's all. A winter harsh stifled our spring.
Perhaps, in future years, some great Moravian
    Scion will arise to liberate our nation.'

A deep silence fell then, as Svatoboj's
    Words died away. And for long no one spoke,
Until at last, the three hermits took voice
    Again: 'And yet, indeed there still is hope:
Capable youths develop from orphans,
    And faithful mothers form them into men.

> 'Such shall, perhaps, be the nation's saviours.
>   But where a proper leader will they find?
> You, Svatoboj, abandoned Great Moravia,
>   Yet her salvation's always on your mind.
> So years can pass… Its ancient ardour gone,
>   Why, all of Christendom might be undone!

This is one of the most intriguing and well-handled aspects of the poem. Svatoboj is an anti-hero, but not because of what he'd done. Rather, it is because of what he refuses to do: shrug off his despair and return to the fray. If all the Slavs were to get up off their backsides and put their shoulders to the wheel, what might they not accomplish?

ŠTÚR THE PAN-SLAV: PRAGUE AND THE AUSTRO-SLAVIC DREAM

Indeed in that year of revolutions that shook all of Europe, the so-called Spring of the Peoples in 1848, it seemed as if the time had come for practical work on behalf of the Slavic nation. In his circular letter 'Slavs, Brothers!' calling upon all the Slavic nations to gather in Prague at the Slavic Congress summoned for that May, referring to other practical nationalist stirrings, such as the Pan-German National Assembly in Frankfurt, he says:

> The time has arrived for us Slavs, as well, to come to an understanding and to unite together in a common enterprise. Accordingly, in enthusiastic and joyful agreement with the many requests that have been sent to us from the various Slavic regions, we call upon all the Slavs of the Austrian monarchy, appealing to all who enjoy the confidence and trust of our nation, all, to whose hearts our general welfare is dear, to gather together in the age-renowned Slavic city of Czech Prague on 31 May of this year, where we shall deliberate together all matters which pertain to the good of our nation. And should any Slavs who live beyond the borders of our empire wish to honour us with their presence, they shall receive a cordial welcome among us.

One of the currents of thought aiming at an autonomous political system for the Slavs in those heady days, when all the world seemed moving toward a juster, more representative form of government, was known as Austro-Slavism. This political movement, acknowledging the numerical preponderance of Slavs in the Austrian Empire and Hungarian Kingdom, sought to effect a tightening of the bonds between these 'tribes' and the eventual formation of some sort of statal organisation in which it would be they, not Germans or Magyars, who would be in charge of their destiny, their educational system, and their internal matters — though with a Habsburg monarch at their head. (Curiously enough, the 'trialism' of which Franz Ferdinand was suspected might have realised this, had he not been assassinated in 1914). At first, Štúr was cautiously supportive of such a scheme. In his 'Address to the Slavic Congress,' he said:

> Up to this very day, we have had no autonomous Slavic commonwealth within the borders of Austria. Let us express ourselves as follows: *We wish to remain in the Austrian Empire as autonomous Slavic commonwealths.* Let us neither say that we desire the preservation of Austria, nor that we wish to create an Austro-Slavic realm. Such a statement would deprive us of the sympathy of the European nations. Let us rather say that, as autonomous Slavic commonwealths, we wish to remain under the Austrian government. In this way, we shall place the accent on the Slavs — following this, the Austrian government will find itself able to live with us on this basis.
>
> For this reason, we must crush the power of the Magyars. As long as the Magyars are in the ascendant, and the Czechs are paralysed, all attempts at inducing the Austrian cabinet to busy itself with Slavic politics will be vain.
>
> I suggest:
> 1. That we desire the creation of autonomous, united Slavic commonwealths within the bounds of Austria.
> 2. Immediately thereafter, to impel the Austrian government to move to shatter Magyar dominance.

Just how cautiously he moved in support of Austro-Slavism is evidenced by the words which bring his 'Slavs, brothers!' to a conclusion. It is perhaps not without significance, that heartfelt invitation to 'the Slavs living beyond the borders of our empire.' Štúr never let his eye shift too far away from all of Slavdom; it's as if he were carrying that *zemĕvid slavjanský* of Šafařík's around in his heart. Even had the Austro-Slav plan been realised, it is hard to imagine that he would ever quite renounce striving for unity with all of the Slavic lands. As it was, the guns of Windischgrätz, which quickly dispersed the Slavic Congress, and the repression which fell upon the participants of the Prague Uprising in June of that year, confirmed him in his mistrust of Austria. The Slovak uprising later that year, in concert with the Croats and aimed at the Magyars (who were themselves in revolt against Austria), was at first supported by the Austrians (and achieved quite a few military victories) before the Magyars, regrouping under Kossuth, began to repel them, retake the Slovak counties, and reimpose Magyar government. What seemed promising to the Slovaks at the beginning of the conflict — perhaps even the separation of Slovakia from Hungary as a crown land in its own right — evaporated once the Russians entered the conflict at the behest of Vienna. The Magyar revolt put down, the Austrians no longer needed the aid of the Slovaks, and the situation returned to the *status quo ante bellum.* Thus Gilbert Oddo sums up the result of the Slovak uprising:

> Vienna knew full well that the Magyars had come within a whisker of making their revolt stand up. To incite them again now, by dismembering Hungary, would insure that anti-Habsburg resentments in Budapest would continue to smoulder and grow. And then next time the Magyar revolt might succeed. [...] Accordingly the emperor, perhaps swayed by this kind of 'real politique' on the part of his chief advisors, very neatly forgot his proffers of support for the Slovak cause. They were made, after all, in ambiguous fashion and during the flush of revolt and couldn't be considered binding. Thus Slovakia was thrown back to the Magyar wolves.[36]

And so: intensified magyarisation. In this context, it is easier to understand the rather harsh-sounding words pronounced by Štúr in his address. He saw clearly, at least as far as the present and near future were concerned, and read the consequences of disunion and failure correctly:

> It won't suffice for all the regions merely to have equal political rights, they need to be autonomous. First, the Magyar must be destroyed, and then, let the Danube unite our regions. We want to govern ourselves. The rest will be self-evident. You want equal rights for the minority along with the majority — but that's just not possible. If the Czech does not prevail in the Czech lands, the truly Slavic life will not take root here. And if the Magyar is not destroyed, then we'll merely be talking about

---

[36] Oddo, p. 120.

a Czech culture, for we would have lost the organ which unites us with the Yugoslavs. The Danube is a Slavic river. We must become masters of the Danube, which would provide us with a road to the south of Europe.

It would be wrong to read such statements calling for the 'destruction of the Magyar' as a call to genocide. If Štúr had, as we do, the experiences of the twentieth century behind him, he certainly would have chosen other manners of expression. What he is doing, however, is using drastic language to address a drastic situation. If the Magyar power to oppress the Slavic nations inhabiting Hungary is not destroyed, that will lead to the destruction of the Slavic nations themselves. As he notes in his 'Glance at Current Events in Slavdom, 1848:'

> In these days, when nearly all the nations of Europe are acquiring their liberty, when equality and fraternity are being vowed to all, the Slavs subject to the crown of Hungary are also yearning to cast off the ancient and unfair Magyar yoke. But that the Magyars, fellow-countrymen of the Mongols, comprehended the spirit of this age, can be seen from the fact that, not only did they not concede anything to the nations inhabiting Hungary in respect to their ethnic nationality, but, what is more, they began repressing them more than ever before and imprisoned all who dared speak of the sacred rights of their nation.

And in *Slavdom and the World of the Future*:

> But let us be clear about one thing: Magyar liberalism, which by its own definition sets itself to the task of establishing enlightenment and liberty in Hungary, has suffered up to this very moment from one great wound — a wound, which from its very inception was fatal, and made of it a laughing-stock in the eyes of the world and suspicious and hated in the eyes of the Slavs. And that wound is this: the enlightenment and liberty for which the Magyars profess to be fighting is intended for the Magyar nation alone. Magyar liberalism is, therefore, to the highest degree, nothing but egoism and tyranny.

In this situation, it is easy to understand the bitterness that emerges, time and again, from Štúr's writings, especially *The Slovaks, in Ancient Days and Now*, despite the fact that this particular text was composed in 1841, nearly a full ten years before the rollercoaster of 1848:

The wind that booms, echoes with the voice proper to him; the bird sings in his own voice and the beasts refuse not to bellow in their natural voices, but You, man! are forbidden to speak in your own tongue!

Your oppressors set you lower than the brutes, lower than the birds and lower than the realm of things incarnate, yet you look upon this with apathetic eye.

[...]

Now what Greek, I ask you, will address a fellow Greek in Yiddish? What Italian will turn to another Italian in German? How then is the Slovak to address his fellow Slovaks?

The situation of the non-Magyar nations in Hungary was untenable. After all attempts at creating autonomy for the Slavs proved futile, the term Pan-Slav was used as a cudgel against any and all Slovak attempts at accentuating their ethnicity. In words that foreshadow those of Janko Jesenský two generations later,[37] Štúr, in his *Slavdom and the World of the Future* (1852), notes with gall:

Should someone or other retire from public to private life, they cried: Suspicious! What's he conspiring? Should someone else emerge from private to active public life: Suspicious! He's looking to work up a cult of the individual and undermine liberty! That fellow there is a poor man: Suspicious! He'll sell his services to those who would fight against liberty! That other fellow is wealthy: Suspicious! He'll be using his money to assemble hirelings for the fight against liberty! This one's like that, that one's like this — to the guillotine! Off with his head! Such was the situation to which the frenzy about Pan-Slavism arrived in our own country. Someone wanted to reform our wretched Slavic schools — Pan-Slavist! Someone published a book for our neglected nation: Pan-Slavist! Someone founded a charitable association — Pan-Slavist! That's a conspiracy of Pan-Slavists! Someone's arranged a Slovak entertainment for us Slovaks: Pan-Slavist! Voices were raised in pain at the injustices done

---

[37] 'What's with the Pan-Slav! Instead of saying *kissaszonka* for 'little miss,' he says *slečna!* For 'I kiss your hands' he pops off with *ruky bozkávam* instead of *kezítcsókolom*; calls himself *služobnik* for 'your humble servant' and not *alászolgája*, and when you say 'Praise the Lord,' *dicsértesék*, he comes back at you with *naveky ameň* 'for ever and ever,' just as he should, but... in Slovak!... He uses the plural in formal address... And did you see how his name is spelt on his shingle? With an *S, not SZ!*... Pan-Slav... He takes his dinner and supper at Heindl's, where he orders in Slovak...' Janko Jesenský, *Cestou k slobode, 1914-1918* [On the Road to Freedom] (Turčiansky svätý Martin: Matica Slovenská, 1933), pp. 7-8.

to our nation: Pan-Slavists! In the end, anyone who dared say any word about the Slovak nation was already called a Pan-Slavist.

That such should be the case is not surprising, though one might say, following Július Mésároš, that the situation of fear in which the Magyars lived was created by themselves:

> The more that the Magyars pushed through their idea of a reformation of Hungary into a Magyar nation-state, thus increasing for themselves the resistance of the non-Magyar Nations against this politics of hegemony, the more the Spirit of Pan-Slavism waxed in Hungary, and consequently the struggle against the Plan-Slavic danger.[38]

With Austria out of the question, and the attempts at uniting the Austrian Slavs under the Habsburg crown proven to be pipe-dreams, Ľudovít Štúr plays his last and final card: the only hope for Slavic autonomy is in the annexation of all the 'tribes' of Slavdom under the sceptre of Russia.

ŠTÚR THE PAN-SLAV: IS IT NOT RUSSIA, INDEED?

Despite all his disappointments, Štúr never seems to have lost his optimism. His work *Slavdom and the World of the Future* foretells the advent of great things for the Slavs — something that Halina Janaszek-Ivaničková feels was influenced by his contact with Hegel's philosophy during the two years (1838 – 1840), which he spent at university in Halle:

> At the current stage of historical development, the Absolute Spirit is incarnate in Slavdom, more precisely: in its historical core, which, Štúr was convinced, was Slovakia. For just as once — according to Hegel's theories — at the height of its development, the ancient world of the Greeks and Romans realised the idea of beauty, and the Romance and Germanic nations became the representatives and incarnations of the

---

[38] Július Mésároš, 'Magyaren und Slowaken. Zur Frage des Panslawismus in der Vormärzzeit' [Magyars and Slovaks: On the Question of Pan-Slavism in the pre-March Period] in Ľudovít Holotík, ed. *Ľudovít Štúr und die slawische Wechselseitigkeit* [Ľudovít Štúr and Slavic Reciprocity] (Bratislava: Slovak Academy of Arts and Sciences, 1969), p. 189.

idea of truth, according to Štúr, the current Slavic world shall become the bearer of the idea of the Good.[39]

Yet this will not come about by itself. As Štúr appealed to all Slavs to take responsibility for the development and defence of their 'nation,' he came to believe that the only practical manner of assuring the advent of the Slavs' brave new world was through their submission to Russia. The manner in which he expresses this in *Slavdom and the World of the Future* sounds almost like a sigh of relief, as he finally gives expression to something he has long carried about inside himself:

> Come, my brothers, rest your hands on your hearts and admit it: Was it not Russia, indeed, that, throughout the sad ages of our past, shone like a beacon in the dark night of our existence? Was it not Russia that enlivened our hope, sparked our courage, revivified our will to live when it was all but extinguished?

This is no mere sentimentalism. These warm lines are immediately preceded by something amounting to a cold, logical syllogism:

> Since neither the first, nor the second of these options is practical, since the Slavs cannot organise themselves into a federation of states, independently or under the aegis of Austria, there remains only the third option: that of annexation to Russia. Only this project is reasonable; only it has a future.

Whether or not his reasoning is correct, whether or not all other options had been exhausted, these expressions certainly ring true to anyone who has considered his writings. Loyalty to the Habsburg crown, the 'king' (since he is writing from the perspective of a Hungarian citizen) who works tirelessly on behalf of his beloved subjects, is a theme that runs through *The Slovaks, in Ancient Days and Now*. As long as he could believe that a bettering of the situation of the Slovaks, and the Slavs of Austria-Hungary, was possible under the Habsburgs, he was more than willing to remain *treu und bieder*. The narrator of that work reacts with astonishment and anger to suggestions that what the Slavs of the monarchy are really aiming at is annexation to Russia:

---

[39] Janaszek-Ivaničková, p xxxiv.

It was also said in that speech that the Slovaks are to be magyarised so that they should not seek to ally themselves to the Russians, who are of the same Slavic tribe [sic] as they, and so that on the mere grounds of kinship they not call unto them, those northerners.

O man — you who made this statement, how could you so shamelessly accuse the Slovaks of disloyalty? When have the Slovaks ever shown themselves to be disloyal to their motherland? Have they not waged war in the ranks of her warriors against any and all of her enemies? Have not thousands of them fallen on behalf of their Hungarian motherland?

And you — are you concerned with the defence of the motherland, man?

Is the King not concerned with us, and does he not defend us from all our enemies — does he not call our Slovaks, thousands of his sons, to the glorious standard of the monarchy?

[...]

Rivers flow down from the Tatras, booming and uniting into one, and thus do they flow on to the sea, their roar resounding on all sides.

Rivers flow in the north as well, flowing into the deep sea with a roaring that fills the air.

And who of sound mind will curse the Tatra rivers for roaring in the same fashion as the rivers of the north? And who shall be so crazed as to believe that the Tatra rivers will call forth the rivers of the north with their roaring, so that they should flood these regions with their waters?

But now, all that has changed. In 1848, the good king Ferdinand had been shunted aside in favour of the young Franz Josef, and the devotion of the battle-scarred Slovak veteran and his strapping young cousin, who regale Štúr's narrator with tales of Slovak bravery in their battles under the yellow and black banner, are no longer worth as much in the eyes of Vienna as a docile Budapest. Austria has let her Slavs down, and in the early 1850s, the scales have fallen from the eyes of Ľudovít Štúr. 'Away then with utopias,' he exclaims in *Slavdom and the World of the Future*, and let us set ourselves rather to work with knowledge of the conditions and course of history.'

The Slavs wish to join in spirit with Russia, the only independent, organised Slavic state, and their global representative. We may now state this openly: that following our most recent negative experiences, the harsh disappointments of these latter days, our hearts have opened wide to Russia.

Štúr's maturing to a Russophilism, which progresses from a respect and fascination with the one Slavic 'tribe' that still plays an independent role on the European stage, to an active propagation of political union with the Tsarist Empire, is a curious mixture of a cold, logical thought process, and an urge toward idealism that seems at times wilfully uncritical. In 1852, at the mature age of 37, Štúr has eaten from more than one dish, as the Slavic saying goes. Having dedicated his life to the cause of his nation — be that Slovakia or Slavdom — he now sees what works, and what doesn't. As noted above, he has proven that neither an autonomous federation of Slavic nations, nor an Austro-Slav confederation under the Habsburgs, is a workable option. Alone, 'in their separatism,' as he puts it in *Slavdom and the World of the Future,* 'it is simply impossible for them to capably establish their own states. At the very least, no reasonable man can believe it possible.' There remains nothing now but to put an end to that separatism by rushing into the embrace of Sankt Petersburg. Notice, however, how clear-sighted this formulation of accession to Russia is. In the paragraph we are about to cite, there is no sentimentality; it is an argument from *Realpolitik* such as one is surprised to find in the mouth of a tempestuous Romantic such as Štúr:

> Let us assume that these tribes, by some miracle, actually succeeded in overcoming all of the above-cited difficulties. How then would Russia react to the appearance of a federation of Slavic states? Above all, out of principle, and with all her might, she would fight against the rise of such an independent Slavic state; she would not allow it to happen, for one simple reason: every non-Russian Slavic state would inevitably set itself up in opposition to her, and would either seek to influence her, in principle, or would have to fight against her, with the aid of western ideas and western nations. Russia is well aware of this. Only thus can we explain why she has up till now so little supported Slavic tendencies.

It is an amazing flash of clarity; it has something of the practical calculation of a Churchill to it, who, despite all his fondness for the nations of Central and Eastern Europe, recognises that his hands are well-nigh tied by the *fait accompli* of the Red Army's advance, and acquiesces to the falling of the Iron Curtain he was later to fulminate against. I say this neither in support of Churchill nor Štúr, by the way — I simply wish to point out something that is obvious to us all. There is right and wrong, there is justice and injustice, and then there is practicality and making the best of a bad situation. The Polish nation has been faced with such difficult choices between despairing justice and compromising practicality again and again — from the uprisings against Russia in the nineteenth century to the Warsaw Uprising against the Nazis in 1944. In a group of people who have a common goal — the reacquisition of independence — there are always those who wish to roll the dice and rush to arms, damning the torpedoes, and those who urge caution. What is surprising here is that the passionate Pan-Slav Štúr should begin to argue from a position so calculating:

> Our tribes have been completely lacking in any sort of unifying and elevating ideal. A common origin is no such ideal. It cannot even bring about a turning away from disunity and a discontinuation of inter-tribal quarrels. For it can certainly come about that brothers inhabiting the same house can fall to quarrelling; how much more frequently does this happen amongst tribes who, over the course of time and due to physical separation, become ever more alienated one from another in customs, speech, and much of their establishments.

This practically amounts to a rejection of everything that had motivated him up to this point. Common language, common heritage, common origin, all well and good. The best that can do, Štúr now understands, is the sort of cultural reciprocity that his former oracle, Ján Kollár, urged — a common sharing and support between the Slavic tribes in the literary sphere, which, however, Kollár emphatically asserts '[lies] not in any political union of all Slavs, or in demagogical babble or revolutionary resistance against the rulers of the earth and our governors, from which only chaos and misfortune can result.'[40] This was never Štúr's policy; according to Osuský, as early as the Prague Congress 'Štúr had certainly progressed from cultural reciprocity to the political unification of the Slavs.'[41] Poet, priest, but political activist above all — to perhaps even greater an extent than Adam Mickiewicz, whose life as a literary figure and active freedom fighter Štúr's seems to mirror — no, he was not satisfied with merely being pen-pals with his Slavic 'brethren';

---

[40] Kollár, p. 3.
[41] Osuský, p. 177, and: 'Štúr was opposed to all petitions and moaning; he burned for action,' p. 167.

he always sought to move past this, eventually, and 'inhabit the same house' with them.

In this respect, no less striking than his calculating arguments for the advantages of becoming allied to Russia is the bitterness he begins to direct at his 'brothers' for political timidity, or, at least, their satisfaction with a Kolláresque effetism and antiquarianism. Those same Lusatian Sorbs over whom he gushed in 1839 for their literary pursuits and Slavic linguistics, now, in 1852, he speaks of as being 'abandoned to an insignificant literary dilettantism which is praiseworthy, but all the same unable to produce anything grand until the sun of Slavdom should burst forth at morning.' He has even harsher words for he Croats:

> What has become of your leaders, your *bans,* O Croats? What has become of your mighty military slogan, *Vivat banus cum Croatis*? Your *ban* has been shrunken into an Austrian bureaucrat, who already lacks even so much vinegar as to shout down a wretched constable, for fear of endangering his cushy position. Your song has grown silent! But what's there to sing about, anyway?

Yet Štúr is nothing if not fair in his distribution of thwacks, for he does not spare himself either. In his earlier idealisation of ancient Slavdom, one of the things he points to, in *The Slovaks, in Ancient Days and Now*, is the dependence of an elected leader upon the commonwealth that has raised him to his position. Unconsciously perhaps channelling the spirit of the words addressed to Polish King Stefan Batory (a Magyar elected to the throne!) by one of the noble electors — 'I am a maker of kings and a dethroner of tyrants,' he underscores the possibility of the ruler 'descending' from his position 'if he were not to rule his people with righteousness and justice.' Now — although he still values the Slavic political organisation of representation by heads of family which still (of course) exists among the Russians and Serbs, he sees his earlier ideas of Slavic democracy as naive:

> O model democracy of our forefathers! To allow itself to be dragged about and torn apart without a whimper of protest! To tamely bend its neck beneath the yoke and bind its descendants in the fetters of a millennium of slavery! O cut it out already, with those paeans sung of the democracy of the ancient Slavs! Stop shedding those tears over the sufferings that our nation underwent at the hands of the barbarian Asian hordes and express, rather, a righteous repulsion to the weakness, the recklessness and the helplessness of our nation!

In place of this, now, he values Russian authoritarianism, replacing the idyllic myth of government moving upward from the family through the village to the county and so on, a democracy of wizened fathers, with the no-less idyllic myth of the benevolent, absolutist *batyushka*: 'There is not the same sort of discord between ruler and people in Russia as there is elsewhere. In this respect, there one finds more concord than perhaps anywhere else in Europe.'

Just how much contact Štúr had with Russia and Russians is worth study; just how well he understood the conditions prevailing in Tsarist Russia is debatable. He certainly never experienced them on his own skin, never having travelled there as did his erstwhile Czech companion in arms, Karel Havlíček-Borovský. Having accepted with rejoicing a teaching position in Moscow through the good offices of Pavel Šafařík, he set off for Russia enthusiastically in February of 1843, only to return to Prague as fast as his legs could carry him in July of 1844, 'having learned that his boundless ardour [for Russia] had been merely nourished by unhealthy fantasy.'[42]

Whether Štúr would have come round to the same disappointing recognition or despair in connection with the Tsar as he did with his own Emperor, had he lived long enough to see Russia for himself, or consider the matter more closely, is impossible to tell, as he was to die in a hunting accident just a few short years after writing *Slavdom and the World of the Future*, a magnum opus of his political thought, so to speak, which unfolds as a more or less reasoned defence of Russian political hegemony over all the Slavic nations.

We say 'more or less' for, in the breast of the wizened old revolutionary of 1852 there still beats the heart of the twenty-four year old pouring his sacrifice of tears upon the stones of what he allows himself to be convinced are ancient altars of his vanished brethren in Lusatia. He never really moves past his idealism, he merely transfers it from the Slavs as a whole to the Russians in particular:

> Now, despite the fact that her power has reached such heights, it is not chiefly on account of this that the Slavs ought to join themselves to Russia. The chief reason, rather, rests in the creative might of the Russian nation, and their ability to maintain all that they have achieved. Besides

---

[42] František Sekanina, 'O našem Karlu Havlíčkovi Borovském' [Concerning our Karel Havlíček Borovský] in Karel Havlíček-Borovský, *Životní Dílo* [His Life's Work] (Prague: Věčné prameny, 1940), p. 17.

the fact that the Slavic spirit is best preserved in the Russian character, and in the Russian civic system, in Russian customs strength is wedded to humility and good-heartedness. The Russian state has avoided the greatest errors of Slavic nation-building and has proven itself capable of establishing a strong, united realm.

Earlier, we read of the natural moral propensities of the Slavic people being such that even traditional legislation was unnecessary to them. Now, it is the Russian people who have preserved the 'Slavic spirit' to such a great extent that in them, 'strength is wedded to humility and good-heartedness.'

It would be tiresome to list here the many examples of Štúr's blanket idealisation of the Russian Empire found in *Slavdom and the World of the Future*. The interested reader will be able to conduct a tally-sheet for himself, if he so wishes. For one last example: 'The people and the Tsar are united in Russia — and in this lies the main strength of the country. Her nobles are selfless even if they do not enjoy political freedoms.' Anyone willing to say that that's a reasonable trade-off? This aspect of Štúr's new enthusiasm for Russia is adequately summed up by Samuel Štefan Osuský: 'Štúr looked at the situation in Russia with exaggerated idealism. He was blinded by his Slavic evangelisation, so that he did not see the horrid inadequacies, the flaws, the wreck of it all.'[43]

Suffice it to say that this essay of Štúr's is certainly to be listed among the greatest works of Russian propaganda that has ever spilled forth from the pen of a foreigner — John Reed's *Ten Days that Shook the World* notwithstanding. The entire thrust of the essay is both an argument for Russian dominion over the Slavic world — for the Slavs' own good — and something of a travel brochure. When Štúr turns to his enumeration of the mineral wealth of Russia, its gross domestic output and (supposedly) state-supported progress in culture and science, it almost reads like one of those American newspaper ads of the same period, extolling the riches of the unsettled lands beyond the Rockies to adventurous Easterners looking to make a fresh start. With one major difference, of course: where the European Americans from the Anglo Eastern Seaboard were enticed to head west and build up a paradise of their own, Štúr is inviting the Slavs to a paradise ready-made — or, more precisely, a landing of Russian angels on the beaches of their lands, to bring that paradise with them.

---

[43] Osuský, p. 176.

It would be just as tiresome to list here the errors, accidental or wilful, that pop up throughout *Slavdom and the World of the Future*. To mention just one, as it touches upon Štúr's idealisation of Russia, we note his description of Slavdom writhing in the torments of foreign subjugation:

> Indeed, it is a heartbreaking spectacle to look upon, this nation, the most numerous in all of Europe, shattered, divided; as in its atomisation it groans here beneath the Turkish yoke, there in long ages of servitude to the Germans: first to the Holy Roman Empire, and now to the Austrians, Prussians and Saxons. And there, she is engulfed and enslaved by Italian or Magyar. Everywhere she is dragged in triumph, bound to the chariot of foreigners.

It is a comprehensive catalogue of woe, so much so, that along with the usual suspects of 'foreign' invaders, the Germans and Magyars, even the Italians are pilloried — for their pretensions to Dalmatia, one suspects. But who is missing here in this rogue's gallery? Who, if not the Russians themselves. In his treatment of Poland, Ľudovít Štúr displays a flabbergasting depth of wilful ignorance. If there was any group of 'foreigners' at the hands of whom the Polish 'tribe' suffered, from at least 1795 onwards, it was the 'fraternal' tribe of the Russians. And so, it is difficult for Polish eyes to read such comments as:

> Now, in this lonely night, in this barren, sad time for the Slavs, when their body lies as if without sense or feeling and foreigners all the more rend and tear at the ligatures that bind their limbs together, drawing ever closer to the beating heart of Slavdom, not one single tribe has given thought to the sufferings of another, but rather, crammed into alien slops and tied to leads in the grip of alien proprietors, they have been made to serve the comfort of their lords, like instruments for the oppression and further enslavement of their own brothers.

Although surely not intentional, it is hard to read these words of the well-informed Ľudovít Štúr as anything else but a rubbing of salt into Polish wounds — something that would not be out of character after all, as he agreed with Pushkin's warning to western powers not to stick their noses into the 'family squabble' of the November Uprising of 1830, declaring somewhat triumphantly 'Who bears the blame, then, for the partitioning of Poland? The Poles themselves!' For if there was any group of Slavs whose body lay torn and bleeding, it was the Poles, and if there is anywhere that

Štúr ought to be pointing the finger for 'giving no thought to the sufferings of another,' it is at his own breast.

If there are any villains to be found in the writings of Ľudovít Štúr beyond German, Magyar and Turk, they will be Poles and Catholics. The 'arrogant separatism' of the former irks him as a Pan-Slav, and the character of the latter as one more tool of oppression introduced into Slavic lands by Germans (and Italians) sends him into a paroxysm of zeal for the Russian Orthodox Church. We mention it here as one final example of Štúr's unqualified idealisation of all things Russian, and one final bit of literary sleight of hand employed in his polemics of persuasion:

> O holy Church of our fathers, who first blessed our tribes with Christianity from the summits of Nitra, Velehrad and Vyšehrad! Who was once set to unite in spirit the entire family of our nations! O, return Thou to us! Lift up our hearts toward the Eternal and nourish our soul, so that it might realise its magnificent calling. [...] Let no one charge us with advising the Slavs to exploit their Church as a means of political unification. Nevertheless, it is clear what we wish to accomplish by the means of Slavdom — and only that Church is in accord with that mission. Slavdom will never be associated with Roman Catholicism, while the eastern Church was once common to nearly all of our tribes, their true treasure. We are only drawing their attention to what already belongs to them.

This from the lips of a Lutheran minister. With such words Štúr brings a long discussion of the virtues of Orthodoxy to a close, after comparing it favourably to both Catholicism and his own Protestant tradition. What is interesting here, however, is how he identifies Russian Orthodoxy with the mission of SS Cyril and Methodius. This of course flies in the face of all historical truth. The Thessalonian Apostles to the Slavs did set out from Constantinople, it is true, and were shaped by Greek traditions, rather than the Latin West. But this argument conveniently overlooks the fact that the Church had not yet been split between West and East, and in their labours on behalf of the Slavs of the Great Moravian Empire, they had recourse to the authority and support of the Pope. Although part of the treasure of the entire Church Catholic, East and West, SS Cyril and Methodius, who visited Rome twice on behalf of their new flock, were most certainly obedient priests of the Western, Roman Catholic Church, and the liturgy they translated into the Slavic tongue, was that approved by the Successor of Peter.

The Great Moravian Empire, and its constituent peoples — Slovaks, Czechs, Moravians and Poles — were not evangelised by the Russian Orthodox Church; the Patriarchate of the so-called 'Third Rome' was neither once common to these tribes, nor, necessarily, their true treasure. Štúr's preference for a national church is understandable, as is, as far as his propaganda is concerned, his deception in conflating Russian Orthodoxy with the parishes established by Cyril and Methodius. For in so doing, just as Virgil shows Aeneas and his Trojans to be no foreign invaders landing on the shores of Latium, but a group of destined shipwrecks returning to the homeland of their protoplasts Teucer and Dardanus, so here: an annexation to Russia, and a submission to the Russian Orthodox Church, would not mean the assumption of a new identity, but a returning home, to authenticity.

ŠTÚR AND HAROLD CAMPING. OR, NOBODY KNOWS THE FUTURE

We all know that one day the world will come to an end. We also know that nobody knows when that will happen — poor Harold Camping, to give just one example, has proven that conclusively, after predicting its end — twice! — in 2011, and… here we are. Thank God. Maybe.

Štúr's predictions also came out wrong, in the main. Russia certainly was able to flourish, after a fashion at least, without the Tsar, something he thought impossible; Poland did survive the partitions, reuniting the territory that had been taken from it by Russia, Prussia and Austria — following the Great War which realised to the full Štúr's dreams of a Slovakia liberated from Magyar control, and in part, his Pan-Slav longings, by uniting Czechs, Moravians, and Slovaks in one statal whole, which would last, with one brief interruption, until 1993, nearly a century and a half after his death.

That all this would occur without the help of Russia, and even against its wishes, would perhaps surprise him; the fact that, having once achieved political union, the Czechs and the Slovaks would want to *part* from one another, would certainly have knocked him for a loop. As would the fact of the Slavs closest to him — Czechs, Slovaks, Poles, Slovenes, Croatians — being attracted, not to the East, but to the western European Union, *along with the Magyars*. Bulgaria is in the European Union as well, and two nations of which Štúr speaks with great fondness, Serbia and Montenegro, are knocking on the door. How happy Ukraine — the once-termed 'Little Russians' — would be, to tear themselves from the jealous embrace of their big brothers, idealised by Štúr, and annex themselves not to any Slavic super-state (been there, done that), but that Western European Union, with all its western ideas! And the only thing that is blocking that access, to the EU and NATO, is Europe's fear of provoking Russia. At least Štúr got one thing right:

> How then would Russia react to the appearance of a federation of Slavic states? Above all, out of principle, and with all her might, she would fight against the rise of such an independent Slavic state; she would not allow it to happen, for one simple reason: every non-Russian Slavic state would inevitably set itself up in opposition to her, and would either seek to influence her, in principle, or would have to fight against her, with the aid of western ideas and western nations.

I am far from chuckling at Štúr here. Rather, I'm returning at the end of this long introduction to some ideas I broached at the beginning. When we experience long periods of prosperity and comfortable stability — let's say, for many people reading this, from 1969 until 2001 — it's easy to succumb to the illusion of progress, the one central tenet of Štúr's thinking that continues unchanged throughout his writings: that of a continually upward-pointing graph of human progress. How many people of my generation, born in the early 1960s, died, prematurely perhaps, before 11 September 2001, never having experienced the horror of that day, or the consequent fallout, knowing nothing but security, comfort, and the idea of a steadily broadening, steadily 'progressing,' good life?'

Even people of my generation, or my sister's generation, who were born in the early fifties in Central Europe, have experienced the same thing — even more intensely. While their standard of living was much different from that of their peers in Western Europe and the Americas, still and all: the end of Stalinism, the unprecedented uprisings of 1956 and 1968, the rise of Solidarity in 1980 — even if all of them faced setbacks, sometimes violent ones — unto the revolutions beginning in Poland in 1989 and then spreading throughout the Soviet Bloc, until — now who would have thought *that?* — the disappearance of the Soviet Union! To people like them, to people like me, Štúr *made sense*, at least in so far as his faith in progress was concerned.

But here I am, in the middle of the Covid-19 crisis, watching protests — violent or not — wreak havoc upon the social fabric of the country (I almost said 'nation') in which I find myself at the moment, unable, because of the pandemic, to be anywhere else — and, as I said at the start of this essay, unable to read Štúr in the same way as I read him before. Social progress, really? An ever upward ascent toward more justice, more brotherhood, more peace... *really*? Who do you think you're kidding?

Štúr's optimism, for me, is now as quaint as the *shantis* and *oms* of the flower children, who have been on the wilt now for at least twenty years, if not longer. I'm coming to think that maybe that germanified Slav Nietzsche was right. Time is not proceeding in a linear fashion; we are stuck in an eternal return of the same. Liberalism pushes and pushes until Conservatism is provoked into pushing back; Conservatism tightens the screws until the threads are stripped, and the pressure of Liberalism starts popping them out again. My Christian nature, as faulty as it is, is still deeper than my Slavic identity, and it recoils at this. But if there is a linear nature to time, after all, it can only progress, as St Augustine says, from the creation of the world to its end by constantly turning back upon itself in 'eddies.' And how tiresome it is, to be caught in an eddy such as this one.

Change is the element of human history: nothing is stable, there is no 'once and for all' state of stability, which, once achieved, will usher in a continuum of enduring peace; 'progressivism' is a myth. Goals and freedoms achieved by progressives can be toppled just as easily as the monuments of 'unawakened' reactionaries. The most recent history of the West shows us that the progress of humanity *can indeed* be stifled; the only progression that cannot be held back is that — Augustinian — progression through time. What the future holds may not be better than the present at all. There is no guarantee.

One of the greatest fallacies shared by many citizens of the land in which I am writing these words is their naive American Exceptionalism — the gullible perception that 'it can't happen here;' that the United States is some kind of *ne plus ultra* political community, which, having attained the summit of liberty and social perfection, is somehow immune to the slings and arrows that take other empires down. The greatest empire of all, on which all of our Western systems are based, the Roman, saw its greatest period, that of the Pax Romana, expire after the passage of some 207 years. As of this moment, the ticking clock of the United States shows 244...

I do not intend, God forbid, to offer any predictions of my own. Quite simply, using myself as an example, I'm laying out how literary texts change over time — or, at least, our perceptions of them do. Writing in *Slavdom and the World of the Future*, at a time when the weaknesses of the Austro-Hungarian system were apparent, and the forces that would eventually burst the Dual Monarchy apart rising before his ken, Štúr correctly foresaw the following:

It is as clear as day that if the majority of her nations, the Slavs among them, were to turn against her, it would no longer be possible for her to resist them, and Austria would disappear from the face of the earth. Then no power on earth would be capable, however mighty it be, of gluing back together the parts of Austria dismembered. They would no longer belong together, and no spirit of life could then be breathed into her nostrils.

Where he got it wrong was using so strong a negative formulation there, at the end. We should know by now never to say never. Let us consider one final aspect from *Slavdom and the World of the Future*. I would not blame the Reader if he or she finds the following citations concerning Russia and the West patronising, and even out of step with the general tendency of history — especially considering what I have mentioned above concerning the key dates of the latter twentieth-century:

> We have shown how all of those Western ideas are worth nothing to that nation, and can merely lead it to the edge of the abyss [...] The Russian government does not allow many western products into the country, which are abhorrent to the people — and both the people and the government are quite within their rights to do so.

All one need do is substitute 'Poland' and 'Hungary' — those favourite whipping boys of Western European progressives — for 'Russia' in the citation above to place the matter in a more immediate, relatable, context. Who is to say that the European Union is a be-all and end-all, the final, and ideal, terminus for these countries in their journey through time? Who is to say that the ever more open, ever less Christian, philosophy of the West is an objectively better approach to the world, and reality, than the traditional outlook shared by less 'progressive' nations? We have already seen the unthinkable — Brexit — happen; does anyone remember the 'Grexit' threat that preceded it? Given the wide gap that separates Western attitudes toward refugee rights, life issues, and sexual morality from those in countries such as the more conservative Poland and Hungary, who is to say if, or when, a critical mass might be reached that would impel the Vyšehrad Group, or at least portions of it, say, Poland, Hungary, perhaps Slovakia and Moravia, to withdraw from the EU and form a different sort of *polis*, repellant, perhaps, to those looking in from without, but more convenable to the outlook of those within?

I hasten to remark here that this is *not* something that I advocate, or would necessarily even approve.⁴⁴ What I must say — and this I have just learned from Štúr — is that no one knows anything about the future except: it will in some way repeat the mistakes of all past human existence. Progress? *Plus* ça change, plus c'est la même chose.

Pan-Slavism is an important aspect of the culture of East and Central Europe during the nineteenth century. It has long been my dream to make at least some of the writings of Ľudovít Štúr, one of the great theorists of Pan-Slavism, and one of the greatest poets of Slovakia, a nation dear to my heart, available to the English reading public. This anthology proposes to do little more than that: to present Ľudovít Štúr under the aspect of Slovak, Slav, and practical advocate for the peoples to whom he was devoted. Still, Štúr is more than just a Pan-Slav; his horizons are wider than his focused struggles on behalf of Slavic autonomy and fraternity might suggest. I regret that more space could not be devoted, at present, to Ľudovít Štúr the poet and Ľudovít Štúr the cultural explicator; I wish I could have included at least some fragments of his O národních písních a pověstech plemen slovanských [On the National Songs and Tales of the Slavic Tribes], but that would have swelled this volume, already hefty, to unimaginable dimensions. Perhaps, in the future, I will be lucky enough to have the opportunity to return once more to this fascinating Central European Romantic.

As always, I owe a deep debt of gratitude to Glagoslav Publications, my editor Ksenia Papazova, the Slovak Literárne Informačné Centrum, and all who have supported this translation.

Tento preklad venujem svojej babke blahej pamäti Juliane Kožarovej.

Virginia Beach, VA
17 September 2020

---

[44] To argue against this, one need only point to the current intra-Vyšehrad quarrel between Slovakia and Hungary over dual citizenship, and the cultural wars (the 'Women's Strike,' for example), which is polarising Poland as much as any other western country.

SLOVAKIA

A Journey through the Region of the Váh

The Slovaks, in Ancient Days and Now

Svatoboj

Matúš of Trenčín

A Letter from a Hungarian Slav to the Editors
of the *Literary Weekly*

At Ján Hollý's Monument

A Journey Through the Region of the Váh

As I made my way from Bratislava to my native region in the Tatras, I made a stop in Trnava, that free royal city some six miles distant, and so noteworthy in the history of Hungary,[45] known as 'little Rome' on account of its many churches, where I wished to spend at least some time amongst my friends. I must admit that it never crossed my mind what was waiting for me there. For immediately after a rapturous welcome, my friends produced a letter of King Matej's, he known as Korvin, dated 1483. It was written in Czech and addressed to the Trnava city council. The salutation reads: *Opatrnim Richtarzi a Radie Miesta našeho Trnawy wiernym našym milym* [To the providential Reeves and City Council of our Trnava, our beloved faithful subjects]. The letter itself is not especially noteworthy, historically speaking, but it is quite important to us, as the earliest Slavic letter discovered in Hungary — a weighty, crucial document in the context of our contemporary relations with our Magyar neighbours in this our motherland. For it proves that even the Kings of Hungary addressed their Slavic subjects in the Slavic tongue in matters of public importance, and it also testifies to the fact that the Czech tongue was familiar to, and favoured by, the courts of the Hungarian kings. The use of the Czech language at the court of the Hungarian Kings was the natural result of education in Czech in the Czech lands[46] themselves, for through its conscious employment there, the Czech

---

[45] Traditionally, Hungary was a multi-ethnic unit in which Slovaks, Croats, Romanians, and Magyars coexisted. The contemporary conflation of 'Hungary' and 'Hungarian' with Magyar is the result of the breaking up of the Austro-Hungarian Empire along ethnic lines following World War I. We will follow Štúr's usage throughout. 'Hungary' and 'Hungarian' refer to the broad geopolitical concept; Magyar to the dominant ethnic group which today is commonly referred to in English as the 'Hungarians.'

[46] *V samých Čechách.* In the Slavic tongues, the regions inhabited particularly by the Czechs — Bohemia and Moravia — are referred to as Čechy (Czechy, and so on). This general name of both regions has never been adequately translated into English; modern-day usage 'Czechia' is both awkward and anachronistic as a geographical description for times preceding 1993. In our text, we will use 'Czech regions' or 'Czech lands' when Štúr is speaking of both areas in common, and

tongue acquired an influence and importance that stretched into the farther countryside as well. Further, through the military incursions into Hungary of the warring Hussite regiments, under the leadership of the successful Jiskra, who, ensconcing himself in the fortified position of Trenčín Castle and defeating the multitudinous Hungarian regiments who had been sent against him, ruled the northwestern portion of Hungary firmly — the Tatra regions. It is also well known that Matej Korvin had been brought up at the court of King Poděbrad, whose daughter Kunhuta, a beautiful Czech girl, he married upon reaching maturity. Finally, the Hussites, brimming over with Czech books (mostly of a sacred character) made the Czech tongue all the more popular in Hungary by spreading those books throughout Slovakia, above all in ecclesiastical circles. The letter in question may be found in the city archives of Trnava, where it was faithfully copied by the hand of one who is my personal friend, and a friend to all Slovaks. I shall publish it in print at the first opportunity, for the consolation — I reckon — of all my fellow countrymen in the Tatras and along the Danube, as well as my brothers living along the banks of the Vltava.

Leaving Trnava, I hastened to the region of the River Váh, which spread out before me from afar, ringed by all its summits. The autumn weather was beautiful. *Nolens volens* I passed by the cities and villages along the highway, to which many of my friends inhabiting those parts invited me with friendly words of greeting. Alas, not having time enough to turn from the most direct route, I pushed on ahead. After the roads I had seen in the Czech lands and in Germany, these here did not please me too well, although, deep in the Tatras, in Orava and the Turčianské region, one finds roads of comparable quality. I arrived in the Váh region proper at Nové Mesto nad Váhom. The deserted castles that climb the broad slopes on both banks of the Váh, as well as the Tatra summits wreathed in clouds, moved me deeply, to my very soul, as a man returning from distant foreign parts. But instead of joy, I felt a sadness, and fell to musing; the loud-sounding Váh, flowing alongside the highway, accompanied my thoughts in a minor key. A few hours later I found myself in Trenčín, upon the steep summit of which stands the great, legendary, and presently desolate castle, one ancient wing of which revealed itself to me from afar. More than one thought passed through my soul at that moment. That castle is of archly important significance to history, especially the history of the Slovaks, although few they are who are aware of this fact.

Bohemia or Moravia, as the specific case requires.

In Trenčín, I visited my relations and my friends, after which I betook myself to the local alderman, Pavel Vaďon, so as to enquire about the possibility of my accessing the city archives, in which I thought to find many items of importance to us. However, because access to the archives may be granted only by a vote of the entire city council, and because the process must be initiated by written application, this proved impossible due to time constraints. So I set aside an inspection of the archives to the coming summer. Mr Vaďon promised his unfailing aid. It was, however, a consolation to hear from his own lips that he himself has been poring over the Trenčín city archives for many years now, working through the entire collection, from which, he assured me, everything of importance had already been selected by him and employed on our behalf. He has brought his history of the city up to the XVIIth century. When I asked him what language these documents were written in, he answered, in Slovak, at which I rejoiced more than a little bit. From his patent collecting of such items over so many years, with such great effort, we can expect much. Afterwards, Mr Vaďon spoke to me of many important matters dealing with the history of Trenčín, reminding me as well of the fact that the municipal books were once composed in Slovak — and he promised me access to these. What a surprise! In the past, our nation once enjoyed more rights and respect in Hungary than it does in these days of ours!

After urging him earnestly to publish his work — and without delay — I ascended Trenčín castle and, in particular, its highest point, the legendary Matúš Tower, which still today keeps alive among the people the memory of that extraordinary Slavic man. I asked around among the local inhabitants for stories concerning Matúš, but they were unacquainted with any. One of the most pleasing views I have ever experienced is that from the Matúš Tower upon the far-spreading Váh region, toward the summits soaring at various distances toward the north, the west and the east. The northern Tatras, which lift their brows the highest, were already covered in snow, while the Váh valley and the mountain glens were still almost completely green. With the rays of the setting sun falling on the summits in neighbouring, fraternal Moravia, I descended from the castle, deeply sunk in thought concerning our contemporary situation, and these thoughts bore me far on their wings into Moravia, the mountains of which rose in the distance, and to your beloved Bohemia as well.[47] Having spent the night in Trenčín, a city

---

[47] As becomes apparent here, 'A Journey through the Region of the Váh' is conceived as an epistolary report intended for Štúr's Czech friends.

approximately as large as Hradec Králové and constructed like it in the Old Slavic manner, that is, built in an arc all along the one side, I was in a hurry to get on my way at last in the beautiful, early autumn morning, to the place of my birth. The snow-covered Tatras sparkled pleasantly, greeting my eyes with joyful pleasure.

On my return journey to Bratislava, I visited our renowned singer of the Váh region, Mr Ján Hollý, taking with me the books that Mr Vinařický was sending him as gifts, along with the 'Poslání z Čech' [Czech Message]. It so happened that, but a few days beforehand, he had received a letter from Mr Vinařický along with many copies of the 'Poslání' and other books, for which he was very grateful. As always, now too I was greatly struck by his colossal and at the same time magnificent frame, from which radiates the aura of an exceptional man. When his great, blue eyes fix themselves upon a person, their fiery flashes pierce one to the very soul, testifying to the quick sagacity of his spirit and his lively imagination. The pleasant countenance and grey hair of this old man of fifty-six years lend him an especial charm that enchants the person who gazes upon him. His powers of memory are phenomenal, and his imagination, as I have already stated, is quite lively and doesn't seem to have grown weaker at all over the passing years. He discourses upon the most varied topics with great adroitness; the experiences of his youth, which he fondly recalls, and the places he once visited, these all he describes in the greatest detail. His conversation sparkles, shifting from topic to topic as if driven; often, there is no connection between the topics, so one must take special care to follow the thread of his conversation.

Matters vital to the Slavic people, on whatever topic, are of the greatest interest to him. I should never have found him so eager to talk as today. The reason for this was that he had been ill before, but now he is in perfect health. He was greatly gladdened at news of the contemporary development of Czech literature, and the industrious activities of the Czechs in general. He was genuinely interested in the doings of Messrs Šafárik, Palacký, Vinařický, Pešina, Hanka and Čelakovský, and asked that his sincere compliments be passed on to them. Then we moved on in conversation to the contemporary state of things among the Slovaks, as well as the fact that so many have become renegades in relation to their ethnicity. Whenever this topic was broached, the reverend old man would emit a deep sigh and the pain that then appeared in his eyes and on his face pierced the spirit through and through.

His poetry arises from the most candid and cordial of hearts, and thus it is no surprise that it so moves the Slovaks. But now he has set aside all poetry, except for religious verse. 'I've hung up my lyre on an oak tree, and its strings are now touched only by the empty wind,' were his own, somewhat painfully uttered, words. When in the name of all sincere Slovaks I begged him to take the lyre back down from the oak, once more to sing to us from the banks of the Váh, heart to heart, to its charming accompaniment, he brushed aside any chance of once more raising his voice in worldly song — to my profound grief. Yet my sadness was soothed when he extracted from his chest some highly-wrought devotional verses, a full seventy of which were ready for publication. I read some good half of these and soon became convinced of the fact that the same spirit that created *Svätopluk, Sláva,* the *Bucolics* and the *Threnodies* was the author of these poems. In these too he proves himself a poetic genius. The content of these songs is broad. The great number of them are written in praise of Slovak, Czech, Polish and Croatian saints, in the selection of whom, here too, the author gives determined testimony to his Slavic nature. They are composed in the Slovak dialect and shall be printed, generously augmented still with other of his works, the collected publication of which is occupying the diligent Mr Hamuljak, who has already shown us such great service. Our songster is already at work combing through his writings for this very purpose. At length, he joked that he ought to become a hermit. When I remarked in response that indeed he was a hermit of sorts, secluded here in the pensive region of the Váh, he set to praising the peace he enjoys in Madunice and its groves, which he finds so pleasing. He had been offered a much more significant parish, but he turned it down, as he said, because of his great preference for the peace and quiet he enjoys here. It has been reported, nonetheless, that he would have allowed himself to be transferred to a certain parish, but because the curate there was devoted to the Magyar cause, he elected to remain here, being as he is the confirmed enemy of all renegade attitudes. And finally, he can't hope for much longer a life on this earth. According to his assessment of the time left him, he reckons that not much remains. My words of comfort were unable to arouse in him a different opinion. Noting how downcast I had become at his words, he produced two cups, and filled them with an excellent Hungarian wine. Handing one of these to me, he raised a toast to the health of Slovakia, and ourselves. My great desire in clinking my cup with his was that his words should be fulfilled. I spent that night with him in conversations of the most varied sort. At the break of dawn, pressed for time, I bade our beloved poet farewell, with pain. — I here pass on to Mr Vinařický the poet's sincere thanks for the 'Poslání z Čech.'

The Slovaks, in Ancient Days and Now

Which
BEDLIVÝ LUBOROD
addresses to his countrymen
toward summer's end, 1841.[48]

Give ear to me, O my countrymen, as I speak to you of your ancient motherland, and of your motherland today. And consider carefully my words. For they come of a vigilant, careful mind, an unsullied bosom, and a heart that wishes you well. For my eyes have gazed far into the past; before them stands the present age. My mind has brooded over the days of yore, and plunged into the present. My heart has beat in time and compassion with those and with these, therefore, hear me! Indeed, who among you will not gladly give ear to a tale told by a herald who announces things true and moving, things that he brings forth from his heart — especially when they concern you, O my listeners? Just such things do I address unto you, my fellow countrymen!

Long ago it was, O long ago, a thousand years ago, when on this land, over which you now tread, and in the bosom of which, your hard labour done, you shall lay down your bones, adding them to the bones of your fathers, that a great nation came to be — great and populous, rich and widely-famed. And the name they called it by was Great Moravia: and this was the land and patrimony of Your Fathers.

From the river Torysa, there near the Tisa, it stretched toward the broad Danube, and from thence to the Tatras, and beyond the Tatras it stretched far

---

[48] *Starý i nový věk Slováků.* The manuscript, originally written in Czech, seems to have been conceived as an addition to *Das Slawenthum und die Welt der Zukunft* [*Slavdom and the World of the Future*]. Although composed in 1841, it did not appear in print until the 1935 edition prepared by Josef Jirásek, from which our translation was made. The pseudonym 'Bedlivý Luborod' is rather corny: 'Watchfuleye Nationlover.' The quasi-Biblical voice in which Štúr composes this work is based on Adam Mickiewicz's *Księgi narodu polskiego i pielgrzymstwa polskiego* [*Books of the Polish Nation and the Polish Pilgrimage*, 1832], which served a similar purpose.

and wide, with Poland and Bohemia and Silesia, toward the farthest bounds of land: a great country it was! Great, as is the Danube among the rivers of Europe, and the Tatras among the mountains!

Her name and glory spread wide through all other lands, and all did her proper homage; many were they who fled to her for succour and protection beneath her defensive buckler, seeking her aid: a glorious, wide-famed nation she was! The Danube carried her fame to the south, and the high Tatras broadcast it to the nations of the north!

There were no desert wastes in that land. She was sown with villages, cities and castles, just like a meadow in springtime with multifarious blooms; the citizens of these towns traded far and wide, enriching their motherland justly and fairly: a populous land she was, and rich! The neighbouring lands gazed upon the abundance of her cities and castles, of which she rightly swelled with pride.

Your Fathers settled this land in times immemorial, times so ancient that even legend no longer remembers them; it was a thorny and unkempt, wild land they settled! But having settled there, they began to develop it little by little; they cleared it of thorn and thistle, carved it with plough in the sweat of their brow, sowed it and planted, so that it would give forth grain and fruit. And the land indeed bore them generous grain and tasty fruit, and your fathers were gladdened with the fruits of their labours!

Forests thick and impenetrable spread far and wide, filling the people with dread of their dark shadows and giving refuge to wild beasts in their dens. And they cut down the thick forests and built dwellings upon the clearings, in which they dwelt with their families, and they found it good to dwell there and had joy of the work of their hands.

Their families grew in size and with their growth, the number of dwellings grew, drawing close to one another; from the thickly huddled houses grew villages and the villages in turn grew into towns and cities. Thus did your fathers prosper, for which they gave thanks and sacrificed to their gods with glad hearts. They had not yet been enlightened by the divine teachings of Christ, for they bowed low in prayer before gods and goddesses, which they had fashioned themselves of wood and stone. Many times as the year rolled on did they gather in the presence of their gods, in large numbers, and having done their service, they gave themselves over to gaiety, and the forests echoed with their graceful songs. And the forests gave ear to their singing, murmuring along with them, and carrying the melodious echoes afar. And peace and happiness reigned in their families.

But the day is threatened by the night, the burgeoning grain by storms, and your fathers too were threatened with danger from restless and lawless nations,[49] and for this reason they found it necessary to bind themselves together more tightly, so as, thus united, they might oppose the invaders and defend themselves. and for this purpose they elected a ruler, to whom they swore obedience, blessing and anointing him.

Who might that be walking there, staff in hand, wrapped in a cloak tatty and worn; who climbs up on the rock that stands lonely in the empty field; and what host is that, which gathers round him, gazing with respect at his noble figure? The man on the rock is the chosen leader of the people who surround him, the leader who is to remember whence he came and whither he may descend, if he were not to rule his people with righteousness and justice. And such leaders as he indeed ruled their people with righteousness and justice, and the people preserved unto their rulers their loyalty,[50] serving them and singing of their glories.

King Mojmír assumed rule of Great Moravia in the year of our Lord eight hundred and sixteen. The chronicles speak of him as the first to ascend the Great Moravian throne. He had already accepted the holy sacrament of baptism, and many of his people willingly followed his example. He ruled his people solicitously and wisely, like a good father cares for his household.[51] Firmly, too, did he grip the sword, so as to preserve his land from attack and ruin. Now, Mojmír's noble and manly acts were not to the liking of the German emperor, nor was that emperor pleased with the manner in which the land of the Slovaks was growing in power. For this reason he invaded it with his army and deposed King Mojmír from his throne. And the nation bewept the dishonour done to them, and the toppling of their good king; bitterly indeed did they lament their loss.

After him, Rostislav, his nephew, ascended the Great Moravian throne, and the nephew surpassed the uncle, exceeding him in both the wisdom of his rule and his heroism on the battlefield. He waged a bloody campaign against the Germans, and liberated the country from all subjection, which the Germans had imposed upon the land of Your Fathers. Nor did he busy himself solely with warring, for he likewise cared for the salvation of his people. For he summoned unto his country Cyril and Methodius, two brothers

---

[49] The original text has a misprint here: it reads *nároků* ('of claims') where obviously it ought to be *národů* ('of nations').

[50] In the original, *šetřit*.

[51] *Jako dobrý otec čelední nad domem svým.*

from the land of the Greeks, that they might traverse the country preaching unto the people and teaching the divine Word of Christ. And as they went about instructing the people, they gave ear to them as they spoke of great things, and of the wonders of God. And they toppled over all the pagan idols, bowing their heads before the Lord. And the Lord was pleased with this people, for he made them to multiply and spread wide the borders of their land. But Satan drove on the Germans, inciting them to the ruin of a king so devoted to God, causing that Rostislav be plagued with treachery and fall at last into the hands of his enemies. Then was the king, that pious and heroic old man, beladen with frightful fetters on his hands and feet and dragged off to the land of the Germans, where they set him before a judge and passed sentence upon him, that he be put to death. Yet they did not murder him; rather, moved with the sort of mercy that only the devil might inspire in them, they put out his eyes and cast him in prison. There, suffering in his dark dungeon, the king expired. He had no one to dress and bury his tormented corpse, for he gave up the ghost far away from his own land and people, amongst foreigners and murderers. The nation trembled in horror at the fate of the good king, and there was no one who might comfort them in their sorrow and bitter lamentations.

After him came Svätopluk, his nephew, who towered over kings and princes in wisdom and martial valour like a poplar amongst willows. War with the Germans once more burst into flame. But its fire fell upon the heads of the Germans, as Svätopluk battered their regiments,[52] smashing them and scattering the survivors. And great fear fell upon the Germans, seeing that they could not oppose so strong a king, and so they began to consider how they might bring him to ruin. At this very time there arrived in Transylvania[53] fleeing bands of nomads[54] known as Magyars, who were escaping in fear from other nations. For they had stolen away from their own homeland in the Urals lest they be enslaved. On their escape they lived from banditry and upon horse flesh. These then the Germans approached, saying: 'Come, let us fall upon the land of the Slovaks together. For you shall be shattered if you fall upon them by yourselves. Neither we nor you can do anything

---

[52] There is possibly a play on words here in the original Czech. *Pobil Svätopluk pluky jejich* — note the similarity of the word for regiments — *pluky* — and Svätopluk's name, which adds the modifier 'holy, sacred' to a syllable identical with 'regiment:' Svato-pluk.

[53] Štúr uses the Slavic term *Semihradsko* here — intimating that Transylvania was part of the Great Moravian Empire too.

[54] *Ouskoci*.

with this warlike people on our own, but if we strike them together, we shall overcome them. You shall obtain a lovely and fertile land to call your own, and we shall be delivered from our fearsome enemies.' And the vagrants gave ear to these words, for they had no land whereupon they might spread, and pasture their horses.

And so the Germans gathered their troops and, joining with the vagrants, fell upon the kingdom of the Slovaks. But this first attempt ended badly for them, for Svätopluk shattered both the Germans and the vagabonds — spurning them head over heels. The glory of the great leader and king then rang out from the Danube to the Tatras, and the Tatras echoed it far and wide, far to the ends of the earth. The Germans were beside themselves in fury, whilst the wanderers scattered in fear to hide themselves in the forests, where they lurked in wait for better days of banditry.

Then it came to pass that Svätopluk fell ill. Sensing that the day of his departure from this world was near at hand, he called his three sons to his deathbed and, dividing his land among them, exhorted them to concord and the fear of God. And the princes having accepted their apportioned lands from him, the great king expired. O great, but unfortunate king! 'Twas Thou didst found the kingdom of the Slovaks, and Thou who didst undermine the foundations of the same by dividing it amongst Thy sons! We praise Thee on account of thy deeds, but raise our complaint against Thee, for having thus plunged Thy descendants into long ages of misfortune, digging the grave of the motherland which Thou thyself didst engender by Thine own might!

Svätopluk's oldest son Mojmír, having obtained the greatest share of his father's divided state, assumed his father's throne. But his brothers envied him his place, and, rebelling against him, enkindled a civil war, the flames of which consumed the land at last. At this was Satan delighted, seeing that all was proceeding according to his intentions. So, swiftly he drove the pagan Magyars forth from the hills and against the Christian Slovaks, inciting also the Germans against them, to their destruction. And drawing upon them in great numbers, and seeing that the might of the Slovaks had been divided into three, they fell upon them quickly and shattered their empire in pieces. Ah, what a misfortunate hour then tolled for the Slovaks! Those miserable sons of Svätopluk came to their senses — but it was already too late. For their armed might had been squandered, and the vagabond regiments overgrazed their meadows and farms, fattening themselves upon the sweat of Slovak brows. Mojmír fell at the battle of

Prešpork, which was then known as Břetislava,[55] in the year of our Lord 907 — and along with him the Great Moravian Empire died as well. His younger brother doubtlessly fell in battle too, while the third, in penance for his sins, retired to Zobor[56] where he dwelt in secret in a cavern. He became a hermit, and from his lonely peak he would gaze down upon Nitra, ever calling to his mind his impious acts, in this way sincerely sorrowing for his sins. Ah, but just as much as the tears of a child are worth, spilled at the grave of the mother he will never see again, just so much was your penance worth, you godless man, to your countrymen!

And the Danube murmured in sadness, foaming in its banks, moved at the fall of the native realm, and the Tatras covered their brows in sadness, while a voice, yearning and dark like the voice of the owl at midnight, tolled from its cloudy summit 'Slovaks!' That voice echoed through mountain and vale, from all sides darkly resounding, 'Slovaks!' And the Slovaks bewept their empire, and their glory!

There had been seven kings of the Great Moravian Empire, and from the beginning the capital region had been the cities Velehrad and Nitra. O Nitra, Nitra, who can call Thee to mind without amazement; who can call to mind Thy ancient glory without shedding tears for Thee? Over and over they have told us: rejoice and be glad, dance! But how can we be joyful, how can we gladly dance, when Thou ever standest thus before our eyes?[57]

Thou wert set in a high place amidst cities and nations, like a tower looming over dwelling places, like the mast of a ship above the seas, like a swan upon the bosom of the waters. And now Thou art stretched low upon the dust!

Thou hadst wide-spreading lands as Thy footstool, gazing upon Thee with respect as their queen — and now Thou art bent low to the earth, Thyself!

In praise of Thee there once resounded countless songs, and minstrels came unto Thee from far and wide to do Thee homage through the voice of their lyre, prostrating themselves before Thy glory: while today hardly a single faithful scion of those old, chosen ones[58] of Thine intones a song of sadness for Thee!

....

[55] Bratislava, today; formerly known by its German name Pressburg.
[56] A mountain looming above Nitra.
[57] Cf. Psalms 136: 3-5: 'For there they that led us into captivity required of us the words of songs. And they that carried us away, said: Sing ye to us a hymn of the songs of Sion. How shall we sing the song of the Lord in a strange land? If I forget thee, O Jerusalem, let my right hand be forgotten.'
[58] Štúr uses the term *vyvolenec* here, meaning 'elect' or 'chosen' one — continuing with the Old Testament parallels.

The rising sun was wont to cast its light upon Thee swiftly at its dawning, and set slowly, its lustre ebbing lazily from the domes of Thy towers and Thy fastness: but now it rises late to Thee and sets quickly, for today Thou liest prone in a vale and Zobor bends over Thee, like Thy willow, weeping!

O Nitra, Nitra, who can think of Thee without astonishment, and who, mindful of Thy ancient glory, can refrain from shedding tears over Thee?

And thus passed away the country, the fame, the happiness of the Slovaks — although their strength had not yet been destroyed, wherewith they might have liberated themselves, redeeming their land from those cruel ones who laid it waste.

The vagabonds took note of this, and because they valued the land of the Slovaks above all else, they said amongst themselves: 'Let us settle in this land, but let us not oppress the Slovaks, whom we conquered only with great difficulty, lest, rising up in arms against us, they should expel us from their beautiful land and we should again be made to wander the earth homeless, without a land to call our own. Let us take them to ourselves, bind them to us, so that it should seem to them as if they were still living in their own country: thus it shall be good for us to live in the midst of a nation so industrious, diligent and peaceful.' And they did as they had determined upon doing, accepting for their own the laws, with which the Slovaks governed themselves, upholding the old administrative divisions of the land, as well as the original nomenclature of these regions, and accepting the more excellent fathers of the Slovak clans amongst their landed gentry. The Slovaks agreed to the terms of this covenant and swore by their God to preserve the peace and not to take up arms against the Magyars. And these last, joyful at having achieved what they desired, quaffed blood to seal the agreement, for they were still pagans. To the covenant it was further ratified that the Slovaks would not be hindered in their worship of the one true God, and that they would have the right to carry out all business, private and public, in their own tongue, and according to their own customs. And the Magyars settled beyond the Danube and on the banks of the Tisa; the Slovaks remained in their beloved Tatras, and those Slovaks who had been living beyond the Danube moved to the Tatras, so as to live peacefully amongst their fellow countrymen.

Now, both because they were prohibited by the pact from plundering among the Slovaks, and because they feared to do so, lest they be banished from the land again, and also because they somehow could not get used to a settled life and labour, but were accustomed to live from the sweat of the brows of others, the Magyars set out to plunder the Italian and German countrysides. After their expeditions they would return home to live off their loot for a certain time. But they met with misfortune in Germany. For the Germans gave them a sound thrashing, and took away from them all that they had previously accumulated through banditry. Their most stinging defeat occurred near Merseburg, where all except seven were lain low by the sharp swords of the Germans — and these seven the Germans sent home, having first lopped off their ears, to bring the news of their whipping to their countrymen and to announce that they needn't expect any profit from such expeditions, as all of their booty had been lost.

Those who had remained at home were stunned at the horror of the unheard-of catastrophe that had befallen their countrymen, and they sorrowed that they would no longer be able to live from plunder.

For this reason, they now approached the Slovaks and begged them to teach them how to plough and tend the fields, and provide themselves with food. The Slovaks acceded to their request. They taught them farming, and provided them with a large number of ploughs, with which to commence their labours in the fields, and which to use as models for the construction of further ploughs. And the terrified Magyars thanked them for such charity, and they adopted a great number of Slovak terms descriptive of husbandry and fieldwork, for they had no such in their own tongue. For they knew nothing of farming before this, as heretofore they had only busied themselves with brigandage.

And it was difficult for the Magyars to accustom themselves to work in the fields and to rise to toil in the heat of the summer. And thus, once more they yearned to take up banditry. But the Slovaks restrained them from expeditions of plunder, showing them what they themselves had elicited from the bosom of the earth by the labour of their hands, assuring them at the same time of like success, if only they would apply themselves to labour. Thus they encouraged them by their good example.

At last, the Magyars set themselves to work. Seeing that the earth bore them grain as a reward for their toil, they were persuaded, and grew accustomed to it. At this the Slovaks rejoiced, seeing the Magyars commence toiling, for well they knew that, only in this way might they be weaned from their previous savagery, and begin to live with them, peacefully sharing one land.

Before this time, the Magyars had no permanent buildings or houses, for leading a nomadic life, they knew only quickly erected hovels and lean-tos, in which filth reigned and no implements were to be found. It was the Slovaks who taught them how to construct clean, spacious dwellings and how to fashion various tools and implements for household use.

At this time, the Magyars were pagans. In their blindness, they called upon various creatures in prayer. It pained the Slovaks to behold a people knowing nothing of the true God, the Creator of Heaven and earth, above Whom there is no other Lord, Who reigneth over all, Whose throne is the heavens and whose footstool the earth with the waters of the seas. And moved with pity, they said amongst themselves, 'Let us send teachers unto that nation, whom the Lord doth not hold in such contempt that they should continue to err in the darkness, that they might raise their countenances unto Him, from Whom cometh all goodness, Whose love is greater than the love any father beareth unto his children.' And this they did, sending unto them teachers, so that they should preach unto this people blundering in darkness. They brought to them the Word of the Lord, announcing unto them His awesome works, which manifest His glory. But the time had not yet come to its fulness for that people, blind in their paganism, that they might behold the light.

And thus were the Slovaks struck with fearsome wonder at this stiff-necked people. And they said unto themselves: 'His time hath not yet come among them. But we shall not cease in our labours, beseeching still the Lord to show His mercy unto this benighted people, that He should not withdraw His hand from them.' And so again they dispatched teachers among them to preach the true God; to show the wondrous works of His hands to the deaf, and to speak unto the blind of His endless love and immense mercies. And God did bless their works, for the Magyars, seeing that the Slovaks were doing them so much good and that whatever the Slovaks advised or enjoined them to do, turned to their profit. In this way did they accept their God, slowly, and they began to humble themselves before Him. Then did the Slovaks dance for joy, seeing that God had shown His mercy unto that people.

At this time, 980 years after the birth of Our Lord, Hungary was ruled by Géza. When he saw that the Christian faith was spreading among his people, he betook himself to aid its propagation. And so he summoned unto his land Vojtěch, the Archbishop of Prague, a pious and learned man, to act as an apostle in that land. He gave his son István, that is Stephen, to be baptised by him. Stephen was to succeed him on the throne. There was great joy of this in the neighbouring lands, because even the Hungarian governors accepted baptism, and because the man who Christened them was a Czech, of the same blood as the Slovaks. Along with Vojtěch, more priests came from the Czech lands, and these spread about over the country preaching to all the people the words of God in the Slovak tongue.

Stephen succeeded to the throne in 997. As soon as his reign commenced he set himself to the task of spreading the teachings of the Lord with all his strength, going about with the priests himself. From them he had learnt all the precepts of the Christian faith in the Slovak tongue, and these he proceeded to explain to his people in Magyar. He built churches and founded monasteries, establishing pious people, native Czechs or Slovaks, in them. And because he laboured himself like an apostle in his land, for this reason he is known as the Apostolic King, and after his death, he was declared by the Church to be a saint.

Now indeed there had arisen against the ardent king a man named Kupa, who was the leader of the rebellious Magyars, those who grumbled against the word of God, wishing to continue their stumbling about in the darkness of paganism. But the king crushed the rebel and his band — something in which the pious Slovaks especially aided him.

And behold, in this way did the teachings of the Lord arise and spread among the Magyar nation, slowly making firm the commonwealth established in such exemplary fashion. And the Slovaks rejoiced in the progress made by their neighbours in Christianity, as the faith took root amongst them, and in their development in farming, crafts and commerce — all of which they had learned from them. And thus they grew united to them in one, Hungarian homeland. Now, she was to be the common mother of all — Slovaks and Magyars — who were equal to one another in all laws and privileges.

And from that time forward, both Magyar and Slovak lived proudly, in one land, both being faithfully devoted to that common mother. They elected various kings to the throne for the government of the land and showed unto them a loyal fealty and a steadfast faith. And they found it good to reside here, for the land waxed in prosperity and brotherhood.

Indeed, from time to time the motherland was threatened by various savage and murderous nations: Mongols, Tatars and Turks. But the conjoined swords of her united sons swiftly vanquished all these hordes — all those who had come intending to pasture their steeds and herds on the fat meadows, on the fields covered with thick stalks of grain, and to spill the blood of the citizens of our land. But it was especially with the Turks, who terrified the nations of Europe with their savagery, that the bloodiest battles were fought, and most frequently resounded the clash of swords opposing on the fields of Belgrade, which is on the lower Danube.

Belgrade, Belgrade! How often hast thou beheld upon thy plains the mortal clinches of armed regiments? How frequently has the choking, throttling smoke of war wafted about thee! Thou, who wert like a ball kicked about between the warring sides, whose fate was decided over and over again as victory wavered from side to side, battle by battle. Thou who hast felt most keenly their wounds, Thou mightest speak most knowingly about those wars!

Belgrade, Belgrade! How many thousands of tears have been shed by Slovak mothers at the mention of thy name, the mothers of sons who had marched off to battle beneath thy walls, never more to return!

About thee rushes the Danube, her waters dyed with the blood of our heroes, and those waters flow into the sea, changed into blood. Thy fields are graves and those graves were once pyres, upon which Slovaks were consumed on behalf of Hungary, our common motherland.

But I will raise no bitter lament for the fall of thousands of heroes, our countrymen, for their death was a glorious one, on behalf of their motherland.

Behold, my fellow countrymen, how much our fathers laboured on behalf of the land where we reside, how much they sacrificed on behalf of Hungary! Who might enumerate them all, who might be able to recount them all? I shall not be carried away with such a narrative, for the items to be retailed are without number; for the Slovaks were renowned for industry, bravery, and swiftness of intelligence from age to age, so that were one to count up the men most signal in talents in Hungary, only a small number of them would not be of the Slovak nation — your nation.

And now the Magyars too rejoiced in having such a nation within the bounds of their country, upon whom they could always rely and depend, and they lived with them in peace, for they recognised their services on behalf of the motherland, Hungary, which nourished them, the Magyars, as well as the Slovaks.

And yet the superiority of the Slovaks over the Magyars, and, what is more, the wealth they accumulated by their hard work, aroused jealousy toward them on the part of some of the Magyars, and these grew angry at the fact that they were unable to equal the Slovaks in ingenuity and wealth. And these envious ones began to invent many a calumny against the Slovaks, and to think up ways of rising above them. But as they were unable to accomplish the same at first, this only made their hatred of the Slovaks increase and stiffen. But the Slovaks, not being such themselves as, being unable to elevate themselves by their own efforts, mock and scorn those who do so excel (and in this way give witness to their own baseness) took no notice of the machinations of their enviers, who burned with hatred toward them.

So now you have heard, my countrymen, my tale of the ancient age of the Slovaks; and now it is only fitting for me to speak to you of the new age, in which, unhappy ones, it has been given us to live.

I do so unwillingly, for painful are the things I must relate to you. But as your fellow countryman, careworn on your behalf and faithful to you, so must I make you aware of everything that concerns you, and what the future holds for you. Therefore, give careful heed to me, my fellow Slovaks! Give ear!

* * *

The new, frightful age of the Slovaks commenced at the beginning of the present century.

The spark of hatred, which the Magyars kept burning for the Slovaks, was fanned and fanned ever more as the ages passed until it burst into flame — a flame that began to rage in this century of ours.

Pride elevates itself alone, holding all others in contempt. Wherever possible, it treads others underfoot. Thus the pride of the Magyars grew and blinded them utterly.

And so their leaders gathered together with all their chief councillors and they said to one another: 'This land is our land, and all who reside herein are in our power. Thus we may encumber them, and do unto them, according to our will and pleasure.'

And then did there resound the voices of the loudmouths and the fools there assembled: 'Bravo! You say well! Let it be as you say!'

The leaders and chiefs were greatly pleased that their advice was received as wise, and thus they boldly declared: 'Whosoever shall not recognise our rule as wise and legitimate will not be considered worthy to sit on our councils, and whoever shall oppose himself to our determinations will not be considered worthy of the protection of our laws or entitled to whatever is good in our land.' And once more the voices of the reckless landowners resounded: 'Unworthy! Unworthy! Long live our leaders and our chiefs!'

Now the leaders, wishing to rationalise these unexpected and peculiar determinations of theirs, cried out anew: 'Rule over this land properly belongs to us, according to the rights of conquest won by our triumphant forefathers. The nations that we find here are as conquered peoples, subjected to us; servants, for which reason it is just for us to deal with them as we see fit.'

At this much noise and revelry resounded from amongst the loud-mouthed toffs, for these words of the council's tickled their pride and flattered their desire for rule.

And so they continued, saying: 'Because the Magyar nation is that which conquered this land and took unto itself the rule thereof, it is only right and just that their language should take precedence over all others and broaden its reach, while the languages of the subservient peoples should humble themselves before it. In time, they should be swept away, for good it is, and needful, that there be but one tongue in our motherland, and that one language that is to be spoken, that is to dominate all others, should be, by right, the tongue of the Magyar nation.'

Then, following these words, the council hall was filled with unending screeches, for the toffs were very pleased at the thought that henceforward they would not have to learn any more languages,[59] but have need of just one and one alone.

The council went further and declared: 'The Slovaks are a subject people. Let them learn the language of their masters which, once they have done, they will forget and abjure their own tongue and become Magyars themselves.

'The same is true of the Germans, whom we accepted into our land after their wanderings, and unto whom we showed all kindnesses, without which they would have gone away in starvation and need. The same must be true of all other nations living in Hungary. Let us therefore legislate strict laws to this end — let us begin this work of ours!'

And the noise and revelry of the loudmouths knew no bounds. For now they had been given the hope that they should be lifted above all other nations by their hatred.

Then the leaders and the chiefs added this to their determinations: 'Slovaks and Germans and all the other petty nations are furthermore bound by gratitude itself to renounce their mother tongues, for it is the Magyar land that nourishes them; it is Magyar bread they receive from it, and all the good they have comes to them by the good graces of the Magyars.'

'That is so! That is so!' leapt from the throats, by now raw and hoarse, of the loudmouths ranged about the hall, 'Long live our leaders and our chiefs!'

Here ended, for a time, their council, and they all dispersed, to the cheers of all, who cried:

....

[59] Up until 1844, when Magyar was pushed through as the official tongue, Latin was used as the administrative language of Hungary.

'How great are these men of state; just councillors they, for at heart they have nought but the happiness of the motherland, and truth. Long live our leaders!' echoed abroad, as they led them out.

Now at this council there had also been a considerable number of Your fellow countrymen, O Slovaks. But some of them were skittish and bent at the merest breeze; others were like reptiles, picking their careful way along in the dust, while still others were puffed-up braggarts. And all of these approved of the determinations of the leaders and chiefs of the Magyars. The first did, so that they would not be oppressed by the voices of the loudmouths. The others wished to lick up to them, and the third thought themselves to be masters of this land as well, and felt that they did not belong amongst those who were to be shunted aside. And they set themselves to such a loud crying, insulting and crude, as was above and beyond those of the Magyars themselves.

And musing upon the determinations of that council, I set forth, brooding, to walk about the Slovak lands, over which my feet so delight to travel. Without even noting where my legs were bearing me, I suddenly found myself upon the banks of the loud-rushing Váh, the booming current of which shook me out of my meditations. And then I saw upon its banks the mounds and hillocks which are said to contain the ashes of our long-departed forefathers. Wondering whether the statements of the Magyar councillors and chiefs could be true, and whether I had been misled by the testimony of what has been written concerning the agreement between our ancestors and theirs, I was moved to call forth the shades of our long-departed forefathers to hear their testimony. It was that hour when night just begins to spread her bed upon the earth, when the heavens begin to roll the dusk into the valleys, when I began to cry out:

'Arise, spirits of our forefathers! You, who during the reign of Svätopluk walked the earth, who lived in King Mojmír's time, arise! We conjure you from your graves, for we would learn of you — did you preserve unto us a motherland, and a secure place therein, or did you sell it out, to God's disgust, to foreigners?

'Arise and speak! That we may either rejoice in our inheritance, or pile our curses upon you in your graves!'

And at this I saw, flashing from the earth of the tumuli on the banks of the Váh, something like tongues of flame, which grew and grew until at last entire figures of *manes* could be seen, at the appearance of which the winds of the vales began to blow. And so these shades stepped forth and stood there, motionless. For it had been nine hundred years now, since they'd forgotten this earthly life, and now, the piercing voice of a son of theirs had called to them, calling them forth.

'Are you the *manes* and spirits of our forefathers?' At this, the shades nodded their heads.

'Have you handed over your motherland, the land of our inheritance, to strangers such as would deprive your descendants of their rights, allowing those foreigners to treat us according to their whim and pleasure?'

And all grew silent, and not a single shade from amongst those assembled there made sign of assent.

'Therefore, you so compacted with the strangers that you would remain such citizens of the newly founded motherland as you had been in earlier days? And you have handed down such rights unto us, your descendants?'

And each and every one of the shades nodded his head.

'Descend once more into your tabernacles then, in peace, O spirits of our forefathers, and may nothing disturb your rest ever again. Blessed is your memory amongst us, as is reflecting upon our past.'

And the shades disappeared once more into their graves, until they had all vanished, glimmering; yet the wind continued to sigh mournfully through the valley.

But because in the meantime the night had spread thickly over the earth, and there was no domicile to be seen in the vicinity, I lay myself down to sleep upon the mounds in which our forefathers rest.

But I could not fall asleep for a long while, for my mind was full of the vision I had just experienced, until at about midnight, finally, I fell into a deep slumber and behold — a new vision came unto me, but these were no longer shades I looked upon, but skeletons, capering. To them I posed my questions again, in answer to which they all nodded their heads in confirmation, thumping their feet against the turf, so that one could hear the rattling of their bones, after which they took me up and carried me unto a high place and showed unto me the land stretching round and about; once more they thumped their feet and, carrying me down again, placed me once more upon my bed. And I slept deeply and did not awaken until the sun shed its light over the land and the labourers were at their toil in their fields. Then, I went down thinking of the strange things that I had been permitted to experience, and I walked along the banks of the roaring Váh. And as I so walked, I came across a farmer, toiling at his labour in the fields surrounded by cliff and chasm. So I went up to him and wished him the help of God in his toil, for which he thanked me. And then I entered into conversation with him, as the time of his breakfast had come round.

'From whom did you obtain these fields, my good man?'

'I inherited them from my forefathers, and each week I labour upon them, for their upkeep.'

'And no one else works these fields except you, farmer?'

'Now, who would work them, toiling in the sweat of his brow, except me? You pose strange questions, sir, such as I've never heard before. The owner of the fields must work his fields by himself, or with the help of his household, if he wants the fruits of the labour to belong to him. Should he give over the labour to others, he should deprive himself of the profits of his own fields.'

'And who is it provides you with the seed, with which you sow your fields, farmer?'

'Who else if not myself? If the seed from last year's harvest is not sufficient for this year's sowing, I must buy the seed. It so happens that this year I bought rye for seed down there in Nové Zámky, and dearly, from the Magyar merchants.'

'And so you do not eat the bread of strangers, farmer, nor do you take the charity of others for your nourishment? May these questions of mine not anger you, for indeed it has been said that you and others like you live upon the charity of others, and not from your own wealth and labour.'

'May God preserve us from the charity of others! We neither need nor desire any such!'

'May God be with you, my good man; may the work of your hands be blessed one hundredfold!'

* * *

Once, it came to pass that a certain farmer, rich in fields and vineyards, fell ill. In his illness, he was unable to manage his wide-spread lands. And so he called his sons unto his sick-bed and, dividing his fields amongst them, apportioning each something to care for, he thus said unto them: 'Toil diligently, my sons, each upon his own allotment, so that the fields should give back a generous yield, and none lie uselessly fallow. I have divided my lands amongst You, not with the intention that each of you should labour only for himself, but rather that each of these divisions, well-worked, should bring a generous harvest to all, so that your common farm should grow day by day, rewarding you generously for your labour.'

The father died soon thereafter and his sons began to work the land. Yet each of them wished to be his own lord and master, and each thought himself wronged by his father's division of the farm. Thus, before long, they began to quarrel, sowing dissension amongst themselves, for they had forgotten that they were to farm together, and that the lands thus held in common were to bring each of them more wealth than they would, otherwise, each on his own. And it so came to pass after a little while that a certain foreigner came to settle the fields neighbouring theirs. And when he saw the discord amongst the brothers, he usurped unto himself a portion of the lands of one of them, who of his own power had not the strength to expel the stranger from his land. For the other brothers paid no heed to the wrong done unto their sibling, for each one thought 'now shall I be wealthier than he.' But then, other foreigners, noting the success of the first usurper, began to ready themselves as well to fall upon the lands belonging to the other brothers, and take unto themselves each as much as he could of their lands. Seeing this, the brothers said amongst themselves: 'Lo, we have done wrong in quarrelling over our father's lands divided, and sowing dissension amongst ourselves. For behold a portion of our brother's land has been taken from him, and now the same fate nears us, day by day, according to the maxim "Today you, tomorrow me." Therefore, let us unite once again, with one will, and reunite our farms, so that they be held in common among us.' And so they did, the farmer's sons, and when they had reunited, they planned to fall upon the foreigner who had usurped that portion of their brother's apportionment. But as they discussed how they were to do so, they came together in council and said, 'Let us allow the foreigner to retain what he has already taken. For after all he has begun to accustom himself to our ways. Let us invite him, then, to join with us in common holdings, and stand with us, so that together we might be all the more able, with his aid, to resist the other strangers looking to ambush and usurp our lands.'

And so they did, and the foreigner being summoned to the common administration of the farm, in answer replied: 'I will administer all with you in common, for it pleases me to be amongst you, and I shall be with you as one of yourselves.'

And from that moment forward, the farmer's sons cared for the farm in common with the stranger, and they lived as friends, the brothers, their sons, their grandsons and their descendants, meeting in council together to decide all matters that concerned them, and defending the farm together against all foreign attack. And God sent blessings down upon them.

These quarrelling brothers are your ancient forefathers. Their father is the ancient ruler of this your subjugated country, and the foreigner who arrived and with whom your fathers began to administer their holdings in common are the Magyars. Those common lands signify this our homeland,

and the descendants spoken of, these are You, Slovaks; the descendants of the foreigner: the Magyars, united in the bonds of a common homeland. Those foreigners lurking at the frontiers of the farm, threatening attack, are the barbarian and enemy nations, which you, along with the Magyars, have victoriously repulsed from your borders.

And the Slovaks diligently worked the common earth from age on age, faithfully keeping their word as agreed upon with the Magyars, for how where they not to keep it, for the good of our ancient homeland?

Now, he who has worked diligently and conscientiously for so many years on the fields of the common farm, bearing the burden of the swelter of summer and the inconvenience of winter, is he not deserving of a proper reward for his toil from the common granary? Has he not the same rights as his associates, to a like share? Now, the granary of our common earth is the welfare of our motherland. We are the associates, equal to one another, to all of our fellow countrymen, and are we not to enjoy an equal share in the welfare and happiness of our homeland, such as she distributes to those who toil upon her behalf? Who would dare deny us this, claiming to do so on behalf of the motherland, who loves all of her children with an equal love? But lo — false prophets have arisen, who proclaim 'in the name of the motherland': 'We call upon you to reject your native tongue and customs, and to transform yourselves into Magyars.'

Don't you dare say such things! Don't make your claims in the name of the motherland, you false prophets; don't try to deceive us with the suggestion that you're acting for her happiness! For she cannot be happy unless her children are happy, and her Slovak children cannot be happy unless they be educated for the common good, and serve God, in their own dialect.

Don't you cry out, and don't demand in the name of the motherland such things as she does not demand herself. For it is You, You who demand our denationalisation for the satisfaction of Your own hatred and pride, insolent and empty ones!

Many have been the motherlands in which multiple tongues were spoken — and they were happy lands.

Even now there are many motherlands in which more than one language is spoken, in which more than one nation exists, and these are happy lands! For the welfare of the motherland is sacred to all her citizens, nor do they seek to rise above one another, nor do they hate one another, but rather they live together in unity and concord, so that their common motherland should be happy, and they along with her. Lo: varied are the nations you will find in Switzerland: Italians, French and

Germans — and each of these you shall hear speaking in his own mother tongue. And yet all throughout their motherland peace and welfare have their domicile; for none of these nations strives to dominate the others; rather, all are obedient to their common motherland, to the one mother of them all.

In Britain too various are the languages that are spoken: the English, the Scottish and the Welsh, according to the various nations that inhabit Britain. And their motherland is great and happy, for none of these cries out: 'This land belongs to us alone! You others are subject to us!' No, the motherland is constituted of all who live within her borders, who are obedient to her societal laws, and who bring their offerings to her.

*　*　*

Now, when the news had spread abroad, that the chiefs and leaders of the Magyars had decreed that the Slovaks, Germans, and all the other small nations inhabiting Hungary were to be magyarised, the rascals and deserters among them began to swarm and take counsel as to how they might further these plans. And in a short while, the deed was accomplished.

They debated various means for doing so, for they said, whatever law they choose to enact, decreeing that these smaller nations learn the Magyar tongue, they themselves would not be able to enforce the statute until such a time as they aroused in the Slovaks a desire to cleave unto the Magyar tongue, of their own free will. Among the suggestions, the following was offered by one of them: 'Let us gather together much money and take it to the leaders of the Slovaks. Then, bribed with our funds, they will tell their people that it is unavoidable and necessary for them to learn the Magyar tongue.' This language they praised above all others for its beauty, imposing it upon all the sons of the Hungarian motherland, saying that 'A Hungarian and a Magyar have always meant one and the same thing. Thus, because we are all Hungarians, we must all be Magyars, too; we must all of us be Magyars if we wish to be seen as good and faithful sons of our motherland.' And all of the scoundrels present cried 'Vivat! Vivat our wise advisor! We shall carry out his plan!'

But when it came to the collection of funds, when each was to give what he could, and what he wished, they learned that they had no such money; and where should they obtain it, these rascals and deserters? All the same, they continued to cry full-throatedly for money, while others urged that they seek out some other plan.

Now, upon seeing that no one wished to give anything, the advisor who had put the suggestion forward set a few gold pieces on the table, in such manner laying the foundation for the funds for the magyarisation of the Slovaks. But when no one followed his example and added to the pot, the rest began to cry, 'Let us set aside that counsel and enact some new means, to which everyone might set his hand, according to his capacities.' Then one of them spoke up and said: 'Listen to me, my good men, my brothers! There will be no better plan for the magyarisation of the Slovaks than to think up invectives of all sorts against them; to hold the Slovak nation in contempt, along with their tongue, their ethnicity, their national costumes and mores and their whole way of life — for then, soon, the Slovaks of their own free will shall begin to condemn their heritage, cleaving unto our nationality, so that they should not be laughingstocks, held in contempt. In this way, I reckon, we shall encompass all that we desire, without any expense of funds.'

And all of the gang cried and howled with many voices: 'Vivat! Vivat he who brought forward such advice!'

Resolving thus at their council, everyone set about apportioning amongst themselves the labour of sowing such tares among the Slovak wheat. Since now they had no need of money, and some funds had been donated toward the first stratagem, they determined to take that money and make merry with it, rewarding themselves with a gay celebration after having laboured so hard on behalf of their motherland. And so they went, rejoicing and revelling lavishly as long as the hellars lasted. Then, having slept off their rout, they bade one another farewell, each departing to his own corner of the motherland, where it was determined that they should go and preach to the shame of the Slovaks.

Yes, these apostles scattered through the various Slovak regions, commencing their labour, announcing to all and sundry the disgrace of the Slovaks!

And some of them would not even deign to call the Slovaks human beings, declaring only the Magyars to be a chosen race.

And others mocked with laughter the customs and mores of the Slovaks, saying that they were stupid and raw.

Still others made laughingstocks of the ancient Slovak state and their King Svätopluk, painting hideous caricatures of him and spreading these in large numbers about the land.

And other of these clowns mocked Slovak foodstuffs, saying that only Magyar bacon is proper food.

Others yet guffawed at the mountainous regions inhabited by the Slovaks, saying that God was not to be found there, and aggrandising at the same time the Magyar wastelands.

And others distorted and ran down the Slovak tongue, declaring the Magyar tongue noble, elevated in comparison to the supposed coarseness of Slovak.

Others still made fun of the Slovaks on account of their kinship with the 'impure' Moravians and the 'deceitful' Czech beggars.

Such things and others of this sort did they spread amongst the people as they travelled the length and breadth of the land.

Ah, but you have heaped up coals upon your own heads,[60] you mockers, you evil-doing, thievish scoffers, you worms burrowed deep in horseradish, who believe there to be nothing sweeter than horseradish, and no better habitations than such burrows as you call home.

From whom, I pray, did the nation you so adore learn what it means to be human, if not from the Slovaks? Who christianised you, who taught you to construct houses, work the soil, settle the land and be governed by laws, if not the Slovaks?

Thus when you state that the Slovaks are not human beings, you say as much as: 'We come from cattle, for such were our masters.'

Who was it that polished your wild manners, when you pushed into our lands on your horses, if not the Slovaks, who never thirsted for human blood? By exclaiming that the manners of the Slovaks are raw, you but proclaim your own rawness, for it was they who pacified your manners, although — unfortunately, you were not, nor are you yet, the most diligent of pupils.

Cast not your mockery upon Svätopluk, who was the glory of his age. The Germans had a taste of his might, and you yourselves would have had a proper mouthful, had he not fallen victim to the deceptions of a strong foreign king. No — just glance into the chronicles and, as in a mirror you will find reflected there your ignorance. By distributing shameful images of Svätopluk you act as children flinging mud upon the monument of a great man.

Leave our foodstuffs to us, for they please our palates. It is not for us to smear and dribble ourselves with your bacon and half-raw flesh, which you find such a delicacy. O, that you were never in need of our crumbs!

....

[60] See Proverbs 25:22 and Romans 12:20, although *Na hlavy své sypali ste oheň* may have more of a sense of 'calling down fire upon your own heads.'

The regions we inhabit are beautiful and we love them, as the falcon his high cliffs and the stag his deep woods. We have no interest in your deserted and windy wastelands, over which one scarcely catches sight of a solitary bandit skulking. God speaks to us in each tree, each hill, each stream; in every storm brewing over our Tatras, which light up with their flashing the vales we love. What has the dumb *puszta* of yours to say in response to such heavenly voices?

Our tongue is smooth and polished. It possesses none of your un-European ö-kus. It wounds the ears of no one, unless it be the ignorant, amongst whom you are surely to be reckoned. It is an intuitive and rich language, and you have used it to enrich your own! Erase from your language the words of ours that you have borrowed from us, so that you should no longer bruise your tongue against them. Ah, but your daily repetition of them shall be penance for your mockery.

We are not ashamed of our kinsmen the Czechs and the Moravians, however much you would like to make laughingstocks of them, so that we should break the bonds between us, bonds which are salt in your eyes. Have a look into Moravia — you shall find there such cleanliness as is never seen in the hovels of your people. Tell us, in what way have you ever been deceived by the Czechs, unless it be their surpassing you in art and science and industry that you call deception?

They never expected anything from us, and when they settled amongst us they but amassed fame on account of their industry and creativity, which you envy them, you vain prophets.

Such are the apostles who have come amongst you, Slovaks, preaching Your opprobrium. To this day they wander still in your midst, seeking their own advantage. And indeed, they have been successful in tempting, and with disgraceful words, splitting away from the nation the ignorant, the weak, the pot-lickers and the vainly puffed up, who, united unto them, carry out their shameful missions along with them, burrowing like very worms into the depths of their own people. Oh, you wretches! Far better had it been for you, had you never been born![61]

Now, after the passage of a certain amount of time, the chiefs and leaders of the Magyars came together once more, so as to proceed in their deliberations, how best and most quickly to magyarise the Slovaks. The terms Magyar 'council' and 'leaders' are not to be understood here as if they indi-

---

[61] See Mark 14:21 and Matthew 26:24, where Christ uses this phrase in reference to Judas.

cated some sort of real corporate body; rather, these words signify the whole chorus of those who think, speak, and act as described above.

And when the deliberations commenced, one of those present arose and spoke thus: 'It is not enough to direct the Slovaks to learn the Magyar tongue, for mere commands are not always strictly cleaved unto in these lands, and so in this way the magyarisation will progress very slowly. We must therefore take other, more powerful, means in hand that we might arrive at our desired ends.'

Then from all sides voices rang out: 'Vivat, vivat your wise counsel!'

In response to this challenge, one of the councillors arose and said, 'Let us so decree that in all schools, both small and great, teaching should take place only in the Magyar tongue, and all the pupils must be trained in Magyar alone.'

'Splendid is your advice!' innumerable voices cried out.

'If we wish to realise this proposal,' another councillor stated, 'let us establish a reward for all those teachers who, in their sedulousness for instruction in the Magyar tongue, distinguish themselves by heaping opprobrium upon the Slovak language and forbidding their pupils to speak it.'

'That is wise, so very wise,' resounded numberless voices, raucously pealing.

'Now, so that our efforts to magyarise the people be supported from another side and take root in their hearts,' said another, 'let us impose upon all pastors in those parishes where both Slovaks and Magyars reside that they preach in Magyar alone, whereas in parishes inhabited solely by Slovaks, at the start, let us impose the use of Magyar in church only several times a year. Later, this will of itself grow, once the people recognise the excellence of the Magyar tongue and the purity of our intentions. But so that we should bring our designs to fruition, let us establish a reward for all preachers willing to preach in Magyar, threatening on the other hand with penalties whomever amongst them should hesitate to preach the word of God to the Slovaks in the Magyar tongue.'

Now, there were several present at the gathering who sighed quietly at this suggestion, but out of fear of contumely and provoking stormy cries, they held their tongues and allowed the suggestion to pass unopposed, at which the entire hall thundered with applause.

And when the applause had ceased, yet another one arose and said, 'Wise are those suggestions, but we will never achieve our ends unless we go even further. And thus I propose that children from Slovak towns be taken from their homes and transferred into Magyar settlements, there to remain until such time as they forget their native speech and become fully magyarised.

And there was no end to the clapping and riot at this suggestion.

But even this did not satisfy the chiefs and leaders of the Magyars, for yet another arose and said: 'We must take in hand still other means for the magyarisation of the Slovaks. As I see it, it would be best to station Magyar soldiers amongst the villages and towns of the Slovaks, and when one of these should be magyarised, to send them on until the entire region has been magyarised, all of the Slovak inhabitants, to the very last man. Now, so that these means might be effected, let us promise a monetary reward to each of their head men who should conduct his business with his underlings and workers in Magyar only, for the space of three years. Thus shall we encompass what we desire.'

'Wise, wise, vivat your counsel,' echoed throughout the hall.

'So let us accomplish our goal,' said yet another. 'Let it be forbidden to the Slovak youth in the schools to be educated in their native language, so that the Slovak nation should be deprived of an educated élite. In this way they will be joined to us. For they shall have nothing written in their tongue; they shall not be able to teach independently of our writings. For the nonce, they can express themselves in sermons, but this too will come to an end as soon as all the Slovaks are magyarised.'

And there was enormous applause and whooping throughout the hall, all in praise of the triumph of the Magyars and the destruction of the Slovaks. The council was thus brought to an end and the councillors paraded out to shouts of joy, the faces of councillor and cattle shining triumphantly.

* * *

Now, when this council was over, I took myself again into the Slovak regions along the banks of the Váh, so that I might cheer my eyes with the beautiful riverside regions and soothe my suffering heart.

And as I progressed through the lands, passing through one village after another, the evening fell. And catching sight of a group of husbandmen who were conversing amongst themselves on matters that concerned them — since it was not a work day — I drew close to them in order to speak with them myself, since I have always enjoyed such conversations.

'God grant you a good evening, village fathers!'

'God grant, God grant — welcome amongst us, pilgrim! From whence are you travelling to us?'

'I come from the low valleys to draw refreshment from these Your mountainous regions.'

'Indeed you may well find refreshment here, among our mountain summits, in our clean air, drinking from our bright streams of water! Come, sit closer, join us, pilgrim!'

'Thank you, village fathers! What is the news in your village? How are your affairs getting on?'

'Everything in our village is peaceful and quiet, though times are hard. May the heavens grant us better days! And yet duly we discharge our obligations to our king and our lord, to the commonwealth and to our holy ministers.'

'It is right and good to discharge your duty in all points to the King, all that belongs to him, for he labours for your good, and all that you give him, he returns in fulfilment of your needs. Right and proper it is as well to support your ministers, for they have care of your souls. And so it is you yourself who pay the salaries of your ministers?'

'Of course. Who should pay them, if not we ourselves? And we pay them with good will, for they serve us well.'

'And have you also a school in your village, my good fathers and husbandmen?'

'Of course we have. How should we not? It is to our ghostly teachers and our school that we owe a debt of gratitude for being able to read and write and reckon our sums, to sing sacred songs along with others in church, to the glory of God, the Creator of Heaven and earth, of Whom we have all necessary knowledge — and all thanks to our school, especially, in which we learned such things during our youth. And beside these, we have learned many other things as well, such as the history of our Hungarian motherland, and that of other lands, of economy, and other such matters. And the things that we have learnt ourselves, we want our children to learn as well — and even more! We would that they should know more than we do. For in today's world, one cannot be happy and successful without the requisite knowledge.'

'And in what language was it that you learned these things, my fathers?'

'What language, indeed, if not Slovak! We understand no other, and around here there live only pure Slovaks!'

'And who was it that built your school, my good husbandmen?'

'We built it ourselves. Whom might we have asked to do it for us?'

'But listen — now your children are to learn in the Magyar tongue those things that you learned in Slovak.'

'God preserve us from such misfortune! For then they would learn nothing of these necessary things at all, and would grow wildly, like the trees on the mountainsides, without any knowledge of God, without learning to read or write, without any knowledge of their own motherland and their obligations toward the King, toward their country, and toward their fellow men.'

'True enough, good fathers. May God spare you such misfortune.'

'But who would ever contemplate handing our children over to be educated in the Magyar tongue?'

'Such people exist, and indeed I come from a council during which such things were discussed. But from the words and gestures of those people there, it was obvious that they are not concerned in the least whether or not you should learn anything at all, as long as they have their way, and satisfaction be made unto their arrogance.'

'But our King will not stand for such a thing, pilgrim! For he always defends us from injustice, and certainly does not wish his subjects to be stupid and crude.'

'Such is not his will, fathers and husbandmen. Certainly you have a righteous advocate in him; just is his sceptre. Therefore, render all praise and honour to your King!'

* * *

Raise your voices in song, O valleys of the Váh, in praise of your King! Sound, ye winds, through gorge and vale, and incline your brows, O hills and mountains, in earnest honour of the crowned Head!

For misfortune threatens the land and stormclouds gather overhead, but the King shall take his stand in the midst of his people. He shall raise his sceptre, and the misfortune will dissolve, the storm run off, aghast.

Each individual citizen strives for his own happiness; officials look after the comfort of a small number of people, but the King strives for the comfort and well-being of all.

Balls and fêtes are organised all over the land, and the people rejoice at them, casting aside their worry and their care. But even in the midst of dancing, the King is engulfed in care and concern for his subjects.

When the citizen's workday is over, he relaxes with his family, later to lie down in peace upon his bed. But the King keeps watch throughout the night, concerned as he is with the well-being of his subjects. Even when he closes his eyes in sleep, care for his peoples often interrupts his slumber.

Raise your voices in song, O valleys of the Váh, in praise of your King! Sound, ye winds, through gorge and vale and incline your brows, O hills and mountains, in earnest honour of the crowned Head!

* * *

When morning dawned, I set off on my further pilgrimage along the Váh, so as to chase unquiet thoughts from my mind with the soothing beauty of what I looked upon. And I passed through village after village, my eyes skipping gladly from summit to summit, over meadow and murmuring stream sparkling in the sun. Upon leaving a certain village, I came across a man leading some children out onto a meadow. The children were eager to play, for it was a beautiful day in May.

I guessed immediately that the man was the children's teacher. For who else would be leading them out to play? And my heart was filled with joy at the goodness of the teacher, who desired the children to enjoy some innocent fun, which would serve both to refresh them, and invigorate their bodies. But soon my joy was tarnished, upon hearing the teacher order the pupils about in Magyar, for they comprehended not his words, at which they reacted in different ways, searching his face and following his gestures in an attempt to understand him — for they knew not his tongue. And from time to time he bellowed at the children in Magyar, while they never took their eyes off him, trying to comprehend his will. Now, when they did not do what he commanded them to do, he cursed at them so sharply that they shivered in fright! Such a game did the teacher provide for the innocent children!

As I continued to watch the children on the meadow, I noticed that not all were taking part in the game. Rather, some were sitting to the side with sad expressions on their faces. Those who were playing said not a word amongst themselves. Instead, they signalled to one another what they wished to convey, by gestures. From this I understood that they had been forbidden to speak their native tongue — so that they should become unused to it, until they forgot it entirely, learning to use Magyar in its stead.

As I continued to gaze upon what was happening before me, I beheld a man from the village come to join in the games. For in the Slovak lands, adults frequently take part in the recreations of their happy youth. Him I asked why it was that some of the children were sitting to the side, excluded and, as it seemed, sorely pained. Had they transgressed, perhaps, against some rule of their school?

To this the man replied, visibly moved: 'Yes, of course. They transgressed against a rule laid down by their teacher, by speaking Slovak amongst themselves in school, for this teacher of ours punishes, and sharply, such disobedient ones, wishing to bring it about all the more quickly, that they should speak Magyar exclusively, and hold Slovak in contempt.'

Now, when I asked the man why it was that they allowed their children to be treated in such an inhuman and godless manner, which is to their own greatest detriment, he answered: 'This does not depend on us, my good Sir. Our teacher receives an award of twenty guilders yearly, as well as the praise of some, for carrying out such a strict Magyar school regime. And with this we are not able to contend.'

I blushed with anger at these words, and with a torn heart I turned away from the torture on the meadow and continued on my way through the valley of the Váh.

* * *

How low you have fallen, O my people, that you yourselves carry out orders leading to your torment and extinction, which others would have spurned with contempt. You have thrown yourselves abjectly at the feet of your oppressors, who tread you beneath their heels with cruel abandon.

The wind that booms, echoes with the voice proper to him; the bird sings in his own voice and the beasts refuse not to bellow in their natural voices, but You, man! are forbidden to speak in your own tongue!

Your oppressors set you lower than the brutes, lower than the birds and lower than the realm of things incarnate, yet you look upon this with apathetic eye.

How low you have fallen, my people! And who now shall raise you from the depths to which you've sunk? Who shall be your saviour? Get up yourselves, my people, and then shall others raise you even higher, recognising your human rights!

As I passed on from there, I came upon some men speaking amongst themselves in low tones. So greeting them, I joined them.

Having conversed with them a little while, I began to relate to them what I had just beheld in the village not far distant: that May outing; and I spoke with zeal against that unheard-of rigour. The men were moved by what I said, and they declared:

'It is true, it is true, that here and there they have begun to press Magyar into our schools, and where it is not accepted voluntarily, it is forcibly introduced. Not far from here, they also tried to insert the Magyar language into a school,' said one of the men, 'but as the local teacher did not know that language, they hired another, on the cheap. For idle persons are many these days, and they are easy to hire. And when the teacher in question arose against that plan in defence of his own rights and those of the innocent children in his charge, exclaiming that, if this were to be effected, the children would be deprived of learning both worldly and divine, they sought to have him excommunicated, in his old age, from the Church he had faithfully served for many years. But he did not allow himself to be confounded thus; he defended himself successfully, although he was unable to fully deliver the children from the torture prepared for them. And this is how we are dealt with in these times. But God is looking down upon it all from the heavens!'

We had arrived at a crossroads when the man finished his account with a sigh, and bidding one another farewell, we set off on different roads.

* * *

I glorify Thee, O noble man,[62] who defiantly opposed the torture of innocent children, and stoutly defended Thy rights.

Many there are in our nation, so forgetful of itself, who allow themselves to be abused and made sport of by the light-minded: but Thou hast dredged a moat between Thyself and Thy oppressors, forbidding them access, lest Thou be insulted by them, and Thy fields laid waste.

Thou hast set aside Thine own domestic comfort, preferring instead to be persecuted for the righteousness of Thy cause than to wallow in a dishonest, dishonourable tranquility. He who will not prefer to bear insult in defence of righteousness has never savoured her sanctity.

Few at the moment are they who follow Thy example, but Thou shalt be a model unto others, and Thy name shall be blessed by all the just.

* * *

Now, when the councillors had each returned to his home, and had broadcast the determination of the council, immediately there joined unto them many desirous of bringing about those proposals, so fatal to the Slovaks.

---

[62] Štúr has in mind his own father here, Samuel Štúr (1789 – 1851).

Plentiful is the number of settlements inhabited by both Slovaks and Magyars, in the churches of which the people were addressed in both tongues.

But then those who acknowledged the proposal of the council lost all love for that order of things, and they commanded the pastors of such communities to preach in Magyar alone. And hearing of these commands, the Slovak residents of those settlements were struck with great fear, for they saw themselves being deprived of the pious offices of the Church, through which they had lifted their souls and hearts to God, the merciful Father. For they recognised that they were being deprived of those most comforting of all words, with which a man might be presented — the teachings of God. And a great lamentation arose from those villages. And the Slovak citizens of some of them hesitated to continue paying the annual salaries of the ministers of the church, from whom they no longer received instruction in the word of God; but their reluctance availed them not, for they were constrained to pay for their own painful oppression.

And citizens of other settlements left their homes with lamentation, fleeing to other places, where they thought their complaints would be heard. But instead of that, they were met with blows of staves and knouts for asking that the others give ear to the lamentations of those deprived of the teachings of God.

May the earth swallow you, hideous city where pious souls were flogged with canes and pummelled with rods; may the earth swallow you, for within your borders the most hideous act has been committed: when honest souls were thrashed without mercy, all because they wished to lift their voices to God, the heavenly Father, the Giver of love, in their native tongue. May the sun of that merciful Father never rise above your fields, the sun He commands to shed its light and announce His love to the universe entire; may that sun never shed its rays upon the place where the children of the Father of love suffered shamefully for wishing to call upon Him. May the fires of the abyss erupt from the bowels of that place and consume it, that it no longer befoul the earth, that nothing should remain of that place, where God was cursed.[63]

---

[63] According to Josef Jirásek in his notes to the Czech original, this took place in Komárno. Among the Slovaks publicly whipped were Martin Bartoš, who took 64 strokes, Jiří Junáček (50), Pavel Russ (40) and Stefan Vrabec (24).

May a gigantic boulder fall from the skies and propel that place into the depthless chasm, so that no sign remain upon the earth of the place where God was so hideously blasphemed.

In yet other settlements, purely Slovak ones, it was enacted (to please the will of the minority) that sermons be delivered in Magyar, at least several times a year.

The people in such settlements were saddened at their loss, but since such was to be the case only infrequently, they acquiesced to the demands of the few. But the wanton ones did not greet this compromise with generous gratitude, for they demanded that divine service in Magyar more frequently alternate with the Slovak, and after a short while of such alteration, that services in Slovak be entirely eliminated.

And the people grumbled and rebelled against such impiety, refusing to come to church. When the wanton ones saw this, they thought it good not to announce beforehand when the sermon would be given in Magyar, so that the people, deceived, would be tempted to come to service. In this way their impiety would be hidden under the frequency of attendance of those so abused.

The people were stupefied at this shameful stratagem, so that when the sermon commenced in Magyar, they arose and left the church. For why should they sit there, to be offended?

Upon seeing this, the wanton ones set beadles at the church doors, who mercilessly beat with staves and knouts those exiting the church, pitilessly driving them back inside.

And the people rioted against such hideous barbarity, and they thrashed the beadles themselves, for which their leaders were taken and thrown into gaol.

* * *

Whoever has wandered through the Slovak lands and visited their churches has marvelled at the devotion, with which hymns are sung during divine service, and has pondered the piety in which the Slovak people are submerged while they sing.

Their sacred songs are the delightful blowing of the wind, and as the wind swells up to the heavens, so do they rise toward the Lord, bearing upon their wings the hearts of a devoted people.

O my people — your hearts are not to soar toward the Lord! In your tribulations, they are not to broach the heavens where your Father dwells!

The wind should blow down from the mountain summits, fanning your face with delight, descending in answer to your songs, which have arisen to heaven to the solace of your hearts, revivifying you with mercy: but now there is not even this last, paramount comfort to refresh your soul.

Wherein lies your fault, my people, that you are thus excluded from Heaven? But it has ever been the work of the impious to keep the pious from those blessed regions.

The diligent farmer toils a long week on his own fields, and on those of others, longing in pain for Sunday, when he may refresh his parched body with spiritual comfort: but even this joy is to be refused you, poor labourer!

But the Lord God looks down upon your pain, my pummelled and kneaded people, reckoning your suffering!

* * *

As I walked along, deep in thought on what I had seen and heard, I suddenly came across a bit of theatre on a hill near a summer house, such as I had never seen before. There, a man all dressed in black was lying upon the ground, while this other clown was leaping roughly upon and around him, giggling. I paused to watch what would happen next. When the boor paused in his antics, he asked the man whether or not it gave him pain when he jumped on his body like that. And the man replied: 'I haven't felt a thing, and I'm very glad that I can be of service to You, providing You with such fun without being pained by it in the least. I am always at Your service.' For such an answer, he received food and drink from the clown. Setting himself to eat and drink, he praised the generosity of his friend to the skies.

But I could no longer stain my eyes with the sight of that grovelling reptile, that lickspittle, wherefore, aflame with anger, I ran off from there with all speed.

O vile man! You cast away both body and soul like carrion, already chewed upon by worm and buzzard — unworthy you are of the name and image of man. Who thus puts his body up for rent and sells his soul is like the lowly insects, and who casts himself down to grovel in the dust is worthy of being trod upon, like the dust of the footpaths.

O vile man! You have lowered yourself to the level of vermin, shaming in yourself the image and likeness of God and man.

* * *

No longer hast Thou a child to foster, no longer hast Thou a child to give Thee joy, O Slovak Mother!

The mother gives birth to her child and presses the innocent infant to her bosom; the baby wails and the mother soothes him with the words of her mouth, which shall become the child's mother tongue.

The child does not yet understand his mother's speech but his little eyes never leave her beloved countenance.

The child is weaned and grows and the mother chirps and chatters about him; he begins to understand, and to imitate his mother's voice. And the mother kisses her child and plays with him.

The child grows and speaks the words he has learnt from his mother's lips, and the mother's heart dances at the speech of her child.

The boy now plays outside with children his own age and the mother observes her child's games with joy — but she cannot be long without him! She calls him to her so as to kiss him, her little boy.

And she rears him in fear of God, and he learns from his father, and his parents rejoice in their offspring.

The little son has grown, learning from his parents and teachers to fear God; learning all things in his mother tongue.

But no longer hast Thou a child to foster, not longer hast Thou a child to give Thee joy, O Slovak Mother!

They shall tear your little son from your bosom and send him off to a settlement, where he shall have neither mother nor father, where he will have no one to talk with, and where he shall grow up without fear of God, deprived of all that is good.

No one shall watch over your little son in that land, and the house in which he shall abide will remain foreign to him.

They shall mock him there on account of his language, tormenting him, so that he will all the more willingly hold it in contempt himself.

And your little son shall lament a long while, until having learnt to gabble and chatter in a foreign tongue, he shall forget the home of his father. And the foreigners will flatter and blandish him, heaping contempt upon his native blood. In vain shall you gaze about your garden, searching for him at play beneath the linden, O Slovak Mother, for he shall be in foreign parts, unlearning everything you have taught him; unlearning the love he has for you, his father, his family and his teachers.

And he shall return, years later, but he shall not recognise you, though you embrace him and speak to him the words of a mother; for he shall laugh at your speech; he shall make mischievous jokes, and your maternal heart shall wither in sorrow.

His father will threaten him with punishment for his nastiness, but he shall raise his hand against his own father, or run away from his father's house, to become a man of the world.

* * *

Our king has need of his soldiers for the defence of our land, and you need them to teach the Magyar tongue.

The people of our motherland send their sons off beneath the flag, so that they might defend her in danger and preserve the throne of their monarch, who expends his every effort for the good of his subjects: but you wish to employ his soldiers for tasks other than the defence of the motherland and the preservation of our King, for you have something quite different in your hearts.

The words 'Motherland, Motherland!' are always on your lips. Thus you cry until your very throats are raw, as if on behalf of the country, but it is obvious from your intents and your deeds that these are nothing but words, which you use to disguise your real thoughts.

For how can you truly love the motherland, wishing as you do to achieve something quite different from what she wishes, what she yearns for; how can you love your motherland, when the peace of so many millions who speak not your tongue is to you a plaything, with which you toy according to your fancy? The motherland does not wish this, the motherland does not desire this, but you do, demanding it while abusing her name in its support, you vile, reckless ones!

A soldier's duty is to train under arms and stand guard at fortress and city, at his appointed station. However, you wish to make soldiers over into language teachers, establishing a new school such as never has been before, such as might only serve Magyar interests.

The King pays his soldiers, not you — and he, the King, shall be the one to command them, not you, curious commanders that you are, mixing yourselves into competencies, which, thank God, do not belong to you, yet which you would gladly wield according to your own arbitrary will. Ah, such cravings fit well your swollen pride!

But tell me now — how many Magyar sons stand pledged to our King? And what is their small number in comparison to the many Slovaks, who from age upon age have fought victoriously with his crest on the banners that fly above them? And with a handful such as that you wish to magyarise our land! Laugh on — you mouth-workers! Whatever hatches in those thick polls of yours seems possible to you…

* * *

And as I proceeded through the land, I came across an old, bewhiskered soldier coming my way, followed by a young lad dressed in military togs. Now and again the old soldier would burst forth into song, so as to give the young lad heart, whetting his appetite for the warrior's life. And he sang:

> At Leipzig, mates, we were at war,
> Firm-standing midst the firestorm's roar,
> The Slovak and the Croatian,
> The Pole, the Czech, and everyone
> For Motherland and Emperor.
>
> With Alexander in that clash
> The Slovak sabres keenly flashed,
> The cannon thundered up a fright
> And in that long, and noble fight
> Our enemies were soundly thrashed!
>
> The soldier's life's a glorious thing:
> To shed your blood for land and King,
> To stand and fight the enemy
> And boldly, fame and victory
> For King and Motherland to wring.
>
> O faithful sons! Fix now your eyes
> Upon the eagle, as he flies
> The foe with flame and steel to greet
> And grapple with his taloned feet!
> Sons of the Motherland, arise!

'Good day, good day to you, old veteran! How gaily sounds that hymn of fame and glory on your lips!'

'God bless! We old hard-bit warriors love to sing of past deeds, and, especially, of our victories.'

'I believe it willingly. For songs like that refresh the memory of Your glory, and the good old days of your soldiering. In any event, we Slovaks like to sing, and you're one of us, a Slovak.'

'That I am, sir, a Slovak, like all of my family. And old Alexander's regiment, in which I serve, consists entirely of Slovaks. O, that's a doughty regiment, sir, eager for the fight as hawks for chickens. Oh, sir! I could tell you many a tale of our heroism! Down at Aspern[64] we stood to such fire, and took ourselves so to the enemy at bayonet-point, that hardly a whole company remained standing from out the whole regiment. But the King awarded the bravery of his lusty warriors! We got double pay, and the wine flowed like water. Our general praised our bravery to the skies in his order of the day.

'Our regiment was brought up to strength again shortly thereafter, as a great number of our mates crowded to our colours, and gladly, because of our fame. And us old warriors, we take care of 'em, the new lads, as if they were our own sons.

'A few years after that, sir, we marched on Leipzig. O, there was a battle for you — the sort the world had never seen before. A hundred thousand men stood on both sides, facing each other — the cannon roared for three days straight, and for three days straight our sabres never stopped slashing, our bayonets never stopped thrusting — thousands fell, but we won a glorious victory over our enemies. And then, my good sir, we plucked ourselves up and, victorious, entered Paris itself along with our Russian allies — but this was some time later; doughty warriors they, and the Prussians too.

'The emperors rewarded us generously: Alexander awarded daily bonuses to our pay; we had all the wine we could drink, and those French lassies, why, didn't they cast their eyes at us! Because our regiment especially was

....

[64] This, and other of the old soldier's reminiscences, touch upon the Napoléonic Wars of the early nineteenth century. The battle of Aspern (or Essling) took place near the end of May in 1809. The first stanza of Štúr's song sounds odd in Polish ears. While there may have been Poles in the Austrian army, during the Napoléonic era, Poles (Francophile as they generally are) placed great hopes in Napoléon for the restoration of their partitioned country. Poles made up the largest contingent of the Grande Armée, after the French. Štúr's song can be understood mainly as an expression of Austro-Slavism: that political movement in the latter nineteenth century, which sought to win more autonomy and political clout for the Western and Southern Slavs by gathering them under the sceptre of the Habsburgs. Austro-Slavism is in contradistinction to Pan-Slavism proper, which aimed rather at bringing all the Slavs into a tight political union under the lead of Russia — something that Štúr was later to espouse, after growing disillusioned with the former.

made up of strapping fellows, my good sir, brawny and handsome as the wild rose. Now, who wouldn't want to stand to battle like that? We won peace for our Motherland, which recognised our bravery, and we fought for our king, who always strives for the good of us all, and we won glory and renown, we did.'

'Yes, you have won glory, you noble old warrior! Your regiment is celebrated for its gallantry; celebrated too are other of our regiments. Whither are you hastening, warrior?'

'I have been in my native village along with this young fellow, my blood relative, who had requested several weeks of furlough at home. I train him in all things military, I teach him, and now I have accompanied him home, as I too wished to glance in on my village, my people, whom I had not seen for such a long time. And yet they've all passed away, my dear Sir — all of my old acquaintances; hardly one or two yet remain. My father and mother have been in their graves many years now. I was heartsore, indeed, never to see them again, but what can I do, dear God, as I was prepared for that? For who might have foreseen that I should emerge alive and hale from so many battles, that I might one day revisit my native village? And yet, God be praised, here I am, covered with scars, but scars from wounds received on behalf of our motherland and our king.'

'Yours are noble scars, my warrior! But you there, youngster, how does the soldier's life appeal to you?'

'Quite well, my good Sir! I stand in the ranks as if I were poured of bronze; I shoot from a rifle as if I were wielding a pen, and few they are who can match my mark on the shooting range, driving my ball deeper into the target!'

'And you have become so enamoured of it, then, young man?'

'Oh, that I have! And when it shall come to war, we shall all stand as firm as a wall on behalf of King and country, and our enemy will never set a foot within the borders of our motherland, unless it be over our dead bodies.'

'Praiseworthy are your words, youngster! Are there many from your region in the army?'

'A whole army of them alone are to be found in our regiment, and in the grenadiers, and in the hussars. There you'll see lads stout and straight as fir trees, who briskly race upon their steeds, as fast as the wind.'

'Just remain true to your pledge, youngster, for thus you shall keep faith with your motherland and your King. Go with God, my countrymen, my warriors!'

'Go with God, Sir!'

And presenting them with a little something, I went on my way. And the old warrior began his song anew.

* * *

Thousands of your sons, O Slovaks, fight bound by oath on behalf of our King; thousands have fallen on behalf of the Motherland. And have not King and country reason to treat with You, as with other of their children?

Who can count up the thousands of Slovak heroes who fell fighting in manly fashion for their motherland? And you dare oppress us, in the name of the motherland! Say not that such is the wish of the motherland; blaspheme not against its sacred name. It is you, you who wish to stifle us, in your swollen pride, you brazen ones, you mischievous liars!

He who dashes the cup of fresh water from the hands of the thirsty, so that he should continue to suffer thirst, is the enemy of all goodness and mercy.

And he who forbids good to be done unto the needy and afflicted is accursed, for he looks with delight upon misery — the sight of which makes glad only the godless.

And he who forbids people to perfect themselves in mind and spirit — who holds them back from that which makes a man truly human — sins against the chiefest rights of humanity and draws a curse down upon his own head.

Thus upon your heads does it press now, the curse, for you have decreed that it shall not be permitted to the sons of Slovakia to enrich their spirit in their native speech, or educate their fellow countrymen in their mother tongue.

Wherein, I ask, lies your fault, you associations of noble youths, that judgement has been passed against you and that judgement passed after your innocence was made manifest? Wherein, then, lies your fault?

For your catchword was the enlightenment of the minds and hearts of the Slovak youth in their mother tongue, so that in future times they might enlighten their fellow countrymen in turn, giving drink to those who thirst and nourishment to the poor — and such aims as these caused consternation to the godless. For this reason, they passed sentence upon you.

Now what Greek, I ask you, will address a fellow Greek in Yiddish? What Italian will turn to another Italian in German? How then is the Slovak to address his fellow Slovaks? The preacher's voice resounds in the Lord's house, and the people give close attention to it, weighing each word, which seizes upon their intellects like fire — for the thoughts these words express have been transmitted in a tongue the people can comprehend.

The bard intones a song to the strumming of his harp strings, and the words of his song are sad. And the people who listen to him suck forth the melancholy from the words he sings. The hearts of the auditory are burdened with grief and yearning, for the bard sings to them in their mother tongue.

O you, who flatter and blandish with your shining countenances, who swear upon liberty and Motherland and human rights! Felt you no shame when you condemned those who make use of their freedom, preparing themselves to toil on behalf of the Motherland, who bore in their heart such devotion to human dignity?

But you are godless hypocrites in whose souls a fire smoulders that would ravage all that is good, which fire you conceal beneath the rags of outward appearance, so that you might all the more safely feed its flames and those of the other souls who smoulder so. You, it is you who would drive our nation into stupidity and blindness, so that stupid and blind it would cast itself at your feet, begging your mercy, contemning itself to grovel in the dust before you, where you might tread upon it and exploit according it to your own will and all the machinations that your black soul might devise.

But you shall not compass your aims, you snipers, for you have called the curse down upon your own heads. For the schemes of the godless are like bloated foam, which disappears, burst by the lightest breeze that blows from the regions of delight. You shall not compass your aims for they are fixed in your swollen pride; they are rootless trees, houses without foundations, castles made of sand, wills o' the wisp, puddles after the rain.

* * *

What do you intend to do, now that you are growing up, young son?

To make my parents proud, my countryman![65]

O, blessed is your undertaking, young son!

What do you intend to do, now that you are growing up, young son?

To be instructed in all needful things, all useful and lovely knowledge, with which to enrich my mind and feed my heart, my countryman!

----

[65] The word used here is *rodák*. While 'fellow countryman' or 'compatriot' are close English equivalents, *rodák*, as it derives from *rod* (more or less, 'clan') signifies a relationship deeper than the political — it is an ethnic term, a term implying common generation, common blood. Both Slovaks and Magyars are Hungarians, politically speaking; but in terms of the *rod*, both belong to different ethnic nations.

Splendid is your undertaking, young son!

What do you intend to do, now that you are growing up, young son?

To be of use to my fellow countrymen, through the knowledge I acquire, my countryman!

Excellent is your undertaking, young son!

And who are your countrymen, young son?

My parents are Slovak, and so my countrymen are also Slovak — it is to their benefit that I am preparing myself, my countryman!

True are your words, young son.

What do you intend to do, now that you are growing up, young son?

By all the means in my power to become of use to my motherland through the knowledge I acquire, and by my labour, my countryman!

And of which motherland do you speak, young son?

I was born and raised in Hungary, and I am protected by her laws. Thus, my motherland is Hungary, and for her I strive to become of use, by all the means in my power, my countryman!

Noble is your thought, young son!

And will you remain true and faithful to your motherland, young son?

For all times I shall, and truly do I believe that the motherland will repay me for my loyalty, my countryman.

And how shall the motherland repay you for your loyalty, young son?

It shall, if only it support the welfare of my neglected nation, which I love above all things, my countryman!

It is a just thing that you require! May your undertaking be blessed, young son!

* * *

Now, when the enemies of the Slovaks had visited the settlements everywhere in order to ensnare the unwary and inexperienced — some of them raining threats upon them, so as to frighten the meek; others acting with violent force, so as to tame the stubborn — it so happened that a certain respected man, of rare qualities, passed away.[66] He had been a mentor and leader to those citizens of Hungary who confessed to the Evangelical wing of the Christians.

---

[66] Jirásek identifies him as Alexander Prónay, who served as General Inspector of the Evangelical Church in Slovakia from 1819 until 1839.

And they saw in this an opportunity to inflict further ill upon the Slovaks who were resisting them, wherefore they seized upon all means in order to place someone of their own party in that office.

And many of them travelled about the land, touting the ancient clan, the wealth, and the love toward the motherland of the one they wished to be chosen, wheedling in all manner possible to ensure his election.

O, you mischievous ones! That which you asserted in the name of the motherland, and out of love for her, you really understood as relating to your own selves, your own party, and your unrighteous intentions!

For he, whose love of the motherland you extolled to the skies in all conceivable terms attached himself to your party indeed because the motherland had never taken any notice of him and never entrusted to him any office or dignity, which might have elevated him.

Bloated with pride and longing for office and dignity, after having been disappointed for so long, he attached himself to your party so as to be able to revenge himself upon his true motherland and her leaders for having previously rejected him.[67]

Now, what reasonable person will ever expect a desperado to set his personal interests aside, now that he has the chance to be of benefit to his true motherland? Will such a one not rage in frenzy against the motherland, rather, should he come across a little of the power after which he has lusted so immeasurably?

And the wheedlers succeeded in their subterfuges: they encompassed their aims, and their man was elected to the post of advisor and superior to those confessing the Evangelical faith of the Christians in Hungary.

Children sometimes come across a bush with berries, which are similar to cherries. They pick them and eat them greedily, not knowing that they are preparing great pain for themselves — for they are not sweet cherries at all, but Jerusalem cherries. Likewise, the Slovaks elected as their leader a man of the party inimical to them; they were cozened into this choice, for the wheedlers dressed him up in pleasing habiliments, making him comely to their eyes. They knew not that in choosing him they were electing a scourge, an unrighteous double-dealer, a spiteful scandal-monger and an oppressor of all things they held dearest. Such indeed is the nature of a rabid beast that

---

[67] The man referred to is Count Karol Zay (1797 – 1871), whom Štúr knew well, having been employed by him as a scribe for seven months in 1834. Zay strove, unsuccessfully, to win over Štúr to the magyarising party.

it erupts in cruelty toward every being over whom power has been granted it, as soon as it is provided with an occasion for cruelty.

Now, when this party man was elected, there gathered a countless host at the fête celebrating his election, and the eyes and ears of all that host were trained upon him, to consider the upstart and hear what he had to say. At last, he ascended the podium that had been prepared for him, the chosen one, with his partisans ranged below him, and in the deep silence that ensued, he began to speak as follows:

'Elected by you to this office, and raised to this eminence by no subterfuge, without having actively pursued it at all in unbecoming manner, or unrighteous exploitation of your voices, because I have been elected freely, freely I may speak unto you.

'Our Magyar nation must lie at the core of all our efforts. Upon it hangs the maintenance, the preservation, and the spread of our Evangelical faith; upon it depends the defence of all the liberties enjoyed by our motherland.

'Now, because we Evangelicals must be concerned with this above all else, so must we all take care for the spreading of our Magyar nationalism, and because these treasures cannot be preserved in any other way, the chief task of us all must be the magyarisation of the entire Hungarian land, and that as quickly as possible.'

And his speech was interrupted by his partisans' cries, which echoed throughout the halls: 'Vivat! Vivat!' When these exclamations died down, he continued with his speech:

'Every other tongue that exists, and is used in the schools of our motherland, raises its hand against her happiness. The Slovaks are indeed faithful subjects of our motherland, and the first of the nations to inhabit her borders, but education in their tongue, and indeed their tongue itself, constitute a dangerous threat to us. For this reason, their tongue must be extirpated all the more swiftly, and the Slovaks magyarised. And really, they should desire this themselves, for the shield and pavise, indeed the sole possible protection of the Evangelical faith is the Magyar tongue, the Magyar nationality, just as, vice versa, the guarantee of the preservation of the Magyar tongue is our faith.

'The power of the Catholic faith has already been broken, while that of the Evangelicals is fresh and vibrant. If we desire the spread of the latter and the suppression of the former, let us set ourselves to the task of magyarisation with our whole heart and soul — for it is the sole defence of our faith and reason itself.

'Thus do I address you, in all sincerity. No one honours more, and desires less the effacement of the rights of each tongue and each nation more than I. But here, all such ramshackle rights must cease, so that the Evangelical faith, and reason itself, should be triumphant.'

There was no end to the joyous cries of the chosen one's partisans. These cries, that applause, arose because so fiery and passionate were the words of the tatty little fellow, as if they arose from the depths of his heart. Then the host departed. Some of them parted from him with enthusiastic shouts, while others left, profoundly surprised. For had that elected one not been placed on a high seat set upon a slippery floor, such as needs only the slightest nudge for him to be toppled over with a loud crash, tumbled down upon those gathered beneath it, his partisans, who would then fall along with him, smashed to pieces?

So when the hosts had dispersed, the more reasonable amongst them said to one another: 'If things are indeed as the elected one has claimed in his lecture, and if it is the task of the Church to magyarise the nations, would that not mean that there is no equality in the Church among Greek, German, Slav, Magyar and whomever else? But did not Christ instruct His disciples to go out to all nations, to teach and baptise?[68] Is not every good Christian to call upon God often, worthily and reverently, in his mother tongue? Can it be more pleasing to God to be addressed in one language than another? Is it not written in the Scriptures that 'God is a Spirit, and they that pray to Him must pray to Him in spirit and in truth?'[69] And this one would have them pray in their souls and in truth in Magyar, and lead a Christian life only as Magyars?'

And others said: 'Do the things he was speaking of not belong to the saecular powers, which watch over us, and keep our Church in trim?'

'And if the Church has been entrusted with such earthly matters, is she also to oversee the judicial system, and to command the army to keep the borders of our motherland safe from enemy incursions?'

And still others said: 'Our ecclesial assembly is now divided into political parties. It has become an arena for stormy debate and political grumbling. Instead of searching for peace, they have sprung wide the cages of all the passions, and these shall now rush out and sweep our Church and our motherland away, like floodwaters.

---

[68] See Matthew, 28:19.

[69] John 4:24. The citation is almost verbatim; the verb used in Scripture, however, is 'adore' rather than 'pray,' but Štúr is, of course, trying to make a point about language policy.

'It is not proper for us to meddle with the things of earthly government, for the Church is not called to this. We are to be concerned with the good order and instruction in our schools, of the respective governing of our churches and the aiding of our teachers and their assistants, who toil at such meagre wages, doing our best not to embark, ourselves or they, on the fulfilment of political desires.'

But such wise words were echoed not by the majority, who were still seething with the passions of the raving ones.

O you petty man, who know not how to rule your own self, yet in your swollen pride desire to govern others, have you truly weighed the words you have spoken? Are you even aware of what you've said?

In what way will you ever prove that the preservation and spread of Evangelical teaching depends upon the Magyar nation and its tongue?

You have cast up your words just like a little boy tosses a handful of dust into the air. But your words were not intended to be as dust! The little boy cares not where the dust he tosses flies, and where it lands, but you wish with your words to win over the minds and hearts of many men. Now, the hearts and minds of your partisans had already been bartered to your views, and amongst them indeed you find echoes of praise, but were you so gullibly naive as to believe that you might convince others by your bold statements without reasonable demonstration and proof?

Now I ask you, how will you prove unto us that the Evangelical faith cannot stand without the Magyar tongue, but, furthermore, that Magyar is the only means of preserving it in its present state? Set forth your reasons and then await our judgement as we topple them. But will you not deny that with your statements you have spat into the eyes of history, and the present state of things, and all of those who confess to the Evangelical teaching of Germans and Slovaks?

How, I ask you, has the faith been preserved amongst these nations for so many centuries? Will you assert that this was due to the Magyar tongue, of which these nations inhabiting Hungary were completely ignorant, where only a small fragment of their people even learned the Magyar tongue or used it except in case of need? Surely you would not set yourself up so to be laughed at! So tell me how is it that their faith has been preserved? By the people's predisposition to it, and their love for it, I answer you, you ignorant man. But if you were to state, shamelessly, that in these latter days that love has lessened to the point of being destroyed, how do you intend to rekindle it in hearts and minds by means of the Magyar tongue? Does Magyar possess some magical power in and of itself, so that as soon as one's lips touch it, one's heart is consumed with an ardent love for the Evangelical faith? If such be the case, that the Magyar tongue has the power of a sorcerer's ring, you two-faced lackey, why is it that thousands of Magyar Catholics remain faithful to their ancient teachings and do not convert, en masse, under the compulsion of that spell, to the Evangelical faith? Does the Magyar magic not work equally in that manner? O, but your thoughts and intentions are of a different sort, you hypocrite!

You miserable man, so accustomed to babbling as you are, have you weighed your words? Do you even know what you are saying?

For you stated, so absolutely, that the preservation of the Evangelical religion depends upon the Magyar tongue, and that the preservation of the latter likewise depends upon the Evangelical religion.

And so your assertion is therefore that the preservation of the Evangelical faith depends upon the Evangelical faith's preservation! Thus did you gibber in public, stating that as long as a man is in possession of his reason, he is not insane, and as long as he is not insane he is in possession of his reason, possessing the same as long as he possesses it...

Does this not indicate that you were spinning in circles like a drunken man, who has deprived himself of his reason for a space? But you are not drunk with alcohol, of course, but rather with the passion of your vengeance.

Miserable man, have you weighed your words? Know you even what you are saying?

You stated absolutely, that instruction in every other language except Magyar — and which follows, every nation that speaks a tongue other than the Magyar — is a hand upraised against the good of our motherland, announcing therefore that stupidity and blindness constitute the good of our motherland! In so doing, you lost possession of human reason, and pronounced a curse against your own motherland. In so doing, you have committed the most repulsive sin against reason and our national patrimony.[70]

When you stated, absolutely, that the preservation of the Evangelical faith depends solely upon the Magyar tongue, and that Magyar is uniquely governed by reason, of which it is the surest defence, you stated by the same token that all other nations who do not spill Magyar vocables from their lips are not in possession of reason, and such is the same with every other faith except for the Evangelical religion.

---

[70] Throughout, Štúr uses the term *vlast*, which we translate as 'motherland,' because of the writer's frequent invocations of Slovakia as a female entity, and his use of terms such as 'mother tongue.' Here, for the first time, he uses the word *otčina* — 'fatherland' proper.

In this way you wished to heap dishonour upon everyone else, whereas that disgrace actually fell upon your own reasoning powers only.

Wretched man, have you weighed your words, and do you even know what you have said?

You stated that the vitality of the Catholic religion is already passed, although it has endured for many centuries and still today remains the chief religion of our fatherland.

And it shall survive, enduring all of your juggleries, thriving still when all remembrance of you and your comrades has been forgotten. O, I could wish that you would live as long as the Catholic Church will stand, that you might gaze upon her firm foundations with sorrow, and taste of the idiocy and vanity of your prophecy!

Miserable man, have you weighed your words yet? Know you what you've said?

You confessed that no one respects the rights of nations and their tongues more than you, and yet you tread them beneath your feet most foully. Where were your eyes? Where your sense of shame, that you did not flame red with embarrassment to express such a ridiculous thing, considering your actions in reference to the rights of nations? You blasphemed before all righteous men, acting as that wolf who, desirous of filling his belly with sheep, first pretended to be their best friend. But your blasphemies have won you nothing but the condemnation of all the righteous, who cast away with contempt such words, and those who speak them, too.

* * *

Who enters the sheepfold through the gate is the shepherd of the flock. To him the gatekeeper opens the enclosure, and the sheep know his voice, for he calls them by name and leads them out to pasture.

And when he leads them out, he goes before them, and they follow him, for they know his voice.

But they will follow no stranger; rather, they will flee him for they recognise no strange voices.[71]

* * *

---

[71] See John 10:1-10.

Children, the last hour has come. As you have heard that the Antichrist is to come, I tell you that even now many antichrists have arisen — from this we know that the last hour has come.

They have arisen in our midst, but they are not of us. For if they were of us, they would have remained with us. But they arose and went from us, so that it should be clearly revealed that they are not of us at all.

* * *

After one, or two admonitions, flee the man who has fallen away!

Knowing that he is a fallen one, a sinner who stands condemned of his own judgement.[72]

* * *

It was also said in that speech that the Slovaks are to be magyarised so that they should not seek to ally themselves to the Russians, who are of the same Slavic race as they, so that on the mere grounds of kinship they call not unto them, those northerners.

O man — you who made this statement, how could you so shamelessly accuse the Slovaks of disloyalty? When have the Slovaks ever shown themselves to be disloyal to their motherland? Have they not waged war in the ranks of her warriors against any and all of her enemies? Have not thousands of them fallen on behalf of their Hungarian motherland?

And you — are you concerned with the defence of the motherland, man?

Is the King not concerned with us, and does he not defend us from all of our enemies — does he not call our Slovaks, thousands of his sons, to the glorious standard of the monarchy? Yet you, in your pride, wish to cover with your protective shadow — him, who stands before you! And elevate yourself above him, your own benign lord, and that of the motherland entire! Can it be that with your shameless speech you also accuse the powerful defender of our lands of weakness, wishing to make him firm with your strength, you? — to rescue us from all danger yourself?

O wretched man — in your speech, you are like that fly who, seated on a carriage, believed that it was she who had created the very dust of the roads she travelled over.

---

[72] See Matthew 18:15-20; Matthew 12:37.

The Slovaks have warred, and war they shall, faithfully, on behalf of their motherland, but she must deal with them as she does with townspeople — as her own, and not — as some of you would wish — as vile slaves, foreigners and disloyal knaves.

Heed not his calumniatory and iniquitous words, neighbours and fellow citizens! Give them no credit, for they have arisen from a heart swollen with pride and a mind that has strayed from reason; a man that desires the ruin of the Slovaks for his own advantage.

A man whose mind has invented evil-intended accusations and mendacious complaints, in order to destroy the innocent and evilly provide whatever will set them back and prevent them from achieving their aims — all so as to satisfy his swollen pride.

* * *

Rivers flow down from the Tatras, booming and uniting into one, and thus do they flow on to the sea, their roar resounding on all sides.

Rivers flow in the north as well, flowing into the deep sea with a roaring that fills the air.

And who of sound mind will curse the Tatra rivers for roaring in the same fashion as the rivers of the north? And who shall be so crazed as to believe that the Tatra rivers will call forth the rivers of the north with their roaring, so that they should flood these regions with their waters?

Do not all rivers roar, and is this not their natural voice?

Mountain ranges rise in the south, and mountain ranges rise in the north. Those there erupt with fire and spew forth lava, while these here are peaceful and quiet. And who of sound mind would ever claim that the mountains of the north will one day become volcanoes, because they stretch their summits toward Heaven just like those in the south?

* * *

Two villages neighboured one another for many ages, living all the while in firm friendship. But between them stretched an unworked empty field. So the neighbours said: 'Let us go out together and work that field with united effort, to the advantage of us all, after which we shall divide the earnings therefrom equally between us.' So both villages gathered together and set themselves to the common task, working the field and sowing it, and when the harvest came, they divided it justly between themselves. But after a while envy took possession of the hearts of the labourers from one of the villages, possessing their minds so that they formed the intention of gathering unto themselves much more than a just division of the profits should allow them. Indeed, they would expel their neighbours from the common field. But it so happed that the field from which they wished to reap the extraordinary advantage yielded far less crops and their advantage was so much the less, by far. And so the envious ones said — 'The field has given forth no crops, and you there are the cause of this.'

But their diligent and just neighbours thus made answer to them: 'How can it be that we should be the cause of the field's barrenness? Did we not work it diligently and at the allotted times? Did we not see to its care, striving for its yield with all our might?'

But the envious ones said, 'You ploughed it with horses, and not as we did with oxen, and the horses trod flat the field with their heavy hooves. And this is the reason why it did not generously produce the grain, as it was wont to do.'

And their industrious neighbours replied: 'Is it not one and the same thing, to plough with horses or with oxen? Tread they not the earth in equal measure? And does their treading adversely affect the fertility of the soil?'

But the evil ones said: 'You ploughed on Friday, which is an unlucky day, whereas we ploughed on the days that were good.'

And their pious neighbours replied: 'Blaspheme not against the Lord God, ye envious ones! For does He not cause his sun to shine on Fridays? Does He not send down His rain from on high to moisten the earth on that day?

'How can you say that it is an unlucky day?'

'You are to blame for all of our misfortune,' said the envious ones to their righteous neighbours, 'and thus you must forfeit your rights to the field. And if it be not given over to us by the verdict of a judge, we shall take possession of it ourselves.'

* * *

You sow, you reap, you mill, and you are not to receive of the flour, the recompense of your labour, my good people!

You have done nothing harmful or evil to the detriment of your neighbours. You are just and God-fearing. But because you simply are as God wished you to be — in their eyes, you are guilty, and deserving of condemnation.

Trust in God, my good people, and permit not that your rights be taken away from you, which the godless would shamelessly deny you. Permit them not to take away your rights, but stand up boldly in their defence and take comfort in your innocence! For the fortunate hour will strike for you as well, when all of your troubles will vanish!

* * *

Now, when the chosen one saw that he had obtained the eminent position, which, petty fellow as he was, he had no chance of being raised to on the strength of his own talents and virtues alone, and which he so greatly desired, he began to ponder how he might exaggerate his powers and reward his partisans.

He grasped after all possibilities. Chiefly though, he turned his mind toward the unification of the Evangelicals, that is, the Lutherans, with the Calvinists, who, in Hungary, were entirely made up of Magyars. For he considered that, if the Evangelicals — mostly Slovaks and Germans — were to be united in one Church with the Calvinists — pure Magyars — the Calvinists would easily dominate the Evangelicals, for they were more numerous, and thus the minor party would be obedient unto them, as a matter of course, being weaker. It would be easier to command them thus, and direct them, at will.

Furthermore, because the Calvinists are Magyars, in this way the Slovak Evangelicals should be oppressed, which would lead, slowly but surely, to the extinction of their tongue, and their nationality. 'Such means as you propose are excellent,' exclaimed his partisans, and he set himself to work.

And so he began with pretence, chameleon-like, to put himself forward as the most pious of Lutherans — which was announced throughout the villages, and in the cities by all his partisans.

Now, he who is faithful does not trumpet his faithfulness abroad at the street corners; rather, he gives proof of it by his actions. But he who wishes to deceive and cozen others screams his own throat raw so as to drown out the voices of the faithful and then, at last, all the more easily, tangle them in his web.

We know what you had at heart, you hypocrite, when you so sought to persuade us! But all of your plots will dissolve as so much smoke and ash — just like your very name.

But the chosen one continued to cast abroad his desire to persuade the Evangelicals to unite with the Calvinists, claiming that there was no distinction, in fact, between their two parties. But the Evangelicals replied: 'Why is it that we have been separated for so many years, until this very day, if there be no difference at all between us? Why do we have separate churches, separate liturgies, everything different from the Calvinists? Because there is a difference, and that a great one, between them and us, and we are quite conscious of that fact.'

Now, when the hypocrite saw that he was getting nowhere, he said, 'Yes, of course there is something that divides us, but that division is a petty thing — so small that, if each side were to give in just a bit, we should all at last be unified.'

And this the two-faced fellow tossed out with such insouciance, as if the whole thing were nothing but bargaining at the market, haggling over trash, and not theological and ecclesiological matters, which touch upon and express the most sacred sentiments of man, those most deeply rooted in his heart.

But the Evangelicals said: 'We wish to remain true to the faith of our fathers, and we will not compromise any one of our principles. Just as we do not desire that anyone else compromise his principles on our behalf.'

When the hypocrite saw that he was getting nowhere with his proposal, he began counting off on his fingers the many advantages, and the sort of benefits, that would supposedly fall to the Evangelicals from such a union, drawing their attention at the same time to the Catholics, who would crush their Church, he said, if they did not join forces.

But the Evangelicals replied: 'We have always held fast to our Church, governing ourselves happily, as we do now — and our king has ever protected us, as he always will, from all that is evil and horrid, by the force of his laws, decreed on our behalf. What is more, our Catholic brethren leave us in peace — for they know that together we worship one God, and that we are citizens equal to them in all things, the sons of the same motherland.'

Seeing his hopes dashed in this respect as well, the hypocrite commenced to try and show them how many Evangelicals were favourable to the union. In this manner, he wished yet to influence the people, who up until then were not allowing themselves to be seduced by his underhanded words.

When once again the Evangelicals gathered in assembly to discuss matters of concern to their churches, the chosen one set his proposition before them. When he had finished speaking, a great shout erupted in praise of him — but, all those who clapped and cheered were his partisans and followers, who had elected him for the sole purpose of using him for their own evil-minded plans. But all the faithful and good Evangelicals turned away, shunning his words, his counsel and his suggestions, departing from the assembly in sorrow and pain, for they saw that the Holy Church and its synod were being made over into a den of party-men and deceivers, a shop of unclean and evil spirits.

Then, in his swollen pride, the chosen one began to broadcast the idea of a union between Evangelicals, Calvinists and Catholics, for he wished to make a name for himself as a church reformer and the founder of a new, unified Hungarian church. But the Catholics, true to the ancient faith of their fathers, swept away from them in exasperation and indignation the prating of that blowhard, for they too saw that what he aimed at was the destruction of their faith.

* * *

Don't allow yourselves to be fooled, you, who cleave unto the Evangelical teaching. Don't allow yourselves to be cozened and exploited, I say, by this hypocrite, lest your faith be dashed to pieces!

Your Faith is purer and truer than the faith of the Calvinists, who have many erroneous and unbecoming theories in their teaching.

For indeed the Calvinists teach that God created a large portion of the human race for the express purpose of damning them eternally, and so determining not on account of their sinfulness or guilt, but because it has so pleased Him to testify to His might and His ire through the condemnation of these souls.

And so the Lord does not wish to save all of the people, even if all people wish to be saved.

Furthermore, they teach that he who has been predestined to eternal life simply cannot fall away from the grace of God and perish, no matter how gravely he sins.

Moreover, the Calvinists believe that God desires the impious to sin, disposes them to sin, and even forces them to sin Himself.

Thus they hold that our Lord Jesus Christ did not come into the world on behalf of all, nor did He suffer and die for all men.

Now I ask you, how can this impure doctrine compare with the love of God, of which the Lord Christ is consistently speaking, to which all of His teaching refers, and upon which He founded His Church?

God is love, and he that abideth in love abideth in God, and God in him,[73] says the Holy Scripture, and does not that Calvinist teaching stand in contradiction to the clear voice of the word of God? God maketh His sun to rise upon the good, and bad, and raineth upon the just and the unjust[74] — so how could God, the Father of love, find pleasure in the godless, and in the spreading of godlessness, being Himself the wellspring of love, and all that is good? Is it not that the God of Calvinist teaching is a spirit unclean, who derives delight from the prospering and multiplication of the godless? Is not such delight a devilish thing? And to whom, I say, are people — the children of God — to run for refuge if not to Him, the good Father, Who watches over us all? But how are we to appeal to such a God, who wishes the perdition of many and fosters the impious, godlessly?

And for what reason, in the light of Calvinist teaching, should a man strive to be virtuous, if his virtue aids him in no manner, nor delivers him from damnation if such be predestined him? In such a case virtue would profit nothing in the eyes of God, to Whom, according to the words of Christ, faith is most pleasing. But they assert that if one has been already promised eternal life, his impiety and his sin is worth just as much in the eyes of God as faith and virtue, although we know that God detests evil. Is not their teaching impious grumbling against God?

Nor do the Calvinists think worshipfully of Christ, our Saviour. Already Luther himself said of them that they have little, or nothing, of Christ.

For hasn't Christ said of Himself that He was sent of His Father from Heaven so as to reconcile the world with His Father in Heaven?[75]

For God so loved the world, as to give His only begotten Son, that whosoever believeth in Him, may not perish, but may have life everlasting.

And God sent not His Son into the world, to judge the world, but that the world may be saved by Him.

He that believeth in Him is not judged. But he that doth not believe, is already judged: because he believeth not in the Name of the only begotten Son of God.[76]

....

[73] 1 John 4:16.
[74] Matthew 5:45.
[75] See 1 John 4:14, Colossians 1:20.
[76] And God sent not His son...the only begotten Son of God. John 3:16–18.

Nor do they rightly believe concerning the Lord's Table, and for this reason, that they do not accord the Sacred Rite its proper reverence, of old they are known as Sacramenters.[77]

Beware of their teaching, good Christians, lest you stir up the Lord God against you, or do offence to your souls! Beware, I say, lest you fall into the godlessness in which they wallow, who wish to despoil you of your language and religion!

For indeed they wish to make Calvinists of you, so that, having apostatised from your faith, you should all the more easily renounce your mother tongue, just as you renounced your religion.

For he who has betrayed his brother will betray his father and mother as well. Indeed, he will hold nothing sacred any more, and having committed one base villainy, he will commit others from habit and heart befouled. Thus, be watchful and on your constant guard that you be not deceived and seduced, surrounded as you truly are by enemies and tempters. All those who have arisen from your own nation, yet who work for the spread of the Magyar tongue amongst you, compelling you to adopt it, have fallen away from you already and search for ways to entrap you and deprive you of your religion. For they already confess the Calvinist religion in their hearts, that they should be all the more pleasing to the Magyars, for whom they toil as lackey herdsmen. Yes, those who encourage you to accept Magyar seek to clear a path, little by little, for the passage of Calvinism. For the times are evil and many are the seducers who prowl about;[78] be watchful then and take care, lest you fall. Reject such unification as would insult you and suppress your consciousness of who you are, and which would, in the end, deprive you of all that is sacred and natural to you.

Now, who amongst you, Catholic and Evangelical Christians, who amongst you, I say, would like to see your churches without altars and organs, such as prevails amongst the Calvinists, whose temples differ in nothing from common and vulgar places?

The altars of your cathedrals[79] and the organs of your churches enkindle the penitent heart to piety — for the practice of which you come to church in

---

[77] Sacramenters, or Sacramentarians, as they deny both Catholic and Lutheran dogmas concerning the Presence of Christ in the Eucharist. To them, the Eucharist is merely a symbol, a sign, hence, a 'sacrament' and nothing more. Luther argued against the Calvinist view espoused by Ulrich Zwingli at the Marburg Colloquy, which took place in October, 1529.

[78] See 2 Timothy 3:13; 2 John 1:7.

[79] Štúr uses the terms *chrám* (cathedral, large church) and *kostel* (church). The first term particularly is directed to appeal to the Catholics, to whom the apostolic succession of bishops

the first place. The sound of the organs which fills your churches leads your voices in earnest song, lifting them on more ardent, and humble, wings to Heaven. Yet of all of this you would be deprived should you allow yourselves to be drawn away from your faith and accept that of the Calvinists.

* * *

Be diligent then, in avoiding the false prophets who approach you in sheep's clothing, but who within are greedy wolves.
By their fruits you shall know them![80]

* * *

The end of the commandments is love from the pure heart and a good conscience and a faith that wavers not.
From this some have erred, as from their one destined goal, and having thus strayed, they incline themselves to vain speech.
Wishing to be teachers of the law, they comprehend neither what they say, nor what they espouse.

* * *

Take heed, brethren, lest perhaps there be in any of you an evil heart of unbelief. But exhort one another every day, whilst it is called today, that none of you be hardened through the deceitfulness of sin.[81]

* * *

Now, when the chosen one saw that his words were praised only by his own partisans and others who thought along the same lines as he, and that they had no access whatsoever to the hearts of the people, he lost patience, and began to think of other ways to ensnare people, compelling them to apostasy and winning them for the Magyar tongue. He began to terrorise many with threats, declaring that holding to the Slovak language and its instruction

is particularly important.

[80] Matthew 7:16, 7:20; Luke 21:30.
[81] Hebrews 3:12-13. Verse 12 continues from 'heart of unbelief' with 'to depart from the living God.'

were forbidden by law and dangerous. All who heeded not his words he threatened with strict punishment.

But no country might decree laws forbidding any sort of instruction or education, unless it wished to call a curse down upon its own head. For what country, I ask, would wish, or even think of desiring, that its citizens should remain in ignorance and darkness? Would this not be the same thing as if it arose in arms against itself, thus forbidding its citizens to become better and more perfect? Nor did our motherland ever decree such laws; it was you, you fraud, in your swollen pride, who think your notions, desires, and will are the law of the land. For you see nothing beyond yourself and your passions.

Abuse not the name of our motherland, nor her laws, nor those who enact them, and do not set yourself up in opposition to our king, who toils on behalf of the happiness of all his subjects! The deceiver also seized upon other slippery means; seeking to implement them, he sent out letters to the representatives of the churches and published writings, in which he accused the Slovaks and solicited others to do the same, noting not, in his passion, that he was contradicting his earlier words with his present assertions.

For indeed he claimed in his writings and in his letters that the large part of the Slovaks who held to their language were disloyal to their motherland and renegades. But how does this compare to the public testimony he gave before the hosts of Evangelicals in assembly, saying that the Slovaks are loyal subjects to their motherland? Do not his words contradict themselves? Can one accord them even the least bit of credit?

Is it not an ugly thing when a leader, into whose hands the defence of others was once entrusted, begins to persecute his charges? And is it not uglier still, when he has no cause to do so? But ugliest of all is when he exterminates them and fattens himself on their goods!

An orphan was once entrusted to the care of a stepfather, so that he should be taken care of and his inheritance preserved. But the stepfather was a greedy man, and he hankered after his charge's inheritance and thought up all possible means of embezzling them. Unable to destroy the orphan himself, he invented many a false charge against him, many a blasphemous charge against the innocent child, until finally he was sentenced by a judge and the stepfather was enabled to appropriate his inheritance. What that godless man perpetrated against the orphan, this have you committed against those who have placed themselves in your care, you wretch!

He also said that the Magyar tongue is the support of the Protestant religion, and that the spreading of the former would lead to the spread of the latter, as well as the overthrow and destruction of the Catholic religion, the strength of which, according to his words, is already broken. But not long afterwards, he broadcasted in public letters, which served his own ends, the assertion that the Magyar tongue is also the defence and refuge of Catholicity. Now, has he not contradicted himself again, upending his own words? Whence comes such a sudden change in his claims? Well, the old fraud saw that his earlier words, with which he sought to gain the Evangelicals for the Magyar tongue, incensed the Catholics against that language, and thus he noticed that his labours would all be in vain should he not also win those to the Magyar cause.

For this reason he changed horses and twisted his own words, so as to incline the Catholics to the Magyar tongue, in order to despoil them later of their faith. For he wishes to have but one speech and one religion in this land: that of the Calvinists, which is known as the Magyar faith.

Is it worth responding to such statements, which tear themselves up by the roots? Who is there but cannot see that this passionate fellow is blind? A person blind to all things save his own blind passion?

Nevertheless I beg you, leave off already, wretched man, for you have been stripped bare now, and you stand before the world in all your nakedness.

* * *

And thus, O Slovaks, your ancient times and those of the present moment have been lain before you in all truth, frankness and sincerity of heart. We have set them before you, for now the time of temptation has come upon you and our love for you is great. We have set them before you so that in these horrid and disorderly times that so trouble us, no evil should befall our motherland, which, like you all, we cherish with great ardour.

Nor have we addressed you with any intent or motive other than our love of the truth, of Yourselves and of our motherland. The words spoken by the apostle Paul concerning himself in the second chapter of the epistle to the Thessalonians can be applied to us as well, though unworthy.[82] Read them

---

[82] Štúr does not indicate which of the letters to the Thessalonians, 1 or 2, he has in mind here, but 1 Thessalonians 2:1-9 seems germane to his topic: 'For yourselves know, brethren, our entrance in unto you, that it was not in vain: But having suffered many things before, and been shamefully treated (as you know) at Philippi, we had confidence in our God, to speak unto you the gospel of God in much carefulness. For our exhortation was not of error, nor of uncleanness, nor in deceit: But as we were approved by God that the gospel should be committed to us: even so we speak, not as pleasing men, but God, who proveth our hearts. For neither have we used, at any time, the speech of flattery, as you know; nor taken an occasion of covetousness, God is

with care, O fellow countrymen of mine who give ear to my words, and understand them in the context of our times and circumstances.

* * *

What saddens you, dark clouds spread above the Tatras, those Slavic mountains?

The sad state of those who live among them, young man!

You are right to be sad, dark clouds!

What saddens you, turbid hills and Tatra summits, O Slavic mountains, who stretch aloft so freely to the skies?

The fact that our human countrymen are unable to arise into the pure aether, but are pressed to the earth, young man!

You are right to be sad, hills and Tatra summits!

What saddens you, boulders split from the Tatra cliffs, who endure a thousand years as if they were but one day?

That our human countrymen are mutable in their minds, and know not how to endure in their resolution, young man!

You are right to be sad, Tatra rock-faces!

What is it you bemoan, you winds, stormily sounding over the Tatras?

The fact that our human countrymen know not how to live, nor do they embark on action, young man!

You are right to be sad, Tatra winds!

What grieves you, breezes gently floating over the Tatra meadows and lowlands?

That our human countrymen do not take their nourishment, as do we, from the breaths of the flowers, but seek out rather material things instead of spiritual freedom, young man!

You are right to be sad, gentle breezes!

Why do you whimper and wail, O Tatra streams and rivers, who carry your plaintive lament resounding to the sea?

Because our human compatriots do not join together in memory, as we our waters mix with our origin, and because their lives do not resound

---

witness: Nor sought we glory of men, neither of you, nor of others. Whereas we might have been burdensome to you, as the apostles of Christ: but we became little ones in the midst of you, as if a nurse should cherish her children: So desirous of you, we would gladly impart unto you not only the gospel of God, but also our own souls: because you were become most dear unto us. For you remember, brethren, our labour and toil: working night and day, lest we should be chargeable to any of you, we preached among you the gospel of God.'

booming, but roll on unconsciously, like hidden streams, silently to the sea of the life of the nations, young man!

You are right to be sad, Tatra streams and rivers!

Why are you sad, you slender firs and powerful oaks, stretching high above the Tatra foothills?

Because our human countrymen permit themselves to be trod underfoot by villains, rather than standing to face them like men, as we bravely breast the wanton winds, young man!

You are right to be sad, you slender firs and mighty oaks of the Tatra foothills!

SVATOBOJ

To his first companion, in life as well as feelings and thought, lover of song and creator of songs, to his dearest brother Karol, now separated from him by the grave, the author dedicates this poem with loving heart unchanged.

The kingdom of the Slovaks shorn of might,
   The rumour of defeat from Pressburg flies —
There on the battlefield — O mournful sight! —
   Mortally wounded, King Mojmír now lies,
His gaze fixed on Nitra, ere he expire,
   Where dies his Great Moravian Empire.

The corpses of his men around the King
   Are strewn, and brave they fell, where brave they fought;
Old warriors and youths as fresh as spring,
   Run through with sword, riddled with crossbow shot,
While myrmidons victorious howl and skip
   Couping the crippled as they trophies strip.

Across the way, on grey steed galloping,
   Someone speeds off, as swift as a simoom.
'Tis Svatoboj, the brother of the King.
   Alone he flees the blood-soaked field of doom,
Without a backward glance rushing from there,
   While his heart shrivels in sorrow and despair.

Such guilt and woe his heart, rent, feels,
   It flutters wildly in his breast pinched tight.

The dead call to him from the battlefield
   While Hell itself is laughing at his plight.
He speeds o'er hill and vale, fast as he can —
   For Hell can terrify a mortal man…

He vanishes. The looters having gorged
   Their bags with spoil, now slowly leave the field
To gallop inland, ireful, greedy, urged
   By lust to see what loot the towns might yield.
They leave all still behind, except the cry
   Of man expiring, as day, and kingdom, die.

Those moans reach Slovak ears like peals of doom,
   As tolling bells oppress the orphaned heart.
Slovakia! They bear you to a tomb
   Where you shall lie, benighted, set apart,
Though lifeless, in the world for all to see —
   To toil, die, toil, and perish endlessly.

In hordes triumphant the marauders roil
   Like locust swarms that plunder with a will.
They strip, consume, and carry off; they spoil
   All that men foster, but they do not kill —
They leave them to repair their loss, and then,
   Like locust swarms, they'll plunder them again.

There's no help for it; on the Pressburg plains
   The bulwark of Slovak manhood crumpled rests.
No wounded heart there now throbs on in pain,
   However fiercely Fate their loves might press —
Their wives and children cannot bear a shield;
   Prayer, tears and trembling are the arms they wield.

For lofty Nitra fate decrees the same:
   The mob rushes upon her, mad for looting.
Ah, royal seat! There your pride and fame
   The horde is burning, smashing and uprooting!
Commands fly on all sides, while on your walls
   The vicious predator clambers and crawls.

To Zobor meanwhile Svatoboj is racing,
   Still on he spurs his broken winded steed.
Then, seeing that no one behind is chasing,
   Dismounts, broken with shock and dread, indeed.
Silence broods over Zobor's widespread swale;
   He climbs the crag that overhangs the vale.

There in the distance, mournful Nitra stands.
   From time to time the wind wafts near a groan.
The horde of dragons swarms about the lands
   About its foot — now here, now there, they roam —
What skill had raised, they roughly overturn,
   And town and hamlet smoke like pitch, and burn.

Svatoboj hears the cries from his high place —
   The looters' laughs, the people's screams and moans;
He sees the roaring fires swell and race
   As flames consume the valleys and the towns,
And with eye wide in fear, from his high perch
   He looks on as they fire God's holy church.

Towers collapse, the raging firestorm howls.
   His eyes are mirrors of the shame and fright
Regret and anguish that consume his bowels —
   His face is drained of blood, like linen white.
He looks on, with many a scalding tear
   And seems, in spirit, to be far from here.

He stands distracted as, aghast, the son
   Stands by his bleeding father, whom he's killed,
Trying to grasp the sense of what he's done,
   What devil was it, who to crime impelled
The trembling youth — such an unholy deed!
   Meanwhile, his horse strays, calmly crops the mead,

And casts a quizzing eye upon his man:
   Why have we stopped? Refreshed, again he'd race
To the world's end, but still Svatoboj stands,

Possessed by something, rooted to the place,
Unable from the fray to turn his eyes,
   Until, kneeling, he lifts them toward the skies.

'Heavenly Father,' he cries, 'before Thee
   A sinner most foul cringes in the dust!
The devil drove me to a villainy
   To which I was not destined; it was lust
For rule that prompted my unhallowed dare,
   For which I grovel here now, in despair.

'Mojmír, as eldest son, rightfully took
   The sceptre from our dying father's hand,
Who then me, and my brother Svätopluk
   Entrusted with our own share of the land,
Anointing Mojmír as our sovereign lord,
   But urging all to brotherly concord.

'Impious lust for rule upon us fell;
   Our Father's words so eager to forget,
We took such counsel as was spawned in Hell!
   Our feet upon the paths of war we set,
Against Mojmír our thanes basely inciting,
   And in our evil cause, with foes uniting.

'O, eagerly they hastened to our side
   To aid us in the fratricidal stour!
'Twas in their interest, us to divide,
   To conquer, at last. And now we're in their power!
Of our old freedom nothing now remains —
   We'll chafe in cruel — long forged for us! — chains.

'Our allies called up allies of their own
   — The savage pagan bands known as Magyars
Who wander the wild steppes with no fixed home —
   Unto this weakened, squabbling land of ours.
So Christians serve their brothers in the faith
   By urging pagans to put them to death!

'We turned back to our brother then, too late
  Joining his lines to stem the tide of doom:
For Heaven left us sinners to our fate.
  Already we'd been dealt our mortal wound.
There on the Pressburg fields raged the fierce war;
  The Kingdom of the Slovaks was no more!

'Nothing is left now, everything is lost.
  The Slovak army, crushed beneath the blow
Of treason, mown down, the entire host
  There with their chief and king, Mojmír, lain low —
Yes, he, my brother! King Mojmír the Great!
  So great of soul, and so unfortunate!

'There Svätopluk lies dead upon the ground
  Who found for his great crime a fitting end.
Only this sinner — I — slipped away sound
  To pine in anguish and endless torment.
A harsher penance might not be imposed!
  How gladly I'd exchange it for death's throes!

'My sin — is it so great? I, a king's child,
  A king's brother! Banished! what could be worse?
Harried by vengeful ghosts through barren wilds,
  And by the living of my nation — cursed,
Prey to the thug that burns and loots and slays,
  And on my nation's torment, I must gaze!

'I search for peace and comfort, all in vain.
  Wherever I run, danger is set to fall.
Behind me race a gibbering ghoulish train;
  Before me horrid monsters form a wall.
Enough of this! I would this world renounce
  And end my life here, on these barren grounds.

'Yet steady me, Lord, with Thy mighty hand,
  O God most merciful, and I'll find peace.
For hurricanes are stilled at Thy command,

And at Thy nod the fiercest tempests cease.
Yes, I shall serve Thee in the wilderness,
   Think of Thee only, and in Thee find rest.'

Thus Svatoboj with earnest sorrow prays.
   Blessing himself, up from his knees he stands;
His eager charger rears his head and neighs,
   But Svatoboj just stretches forth his hands,
Caressing Sivko's neck and flowing mane
   But mounting not, he says, in heavy pain:

'Go now, my friend. Now must we say goodbye.
   You shall bear Master Svatoboj no more.
Where to, my dear? Where would you have us fly?
   Into the wide world? or again to war?
What good in war, the two of us alone?
   As for the world, I'm hated, spurned, disowned.

'Together, we'd be quickly recognised;
   Our enemies are prowling yet for prey.
If caught: you're slaughtered, and your master dies.
   O, such a murder would make our foes gay!
But should someone see you astray, alone —
   Who wouldn't want such a horse for his own?

'Take care to seek to fall into the hands
   Of one of ours — toward Trenčín go! Our folk
From off their knees may one day boldly stand
   To toss from off their necks this foreign yoke —
Then once again you'll prove your might, your troth;
   Stand to the fight reprised — fight for us both!'

He said no more. Tapping his horse's flank,
   Svatoboj turned and parted, sunk in woe.
The grey stood still there, on the grassy bank,
   And, sad himself, just watched his master go…
Thinking he'd turn back… But he never will —
   The true steed gazed; the man grew smaller still,

Till near a thicket, dark and far away,
   He saw him turn, take one last, longing look
Before he plunged into the copse. The grey
   Then let his head sink. Sadly, thus he took
His way, alone, unto the high mountains —
   Thus friends must part, when they have no more friends.

Deep in the glade, a sheer cliff skyward soars.
   Up this, Svatoboj scrambles, suddenly
Moved by the urge to look upon his horse —
   — His friend, beloved, once more — but though he see
For miles, in vain he searches far and near —
   Only dim echoed hoofbeats reach his ear.

Alone he stands upon the summit then:
   Alone up there, alone in the wide world,
Like the last leaf in fall, when thunderous wind
   Upon the ground all others, dry, has hurled.
'Now I've lost everything,' he sighs, forlorn.
   'All treasures, one by one, now Fate has torn

'From me. One sacred relic still remains
   From all the birthright that I once possessed:
Faithful companion through glory and pain —
   And now I've brought you to this wilderness,
My blade, who still sowed fear and death appalling
   Though Great Moravia's banners thick were falling.

'What use shall we be now, in such sad days
   When nothing of our Fatherland is left?
With you, my dear, now I too must part ways,
   Each now, alone, of the other bereft;
In such wastes I'll have no need of a sword
   For beads I'll wield now, and serve but the Lord.'

Then he unsheathed the broadsword from his side
   And, standing at the edge of the abyss,
Gazed at the blade — his father's gift, his pride…
   Then from the summit of the precipice

After his eye, and heart, had fully fed
   Upon its beauty, whirled it o'er his head

And flung it far away. He watched it fly
   Through empty space, into the depths below;
It struck the rock-face — its unvanquished cry
   Booming, he heard through vale and gorge echo;
He groaned to hear that manly clashing, for
   When last he heard it sing, it was in war.

Then from the summit Svatoboj's descent
   To stillness leads back through the gloomy brake;
To serve the Lord now is his sole intent,
   And for his sins, meet reparation make —
A sinner penitent, in search of peace;
   The warrior seeks no more war's cruelties.

Onto a dusky vale his path now gave.
   Above this rose an altar-like cliff, sheer
And moated with a ditch. Atop: a cave.
   A better place could not be found, for years
Beseeching God in solitude, on high,
   The while the world's vain pomp should pass him by.

            *

Soon to this hidden hermitage withdrawn,
   His soul's salvation is his only care.
The thick oaken glades echo with his psalms.
   Often he faints, worn-out with ceaseless prayer;
Scant notice takes he of his body's needs:
   On crab-apples and roots he daily feeds.

The long, dark nights he puts to pious use,
   Chanting the vigil with antiphonal breeze.
Still, on Moravia he will sometimes muse
   By his small fire, that crackles amidst the trees.
He sees strange figures as he trance-like dreams
   While through the dark, the mocking marshlight gleams.

The days are long, but longer still the hours
　　That drag through his wild hermitage the nights;
He'll pick his way then through the tangled bowers
　　To gaze on Nitra from the rocky heights;
Some rumour from the ruined castle flies —
　　And to its black mass turn Svatoboj's eyes,

Where, sometimes, he'd behold a wondrous thing…
　　Now, Nitra's walls flamed with a flashing light.
There — in the church — a crowded gathering:
　　Father Methodius, preaching… or the sight
Of his own royal father, on his throne,
　　Or pacing the broad ramparts. Then, a groan:

Two figures rush before the noble man,
　　Fall to their knees — they're bloody, it appears_
They reach out to him, both, with their right hand,
　　While with their left, they wipe away their tears.
What will he do? Comfort them? Or reprove?
　　He stands there sad, austere… by pleas unmoved.

At once terror upon Svatoboj fell!
　　But then these visions melted, and were gone;
And black shades once more around the castle swelled
　　And as before the night was quiet, calm.
Nitra in ruins, forlorn, sunk in night:
　　Svatoboj groans in sorrow at the sight.

The Song of Svatoboj on Zobor.

Tornados, who about these summits fling
Yourselves against their granite brows, with might,
Who race toward Heaven on unburdened wing,
Surmounting lofty peak in unmatched flight,
O, carry heavenward, ye mighty winds
My sighs before the all-merciful Throne,
The fresh confession of my many sins,
As, drowned in tears, I for His pity groan.

A nation, faithful, true, and reverent
Now chafes beneath a pagan yoke abhorred;
Our tabernacles fouled, where saintly men
Had preached to us the Gospel of the Lord.
A freeborn people, now enslaved, in chains,
Ground beneath the heel of the invader,
Our king is fallen, and with him scores of thanes.
Of all the sins of man, can there be greater?

Mine is this grievous sin. The guilt is mine —
Such are the rotten fruits of hellish greed;
My soul, whenever this I call to mind,
Shivers in terror, and in sorrow bleeds.
And who am I, this criminal? None other
Is marked by such titanic guilt, so base,
Than poor, unfortunate King Mojmír's brother —
A scion of Moravia's royal race.

Bedim your fire, O stars! Send down your sheen
Upon this wasted sinner's cheeks no more!
You flame like judges' eyes, searching and keen,
That pierce my wretched soul unto the core!
Turn your just eyes away! Put out your light!
By thickest clouds now be you overcast —
And you, mists of the earth, clouds of the night,
Hide me from all, and from myself, at last!

*

Such were the songs his soul repentant raised,
   Which no one but the night heard, still and calm;
Upon the swirling mists Svatoboj gazed,
   Which were to his heart sorrowful a balm.
His hymn resounded from that rocky spire
   Like to the chancel echo of a choir,

The last voice, dying. Many a long while
   Svatoboj spent, alone, cut off from men;
Hearing no speech, but the voice of the wild,

The song of birds, the mighty soughing wind,
Which swept from mountain top through woods of oak
  And long and earnestly to his soul spoke.

So wide and far the Zobor wilds extend:
  Svatoboj's realm now, shared with bird and beast;
When the dusk falls, a lonely way he'll wend
  From place to place, mournful, in search of peace.
One evening as he erred thus cheerlessly,
  A song irrupted on his reverie.

It was a pious song, low, but heart-rending.
  Svatoboj held his breath and pricked his ear —
The notes swelled, died away, with woodsong blending…
  Softly, intently, Svatoboj crept near,
Lured by the hymn, which rose and fell again
  And then his eye caught something on a plain

From which a high cliff soared… nearby, there stood
  A solemn oak and, near this, on the sod,
A skull was placed, while, stretched upon the wood:
  The image of the humble Son of God.
Beneath it knelt three men, engulfed in prayer —
  It was their song that thrid the forest air.

The darkness now was spreading through the height
  Of heaven; here and there, fiery traces
Of the sun's embers glowed still, flashing bright
  Upon the lawn, upon the pious faces
Of the three men, and as Svatoboj turned
  His eye upon them, he felt his own heart burn.

Their service at an end, the three men rise —
  'Tis then the prince appears upon the lea.
The three men look at him without surprise,
  And he approaches them — like family.
As if it were a rendezvous of friends,
  The three invite Prince Svatoboj to spend

The night in their retreat among the rocks.
  Around a cheery camp-fire at rest
Through the dark hours, at first, nobody talks —
  Curious all, about their hermit-guest.
He, trusting the good men, starts to relate
  The story of Moravia's hard fate.

So, of the cruel invading horde he speaks,
  How from some far-off land they pillaged near;
Of evil such as greedy vengeance wreaks,
  Of damage to the realm beyond repair.
He tells them of the catastrophic war…
  Through which the Slovak state is now no more.

Further, of the king's death speaks Svatoboj,
  The fearful cruelty of the pagans,
Of church after church by that mob destroyed,
  Of how they loot and exploit good Christians.
All this, the pious men in terror heard,
  And shocked, they blessed themselves, without a word.

Then comes Svatoboj to speak of himself —
  Of his own crime — by some devil possessed! —
For which he earnestly begs Heaven's help,
  Doing rough penance in this wilderness,
That God might him absolve, in His mercy,
  Beholding his tears and his misery.

Svatoboj ended. Slowly then, he lifts
  His eyes to meet their empathetic gaze.
A brooding silence reigns among the cliffs,
  Broken only when twigs snap in the blaze.
At times, the wind through the oak branches sighs
  As if it mourned Great Moravia's demise.

So long the silence lasted. Nothing stirred
  While Svatoboj sought comfort of the men;
Those ardent servants of God's sacred Word
  Assured him, and absolved him of his sin.

They urged him to remain in their retreat,
   And thus the penitent did they entreat:

'Here, Svatoboj, a hermit's life we lead,
   Passed down to us from those who came before.
Like to our founders, those who will succeed
   Us here, in prayer and psalm we serve the Lord.
And here among us, you too may retire
   To contemplate Him, as your sole desire.'

Svatoboj's heart warmed at the things they said,
   And gratefully he responded to the call.
And then each hermit made his humble bed,
   The while the camp-fire flickered, and grew small.
Still they recited one last, pious prayer,
   Then all took to their cots, cold, hard, and spare.

Here, calmer days for Svatoboj begin,
   Pious and penitent, among warm friends.
He senses as the stiff bonds of his sin
   Loosen, as his purgation slowly ends.
His brother monks help him his load to bear,
   Storming the heavens with their constant prayer.

Svatoboj often spoke long through the night
   Of Great Moravia's deeds, and odious
Fall; of his father's glory, and his might;
   Of the holy Father Methodius,
How to the faith he did the Slavs convert,
   Baptising them, preaching Christ's holy word.

When once he spoke of how the holy faith
   Was being uprooted throughout the land,
Toppled, like altar-rubble ground beneath
   The evil heel of the conquering pagans,
The men themselves, crushed beneath sorrow
   Sighed deeply, and then addressed him as follows:

'Your body, Svatoboj, a mere few days
   In simple hermit's robes has been adorned.
Before then, in the fierce midst of the fray
   'Twas mail and bevored sallet that you'd worn.
You here, withdrawn, is something of a waste
   While out there, the Lord's flock is slain, disgraced.

'Go, Svatoboj! Where hands in prayer are clasped,
   To shield them, with your sword drawn at your side;
Arouse them, who beneath the foul yoke gasp,
   And at their head, upon the pagans ride!
Thus will your father's ire at last be stilled
   And all your debts toward Heaven be fulfilled.'

As lightning sets a black stormcloud ablaze,
   So Svatoboj's dark cheeks now flashed with flame
As he recalled Moravia's glory days,
   His father's majesty, and martial fame,
And he thought on his Grey, cast off, alone,
   And on his broadsword into chasm thrown.

Long such uneasy thoughts rolled through his mind
   As when dark clouds tumble through azure skies,
And the sun's darkened, then again to shine…
   So shone and gloomed again Svatoboj's eyes:
Now did he flash with fire, athirst for glory,
   Now was he doused with sadness deep, and worry.

Those embers… died. And once again he grew
   Gloomy, and sad. An overmastering pain
Unpicked the knit of his once brawny thew.
   He dropped his mournful gaze, and sighed again:
'No more have I the wings I once unfurled.
   Here I'll remain, having died to the world.

'God will have none of such a sinner's aid.
   And I am steeped in sin, from heel to head.
Here shall I serve Him, in this quiet glade,

    To all the world's concerns I am quite dead.
       But God the most merciful will never cease
          To pour on the repentant grace and peace.

'And our despoiled land lies like these wilds:
       Deserted; there's no man that I might bring
To war — here a woman, there an orphaned child…
       That's all. A winter harsh stifled our spring.
Perhaps, in future years, some great Moravian
       Scion will arise to liberate our nation.'

A deep silence fell then, as Svatoboj's
       Words died away. And for long no one spoke,
Until at last, the three hermits took voice
       Again: 'And yet, indeed there still is hope:
Capable youths develop from orphans,
       And faithful mothers form them into men.

'Such shall, perhaps, be the nation's saviours.
       But where a proper leader will they find?
You, Svatoboj, abandoned Great Moravia,
       Yet her salvation's always on your mind.
So years can pass… Its ancient ardour gone,
       Why, all of Christendom might be undone!

'In service of the Lord our lives are spent;
       Can we abide extinction of His praise?
Defend us from that, Lord omnipotent —
       For we intend to serve Thee all our days!
Altars may totter through the pagans' ire,
       Yet still to aid Thy flock our heart's afire!

'Listen, my brothers: here we live retired.
       Among these tangled paths no stranger goes.
By our raised voices here no man's inspired;
       Our words all die away in soft echoes.
Let us now venture forth at times, to the nation,
       To preach faith in our coming liberation.

'Let us reveal to them the raging ire
    God feels when Christians to pagans submit;
And promise grace, when they to arms aspire
    To rise, and be of vile servitude quit;
Reminding them of our motherland's glory,
    Recalling her nearly-forgotten story.

'And so that we should not be recognised,
    We'll change our garb as we range through the lands.
And should we not incite them to arise,
    We'll trust the torch to our successors' hands.
God grant our labours meet with this reward:
    Some Slavic champion, sent here by the Lord!'

The hermits then, agreed upon this plan,
    Bound themselves to it with a sacred oath.
Then, in poor pilgrim's rags, throughout the land
    At times appointed, far and wide did go,
From village, to town, to castle, they erred,
    Rousing the people with their ardent word.

In such travail and wandering years passed.
    The people slumbered on — no saviour came —
Long rest the hermits now beneath the grass;
    Time dealt with their successors just the same.
Nothing has changed through the long centuries:
    Vain are, it seems, the Zobor prophecies.

The Slovaks doze, but still they don't forget
    Zobor, where ancient legends still are kept
Like treasures, deep in mountain caverns set.
    Sometimes they wander there with reverent step;
Sometimes from Zobor, so the folk profess,
    A voice calls, sadly, from the wilderness…

A tumulus looms on the Zobor heights;
    Svatoboj's bones rest in this burial mound,
Above which stands the mighty cross of Christ.
    Among the folk, this legend makes the rounds:

At night, Prince Svatoboj can be seen there
    Kneeling before the cross in ardent prayer.

Slowly, he shuffles on his knees (they say)
    Up to the cross, and prays there, drowned in tears,
With hands clasped tightly. Motionless, he stays
    At prayer, until his figure disappears.
The hermits there often see him as well,
    And when they do, they quickly bless themselves.

So treats the legend of this apparition —
    That Svatoboj will never rest in peace
As long as his good folk suffer oppression.
    But when the troubles of Moravia cease,
When her promised saviour shatters her chains,
    Svatoboj, too, will be purged of his pains.

Matúš of Trenčín

Prologue

Who from Turecký vrch follows the flow
   Of the Váh river upstream, or whose eye
Toward the Jastrabský mountains should go
   Downstream through vales resounding, shall espy
A castle on a summit, lofty, proud,
   That soars amidst the heavens like a cloud.

The castle stands there hoary, empty, bare,
   Bereft, just like an old man at the tomb
Of his children might stand, silent, and stare,
   Himself about to tumble in that gloom —
Sadly, it gazes on the Váh, that spreads
   Wide, along which now a sad pilgrim treads.

It's deathly silent there, where once the halls
   Throbbed with a bustling life, of which echoes
Boomed from the uplands whence mighty Váh falls,
   Past where the Tisa, or the Danube flows —
Such was, in days past. Now, there reigns such peace
   As one finds oftener… in cemeteries.

The ages above those high walls swiftly passed
   Like storms that rushed by quickly as they came,
Though the winds roared, and the lightning bolts crashed,
   They brood as if mourning their vanished fame —
For even stone, when long neglected, must
   In sadness crumble into petty dust.

Above these battlements a tower looms,
   Like an old giant, leaning on the walls
Decrepit, flexing still once swelling thews
— An empty spectacle — despite it all;
   Yes, all in vain. For when one's might is gone
The world wastes not a glance, but hurries on.

Who calls to mind, O keep, thy faded story?
   Though at thy feet pulses the human tide,
The world knows nothing of Trenčín's past glory,
   And from cold walls the warm flesh shunts aside.
Only the bard — sometimes — will think on Thee
   And raise a soft, and painful, threnody.

Above Trenčín, above the Citadel

Above Trenčín, above the citadel,
   A storm is brewing, moiling clouds and thunder;
What can this mean? they ask down in the vale.
   An omen, this? Good? Bad? the people wonder.
The sense — if such there be — no one will learn
   From Matúš — brooding, lonely, taciturn,

In Trenčín castle, on his lofty throne,
   He sits, from where the power that he wields
Extends throughout the Váh valley below;
   All that lives in that region duly kneels
Before him; while the mighty Váh his name
   Roars as it flows on, spreading wide his fame.

Long had the halls been peaceful, not a thing
   Disturbed the calm, but now a rumour comes:
Hungary has elected Robert king!
   And in a trice, tranquillity's undone.
Something's afoot — torches flare, an uproar…
   One thing's for sure, that concord is no more.

From all directions now come crowds of men:
   All sorts of visitors — soldiers and lords —
They enter the broad gates, and leave again
   After exchanging many fevered words.
What's all this din and bustle? All this scurry?
   No one can plumb the depths of the mystery.

But all of Trenčín castle is astir:
   The windows are aflash with bright torchlight
Behind which shadows flit — a hasty blur
   Of action all the long and busy night.
The rumours fly, but all know that it means
   Great powers, for some great deed, are here convened.

So Sundays follow Fridays; overhead
   The tumult in the castle doesn't cease.
Of Matúš Čák so many things are said,
   But for all that, Matúš still holds his peace.
The people keep their eyes trained on that height
   Trusting that soon, their eagle will take flight.

Dark and Brooding the Váh Valley

Dark and brooding the Váh valley,
Underneath a pale moon,
Which now hides in the clouds, now sallies
Forth to dissipate the gloom
When she bursts forth through the black clouds —
The helmets flash! The spearheads spark!
Arrowheads glisten — then the crowds
Of men sink once more in the dark.
Who watched the castle that night, saw
Squadrons of horsemen thunder past
From Trenčín, following the Váh,
Hooves drumming field and forest,
The whole valley echoed with them!
And there, upon a stallion grey,
Beneath a flashing golden helm

Races Matúš, leading the way,
Like the swift moon, through the dark sky.
Behind him, squadrons of picked men
Like trailing clouds too, all chase by.
Upstream they're rushing from Trenčín,
Through deaf, dark villages they rush,
Thundering through the black night,
Onward through the gloom they push
Toward a fastness, where a light
Shows that they are expected there —
Toward the torchlight rumbles all
The squadrons, then the calm night air
Is split by watchmen, as they call:
'Unloose the chain, spread wide the gates
Before the horsemen — let them in!
'Tis he, for whom our master waits —
'Tis Matúš riding from Trenčín!'
Then comes a rattle from within —
The chains lift the portcullis, gates
Spring wide, and Matúš of Trenčín
Enters the court, where his friends wait.
Then after him, the armoured swarm
Of his horsemen thunder inward,
Hooves beating like a rumbling storm.
The torches blaze, the castle's lord
Greets Matúš with a glad embrace.
The men are led to a rich board
And when all have taken their place
A silence falls, and all draw near
Matúš in eager expectation.
He speaks, each man athirst to hear
His plans. He speaks, and all the nation
There flushes with ardour, resolved
To set their shoulders to the task.
Strategies are discussed, revolved
Among the resolute; at last
The council's closed, and off again
Matúš swings on his stallion grey,
Galloping off, leading his men

As swiftly as they'd come, away.
Beneath his flashing golden helm
Like the swift moon through the blue sky
He races, trailing his horsemen
Behind him. Like dark clouds they fly
To Podhradie in Bratislava
Up from Trenčín do they speed,
Strečno, Starýhrad, Lietava
See the squadrons visit, fleet
They rush on: Turiec and Orava,
Crisscrossing the Oravian hills
With Matúš ever in the van
To deepest Liptov rushing still.
And as that highest mount, Kriváň
That soars there, high above the sward,
Out-topping other summits, see
How Matúš, Trenčín's doughty lord
Towers above the other men.
And on they rush, that cavalry
From Liptov to castle Zvolen
And thence to Spiš, and farther, keen
To reach where the Torysa flows,
To Brečtan castle at Zemplín,
Where they shall rest. Thus did they ride,
The knights, omitting no fortress,
They covered Slovakia, far and wide,
Conferring by day, on to press
Through the dark nights, beneath the moon
Both at the full, and hidden, new,
When all the earth was wrapped in gloom.
Ah Matúš, Matúš, where are you?
Soar you among the clouds on high,
Steeper than any eagles fly?

*

All Trenčín is astir. Above the walls
   A flag is flapping, as the war-winds blow.
The country roundabout awaits the call,

Ready to take the measure of their foe.
The castle stones themselves seem animate:
Higher, somehow, impossible to take.

Great crowds of warriors to Trenčín come:
Above them, regimental banners fly —
Men strong as oak, who draw their mettle from
The icy streams that flow down mountainsides.
Before them march their lords, all leaders stout
And knights who man Slovakia's redoubts.

The martial trumps are singing since the dawn.
Announcing new contingents, bold and proud:
On laden rafts they navigate the Váh;
Above the highways they raise thick dust clouds.
Whoever in the Tatras can bear arms
Joins now the army that in Trenčín forms.

As when the harvest nears, the wheaten yield
Hums in the breeze beneath the sweltering sun,
So in Trenčín — all the surrounding fields
Are thick with troops, to the far horizon!
A constant buzz arises from the camps
And martial songs mix with their marching tramp.

All of the Liptov lads can be seen there,
Along with cool Orava's flinty sons,
The bold young men that Turiec did rear,
The tall, and wiry legions from the Hron.
The boys from Spiš and Šariš and from Zemplín
Now gather round beneath the walls of Trenčín.

Beneath the keep, the men; within: the great
In quiet parlay. Below, a happy roar —
The army sings, the while their chiefs debate
Questions of country, action, peace and war.
And while the talks proceed, tense soldiers wait
For battle, and think of nothing but the fight.

But now a messenger hastens within:
　　Robert has the support of many lords;
His throne is firm; Hungary belongs to him.
　　This leads to sharper exchanges of words,
Who won't acknowledge Robert king is cursed
　　With exile from the homeland… or even worse.

What more could stir that hive that is the castle?
　　All now take voice, nor wait they for their turn:
'Thus will they force a king on us, unasked?'
　　'What does this mean, to be so held in scorn?'
'Where is our liberty now?' 'Where this land's freedom?'
　　'Matúš our leader!' 'We all stand by him!'

The nobles now spill out the studded doors,
　　Aflame, surrounding Matúš on all sides.
A stream of sparks from burnished helmets pours,
　　But how much brighter shine their angry eyes!
Crested and clad in armour, Matúš stands
　　Tight with resolve, yet calm and in command.

The officers then march before the ranks
　　Of ardent men all thinking the same thing:
The time is now! The officers are frank —
　　'Matúš will lead us — long live Matúš, our king!'
'Vivat!' the troops burst into raucous praise:
　　'Vivat Matúš! May fame attend his days!'

Calmness and strength mark Matúš' face, glancing
　　About the hosts of warriors, and then
He calls out: 'Like the flooding Váh in spring,
　　So shall I rush down, with this river of men!'
'Rush down! Rush down!' the massive army cries,
　　'We shall rush down! For there our mother lies!'

'Our mother!' echoes back the marshalled throng.
　　Amidst the din, Matúš one final word
Addresses: 'Men! Strike up a song!'
　　Then back into the castle with the lords

He goes, to share a final stoup of wine
   With those about to leave Trenčín behind.

Within the banquet hall it's loud and gay.
   The lords and Matúš laugh with lighter hearts.
Now that all's settled, with cups of Tokay
   The health of all is drunk; the toasting starts,
With Matúš, as the chief and hosting lord,
   Then all his faithful mates straight down the board.

Each gives his thanks, in sweet or halting speech
   And sings a happy verse, in tune or out;
Across the vaulted hall, from each to each
   The song skips through the whole good-humoured rout.
Laughter and jokes ring with the loving cup;
   A quarrel breaks out — in a trice made up.

At the head of the board, Matúš alone
   Sings not in answer to the compliments;
His gaze falls down upon his lap, or roams
   About the hall, as if he were intent
In self-colloquy. Concerning what? At last
   He turns his piercing gaze upon his guests:

'Dear brother lords! Each now a happy strain
   In turn, to our great jollity has raised.
As the song passed, I took up no refrain;
   To one more worthy now I cede my place.
I have a bard — let him regale my lords
   At this grave moment, with more fitting words.'

'The bard! The bard!' resounds the happy roar,
   So Matúš nods — and off the servants race.
Soon the tall man appears at the hall door.
   With hair gone grey wreathing a pale face,
His eyes are smouldering with a softer flame
   As if from ages far distant he came.

But now and then, a flame more lively beats
    From them, like sparks from a torch guttering.
The lords, becalmed before him, take their seats
    And wait for him as he prepares to sing.
He tunes his harp. Then slowly, with his hand,
    He sweeps the strings to life, and starts his chant

Song

In ancient songs and legends lies
The might of spells — a frightful force —
For to him upon whom it alights
The gift brings misery, a curse;
The fated man — 'tis not his choice —
Is emptied of himself, and all
That was human within him falls
Away forever, except his voice.

Sometimes whole nations in this wise
Fall victim to a tragic fate;
They still appear to human eyes
Alive, and whole, and animate,
But both their soul and will are gone —
Their arms hang down along their sides,
Their figures mute, immobilised.
Like statues sculpted out of stone

Their heart beats only now and then,
Remembering its pulse in fits;
Their breath breaks forth in sighs of pain
That barely faint beyond their lips.
Thus fitfully, they lift their eyes
Up to the sunlit heavens where
The daystar hangs in the blue air
And send to God their mournful cries.

In countries such as these, where men
Speak not, but whisper, or keep still,

Forests and cliffs speak out instead,
And voices rise from stream and rill;
In countries such as these, the stones
Break forth in song for fame long past,
As when the evening Angelus casts
Afar its voice in echoing tones.

Sometimes, such nations cursed by fate
Win respite from their languor fell;
Someone, a hero,'s born, who with great
Might of his spirit breaks the spell.
Men's hearts again beat strong and bold,
New fire enkindles long-cold eyes;
They raise their hands aloft in praise.
And roar with thunder, as of old.

Son of the Váh, you've heard the great
Roar of the stream that nursed your years;
Son of the Hron, you've hear the plaint
That wets the wheat fields with her tears.
You, Trenčín lad, you've heard the moans
That castle Tematín yet spills
Down from these slopes, this ring of hills,
Beating against these very stones!

The voice of Zobor booms aloud
To you, lowlanders! Hear it calling,
Spreading aloft its plaints, that sound
Like organ-tones, profoundly falling
Through chapel transoms; hear you not
The songs of fame, fled now, so fleet,
The glory of our folk's proud seat,
Our freedom, which is now forgot?

Oh, Nitra, Nitra, when you keen
The mountains thunder back your groan:
Cliffs from Velehrad to Devin
Send on the echoes, stone to stone.
Mountains, forests, and castles all

Reverberate it, on all hands.
It flies through all the Slovak lands
From Orava to Likava.

Whom will it move, her mournful plight?
Who will her thirst for freedom slake?
What great-soulled man, from these great heights
Will call in trumpet-tones 'Awake!'
And whom might we rouse, with our words
To burst the fetters of our chains?
On whom are all our eyes now trained —
Upon whom do you gaze, my lords?

*

The bard grew still. And not one present dropped
   His eyes from him, or Matúš, as the words
Sank in their souls. Matúš gazed at them, and thought
   'What did that song mean to these noble lords?'
They held their tongues, sunk deep in musing, all;
   The stately bard retired from the hall.

Lord Matúš spoke first, breaking the silence
   In that large banquet hall, where nothing stirred:
'And so tomorrow we will be far hence.
   The army merely waits upon our word.
We leave at daybreak. Only war will prove
   If I deserve their reproach, or their love!'

Once more the hall erupts in wild delight.
   Then cries and orders, cheers and loud alarms
Are heard the region round till late at night.
   Each of the regiments prepares its arms,
With Matúš the Czech Boleslavín confers;
   Ctibor is there, Radmír, so many others! —

Oh, River Váh, when last did you behold
   The Slovak flag aflutter overhead?
How long, how long since you last heard such bold

Hymns martial in the Slovak tongue bruited?
But see — the Slovak battle flag is raised,
  And Slovak throats burst forth in songs of praise.

There below Trenčín, beneath the towering keep,
  Off to the battle moves Matúš' armed force.
Soldiers in regiments — whole acres deep:
  Battle-flags, banners, pikes and lances, horse
Squadrons like silver falcons that soar and dive
  So thickly, the very fields seem alive.

With horse in front, next come the infantry;
  The thunder of their tread stifles the roar
Of river Váh. Then Matúš on his steed;
  Higher than all else see his pennon soar!
Proud of his men, he goes, with swelling breast,
  Like his banner, taller than all the rest.

The flower of his friends encircle him,
  Riding with him, their leader, off to war.
The other lords watch over their own men.
  Commands are welcome where eager hearts soar
And soon erupt in thunderstorms of song
  Spreading from troop to troop as they march on.

Beneath Nové Město a plain spreads wide —
  'Tis there the army first encamps to rest.
Beyond the western hills now fades the light;
  The Váh valley is wrapped in thick darkness.
Campfires are lit, which spread a rosy cheer;
  A soldier calls, a horse neighs somewhere near.

The warriors recline upon the sod;
  Spinning their yarns of ghosts and uncanny things;
Laughter and happy banter spread abroad,
  And near another fire somebody sings.
Like smoke above the fields waft all these sounds
  To grow fainter as the campfires die down.

Above the Váh valley now broods deep night;
   Above the river, clouds the stars obscure.
They hide both Matúš, and his plans, from sight,
   His hopes, his person… No one is quite sure
Who Matúš Čák, lord of Trenčín, might be…
   What parts he hails from, of what family?

It's deathly quiet, all are sleeping so,
   Except a few men grouped around one fire.
They cannot sleep, and so they quiz Milko,
   Matúš' servant and friend. 'Who is your sire,
Matúš?' they ply, with curiosity,
   'Come, tell us now, what sort of man is he?

'And tell us truly. Who is he, your lord?'
   There is no need to beg him long; he loves
To speak of Matúš; many a strange word
   Courses about him, and fantastic troves
Of rumours it would take long to relate.
   Some call him a strange man, and others, great.

'What brings him here?' they ask, 'And whence comes he?
   What is he busied with? On what does he found
His hopes?' 'Well do I know his history,'
   Milko responds, 'So listen, gather round!
I've served him long; the tale I have for you
   Whether it's short or long, is wholly true.

'Now, it's not everything, for I confess,
   Some things there are, which he keeps locked up tight
Sharing with no one, deep within his breast.
   Not even the most faithful of his knights
Know these. I'll tell what I know, what I can.
   More, I can't say. No more might any man.

'So, you know Skalka, the castle above Trenčín?
   Monks brought him there, they say, when he was small.
Where he was born, who his folks might have been,
   This no one knows, and no one ever shall.

So the monks left him here. And in the end,
   Not long after they left, I became his friend,

'His friend and servant. Now here, in the Tatras,
   A small and simple chapel stands — first one
Built in Slovakia. Every year, a Mass
   Is said on the day of our Lord's Resurrection.
For in long ages past, Skalka, you see,
   Was kept by monks renowned for piety.

'Now, why the monks brought Matúš there, who knows?
   Why did he take up residence? "For sure,"
The Váh people will swear — "the story goes —
   The young man there stands guard over treasure,
Immense wealth, somewhere buried in the ground,
   Protecting it from theft, lest it be found."

'They wonder that Matúš, far into the night,
   Sits tirelessly on Skalka, in the dark,
And though it's pitch black, if you strain your sight,
   A torch can be seen there sputtering sparks.
That's true enough; I've often seen it glow
   Roaming down galleries, past the windows.

'Now, when he's sated with such lonely walks,
   He broods for hours. Then he's wont to call
Me into his presence to sit and talk,
   Or stare with him at paintings on the wall —
Old pictures, ancient images… These, mind,
   I've seen myself, and more than just one time.

'On one a king sits in his majesty,
   Amidst one thousand men — an army great —
One richly dressed approaches reverently
   Leading a troop of knights in armour plate.
The man takes off his golden-crested helm,
   Before the king, who then confers with him.

'Then off the army marches on a grand
    Campaign, to extirpate all the king's foes.
The flags of one troop are red and white bands,
    Above the other host black banners flow.
The monarch rides clad in golden armour.
    Astride his stallion, eager for the war.

'Upon a cliff stands a massive redoubt,
    Beneath which scattered farms lie, and a town.
There's mountains in the distance, wound about
    By rivers that enclose the keep around
On all sides like a grand watery chain —
    A splendid castle, difficult to gain.

'And then a deathbed scene. The king once hale
    Lies dying; his three sons are drowned in woe.
The flames ebb from his eyes, his face is pale
    And this is mirrored in their faces too.
Behind these someone wrings his hands, and frets
    While beyond the castle the sun, expiring, sets.

'So many, many times Matúš would gaze
    Upon these paintings, through the long, long nights,
And when he'd snuff his lamp at the new day's
    Dawn, still — he said — they danced before his eyes;
Only the monks, he said, knew what they meant:
    The images, and their painters' intent.

'Over these pictures his hungry eyes would rove,
    Attentive to the monks as they explained;
Their words he heaped up like a treasure trove!
    That city was our Nitra, whose great fame
Carried our name throughout Europe entire
    Although its glory long since is expired.

'He burned with ardour to behold in person
    The city that ever stood before his eyes;
To leap astride his black and shining stallion

And fly to Nitra! Then, one day, at sunrise,
He galloped there — none could restrain or stall
　　Him — never slowing till he reached her walls.

'In Nitra — so he often told me — he saw
　　Himself the relics of which the bards had sung:
The church, where first the Slav apostle taught,
　　Methodius, in our own Slavic tongue.
And Nitra Castle — he said — stood there unchanged:
　　Just as it was painted! Round its stones he ranged....

'Zobor — a hill looms above Nitra on high.
　　Strange tales and rumours speak of it; it seems
A prince once laid himself down there to die,
　　Yet in that grave, poor soul, he finds no peace.
At full moon one can see him by the cross
　　In guilt beweeping his dear nation's loss.

'Thus did he expiate the horrid crime
　　Of his abandoning both king and country
In the hour of their need. And yet, a time
　　Would come when from his penance he'd be free:
When some hero should liberate the land
　　Then would his harsh purgation reach its end.

'Matúš rose to the challenge. For, one night
　　See him as up the Zobor heights he climbs!
With darkling clouds obscuring the starlight,
　　The chaste moon hides her face, only at times
Revealed, when the winds part her gauzy veil,
　　As through the desert woods they strangely wail.

'Now midnight tolls. The young man strains his eyes
　　Through thick drapes of nocturnal mist and cloud
Which round the grave, the cross, the castle fly
　　And then, all of a sudden, the moon bursts out:
Beside the cross, a figure, in mourning
　　Appears, and seems its spectral hands to wring.

'Fully upon that face the moonlight shines
   Which pale as it is, still paler seems to glow;
Neither fire, nor spark is seen in those dull eyes,
   That face, in penitence, contorts in woe.
The hair upon his head's wild and windblown;
   And from his shoulders hangs a pilgrim's gown.

'Matúš stared at the spectre, wrapt, intent,
   Although he felt, admittedly, some fear.
And when it seemed his prayers came to an end,
   Like wisps of mist, the mourner disappeared.
Then did my lord descend from Mount Zobor
   Disturbed, more meditative than before.

'Back in Skalka, life went on as before:
   We lived in peace and quiet. Then tidings came
From Hungary, of quarrels and of war.
   The throne was in question. More than one thane
Tempted by what unrest was offering,
   Sought to advance by arms from thane to king.

'My lord drank in the news with eager ear,
   And every time there came to him some word
Of battle, clad in armour, in high cheer
   He raced there toward the clatter of the swords
Until some news came of a better tone:
   Václav, the Czech prince, was offered the throne.

'But soon thereafter, other envoys told
   Of other hosts, another king; they said
That many thanes had risen in revolt
   Who wished to set the crown on Robert's head.
Such plots as these Matúš held in disdain,
   And he prepared for battle once again.

'No sooner had the new Czech king set forth
   Than Matúš raced to battle at his side.
That war was over quickly. The great worth
   Of Matúš' sword (by which so many died

Among the rebels) the grateful Václav saw:
   He dubbed him then Lord of Trenčín and Váh.

'But such was not King Václav's destiny
   To rule this realm, for when he had withdrawn
Dissension flared anew in Hungary
   And Robert seized what he's desired so long:
The throne. And this, brothers, being the case
   Matúš has led his army to this place.

'So here I end my tale. Now you're aware
   Of all I know. If you know more than I
So much the better. But, train your gaze there —
   If you can pierce the dark with a keen eye
To see, far off, shimmering Tematín,
   You see an image of Matúš of Trenčín!'

At this Milko grew quiet. He would love
   To go on, but has quite run out of lore.
Among his auditors, nobody moves —
   Let him speak on! They'd like to hear some more!
But Milko broods in meditation deep,
   And so the campfire dies, the whole camp sleeps.

*

The Camp at Nitra, Broad and Long

The camp at Nitra, broad and long
Lies spread beneath the castle keep,
Where volunteers in numbers strong
Await the word to storm the steep
Escarpment, when a murmur rolls
From camp-centre, like a sea-roar,
When distant waves crash on the shore.
Matúš out through his tent-flaps strolls,
His helmet flashes as he comes:
Tall, proud, and smiling: 'Tatras' sons!'
He calls to his assembled men,

Glancing up at the castle, then,
'Eagles! Glory awaits you there!
Already on that battlement
I see our flag! To those who dare,
Undying fame! To arms! To arms!
Onward, to war and conflagration.
Where heroes roar and sabres rattle,
Fight, brothers, for the Slovak nation!
For you are Slovaks, born and raised —
Far better 'tis to die in battle
Than live in shame, oppressed as slaves!'
Then, just as when the high wind stirs
An ancient stand of mountain firs
And makes the granite tremble, splits
Trunks rooted deep in ancient cliffs,
Thus at the words that Matúš spoke
A roaring cheer from the ranks broke
And then they rushed, like storms of wrath
Crushing, hewing apart, striking
All that chanced along their path,
While, on the battlements, the king's
Regiments, wait, tensed to withstand
The surge — all doughty souls, and brave.
Among them, a captain Roland stands,
Their leader, who like a lion raves,
When cornered, roaring out commands.
Robert's throne will securely stand
As long as Roland doesn't fall
(Great is his fame throughout the land).
Now siege-ladders against the walls
Are set; overhead, arrows fly,
While from the city walls, roll stones
To smash the men besieging. Cries,
A chaos of commands and groans
Arises from the warriors' throats —
The walls are littered with the dead,
And floating corpses choke the moats.
The fierce attack surges, abates,
Only to froth in rage anew.

Oh, how they wish to force the gates
That still they haven't battered through!
Roland is there, wherever foes
Are thickest, bravely hewing hard,
So many fall beneath his blows —
With flesh he carpets the greensward.
The siege breaks down, renews again
But arms and legs grow tired at last;
Matúš fights in a swirl of men
Of this whirlwind of war, this clash
Of armies; he, in valiant deeds,
Outstrips all there, outbattling all:
Urging his men to fight, he speeds
Toward a scrum beneath the wall.
He catches sight of Roland, where
He beats the men down, slaughtering
Whomever rashly calls his dare.
'Tis there in fury Matúš leads
His faithful men, commanding them
To hasten with the utmost speed
To where Roland fights, like death grim,
Sweeping off with his mortal scythe
Whomever stands within his reach.
At this, brave Boleslavín drives
With anger at the bloody breach.
Behind him Radmir, and Ctibor,
Through fields of gore knee-deep they wade
Through scores of dying men, and more
Flesh of the fallen, heroic dead.
Now everyone makes for the walls,
Oh, how they wish that breach to force!
Again the attack weakens, stalls.
As from above fierce slash the swords.
Boleslavín is near the top,
Hewing his way amidst the press,
His sword-arm furiously chops,
Plunging and slicing through warm flesh.
Many a soldiers meets his doom
Thus, many a hero finds his grave

But like a pine, Roland yet looms,
Above him, grand, unconquered, brave.
The clanging swords spatter bright sparks,
Dazzling the eyes: blood flows amain,
Arousing vengeance, fierce and harsh
Within the hearts of all the men.
'Die, foreigner! You must!' calls out,
In raging wrath, Boleslavín.
And from above, with one swift clout
He splits Roland's helmet in twain.
Crumpled in purple blood, fallen
Is Roland — still he lies now, slain.
Throughout the ranks the rumour flies,
Gripping with apprehension all
Who stood there, long breasting the walls
From which they now fall back, amidst cries
That Matúš holds the battlements
Along with his heroic troops:
While joy spreads through the Slovak bands,
Who pour into the town with whoops
'You're ours!' they cheer, 'now you belong
To us, again!' O, happy throng!
'No one shall take you from us now,
And him who is so bold to try
These swords will sweep — quickly! — to hell!'
Exultant cheers burst from the mouths
Of the victorious men, who vie
To bear their leader on the swell
Of shoulders strong again. They cheer:
'Matúš! Matúš, our leader! Here!'
All eyes are raised toward him: all lips
Form but one phrase: 'One hundred years!'
Matúš in turn grins, his eye skips
From man to man with earnest pride.
'A fine beginning that was, mates!
Nitra is ours! Now let this news
Spread through the world — let all relate
Your victory, my comrades true,
Oh, Slovak people! Nitra, now

Is ours again! In Slovak hands!
Let these tidings take root and grow
Within the hearts of all our friends!
In Nitra, here, this city grand
Where our forefathers won their fame,
Where monarchs of King Mojmir's line
Ruled peacefully the Slovak land,
We all, their children, of the same
Blood, start our story here as well.
As long as we are brave and game
To fight, as long as there are those
Among us with Slovak hearts that swell
In breasts to repel foreign foes!'

In pursuit of the routed enemy
   Matúš urges his men. The vanquished scatter:
Whither their eyes latch, thither do they flee —
   To be away, safe, is now all that matters!
Past the broad Danube now the hordes have flown;
   All that remains — kneels at the Slovak throne.

Above Komárno, look! His banner waves!
   From here to Novohrad, and further, now
In rustling lands the river Slaná laves,
   Before the Slovak sceptre castles bow.
Just as the Váh swelling in spring floods wide,
   Thus spreads on all hands Matúš' fame and might.

Nitra revives, blushing with youth restored,
   Her age of glory past returns again;
She governs all the Slovak lands once more,
   As far and wide as Matúš' power extends.
The name and might of Magyar king now melt
   Wherever the warmth of Trenčín's sun is felt.

Matúš begins appointing palatines
   And fixing magnates in trusted tenure
Of border counties, in which he begins

To build fastnesses, well-conceived, secure;
Deed follows concept, deliberate and sage —
   From ancient glory, blossoms a new age.

On daring wings the soul, emboldened, soars.
   This is no time for luxury and rest:
The Slovak regiments, refined in wars,
   Now into neighbouring Moravia press,
Where town and keep submit to Nitra's terms,
   And daughter strayed to mother now returns.

Now unto Danube gaily skips Morava,
   A welcome friend, from infancy well-known;
To Danube too, that summer, comes the Váh
   To whisper, *No more shall you be alone!*
While north to Wisła fleetly hastes Poprad
   To bring her news of Matúš' daring thought.

Amidst these regions, see Trenčín arise —
   Resplendent aerie, Matúš' lofty seat:
His soul far into distant years now flies,
   Musing on future conquests, coming deeds,
While Skalka, the Váh lands he holds so dear,
   Recall to mind the dreams of boyhood years.

Who's never walked upon the broad Váh plain,
   Who's never on that river cast his eyes,
Has never seen true wonder, and in vain
   His soul will strive to picture Paradise.
He's never tasted joy on earth; in truth,
   Earth's sweetest dreams have never fired his youth.

Those Váh lands, like a glass of sorcery —
   Wherever you glance: wonders on every hand
To cheer the eye and fill the soul with glee;
   A glorious theatre, that sumptuous land,
Where beauty beckons from each nook and place
   The soul knows not what first she should embrace!

You like to wander through palatial rooms?
  Just gaze about you in these soaring halls,
Their tapestries and carpets thick with blooms,
  The intricate rocaille of Alpine walls…
All this reflected the crystal stream
  Like emeralds and rubies flash and gleam.

Or, in cathedrals do you find delight?
  Behold these steeples, and the ribbed vaults
Aflash with beams of the Good Lord's sun, bright
  And golden, bays immense, naves and doxals…
At granite altars the Váh chants her hymn,
  And stars, at night, spangle the chancel dim.

Perhaps it's battlements gladden your eye?
  Look there — the massive Váh land's crenellations,
Whose topless barbicans soar into the sky
  As far as deep-set are their strong foundations,
Bastion o'er scarp, tenaille and terreplein,
  And over all, lofty, royal Trenčín.

Who's never set foot on the Trenčín heights,
  Or ranged along the Váh with happy tread
Will find his soul incapable of flight,
  Unable to lift high his sluggish head
Where spirits, borne aloft on wing unfurled
  Soar through the sky, and seem to rule the world,

Over one hundred Mountains as they sweep
  And tremble over myriad pied vales,
Now over Poland to climb swift and steep,
  Above Moravian summits now to sail,
Then down toward the Váh once more to swing
  And, home on Nitra's aerie, fold the wing.

*

Through the Broad Plains Thunders the Váh

Through the broad plains thunders the Váh
As its waves rush on clear and free,
While on its banks a horseman rides,
A young buck, son of liberty,
And the mountain summits soar
Looming above the river-sward,
And upon those rocky cliffsides
Castles stand as if on guard.
While at their feet the horseman flies,
Hey! Horseman thundering on the plains
Through which the Váh flows, someone cries,
Whither, falcon-like, do you race?
Yet nothing draws the young buck's heed,
Nor once does he pause to glance back,
But races on, urging his steed
Onward, along his destined track.
Behind him, cloudy billows sweep;
Before, the mists are thick and deep.
A murder of crows, after him
Sweep gaily, croaking up a din.
Yet nothing does the young buck heed
Nor does he pause to glance behind,
But races on, urging his steed.
Fervent his soul, intent his mind.
And from the castles comes the cry:
Hey, horseman on the river-plain,
Whither do you so swiftly fly?
In gold-chased armour all arrayed,
And at your side, a warlike blade;
Hey! Horseman at the River Váh!
What can your longing soul thus draw?
Here we have stood through many ages,
Looking on as the world changes —
Our clans mope here despondently —
You'll perish, son of liberty!
In us the ancient fire is hid,
Everywhere else, that spirit's dead!

It's not found in your regiments;
This quest of yours is vain! Nonsense!
These dreams of glory past are vain.
No more will the Moravian
Empire arise! Hey, horseman there!
Where do you fly? What would you dare?
Yet nothing does the young buck heed.
He pauses not to glance behind;
Toward Nitra does his stallion speed,
Fervent his soul, intent his mind.
Yet from the castles drifts a keening
Voice: *Hey, young horseman by the Váh,*
Where do you fly? What is the meaning
Of this your haste as you speed on?
You rush unto the conflagration
Young knight, O flower of your nation;
The spirit in your eyes shines bright
As the sun glows red — at twilight;
Alas! Our clans skulk morbidly —
You'll perish, son of liberty!
Once too, our eyes like yours did gleam
On distant glory as we dreamed,
And we have gazed on days of glory.
Ancient those times now, ages hoary...
Springtime was once, but now 'tis fall:
To dust sifts battlement and wall.
So shall it be with you, young man:
None conquer fate, for no one can.
You are the blossom of one day
That wilts at dusk to the cold clay.
Your fate is to be overthrown,
Strong as you are, hero unknown!
Yet none of this the young buck heeds
Nor does he spare a backward glance
As on to Nitra still he speeds,
His eyes fixed on the far expanse
Of future days, the while the Váh
Roars at his side. Yet from afar

The mournful castles echo still:
To your destruction do you speed
At your own choice, by your own will.
Unto the fray gallops your steed;
In battle will your broadsword sing,
But vain shall be your battling —
Our clans wallow in slavery!
You'll perish, son of liberty!

*

Unsettling rumours sweep down on Budín
   Of Nitra's fall, of taken fortresses,
Of the great might of the master of Trenčín
   And of the desire that enflames his breast.
The king is gripped with terror and unease
   To see his subjects rising from their knees.

And so the king assembles all his men
   In council — those still faithful to their liege —
They pact, as their deliberations end
   To aid the Magyar king to lift the siege.
Even the Pope of Rome's almighty hand
   Urges the counts to tame the restive land.

Upon the Trenčín faithful, he inflicts,
   As rebels and anarchic renegades,
The Church's curse severe: an interdict.
   No sacraments, no Masses may be said;
Should any flout this order, dare rebel,
   God's anger he'll incur, and burn in Hell.

What's more, he instigates the German knights
   To ride against those flattened by the curse,
To put the disobedient to flight.
   The power of the Keys he thus asserts
Against such as the common peace embroil,
   And would the Church of her holdings despoil,

While on his part, the Magyar king renews
  His ancient threats, recalling old complaints.
Edicts are cried, assembling new recruits
  For war, by volunteering, or constraint,
And thus he gathers legions to Budín
  Preparing fire and sword against Trenčín.

Matúš of Trenčín is not set aback
  By all these threats and warlike preparations.
He too calls troops, of which he has no lack.
  War is his element — his exhilaration!
As weapon-clatter fills Budín below,
  See lofty Trenčín tense to meet her foe.

To such a fastness now they make their way —
  The thought of glory — for which warriors thirst;
Košice, Prešov, eager for the fray
  Come, led by champions vying to be first;
To Rusin lands as well the courier flies
  In search of doughty, battle-set allies.

Piotr Piotrovich, Bretčan County's lord
  Grips firm the proffered hand: 'We are with you.
My people shall arise. You have my word.'
  He knows of Matúš' glory, and he too
From Rusin shoulders casts the Magyar yoke,
  Redeeming his fatherland for his folk.

The Czech king, too, stands firm at Matúš' side,
  Stirring his warlike people to the fight.
'Nothing, so help us God, shall us divide
  One from the other,' so they vow. In might
Matúš waxes, secured now east and west,
  By scores of fortresses, all battle-dressed.

The clergy of his nation play their part:
  No one's deprived of any sacrament!
The Silesian monk, Stefan, gives Matúš heart:

    Against Rome's curse, a counter-curse is sent.
No man can block the love God pours on men!
    Thus Stefan saves his champion and his friend.

In Budín — ever greater trepidation.
    At each new baleful rumour, the king frets.
He threatens thanes and begs surrounding nations
    To prop him with their strength against these threats.
He sends to Transylvania to ask
    Prince Dansa for his counsel. To the task

The eager Dansa brings his machinations:
    He knows what it would take to tempt the Rusins;
Of old, he knows what grieves the Slovak nation;
    Some men he sends to Prague, the Czechs to cozen.
When bad kings are besieged, some well-placed lies
    Can do the work of numerous allies.

Unto his agents he the task assigns
    Of tempting the confederates from their word,
Reminding them how great a sin and crime
    It is to so conspire against their lord,
With promises of titles, grants of land
    To such as will defect from Matúš' band.

Ctibor begins to waver at their terms;
    Radmír weighs plighted troth and cold, clear reason.
Each to the agent's side would gladly squirm
    But each fears the deserts of open treason.
For Matúš' arm is decisive and strong,
    And justice for such crimes won't tarry long.

With armed men Budín bursts at the seams —
    Varied the banners, varied is the gear.
Count Filipp's men in never ending streams
    March by; Graf Jordán's troops pack full the square.
With legions thick the fields about are spread,
    And clergy too, the bishop at their head.

In cloaks of red embroidered with the cross,
  On heavy horses wait Knights of the Sword:
Fearful to infidel and pagan hosts,
  They in cold armour serve the gentle Lord,
Their Grand Masters Rikkolf and Benedict
  Stand at the head of the warlike elect.

So they advance. But as the battle nears
  Those eager to plunge in the fray are few.
Many a Magyar warrior would despair
  Should Matúš — from afar! — come into view;
Only the German tonsured regiments
  Await the clash eagerly; calm, but tense.

With his squadron rides Filipp in the van.
  He's followed by the king and his knights, fierce
As they invade Matúš' motherland;
  The day of reckoning now swiftly nears.
Where through her broad plains the Torysa flows
  The thunder of war's tempests steadily grows.

Matúš hastes to the field as they draw nigh,
  Accompanied by his suite, faithful and strong.
He gazes at his troops with joyful eye:
  Czechs and Moravians supplement the throng.
Never, since Great Moravia's glory day
  Had one flag led these brothers to the fray.

Along Váh's river plain and roaring banks
  March Matúš' legions with determined tread.
Exhilarating song bursts from the ranks —
  Ardour aflame, by dreams of glory fed.
As brave and gay the clamour fills the air,
  Matúš is thrilled, but not set free of care.

Thus Matúš leads his hosts, and at his side
  Are Boleslavín, Radmír and Ctibor
Shoulder to shoulder, eager as they ride

    To speak, advise, debate the coming war.
Boleslavín's counsel is wise and true,
    But treason animates the other two.

Piotr Piotrovich has fallen away,
    So rumour has it, from his plighted word;
Under the force of Magyar bribes he swayed
    Until — faithless Rusin — his vow perjured,
Purchased, he spurned his honour in the dust.
    Matúš is saddened at this breach of trust.

The angry clouds of war roil over Spiš.
    Filipp the palatine now rages there,
Burning and plundering all within his reach.
    No one faithful to Matúš will he spare!
His sieging army each castle surrounds
    And smouldering ash remains where once stood towns.

So Matúš hastes toward Spiš to aid his friends
    And put a check to Filipp's knavery.
With flaming ire he prods his regiments —
    'Now is the time to prove your bravery!'
'To Spiš, to Spiš!' the angry legions ride
    There with the troops of Filipp to collide.

The Slavic forces, in ranks deep and wide,
    Now fill the field as far as eye can see.
The forces of the Czechs to the left side,
    The crisp Slovaks are drawn up centrally.
Before these, Boleslavín takes his post
    While Matúš rides the line, inspects his host.

The trumpet sounds. The Czech army attacks.
    Their heavy broadswords clatter, sing and slice;
Now wheeling left, they're joined by the Slovaks
    Who fall on the swift Magyars in a trice.
The Magyars swear and threaten all around,
    Meanwhile the Czech broadswords just mow them down.

Filipp runs at his men. Wild, he maligns
   Them, screeching 'Traitor! Rebel! Slovak!'
Hurling whatever insult comes to mind,
   But curses won't force Matúš' young lads back.
The Magyars fall like plums in a high wind[83]
   And Filipp rages like he's lost his mind.

Fiercer yet presses forward the left flank:
   The Magyars crumple, falling back distressed.
The slaughter grows as now the Maygar ranks,
   From both sides, as in pincer tongs, are pressed;
No longer spouting curse or brave slogan,
   Wherever they can, the Magyars cut and run.

Filipp would stanch the rout. He bares his sword
   And froths at them: 'Cowards! Scoundrels! Women!'
But no one heeds the voice of their mad lord;
   Not one turns back of all of these poor men.
Filipp himself, at last, in terror wheels
   And runs, the Slovaks nipping at his heels.

Beside him gallops his still faithful squire.
   Intent to save his master and his friend
Whose livery he wears — splendid attire —
   He reins his steed in, stands fast, to defend
His lord's retreat — and soon is overcome,
   But Filipp's saved indeed. Just see him run!

'We've scattered them!' On all hands, joy abounds.
   Matúš, composed, praises his valiant men,
But has the trumpets for a fresh charge sound.
   'Pursue the stragglers,' comes the firm command.
So on to Šáriš they chase them, pressing hard
   To where the king lurks, with his armed guard,

---

[83] There may be an untranslatable pun behind this curious metaphor. The line reads *Padajú Uhria jako vetrom slivy* in the original; *uherka čerñá* (lit: 'black Hugarian') is another name for the common plum (Prunus domestica). This term still exists in common parlance in the kindred Polish language: *węgierka*.

Besieging on all sides the Castle Šáriš.
   King Robert would subdue it, enter in
Where he'd be covered by Filipp from Spiš,
   And not dislodged by the lord of Trenčín.
The open lowlands are no place to fight;
   Attacks are laughed to scorn from castle heights.

The battlements are manned by the allies
   Of Matúš. Who will batter through those walls?
Robert's repulsed, no matter how he tries:
   At each attack another leader falls
By stone or arrow; even Rikkolf's tamed,
   Knocked fainting from his horse, by missile brained.

Now — see the fragments of Filipp's men rush
   Up, as the knackered count himself limps near;
The anguished news that Filipp has been crushed
   Resounds throughout Robert's camp, spreading fear.
As each new drubbed knight near the castle reels,
   He wails, despairing, 'Matúš… at our heels…'

So Robert quickly forms up in a train
   To flee, and leads away his regiments.
Those who can run, do so — those who remain
   Fall meekly into the conqueror's hands.
Only the Knights of the Sword, steeped in ire
   At cowardice, in dignity retire.

Matúš arrives with his victorious throng,
   Spread wide and deep about the Šáriš plain.
From the joyous legions bursts heroic song;
   From Šáriš booms the welcoming refrain.
Drawbridges lower, gates swing open wide,
   And brother leads brother rejoicing inside.

Amidst the ardent happy regiments
   Only two gloomy, beaten scoundrels stand —
Writhing in worry, trembling in torment
   Lest someone should reveal their treasonous plan.

Deep in their black souls now each villain delves
    For plots to save King Robert — and themselves.

Those felons then proceed to bend the ear
    Of Matúš with invented tales of threats —
That Piotr Piotrovich is creeping near
    And on a treacherous attack is set;
So spin they rumours, none of which are true,
    To make him feel the unease that they do.

Anger, not worry, smoulders in his eyes.
    Honest and brave, it never would occur
To him to think them capable of lies…
    And so he plans on how to meet the traitor.
In halves his troops victorious he divides —
    These shall face Piotr, while he after Robert rides.

The forces of the king, riding in haste,
    Now tired and trembling, have escaped afar,
And only after they've rested a space
    Can they consider renewing the war.
At Rossanovce, on a spreading plain,
    Slowly, in trickles, the men gather again.

Some fresh contingents march up from Budín.
    Grand Master Rikkolf's words are sharp and terse:
'Whoever flees the ranks before Trenčín
    Shall be punished by horsewhipping… Or worse.'
In the van shall be Magyar regiments,
    His men amongst them — for encouragement.

Matúš wavers not, racing toward the king.
    The fate of faithful Košice fills him with care.
As they march on, his men begin to sing —
    Anthems of martial glory fill the air,
Of ancient triumphs, and their own — why not?
    Matúš has swept the field wherever he's fought!

Over the spreading Rossanovce plain
   The winds themselves seem locked in burly war.
Flags flop and twist, their heavy stanchions strain
   Against the blasts that roil the valley floor.
Thus Matúš' flag is buffeted and swayed,
   Yet stands firm like its master — unafraid.

It's quiet now, but hear the waves collide,
   Afar, as the silty Torysa flows,
Frothing its waters over its bankside;
   The farther on it rages, its clamour grows,
But hear — a sigh, like that of those who mourn,
   When the wind lulls, from the river is borne.

Into this warring of the elements
   By which are stifled all the warriors' cries,
In flashing mail and well-wrought basinet,
   On his ferocious stallion, Matúš flies
Casting his eyes on the ranked regiments
   As if he'd make of these mere men giants.

To him at once see Boleslavín race.
   They check their gallop, and the two steeds prance,
While their masters converse long, face to face,
   Watched by their men, who stand there, muscles tensed.
And when the two have set their battle-plans,
   They nod to one another, and shake hands.

And when they turn aside and gallop back
   To lead their troops, Matúš, thoughtful and grim,
Nods for the trumpets to blare the Attack,
   And all the eager warriors raise a din —
Before them all doughty Boleslavín
   Leads forth his Czechs to war, across the green.

In the first Magyar ranks, Filipp, aflame
   To right his Spiš catastrophe, mouths brave
War slogans while crouching behind — for shame! —

A Slovak foot soldier, his subject — his slave.
Once famed throughout Hungary, now, before
  The looming fight, why — see him cringe the more.

Among Boleslavín's men, no one recks
  The might of threats and slogans; on the ranks
Of the big-talking Filipp rush the Czechs.
  In a wink's time they press him from both flanks.
Flashing, their swords with battle-glee resound —
  Soon scores of Magyar corpses are mown down.

The panic grows. The Magyars hesitate,
  Fall back a bit, but dare not run away,
For to the rear the Knights of the Sword wait,
  And for such cowardice they'd make them pay.
Now Filipp to the king a plea sends down —
  He can't repulse the Czechs! He's losing ground!

At once the king into the battle rides;
  With him, the German knights and all his host.
Matúš can be seen on the other side
  Amidst his heroic men, of whom the most
Ferocious — Boleslavín, as he wields
  His sword, sweeping his foemen from the field.

Matúš, at once, rushes upon the king,
  Commanding, 'Forward!' to his regiments;
'Unless that sacred trust away you'd fling:
  This land, your forefathers' inheritance!
The nation would hold us in infamy!
  Slovaks! Know you the price of liberty?

'The enemy that's ranged before you now,
  Resplendently attired, of widespread fame,
Would make you slaves, to labour, cringe, and bow —
  The careless world won't even know your name!
Fight, Slovaks! Or would you prefer instead
  To toil, be whipped, and rot before you're dead?'

Then to the fight Matúš his stallion spurs;
   The Slovaks, like thunderheads in his train —
Swords clash, as from all sides the warriors —
   The Knights most dreadfully — deal death. In vain
The Knights hew, though: the Slovaks aren't dismayed,
   For Matúš leads them, with triumphant blade.

Next to the German orders in the fight
   Is tireless Jordán, who cuts many down.
When mighty Boleslavín catches sight
   Of him, and hears of his battle renown,
He rushes up, hot to chasten his pride —
   At which the other warriors draw aside.

The swords ring out and send sparks spraying clear.
   At the first pass, neither champion is touched;
The stallions neigh in anger, buck and rear,
   But each horseman sits in control, unbudged.
Just as two lions who bristle and bellow,
   Flashing their fangs, take measure of their foe.

Jordán lands the first blow, the other's helm
   Through-splitting, which stokes Boleslavín's ire.
He knocks away the sword. Then, overwhelmed,
   And weaponless stands Jordán; his wound, dire,
Spills forth his soul upon a second thrust,
   And Jordán crumples lifeless to the dust.

Cries doleful, and triumphant, then resound;
   And Jordán's troops in panic leave the fray.
The Czechs, victorious, rush to cut them down,
   And those who can't resist them, sorely pay
In life or limb; as the fierce hosts inflict
   Death on the vanquished, those call for Benedict.

Toward the shrinking mob the master turns
   His steed; see Matúš too, at the cry, race;
In both their eyes the flame of anger burns,

As they arrive and stand there, face to face;
Then both let fly their spears, but both throw wide,
   So they reach for the broadswords at their side.

Well-schooled in swordsmanship, the master wields
   His weapon, as he would a feather weigh;
Proud in attire, he looms above the field
   Just like a hawk that stoops to take its prey.
But Matúš parries each blow. Manly, stiff
   In his resolve, strong as a Tatra cliff.

Benedict swipes and hews, Matúš blocks, feints —
   The duel stretches long, interminable.
The king looks on: 'Sire, neither one relents,'
   They say, 'Both heroes, both indomitable!'
What Benedict serves up, Matúš can take —
   He waits for the string, overtaut, to break.

As his arm weakens, Matúš swells in power —
   Even to parry blows Benedict lacks
The vigour, as now tolls his fatal hour;
   He reels helplessly as Matúš attacks —
His cloak now tinged a deeper crimson hue,
   The Master falls, a sword piercing him through.

He falls, he rolls… he struggles to his feet
   Once more to face his foe, though sorely bled;
Again he parries, but his arm grows weak,
   Uncovering to a horrid blow his head —
This coup-de-grace slays the heroic knight
   Whose hour had come, though manfully he died.

Neighing in grief at having lost his lord,
   Away Benedict's trusty stallion wheeled.
Shrouded in mourning, the Knights of the Sword —
   Their Grand Master! Withdrawn now from the field!
Matúš, meanwhile, takes himself to the king.
   Whomever stands before him, down he flings!

So Matúš hacks and hews in battle-wrath,
  Nor does the Slovak youth behind him lag —
They rush on forward, widening the path
  That Matúš blazes to the royal flag.
There Bondor stands, determined to defend
  The standard with his unit of picked men.

Now comes the harvest! See the Slovak swords
  Mow down the flag's defenders. Where they stand
Is now a gory marsh, through which they ford
  Over corpse, through tides of blood, to the high land
Where the Hungarian flag's fixed. Many fall,
  But it's Bondor's men that perish most of all.

Bondor, the valiant soul, cries out in ruth:
  'Defend the flag! Let her not be forsaken!'
Yet vainly he resists the Slovak youth,
  And soon falls to their ardour, captive taken.
'The flag is ours!' resound the joyful cries.
  See how they shine, the radiant Slavic eyes!

Far from the battle Robert stood, intent
  Upon the distant brawl, eyes open wide;
And when he saw the flag fall, numb, he went
  Toward the knoll, galloping, terrified.
Matúš withdraws, exhausted with the strain,
  Judging the battle to be on the wane.

To the Grand Master then Robert flies on —
  As over the fallen hero in shock he bends,
He calls for aid: 'The Grand Master is gone!'
  Rikkolf rides up, mad, thirsting for revenge,
And with the knights remaining, there he stands,
  Heading their small, but fierce, capable bands.

The Master, dreadful in despair and woe,
  Enters the lists, accompanied by all
The knights, and in their midst, it seems, Fate goes.
  Where they advance, see scores of fighters fall —

They mow like Death herself, beneath whose scythe
   No one she comes across escapes alive.

The youths, on the defensive, bravely fight,
   Yet step by step, withdraw, though loathe to yield,
But, bred to battle is the monkish knight,
   And as a plough slits furrows through the field,
So Rikkolf and his men, with flashing sword
   Drive straight, clean sillions through the tired horde.

When Boleslavín sees them, in the midst
   Of their withdrawal, he cries — 'Slovaks! For shame!'
And racing over: 'Has it come to this?
   Whose sword this tide of murderers shall restrain?'
His cries fill with new vigour each Slovak,
   And digging in, they halt the knights' attack.

Against Boleslavín see Rikkolf race
   In fury; blind with ire, he swipes and thrashes,
But Boleslavín won't withdraw a pace
   And on the knight his heavy broadsword crashes.
Both swords are red; from both, streams of blood flow.
   And yet, it seems, the stronger both men grow.

Biding their time, intent on these events,
   Radmír and Ctibor wait with their reserves,
'Should Matúš need them rush to his defence,'
   They say — yet each one his own self but serves —
Trembling, they spend the hour with bated breath:
   That way — rewards await them; this way — death.

At the decisive moment of the war
   The traitors have their cozened troops retreat.
Throughout the ranks 'Treason!' the Slovaks roar,
   'They sell their motherland to Hungary!'
At this, Boleslavín leaves off his fray
   With Rikkolf, and after Ctibor speeds his way.

In sorrow and in ire he leaves his ground.
  Rikkolf flies after, with his vengeful horde.
Soon do they catch him up, and ring him round.
  Each of the knights against him draws his sword;
Defeat follows defeat: the nation sold,
  Now Boleslavín's last hour has tolled.

Would Matúš were here! But in vain he calls.
  Wounded, he fights on, as his breath grows shorter —
His arm grows weak, and to his side it falls,
  And yet Boleslavín will beg no quarter.
His will fights on — for Slovak liberty.
  If die he must, let him die thus: fierce, free.

He tenses for one last, despairing rush.
  Even the Grand Master feels his sword's bite.
But what can one do in such a crush?
  Soon he's borne under by their massive might —
Pierced to the quick, brave Boleslavín sighs,
  Slides from his horse unto the dust, and dies.

A dreadful cry mourning Boleslavín
  Is raised — And Matúš?... He's not anywhere!
The Slovaks break and run to save their skin.
  To struggle against destiny none dare —
The trickle soon becomes a rout. All flown —
  The field is silent now, save for prayer and moan.

But where is Matúš? all ask. This one heard
  That that one saw him speed across the plain.
That way? No, this... And then pipes up a third
  Who saw him wounded, by a traitor slain...
No, no! He's taken captive!... So it goes:
  Rumours abound, but no one really knows.

Knights of the Sword hunt fleeing Slovaks down
  Though long they flee, and never slacken pace.
At Žabokreky they run them to ground,

And there, the long in coming coup-de-grace:
Their hope all vanished, the leaderless bands
　Fall, one and all, into enemy hands.

The cities, castles, fortresses and all
　Which to the Magyar king never succumbed,
Hearing the ill rumour of Matúš' fall,
　Fall subject to him now, one by one.
Resistance is vain, hope is perished,
　Komárno falls, and taken is Šáriš.

Even the Count of Bretčan (ever true,
　Though slandered by the perjury of men),
Hearing of Matúš' baneful fall, he too
　Could not hold out long by himself, and when
Dansa attacked with all his massive might,
　Piotr fell — bravely — in the uneven fight.

Still one endures, sublimely out of reach,
　Beholding the chaos with unterrored eye.
In vain the enemy prepares his siege;
　In vain he frets around the castle high.
Indomitable before, so it remains:
　The fortress Trenčín, unmoved above the plains.

At each assault, thunder comes rolling down.
　At each assault, more enemies fall slain.
A dreadful rumour starts to make the rounds —
　Matúš himself is fighting there amain!
The fastness… sealed… So who is in control?
　Can it be Matúš? Or perhaps — his soul?

Many years pass, the castle stands firm yet —
　No matter how the foe beneath her walls
Should strain to take her, plan and plot and fret —
　His courage flags, his spirit droops and falls;
The siege lasts far too long, his losses mount,
　While there, it seems that no one's to be found!

The castle seems as if locked in a spell —
   When the assaults break off, deep silence reigns.
But sometimes, at midnight, sad music swells
   About the hill, to spill upon the plains…
Can it be Matúš' old bard, intoning
   Like a nightingale, the last song of spring?

To whom sings he? Or is it that he tries
   To ease with song his heart, burdened with woe?
Who knows? No sooner born the song, it dies,
   As through the valley fades its pale echo…
Quite soon, no voices will renew the lays
   Which so recall, Trenčín, your glory days!

Song on the Ruins of Trenčin

Old legends from an old gravemound
That lies somewhere on Mount Zobor
From pilgrims and poets resound
And spread throughout the world. A store
Of ancient and of splendid tales
That set one young man's heart afire —
To grand exploits he was inspired…
Oh, there is much here to bewail!

Land of our fathers, bitter years!
Where palaces once scraped the clouds
Now only… the huts of villagers
Hunch to the ground. A nation proud
— Once proud — once famed throughout the world
Now lays a-dying in servitude.
Who will its ancient fame renew?
Who will its grand banners unfurl?

A star shone out in the dark night,
A sun broke through the clouds that wrapt
The nation. You, young hero, stepped
Forth to aid us in our plight.

Some greeted you, some turned away,
But you beat down their foreign foes,
And with you, the Slovak nation rose…
But now, that nation moans, enslaved.

Our hope of freedom guttered low
When you, oh hero, found your grave.
Once more, for centuries, we're bowed
Beneath the burden of a slave
And yet, a new age is upon us,
I hear its trumpets blare, thrillingly:
People, my people, look and see:
The morning star of freedom dawns!

A Letter from a Hungarian Slav to the Editors of the *Literary Weekly*

Familiar as I am with other Polish periodicals, it has been my great desire to come to know the *Tygodnik Literacki* [Literary Weekly] of Poznań, all the more so as news of it is constantly spreading through the Slavic lands — and this news is universally good. Eagerly then did I take it in hand as soon as a copy came my way, and I read through all the articles it contained. Nor was I disappointed: I am now convinced that Your periodical, which has as its aim the propagation of culture, and especially the betterment of domestic criticism, is well on its way to accomplishing its elevated goals. Well-chosen are the articles concerning foreign literature and celebrated men: those in the first numbers dealing with Your province's cultural services to the fatherland, contemporary Polish composers, Szymon Starowolski, the fragments of Wybicki's autobiography, the folk-tale of the twelve bandits, and so on. The poem about the stork is honest, and speaks to the tender heart. Ah, but the joy that filled me when I saw that, after the example of *Sławianin* [The Slav] and the Kraków *Pamiętnik Naukowy* [Scholarly Journal], fraternal love, reciprocal Slavic tenderness, echoes in Your periodical too, displaying for all to see Your noble sentiments in relation to Your brothers all throughout the broad extent of Slavdom. This joy of mine only grew the more, indeed, it reached the highest degree, upon my lecture of the important letter from Berlin that You printed treating of sculpture, the detailed letter concerning the direction in which modern literature is heading, and, further, Your defence of the Slavs in response to the ugly words of their enemy H[enschel]. Finally, I come to that important piece, so imbued with the tender Slavic spirit, which treats of Slovak and Serbian song. I am a Slovak. My home is in the inaccessible Carpathian mountains and their valleys, in which, as your author justly notes, ancient customs and mores, entertainments, legends, traditions, sayings and other dear treasures of our nationhood, most especially our songs, are preserved in all of their purity, untainted by any foreign influence. It's true: all of this can be found amongst us in profusion. The Slovak sings hymns to God, and raises his voice in songs of praise of the heroes of past ages; he expresses himself in gloomy meditations and thus lightens the oppression, which the long-vanished heroic ages of which he sings knew nothing. In order to familiarise you with the spirit that beats from the songs of the Carpathian Slavs, I enclose two such along with this letter. One of these comes from those heroic ages when the Great Moravian state shone mightily on the world stage, with its grand cities, Welegrod[84] and Nitra. Alas, on account of the dissension that erupted amongst the sons of the mighty Świętopełk, Moravia vanished all the more swiftly into its grave, and the brutish Magyar nation, whom You are used to term Węgry, or 'Hungarians,' made their way to our beautiful regions. This happened during the period of our fathers' squabbling, and cast barbarian shadows upon the grand age that was just dawning, and upon the gentle spirit of the Slavic people as well, who had but received the Christian faith from the Apostles Methodius and Cyril. The second song is a meditation of the oppressed common people. The melodies of both these songs are sorrowful, and speak eloquently and deeply to the heart. I send them to you in the original, for our tongue is very easy for our Polish brothers to understand. In our periodicals, too, one meets with Polish verses in the original, and our people read them gladly. So I beg You, accept in reciprocity something Slovak (or, better, Slovanian) — for we are all Slavs![85]

I

Nitra my dear, O Nitra, sweet and cherished;
Nitra once blossoming, now, Nitra perished!

Nitra my dear, O mother of all our tribes,

....

[84] Velehrad. Štúr composed this letter in Polish, and thus seeks to Polonise proper names where possible. Poles today use the Czech spelling, although 'Welegród' or 'Wielegród' is possible. Later on, Štúr uses the Polish version of Svätopluk — Świętopełk.

[85] As might be expected, Štúr's Polish is quite good, but in these lines he makes a few mistakes, and expresses himself in an unclear fashion. There are a few Slovakisms, such as his use of *baśnie* for 'poems.' In Slovak *básne*, and in Czech *básně* mean 'poems;' in Polish *baśnie* means 'fables' or 'fairy stories' — *wiersze* is used for verses. The line *przyjmijcie więc i Wy wzajemnie od nas do czasopism Waszych coś Słowackiego (lepiej Słoweńskiego) wszystko jest Sławiańskie!* is a little difficult to understand. Firstly, *Słowacki* is good Polish for 'Slovak,' *Słoweński* would be 'Slovenian' — here too Štúr is using a Czecho-Slovakism: *Slovenský*... To return to the unclarity: the line literally would be translated: 'Therefore accept You as well, in reciprocal fashion, something from us to Your periodicals, something Slovak (better, Slovanian) everything is Slavic!'

Who can behold Thee ever with dry eyes!

Thou once held'st sway, all throughout this broad land,
Wherever Danube, Wisła, and Morava expand.

Thou wert the throne from which King Svätopluk reigned,
A mighty monarch, among his many thanes.

Thou wert the chair from which Methodius taught
When He God's Word to our forefathers brought.

And now thy glory lies hidden in the dust!
The ages pass, alas, as pass they must!

II

O Father, my Father, what a tangled world
Grabs at the feet of Thy poor wretched churl!

He slaves away, and earns nothing but pain;
His master thinks he'll always reign, and reign…

Ah masters! Though you be of noble birth,
We'll all be equals, equals in the earth.

Peasant or prince, once dead, is soon forgot,
And in the grave all flesh will rot, will rot.

Such are the traces of our people's greatness and abasement, and this hard lot of ours is due to the Magyars. When they arrived in these beautiful, fertile regions of ours, they brought their feudalism with them, and with it slavery such as was unknown to our fathers. To this very day the Magyar has not come to terms with the Slav. They are our enemies from time immemorial. And now Magyar fanaticism has set itself to the task of tearing away the national tongue of all the Slavs in Hungary, in Croatia, in Slavonia; they wish to stifle the Slavic spirit, but they will surely not encompass their aim, for each day, throughout these lands, the spirit of Slavic nationhood spreads and takes root. And there might be more of this on Your pages, should our brothers show an interest in learning about the situation of their brothers in the Carpathians and on the banks of the Danube.

At Ján Hollý's Monument[86]

Not far from Dobrá Voda,
See a grave mound arise;
Tell me, O sacred tumulus,
Who in thy bosom lies?

'Deep in my heart is lain
That bard beloved, who first
With song in Slovak, slaked
The Slovak nation's thirst.

His sacred head it is
That lies beneath this stone.
The Slovak nation's glory
Within lies, overthrown.'

Ah, no! 'Tis but his dust
That rests within thy gloom;
His songs resound afar,
Unstifled by the tomb.

And with them too, that eye
Still flashes, soaring grand
Above the length and breadth
Of this our motherland!

---

[86] It is noted that this poem was sung at the unveiling of the monument at Ján Hollý's grave in the cemetery at Dobrá Voda on 11 May 1854. Hollý had moved to Dobrá Voda in 1843 following a severe fire, from which he barely emerged alive, which destroyed his home in Madunice (where Štúr had earlier visited him). Born in 1785, Hollý died in 1849. The poem was sung to the tune of 'Veje vietor, veje, od Tatier k Dunaju' [The wind is blowing, blowing, from the Tatras to the Danube']. In Slovak, the name of the locality, Dobrá Voda, means 'good water'.

PAN-SLAVISM

A Journey to Lusatia

Slavs, Brothers!

from Štúr's Address to the Slavic Congress

Speech at the Slavic Linden

A Glance at Current Events in Slavdom, 1848

The Contributions of the Slavs to European Civilisation

Pan-Slavism and our Country

A Journey to Lusatia

(*undertaken in the spring of 1839*)

The natural affection I have for my nation, which grew stronger immediately upon my acquisition of a clearer consciousness of my own self and my fellow-countrymen, augmented in good time by the lecture of the poetry of our priceless Kollár, swelled year by year, greater and greater in my breast, attracting me to everything that could help me to a better knowledge of our nation, as expressed in all of its tribes. Moreover, this moved me to undertake all that was in my power, as weak as it may be, to offer even the most humble service to aid in the establishment of our slowly awakening sense of nationality.

I had long desired to visit that portion of Slavdom which yet remains in the northwest lands, inhabited and cultivated by our great nation, in particular, Lusatia, which all the more strongly attracted me, because they have preserved the most traces of ancient Slavdom, which once spread so broadly through these lands, whereas in contrast, in other regions, purely Slavic for many ages now, even the slightest residue of the ancient inhabitants has disappeared — but also because of the fact that in our very day and age the sad spectacle of the extinction of all things Slavic and the obtrusive imposition of a foreign ethnicity is especially visible amongst them. Perhaps the final curtain is about to fall upon the once mighty presence of Slavs in the regions beyond the Laba and Odra. These regions — the banks of the Laba and Odra rivers — were the last bulwarks of Slavdom in the face of foreign elements to the west, and it is no wonder that they sustained the most furious pressure on Slavdom, in overwhelming numbers, nor that they (as usually happens to embankments under constant stress of erosion) suffered the most of all Slavs, as a consideration of those regions teaches us well enough. We may boldly assert that in ancient times several million Slavs inhabited these wide-spreading areas. Today, we meet with but several thousand in Silesia, Lusatia, Pomerania, and in the vicinity of Luneburg, of whom the number grows smaller day by day. And thus, at the end of the present century, there shall remain little more than a shadow of ancient Slavdom here, especially in the two last-named places. But although weak and slight these remnants be, still and all, the heart of each ardent Slav must glow with pride and esteem for them. For they, although few in number, have still remained true to their language and the traditions of their forefathers, in spite of all the fierce wars and catastrophes which have been inflicted upon our nation. And so they appear to us as heroes, fighting in the avant-garde against the foreign hosts on behalf of all Slavdom, falling as a sacrifice on behalf of all their brethren, after heroic resistance. It was they who shielded us from the menacing storm. All the more seemly is it for us to hold their worthy remnants in deep respect, and as far as it lies in our power, to come to their aid when they are faced with looming destruction, gathering them to us through literature, enkindling the national spirit in them, and supporting it once it has begun to glow. And this, I reckon, we can best do by seeking to participate, to the best of our ability, in their national literary life, when such should appear, and of which, in Lusatia, we can have a sure hope. We would also do well to encourage our brothers there to nestle close to their more powerful brethren, familiarising them with their literature. For they, being but small in numbers and exposed to the strong and continual blows raining down upon them from foreign parts, could easily grow completely distant from the spirit of Slavic nationhood, should aid from their fraternal tribes not be forthcoming.

And so I set out for Lusatia, bearing in my bosom that sad apprehension which those beautiful, but gloomy words of Kollár long ago enkindled in my heart, in which he compares the Lusatian regions to two sinking ships. On my way there, I paused my journey in Leipzig, that city so famed lately for its many publishing houses, its many and grand repositories of books and bookstores, as well as its international trade. Leipzig is a city founded long ago by our forefathers, and it still bears the name they gave it, although now altered. It so happened that the famous Easter market was taking place at the time I arrived there, teeming with many people from all the lands of Europe and some from Asia and America, too. Among the crowds there were significant numbers of Slavs: Russians, Poles, Czechs and Sorbs — the last of whom were especially numerous. You could make out the Sorbs because of their national dress, which gave me much pleasure, as did their trade establishments, for I thought to myself that nations enrich themselves through trade, and in the end become mighty — as the testimony of so many ages and nations teaches us.

[...][87]

In these latter times, Russia has concentrated her efforts on the broadening of trade and the spread thereof, everywhere throughout Asia, as well as on the perfecting of her industrial manufactures as a necessary condition for commercial success. This will indubitably result in colossal gains. [...] It is true that the Germans often say that, although the Russians possess a talent for bartering and trading on a small scale, they lack the *esprit* necessary for large-scale enterprises. But reality, not words, gives the lie to this, as the British are becoming worried at the development of Russian trade, bristling at its broadening and spread all throughout central Asia. [...] Yet, as far as Slavs are concerned, one needn't fear that trade should grow wildly rampant to the detriment of agriculture, throttling this one branch of the national economy, which involves such great capital. For the Slavs can consider themselves very fortunate in their situation, in which industry must proceed hand in hand with agriculture. Whoever is of the opinion that agriculture is based upon durability and firm grounding, while industry, and especially trade, offer vistas of freer and quicker progress, will easily foresee a happy future for the Slavs, achieved, not by mindless haste, but rather by constant, moderate, and thorough-going progress. I experienced a warm joy upon seeing my fellow tribesmen engaged at the world-famous Leipzig trade fair, amongst whom the Sorbs displayed a particular assiduousness. This innate diligence and entrepreneurial spirit of the Slavs is the reason why their kin in Hungary, with the exception of the nobility, who dispose of greater wealth, are the country's richest citizens — a fact that the languid and clumsy Magyar, himself not venturing into any larger enterprise, attributes to craftiness.

Having some free time on my hands, I revisited Gebhard's garden, which lies right upon the Elster River. It is there that a monument to the unfortunate Poniatowski has been erected. To my description of that statue, first published in *Květy* [Blooms], I find myself obliged to add a few more details and adjustments. Not far from the monument stands a neat little house in which some likenesses of Poniatowski are displayed to passers-by, including one picture that depicts Poniatowski, already mortally wounded, attempting to leap into the Elster on horseback. This last painting is excellently conceived. Mortal agony, as well as a sense of his fatherland's suffering, are so clearly marked on Poniatowski's face, that it cannot but move the sensitive

---

[87] We omit here a long digression into the history of international trade... from the Phoenicians to the contemporary British Empire.

onlooker's heart with strong emotion. His sidearm is also preserved there, from which he fired upon the Prussian soldier who inflicted that mortal wound, as he leapt with his steed into the river. He was buried here, but afterwards the Poles, who desired that the remains of their glorious warrior should repose in his native land, transported them to Kraków, just as Kościuszko's were from Solothurn — which I mention here as a correction to what I wrote in *Květy*. Amongst the curiosities on display at the Leipzig fair that most drew my attention were the animalia collected by the famous Acken, and the skeleton of a whale, ninety feet in length, which gave me a clearer understanding of those oceanic giants.

The university holidays were still going on here, so I was unable to meet with the members of the local Sorbian society, which has been in existence for over half a century, and whose members are active auditors of the university. I made this up on my way back. The market of the German bookhandlers, with its admirable superscription, *Deutsche Buchhändler-Börse*, containing nearly all sorts of business involved with the book trade, elicited a deep sigh from my bosom. For I thought upon our Slavic lands and our own book trade, still so weak and insignificant, to which we would wish a greater energy, vigour and industry. Certainly, our audience is yet a small one. But if we wish that the former grow in strength, we must broaden and multiply the latter. For it is upon the latter that the former depends. As our audience grows broader and takes on a greater role in literature, we shall see that the book industry will become more invigorated. Let this be our sure hope!

I left Leipzig the second day after arriving, climbing aboard a steam train, which transported us along the Leipzig-Dresden railway to the latter city — a distance of almost fifteen miles — in just three hours and fifty minutes.[88]

Dresden on the Laba is also a city once founded by our Slavic forebears. Today, however, there is nothing Slavic about it save its name and its Sorbian wet nurses. The setting of the town is charming. The somewhat distant surrounding hills and the cloudy Laba that flows through it lend it the sort of charm that often appeals to our fancy. The two banks of the Laba are joined by a beautiful bridge, which is yet much smaller than that in Czech Prague.[89]

....

[88] Dresden lies 120.5 km from Leipzig. Today, the distance is covered in roughly one hour and thirty-six minutes by train. Štúr is referring here to the standardised Austrian mile, which was equal to 7.586 km. Fifteen Austrian miles gives us 113.79 km — so the poet was off by roughly one unit of measure.

[89] *V českej Prahe*. It is unclear why Štúr expresses himself thus. In Polish, *Praga* can refer to both Prague and the Praga section of Warsaw; Poles sometimes speak of *Praga czeska* in order to specify which location they're referring to. Perhaps Štúr, in this essay, wishes to underscore the

Steam travel abounds on this river. It is now possible to sail by steamboat from Bohemia to Hamburg and the North Sea quite quickly. What a gateway to trade! Here, I spent more than one pleasant hour with Jan Hraběta, court chaplain and ardent Slavic patriot, who was called to the Saxon court by a curious fate, rather than any sort of lobbying for the office. This is that Jan Hraběta of whom we read in *Květy* some few years ago, who taught Prince Johann, the heir to the throne, the Czech language, which study the prince undertook of his own initiative, remaining steadfast in his application to it, and finding in it much delight. Our patriot told me that the righteous prince took under his personal protection the Slavic tongue in Saxon Lusatia, coming out emphatically against all unlawful attempts at stifling our language in this region. Several years ago, discussions were held in the Saxon diet aiming at the definite suppression of the Slavic tongue in Lusatia, and only Prince Johann's noble defence of it, as well as the courageous efforts of Dr Müller, Minister of Education at the time, successfully plucked her free of the threatened destruction, by decreeing that religious instruction in the grade schools must be carried out in the pupils' native tongue. The rarer such examples of justice accorded to Slavs in German lands are, the more recognition they deserve amongst us when they do occur! The museums not yet being open, after a short stay I set out once more on my journey to Lusatia.

My trip led me through a beautiful, wooded countryside. I passed by village after village, all of which had once been entirely Slavic, but now are completely germanised. Their layout style testifies to their Slavic origins, as do their names, which, like those of the inhabitants, are either deformed or entirely germanised. One can still hear Slavic names here, though most often amongst the simple folk, as among the more educated and on the signage you can hardly make out the original sound of the name, or the village and town nomenclature of Lusatia. The exceptions to this rule are constituted by those that could either not be twisted or completely germanised — their meaning being too obscure for German eyes. Amongst such belongs, for example, Ratibor; among those entirely translated into German we might point out Weissig (Biela). Such as were deformed are many. I give here just a few examples: Uist (Ujezd), Lohsa (Lazy), Bautzen (Budyšin), Görlitz (Zhořelec), and so on. Here I pause to speak of the de-Slavicising tendencies in Hungary too, where our native nomenclature is deformed in exactly the same way, the twisted names finding their way onto signage, for example Bánovce (Bán), Ozorovce (Ozor) and hundreds of others. It is notable that

---

'Slavic' nature of the city, despite its large German-speaking population.

these are taken over into Latin as well, so as to lend them a more Latinate character!⁹⁰ This is an especially important issue for us Slavs, as it makes perfectly clear in what manner our national character is being effaced and uprooted wherever possible.

Wending my way further, I beheld Sloupsko rising on a sheer summit to the right, the appearance of which intensified the ardent pain in my heart, as I spontaneously recalled that sonnet of Kollár's which begins with the line 'O lofty Sloupsko, castle of the Moks,' etc. It is a most powerful feeling to gaze upon the splendid remains of the presence and glory of one's own people, for they best direct our minds toward the happier past, contrasted with our present state of subjection, which latter they allow us to feel most sorely.

Entering the wagon for my onward journey, I found myself in a compartment along with two other Slavs. One of them was Ján Mužík, a citizen of Budyšin, and the other Stanisław Krupiński, a Pole, a wholesale dealer from Odessa, both of whom were on their way home from the Easter fair in Leipzig. These two good men were conversing in the Slavic tongue, each in his own dialect.⁹¹ Amongst other things, they also spoke about the progress that the Poles are making in wholesale enterprises, which gladdened my heart, all the more so as I noted that both of them displayed a particular affection for their ethnicity.⁹² I immediately joined the conversation, explaining in a few words the connections that unite both their tribes, after which I embarked on a broader comparison of all three dialects,⁹³ at which their eagerness to learn and their ability were obvious, for they immediately translated my entire account from one dialect into another. Thereupon we talked about the Sorbs of Lusatia and of the gradual disappearance of their native

---

⁹⁰ Magyar did not replace Latin as the administrative language of Hungary until 1846. It seems that Štúr is making an ironic aside here: nationalist Magyars (speaking a non-European tongue) still wish to underscore their Western affiliations by Latinising Magyar, not Slovak, place names in the Latin language.

⁹¹ The Slavic languages are one of the most closely related language groups in the Indo-European family. It is for this reason that many nineteenth-century Pan-Slavs like Štúr spoke of a 'Slavic' language, designating individual tongues like Polish, Czech, Slovak and Russian as 'dialects' of the same.

⁹² Again, whether that *narodnost* or 'ethnicity, nationality' be Polish and Lusatian, or 'Slavic,' is unclear — and probably didn't matter to Štúr.

⁹³ The Slavic languages possess three sub-classifications: East Slavic (Russian, Ukrainian, Belorussian), South Slavic (Bulgarian, Serbo-Croatian, Old Church Slavonic) and West Slavic (Polish, Czech, Slovak, Lusatian Sorb). It is more likely that the three dialects Štúr is speaking of here are the Polish, the Lusatian Sorb — and whatever he was speaking, Slovak, Czech, or the 'Czechoslovak' language that Ján Kollár advocated.

language, which the Sorb there present confirmed with pain, bemoaning the fact of the various ways in which the national speech is being uprooted. These include: the forcible imposition of German upon all schools, even village schools; the inability to introduce legal actions in court in Lusatian Sorbian, and so forth. In conclusion, he added that they are unable to serve the Lord God properly in any language save their mother tongue, for which reason, it seems, he does not attend the German cathedral church, although the citizens of Budyšin customarily go there, preferring instead to remain true to divine services in Sorbian. There was also among us a certain German lady from Lusatia. Although she didn't understand a word of Sorbian, she began to complain about the godlessness of the Lusatian Sorbs, who, allegedly, in the Upper Lusatian town of Opice,[94] allow the local church to remain completely empty when German services are held therein, but fill it to bursting when God is served in Sorbian. I winced at her words and admonished her for the vanity of her argument, reflecting in my soul how our wagon was like a microcosm of what is happening in the wider world around us, in connection with us and the inferences, which either the antipathy or the light-mindedness of our neighbours customarily make in the presence of the educated world.

Some three hours from Budyšin I began to hear Sorbian spoken and to recognise bright and pleasant Slavic faces, the sight of which filled me with a sort of painful joy. For it came to my mind that perhaps very soon they shall be seized by the cold arms of the foreign elements, which now stretch out to embrace them.

I arrived in Budyšin on the very same day I set out from Dresden. There I bid farewell to Krupiński, the erstwhile companion of my voyage, who was travelling on farther. At the same time I accepted with pleasure an amiable invitation from Mužík, my other fellow traveller, to call upon him during my visit to Budyšin.

Budyšin, the main city of Lusatian Upper Saxony, counts about ten thousand inhabitants, and lies upon the river Sprjewja (Spree). It is the most beautiful place. It is surrounded by nearby hillocks and mountains, which to the west and the north rise to a significant height and bear Slavic names to this very day, such as Černoboh, Prašica, and so forth. At their feet the Slavic nation is still most purely preserved, although the foreign element from the city is making dangerous inroads here too. My first order of business was to visit the chief local clergyman — Handrij Lubjenský, an ardent Sorb, who

---

[94] Oppitz, or in Sorbian, Rakecy.

authored the heartfelt introduction to Zejleŕ's Sorbian grammar. He received me very cordially indeed and expressed a great delight in the fact that Slavs living at even so great a distance keep their Lusatian brothers in mind. Yet his answers to my queries were not very cheerful. For he stated that the Sorbian burghers and the wealthier Sorbian citizens were growing more and more German with each passing day, encouraging their children to speak German, whereby the native language was retreating more and more underneath the village thatch, seeking there sanctuary from the growing threat of extinction. He recalled with sorrow that since his childhood many villages had become completely germanised and, instead of divine service in Sorbian, which was a common event when he was a boy, now church services are held entirely in German. I spared no effort exhorting the excellent man to publish as soon as possible the Sorbian dictionary at which he had been labouring for so many years, so that at least therein the Sorbian tongue might be preserved, which was so important for so many reasons to Slavic linguistics. Indeed, it serves as an heirloom bequeathed unto us from our dying Lusatian brothers — a witness and a warning. The caring and attentive man vowed to preserve that treasure chest for us, but on one condition: that his health, much weakened by many years of labour, be returned to him. In the end, he brought to my attention Dr Klin, an inhabitant of Budyšin, a Sorb, who expended much effort on the preservation of local ethnicity, and who had already achieved much in that respect. He also spoke of the Society of Sorbian Youth which had been newly formed at the local gymnasium.

This encouraging news put me in high spirits indeed. So I made haste to call upon Dr Klin, who received me with a truly Slavic warmth, and assured me that he would aid me in every possible way to come to know Lusatia, especially the history of the city of Budyšin and its surrounding region — which promise the diligent man fulfilled excellently. Immediately thereafter I took myself to the gymnasium where, to my great surprise, I discovered the Sorbian society (which had actually been founded just several weeks earlier, made up of several dozen native Sorbs), having just accomplished the endorsement of their governing body. The chief mover behind the foundation of this society is Arnošt Smoleŕ a native Sorb, and an ambitious young man, whose efforts were rewarded as early as 1832, during his own tutelage at this gymnasium, with the erection of a little Sorbian assembly. This, however, disappeared with his own matriculation in 1835 — most likely for lack of a more independent head and ardent spirit, as well as a lack of support on the part of the authorities. Then, during the vacation of 1838, Smoleŕ became acquainted with several pupils of the gymnasium, and this resulted in the revival of the society which had previously vanished. At the renewed call of Smoleŕ the Society was reestablished in February of this year and, God willing, will flourish more happily than before. The aim and constitution of the society will be most clearly shown by introducing here some of their chief statutes:

Statutes
of the Sorbian Society.[95]

The goal of this Sorbian Society is: that every Sorb might better come to know his national speech; that he might not neglect it, but rather learn it so well as to be a source of advantage to the Sorbs and of pride to Slavdom.

Because no society can endure without statues, we too have enacted the following:

I. Each person who adheres to the society must be a native Sorb, or a German who is to some degree familiar with the Sorbian language.
II. Each member must deliver one lecture in Sorbian each month. Those who are as yet unable to do so are excused from this obligation. All such lectures as are acknowledged by all members to be worthy of inclusion in our books, shall be recorded therein.
III. During meetings, let each member express his thoughts in Sorbian.
IV. So that unity and peace be preserved in the meetings, let there be elected a Starschi or Senior, who shall conduct the books of the society, and compose letters to the friends of the society. In the case of the Senior being unable to be present at a meeting because of illness, let a Podstarschi (Junior Officer) take his place.
V. Let each member also learn another Slavic speech, such as Czech, Polish, Serbo-Croatian, or Russian.

The undersigned confirm these statutes with their signatures:

August Mosik s Aehrenfeldu Starschi
Fried. Immisch Podstarschi
Karl Sauer
Michael Domaschko

---

[95] Štúr appends these statutes to his essay in the original Lusatian Sorb.

Karl Rentsch
Friedrich Stillbrich
Karl Petaw
Bruno Pohlenz
Adolph Schulze
Joh. Lehmann.

Their library, while still indeed modest, is enriched with the contributions required of each member according to the statutes. I was greatly encouraged when, at the very start of my inspection, I came across Czech, Polish, and Russian grammars, the acquisition of which gives obvious testimony to the eagerness of the above-named youths.

Showing me around the notable sights in Budyšin, Dr Klin led me to an ancient tower that still today is known as the 'Sorbian Tower.' It has the appearance of being ages old. It stands alone, unattached to any church. It is round, and at the top ringed with a balustrade, from which the eye has a delightful view of the city and the surrounding countryside. From this perspective, my eager guide showed me where the battle of Budyšin had taken place, during which Napoléon, making astute use of the surrounding hills, fell upon the Allies and won a resounding victory over them. On one of the hills you can still see the lone tree, preserved as a monument, beneath which Napoléon stood, inspecting the field and commanding his victorious troops.

I also made an excursion along with the young Sorbs to a cragged valley not far from town, through which the Sprjewja flows, and concerning which many tales still circulate amongst the folk. In ancient pagan times, the steep, soaring cliffs doubtlessly served as a temple of sorts, since such were frequently located in such eerie, awe-inspiring locales. To this day people still point out the place where, in ancient times, according to popular legend, the idol of the god Flinc once stood, poured of pure gold. This Flinc was thought to be able to raise the dead back to life, but I doubt that he was a Slavic god, as his name has nothing Slavic about it; I reckon that later ages, rather, confused some original Slavic god with Flinc. Allegedly, the Hussites cast this idol into the river and so far no one has been able to retrieve it from the depths. A stone column stands in that place as a memorial to that idol.

Having been provided by Dr Klin with a letter of introduction to the forester in Rochlov, a village nestled at the foot of Černoboh, I set off for that mountain too, accompanied by the young Sorbs. On that mountain, of which there are many tales amongst the village folk, ancient pagan monuments are still to be found. Mount Černoboh lies some two hours distant from Budyšin.

It reaches a significant height and spreads out in two arms, the other of which is known as 'Prašica,' from the verb 'prašiť,'[96] which in Sorbian means 'to inquire.' We passed through purely Sorbian villages, in which my companions continually entered into conversation with the people. They, hearing their native speech, became full of trust and spoke with us freely, indicating to us the most convenient route. It is worth noting that he who wishes to gain the confidence of these people must address them in their mother tongue. Otherwise, they look at one mistrustfully and act craftily toward one — which can be easily understood, considering local history, and how they have been dealt with. A very human reaction, in short. Here we might discover the reason for the charge lain at our feet by the Germans, which accuses the Slavic people of crafty circumlocution in speech and behaviour — the fault of which, however, lies on the other side. Why do our people so willingly and sincerely cleave unto the person who addresses them in their native speech? Because they see in him their friend, judging from the pleasant vocables the mind that expresses them, and it never occurs to them that there might be anything concealed beneath these trappings of sound other than the thoughts as they actually arise. Even the German burghers of Budyšin have assured me that when they have business with the Sorbs, they must speak to them in their own language. And if they are unable to do so, they seek out the services of someone else, fluent in Sorbian, to act in their place. They state that items ordered in Sorbian often come at a cheaper rate than those that are bought using German. And these are the words of trustworthy Germans.

Having arrived at Rochlov, we entered the tidy abode of the forester, a man named Lubjenský. Upon our greeting all there present in the native tongue, with sincere hearts, as is common amongst us Slavs, we too were greeted by the residents and made very welcome. We came upon the elderly man of the house while he was actually reading a book in Sorbian, containing sermons for the entire church year. As our guide to the mountain he entrusted us to his son, a lanky young man of striking appearance. Slinging a musket over his shoulder, he walked on before us, dressed in the costume of his nation (a Slavic overcoat, such as the Magyars call an *atila*) and led us to Mount Černoboh. As I looked at him, it seemed to me as if I were gazing upon some ancient hero setting off to war, or returning victorious therefrom, going off to sacrifice to the gods of deliverance[97] upon the sanctified altars.

---

[96] The proper spelling in Lusatian Sorb is *prašeć so*.

[97] Štúr has here *bohowóm spasám*. This is not entirely good Sorbian; more properly, it would be *bohóm, swým spásám*, although some suggest that he might be citing the 'old Slavic' of Václav

Some half hour later we set our feet upon the summit, where in rapturous awe I inspected the gigantic stone altars, at last satisfying an old longing of mine. They are arranged just as we find them in the Explanatory Notes to *Slávy dcera* [The Daughter of Sláva].[98] Our stalwart guide also pointed out to us some crags and boulders of vast dimensions on which, according to old folk legend, holocausts were performed. Heart-shapes may still be seen carved thereon. After this, we went on to the other arm of the mountain, the aforementioned Prašica, where there is a similar vast, two-shouldered rock — this one sculpted not by human hands, but by Nature — which delights the pilgrim's eye. That like the Greeks — those long-extinct brethren of ours — we Slavs also believed in auguries, cannot be doubted. The very name of this summit (actually, of the boulder that rises atop it) offers ample proof, as do the legends that still live amongst the people. According to these, the priest would stand in the centre of this rock and emit utterances in answer to the questions posed by those enquiring of their future (hence the etymology of the name, Prašica, 'to enquire into'). To one side of the boulder there is a hole. According to folk belief, this was the ear of the god who concealed himself in the depths of the rock. These votives, these stones, which justly might be named the obelisks and pyramids of far-distant Slavic antiquity, are found on the westernmost mountain chain of Slavdom, and, just like their countrymen, are being worn away, gnawed at by the tooth of time and the prying hands of man. Many of these altars have been entirely toppled over; others are preserved only in fragments.

We were very sorry indeed that the gorgeous and distant views from this summit were obscured by the mist, which had just then begun to sweep over Černoboh. The Czech and Silesian mountains were covered in clouds; only to the Lusatian side was it somewhat brighter, and there, with longing, we fixed our eyes. When we had sated our hearts upon these sacred monuments, we descended the mountain again for the village where, having been generously entertained by the amiable Sorbs, we hastened back to Budyšin.

....

Hanka's *Rukopis královédvorský* — like the songs of Ossian, an elaborate literary fraud which many people at the time, especially Pan-Slavs, took as good coin, evidence of the cultural antiquity of the Slavic people. In the poem narrative poem 'Čestmír a Vlaslav' [Čestmír and Vlaslav] the phrase appears as we correct it above.

[98] An expansive cycle of descriptive sonnets dealing with 'Slavdom' by the aforementioned Slovak poet Ján Kollár, originally published in 1824.

In the mountain range where Černoboh is situated, there is also a mountain called Korunný vrch, or Crown Mountain,[99] of which the following tale is spread far and wide amongst the Lusatian Sorbs. Long, long ago, seven Sorbian kings (most probably they were not kings, but chieftains) gathered upon its summit, where they seated themselves upon seven stones — now sunk deep in the earth — and here they held counsel, how they might cast off the German yoke and win freedom for their native land. They decided to rise up in arms together against their common enemy — and indeed they did. All seven fell in the battle and, along with others of the fallen, they were buried, with their crowns, beneath the stones upon which they had sat during their life, when they discussed how to free their fatherland from its oppression. For this reason, this mountain is yet held in special honour amongst the people.

Since Sunday came round during the time I spent in Budyšin, I visited both the Evangelical and the Catholic churches in which the services were held in the Sorbian tongue. Both churches were packed, even though the weather was grim and rainy, and in both I saw much attention paid to the service, and much piety, which made me right glad as conclusive evidence of the godliness of our people. I also had occasion to cast my eyes about the congregations gathered there. The greater part of the men were of tall and robust posture, strong of limb; the women too were of comely form. Their eyes — as is common amongst the Slavs — are bright and piercing. They are fresh-faced, with round features. The fairer sex still mostly clad themselves in their national dress, which does not differ much from the costume of our willowy Slovak women. Among them, the colour white is the colour of mourning, which is supposed to be true of the Poles in Greater Poland and perhaps elsewhere as well.[100]

The people gathered in the cathedral were the residents of the surrounding villages and the outskirts of Budyšin — for, unfortunately, the centre of the city has been taken over by foreigners.[101] So it goes for us Slavs, that we frequently find ourselves pushed out of our main cities by non-residents, and not only in those regions close to foreign parts, and where foreign elements have widely

---

[99] Lubin, Thromberg.

[100] Although this may still be true of the Sorbs in Lusatia, it does not occur in Poland — although the use of white as a colour of mourning is of ancient provenance amongst the Slavs. Therefore, the long continuance of its use in Lusatia, testified to by Štúr, may well be an example of long cultural continuity.

[101] That is, non-Slavs, Germans.

spread, but also in purely Slavic regions. Examples of this are many and obvious: I might point out Trnava and Bystrica in Slovakia, Brno in Moravia and Kraków in Poland, etc. We must admit our own fault here — the first step toward bettering the situation must be a confession of our own sins. The main reason for this state of things is that, earlier, we cared little, or not at all, for industry and trade, but rather, dodging all enterprise, we left it to foreigners, who rejoiced in the advantages this brought them. Industry must be the chief vocation of the city — industry, in the broadest sense of the word — just as agriculture is the chief reason to be of the town and the village.

[…][102]

Thus the foreign element secured a moral superiority over the native, which meant that civic offices and honours fell to their part, while the latter received but cool contempt. The great cities became like the knightly castles of the Middle Ages, from which sorties were made into the surrounding areas, with this difference: that the goal of those campaigns was spiritual gain, while of these — material.

[…][103]

Just before I left Budyšin, I ordered myself some books touching upon Slavdom in Lusatia, and I also received in gift from Dr Klin some sermons that had been printed in Sorbian, along with some nuptial verses, and his speech in German, delivered on 28 June 1836 before an assembly of natural scientists in Budyšin, which is especially noteworthy. Few are the men, I reckon, who have spoken such bald truths to the other side, as Dr Klin did in his speech, in which he speaks of the Lusatian Sorbs. There, before all assembled, he

---

[102] Here Štúr once more engages in a general consideration of the importance of trade to the health of a national group. His thesis is that, for whatever reason, be it 'distaste of trade or devotion to a peaceful way of life,' the Slavs left the development of their cities to foreign elements. Not only did this lead to the influx of a permanent foreign element to the once 'purely Slavic' cities, but also to the development of a high culture — fostered by wealth — in the foreign language. The Slav who wished to take part in that high municipal culture had to become 'foreign' himself, adopting the foreign tongue and assimilating himself to foreign customs, thus abandoning his Slavic nationality.

[103] Here, Štúr bemoans the lack of support for education in the native tongues of the Slavic lands, seen as a threat by the 'foreign elements.' The one praiseworthy exception to this general rule is Dr Amerling in Prague, who, with the blessing of the civic authorities, arranged public lectures in Czech 'on chemistry and technology' at the university, on Sundays.

spoke of the Slavs according to what is contained in Šáfarik's *Geschichten der Slawischen Sprache und Literatur* [History of the Slavic Languages and Literature], and moved on to acquaint them, word by word, with Herder's testimony, wherewith he admonishes the Germans for their unjust behaviour toward the Slavs. The author then turns to the Lusatian Sorbs, of whom he speaks at greater length, relating their good traits, such as piety, industry, love of their native tongue, candour and cordiality, and bravery. All these he splendidly describes, proving at length that the Lusatian Sorbs are the brightest pearl in the Saxon crown. According to Dr Klin, the number of Sorbs in Upper Lusatia, which owes allegiance to the Saxon crown, amounts to 50,000 souls. In other regions, and in Lower Lusatia, which belongs to Prussia, there are 30,000, which all told gives us a total of 80,000 persons. In testimony to their bravery, the good author does not omit to introduce the French saying concerning the Sorbs, which arose during the recent wars. They were called *les bouchers Saxons* by the French, because of their manliness in all the battles they took part in. Amongst the works I purchased here are: Zejleŕ's Sorbian grammar, entitled *Kurzgefasste Grammatik der Sorben-wendischen Sprache nach dem Budissiner Dialekt v. Andreas Zejleŕ*, Budissen bei Weller, 1830 [A Brief Grammar of the Sorbian-Wendish Language, According to the Budyšin Dialect], and Gräve's Lusatian tales, entitled *Volkssagen und volkstümliche Denkmale der Lausitz v. Heinrich Gottlob Gräve*, Bautzen 1839, Verlag v. Reichel [Folk Tales and Folklore of Lusatia], of which up till now only the first volume has seen the light of day. I intend to give a more detailed account of both these books in a more convenable place. I also requested the bookseller to send a few prints of Zejleŕ's grammar to Bohemia, Moravia and Slovakia, so that our fellow countrymen might have the opportunity of a closer acquaintance with the language of their brethren.

After my stay of several days in Budyšin, I hastened to Zhorjelc, where I arrived that same day I bade farewell to former city. Zhorjelc (Görlitz) is a city spreading along the banks of the Sprjewja, inhabited by some 12,000 people, which, just like Budyšin, has a very pleasing aspect. The Czech and Silesian mountains, which can be clearly seen from the regions surrounding the city, afford pleasant recreation to the eyes. The city itself belongs to Prussian Upper Lusatia. It was more than a little dumbfounding not to hear the slightest word spoken in Sorbian there. The city and its entire wide-spreading environs are completely mute as far as the sounds of Slavic are concerned. The greatest portion of the blame for this must be ascribed to the city's close proximity to Silesia, from which, as from the city itself, the foreign element spreads far and wide, more and more.

In this city I paid a visit to Mr Haupt, the chief pastor of the local evangelical church, and a member of the Upper Lusatian Society of Arts and Sciences. Upon my presenting him with the letter of recommendation given me by Dr Klin, he received me with great cordiality. He kindly led me to a grand building belonging to the aforementioned society, where we spent a long while inspecting the great hall, in which the assemblies of the society are held. Here are located its rich library, its collection of various natural wonders, and finally, an exhibit of antiquities. Amongst the natural curiosities, my attention was especially seized by a large vampire bat, and skulls representing the various Asiatic nations. Amongst the antiquities I was most impressed with an age-old ring with the engraving of a lion, of which no one quite knows to whom it should be ascribed. There was also a horned idol, most likely an image of Flinc, and many urns both great and small, as well as a chainmail armour intended for the protection of a woman's torso. Here we have clear proof of the heroic virtues of our lovely sex, which was splendidly in evidence in ancient times and continues down to this very day — of which we have ample proof. By chance, I happened to come across a countrywoman of mine in the library: *Hronka*, sent here not long ago through the careful attention of Mr Kuzmány. This cheered me greatly, as I saw in it the manifest presence of our Slovak nationality before the eyes of the local world. However, my joy immediately vanished when I recalled the unpleasant news, which came to me while I was still in Prague — namely, that that *Hronka* of ours was to expire, shortly, in childbirth. Here, I am not going to indulge in an enumeration of the reasons for this, or the unpleasant circumstances in which the life of our *Hronka*, so joyfully received by the frank souls in Slovakia, was shortened. I will say, rather, that her swift demise is a disagreeable indication of our national life, and presents a bad public image of us to the world. Whoever might suggest that her editor Mr Kozmány is lacking in eagerness and good will would be acting unjustly, or displaying an ignorance of the editor's ambitious spirit. For our zealous patriot would certainly never step away from his enterprise so quickly without steeling himself courageously against all sorts of obstacles and, initiating some changes in her, continuing with her publication.

I was entertained that evening at the home of Mr Haupt, where, at the request of his family, who wished to hear a song in Slovak — despite all my protestations of my poor singing skills — I sang that sad musing on our sacred Nitra, translating it afterwards into German. The words of the song made a very favourable impression upon all. Indeed, it is a beautiful song, which touches the more ardent soul with its taste of a distant antiquity, which our forefathers must have known. Among other things, Mr Haupt complained of the Lusatian Sorbs' disinterest in the collection of folk songs, despite the repeated calls of the learned society. All the same, he introduced me to a generous volume of such songs, which more diligent hands had been fortunate in assembling, thus rescuing them from certain, looming oblivion. The learned society, of which he is a member, has amassed the means for an award for more abundant collections, to be entrusted to his care. Plans have been made for such a collection to be published along with musical notation and translations into German — which will come about, Mr Haupt assured me, in the near future. We can only hope that Slavdom will reward the important fruits of such labour with a generous welcome, and recognise the society for taking care of our songs, something which gives us much pleasure and joy. Lately, I happened to overhear in Lusatia that the aforementioned young man, Arnošt Smoleŕ, along with another, equally aspiring youth named Markus, also intends to publish a collection of Sorb songs, which collection is to contain specimens from Upper as well as Lower Lusatia. We wish this project great success and popularity!

Mr Haupt also complained of the uncertain and halting nature of the codification of Lusatian Sorb orthography. He mentioned that at one time, the clergy of Lower Lusatia assembled with the intent of making uniform the orthographic laws of the tongue, but couldn't come to any agreement, and dispersed without making any progress at all. It is a sad thing when a small handful of people are either unwilling or unable to come together in such a small matter as spelling. Who will not see in this an example of the disunion and atomisation that plagues us Slavs from generation to generation? Such a small number of people, standing at the very threshold of oblivion, who still and all will not join hands so that, gathered into a tighter fraternity, they might stave off the annihilation, with which they are threatened! Much could be said of this, but we shall set it aside for a more convenient time and place.

The next day I had a look about the memorable sights in the city, amongst which is the sublime church of Ss Peter and Paul, the most beautiful of all Evangelical churches that I have ever seen. It has a soaring vault, and many columns of the Corinthian order. The bells in its steeples are gigantic. In the centre of town there is a replica of Christ's tomb in Jerusalem. This is the work of the artist Emmerich, who travelled to Jerusalem twice in order to execute it as perfectly as possible.

After my inspection of the city's historical sites I hastened on my way through Prussian Upper Lusatia. Along my journey I visited the village of Königshain first, near which there is a mound topped by a whole range of ancient stone altars. I diverted from my path in order to see them. The weather was gloomy, but the sun began to break through just as I arrived at the village, and soon the skies grew clear, so clear, that the Czech and Silesian peaks, soaring upward on the distant horizon, beautifully emerged from the clouds before my very eyes, which swept the surrounding countryside with wistful attention. What a feeling it is for a person who has spent a significant amount of time in foreign parts, to catch sight of the least corner of the world inhabited by his dear family! Sending off in their direction my most ardent words of greeting, one after another, I remained a long while amidst these ancient monuments. To these sacred altars I brought an offering of tears on behalf of our race such as, I reckon, had not been poured there for many a year. Over the fields that stretched out on all sides one could already sense delightful spring in the offing, the first stirrings of which I took for a benign response to the questions I posed to the deities hidden in the depths, which still watch over us.

That evening, passing by a long band of settlements inhabited by Germans, I arrived at last at some Sorbian hamlets. In one of these, Koma (Kolmen) I spent the night at the house of Mr Łahoda, the local pastor, an ardent Sorb. While a student at the University of Leipzig, Mr Łahoda was a member of the Sorbian Society there, as well as a contributor to the *Serbska nowina* (Sorbian News), which passed from hand to hand in manuscript amongst the friends of Lusatian Sorb. The contents of the *Nowina*, as I myself ascertained upon inspecting a copy that came into my hands in Leipzig, are made up of songs, tales and short historical notes on various themes. If only succeeding generations had continued in this same manner, there would be no question today of struggling to preserve the love for the mother tongue amongst the preachers of Lusatia. Yet this praiseworthy enterprise evaporated some years ago.

At Mr Łahoda's I met a certain divinity student, a native German, who was learning Sorbian under the tutelage of our patriot, an expert in the tongue. According to his own testimony, the young man was learning Sorbian for very love of the Slavs, and the great progress that he had made in the space of only six months bears adequate testimony thereto. He intends to become acquainted with other Slavic languages as well — the merits of which he judges from the Sorb dialect in which, as he justly noted, all that is tender and subtle can be expressed much better than in German.

Later that evening, Mr Łahoda enquired after his household, and learned in reply that they had all gone off to the forest to burn 'khadojty,' which word the Lusatians use in reference to witches. In fact, it was the last day of April, and this is the day upon which this ceremony is performed all over Lusatia. This rite, I reckon, is a survival from ancient Slavic paganism. All around, hills, groves and forests were glowing with bonfires, which in the dark of night affords a pleasant spectacle to one's eyes. The etymology of the word 'khadojty' is unknown to me. But I reckon that the initial 'kh,' which the Lusatians pronounce as a decided aspirate, derives from 'ch,' which can be clearly seen from other examples, such as 'khorasz' from 'chorý.'[104] Having received from Mr Łahoda a copy of his *Raniše a wečorne modlitwy jako tejž pši wosebnych časach a składnosciach s njekotrymi domjacymi rospomnečami wot Jana Łahody* [Morning and Evening Prayers, as well as those for Particular Times and Occasions, with Some Domestic Recollections], I hastened off on my further travels along with the May morning, leaving behind those pure Sorbian settlements. It is worth noting that in no German region that I passed through did I encounter beekeeping, whereas amongst the orchards of the Sorbs the air abounded with bees, for there were many linden trees to be seen there — such is our inheritance from our forefathers.

The harmful custom of retaining graveyards in the neighbourhood of churches, within the bounds of settlements, persists yet unto the present day nearly throughout Sorbian Lusatia. It is a custom that a wise government ought to do away with.

On my further travels I met up with an old soldier, who was keeping watch over the area now as a policeman. He had once served in the army proper, and, accosting me, inquired as to my homeland. When he learned that I was a Slav from Hungary, he immediately began praising the Slavs to the skies. He was well pleased with the lean and manly build of the Slavs. He said that the greater portion of the Prussian army was made up of Sorbs and Poles from the area around Poznań, who apparently are lacking in nothing, save a certain refinement and external culture. When they perfect this, they become the most excellent of soldiers. I agreed with him, having become convinced of this by my own experiences. What might become of our people, if they had the same instruction in their mother tongue as we find amongst our neighbours? Involuntarily, Kollár's sonnet came to my mind: 'We've everything we need, believe me, dears,' etc.

That afternoon I arrived in Łaz, which the Germans call Lohsa, with great eagerness, for I was looking forward to meeting Mr Zejleŕ, the author of the aforementioned Sorbian grammar, a man with patriotic plans for Lusatia, to

---

[104] The correct spelling in Sorbian is *khorosć*. It means 'illness,' as *chorý* in Slovak means 'ill.'

be taken at his word.¹⁰⁵ I greeted him cordially upon meeting him, at which he, upon learning the purpose of my journey, welcomed me with the same warm-heartedness, natural to the Slavs. To my great joy, Mr Zejleŕ showed me his manuscript of readings in Sorbian, which is to be an appendix to his grammar, as well as his preparations for a compendious Sorbian dictionary and an extensive collection of Lusatian songs. With all my fervour I encouraged the industrious patriot to bend his strengths especially to the publication of the dictionary, as soon as possible, as a work most needful not only to the Sorbs, but also to the other Slavs — which Mr Zejleŕ promised to do. But first he wishes to discuss the matter with Mr Lubjenský, who has been working at a similar dictionary, and for a longer space than he. I also broached the matter of Sorbian orthography to our patriot, begging him to turn his attention to the unification thereof, devoting his talents to the same — of which he has already given testimony in those writings of his that I inspected — in which he has begun writing in the Czech manner.¹⁰⁶ Among other things, Mr Zejleŕ recalled that, during his studies in Leipzig, he had been firmly committed to Slavic language lectures at the university, but had to drop the enterprise for lack of funding.

In this same village I also visited the parents of the aforementioned Smoleŕ, at whose hearth Slavic hospitality also has its home. His father, a teacher at the local school, described to me how strong the pressure had been to introduce German to that school as the sole language of instruction, which he resisted with rational arguments for so long until, at least, religious instruction in the local language was permitted. But all other subjects are required to be taught in the German tongue.

Bidding farewell to these faithful and brave descendants of the ancient Sorbs, I went my way amongst the Catholic Lusatians, as they are known there, on my way to Kamjenc, a town that falls under the Saxon government. On my way there I stopped in at the monastery, wishing to visit the divine Albert, a Czech by birth, of whom I had heard that he blazes with a burning love for our nation and expertly speaks in all the chief Slavic dialects. Alas, to my great sorrow, the diligent patriot had suddenly died some few months previously.

....

¹⁰⁵ *Muža z vlasteneckých plánov po Lužiciach na slovo vzatého.* A pun: A man engaged in the practical, patriotic act of supporting his language by busying himself with its words, is to be taken at his word as far as his patriotism and future plans for serving the nation are concerned.

¹⁰⁶ That is to say, using Czech diacritical marks.

In Catholic Lusatia one hears much less German spoken than in the Lutheran regions, and where one does hear it, it is rather so-called 'broken' German than fluent speech. Whenever I was making my way through Protestant settlements and came across children on their way to school, I was always greeted by them, wishing me a good day in German. In contrast, in the Catholic villages I was greeted with *Dobrý deň* in Sorbian. It surprised me too, when I responded in Sorbian to the children who greeted me in German, that they gaped at me with some sort of shock, bewildered, I reckon, at the exceptionality of my response, which they did not expect from the lips of a man wearing a hat and clad tip to toe in black. From this one can form a certain idea of their education, and the continual progressive confinement of the native language to the cottages of the villagers.

As an example of the abstemiousness and honesty of the Sorbs in Lusatia, I append here the following story. It so happened that, along my road to Kamjenc, the weather grew sweltering hot, which oppressed me so that I was obliged to put aside my overcoat, which earlier I had needed in the cooler days, as well as my satchel of the books that I had purchased and been presented with. By chance, I met up with a Sorb travelling along the same route who — as I noted — was encumbered with nothing. I hesitated not to accost him with the request of lightening my load, a traveller exhausted by the heat, by taking up my things, to which he readily agreed. My companion kept me company all the way into Kamjenc, even though his own road would not have led him so far. We travelled together for several hours. When we reached the city at evening, I paid him a few coppers for his cheerful aid, but when he glanced at the money, he wanted to give me back half of the sum, with the words *jara wele ste mi dali*.[107] Not only did I not take it back, but, moved by the man's disinterestedness and honesty, I wished to give him even more, which of course he stubbornly and absolutely refused. By his clothes I knew him for a poor man, and yet his poverty did not incite him to greed, or even to accepting recompense greater than what was just. Such virtues still find their homeland amongst us, where they abide almost as refugees, banished from elsewhere and serving as one more laughing stock for those who defame us. But come, take refuge here in the regions where our people live, you ornaments of humanity: amongst us, I reckon, you shall be preserved until better times come round!

At the threshold of Kamjenc I parted ways with Lusatia and the Sorbian tongue, for the city itself is completely German. Here I wished to pay a visit

---

[107] 'You've given me so much!'

to Mr Gräve, the publisher of Lusatian folk tales and fairy stories, but I did not find him in. I stayed one night here, and on the next day found myself once more in Dresden, having travelled through the foothills enwreathing Lusatia, by coach.

All of the museums in Dresden were now open. Of these, I was most interested in the antiquities and the art gallery. There, after inspecting the art of the Italian and Dutch schools, etc., I entered a gallery which boasts artworks of the Czech school, which joyfully evoked in my mind Slavic art in general, the evidences of which, shining amongst so many sublime masterpieces, I examined with a great interior pride. I remained in this pleasant city for several days. Afterwards, I took the steamboat for Leipzig, at which we arrived but three hours later. In Leipzig, I came to know Mr Ernest Wanak, the head of the local Sorbian Society. An ardent Sorb, his ambitions are focussed on the maintenance and prosperity of said society, the care of which he has inherited. The chief aim of the association is the formation of preachers, fluent in the Sorbian language, for the parishes of Lusatia. Weekly gatherings are held for this purpose, at which sermons worked up by the members are read aloud and discussed. Beyond this, the more engaged members submit other texts as well, such as essays on the root causes of the disappearance of the Sorbian language in Lusatia, and the means for its upkeep and spread, the preservation of ancient tales, etc. The society has its own treasury and library in which the Slav shall find generous aids toward his mastering of the dialects of Slavdom. It caused me great joy to hear from Mr Wanak that some of the more zealous members, especially Krušwica, are collecting entries for a German-Sorbian dictionary, which is being drawn up in the library. Perhaps it would be better to devote one's labours to a Sorbian-German dictionary, which might prove an excellent appendix to that over which Messrs Lubjenský and Zejleŕ are labouring. The number of the society's members is small, for there are few Lusatian Sorbs at the university. Soon thereafter I left Leipzig, earnestly wishing the society good fortune and growth, for it is small at the moment, yet so important to forlorn Lusatia.

O, Lusatia! In thy regions I beheld my fellow-countrymen; I gazed upon thy sacred historical monuments! These are being toppled over and thinned out, each day drawing them closer to oblivion. O, rouse thyself! Learn thou from the example of thy extinct brethren — that a similar fate awaits thee too, unless thou takest unto thy very soul the inheritance that thou hast received from thy fathers and departed brethren. Protect thy national treasures and preserve them against the dawning of a better future!

Slavs, Brothers!

Who among us does not look upon our past with chagrin? And who among us is not aware of the fact that all of our sufferings are the consequence of our ignorance and our fragmentation, which keep brother from brother? But after long centuries, during which we forgot one another, during which so many misfortunes rained down upon us, we have arrived at the consciousness of our unity — that we are brothers. Exceptional days are upon us. Nations have been liberated, relieved from the burdens beneath the weight of which they had been groaning. These days have relieved us too of a greater fardel, for now we feel able to express what we have sensed for so long, what is to our advantage, what it is high time for us to determine! The nations of Europe are coming to a common understanding, and uniting. The Germans have called a parliament to Frankfurt, with union as its aim. The idea is for the Austrian monarchy to give away just so much of its independence as is necessary for a wider German unification to be effected, which would incorporate all of its non-Hungarian regions into a new German Empire. Now, such a step would not only spell the end of the Austrian union, but also the unification and autonomy of the Slavic tribes, the national essence of which would be endangered. It is up to us, bravely and boldly, to defend what we hold most sacred. Indeed, the time has arrived for us Slavs, as well, to come to an understanding and to unite together in a common enterprise. Accordingly, in enthusiastic and joyful assent to the many requests that have come to us from the various Slavic regions, we call upon all the Slavs of the Austrian monarchy, appealing to all who enjoy the confidence and trust of our nation, all, to whose hearts our general welfare is dear, to gather together in the age-renowned Slavic city of Czech Prague on 31 May of this year, where we shall deliberate together all the matters which pertain to the good of our nation. And should any Slavs who live beyond the borders of our empire wish to honour us with their presence, they shall be cordially welcomed.

Given in Czech Prague, on the 1st day of May, 1848.

from Štúr's Address to the Slavic Congress

Is the preservation of the Austrian Empire to be our goal? Our goal is our own preservation. First we must take care of ourselves, and then we can think of others. Up until now, Austria has stood firm, and we were in decay. What would the world say of us, were we to be more concerned with Austria's preservation than our own? The fall of Austria will not bring us down with her. There are great difficulties in this regard. The government of Austria is found on German territory, and therefore is German. We must compel it to transfer itself onto Slavic territory. The Slavic lands are not yet united; they are not even independent to such degree that they might undertake an effective, concerted enterprise. Only the Czechs, the Moravians and the Poles enjoy some degree of autonomy — the Hungarian Slavs do not. We are beholden to the Hungarian diet. And what can we expect from there? Even the accession of the Poles is none too certain under these conditions. First, the present situation in Hungary must be broken. Our main task is the destruction of Magyar dominance. The Magyars aim to become the absolute power centre of all Austria; accordingly, they are appealing to the Emperor that he move his seat to Hungary. The Germans are afraid of the Magyars; the government shares that fear, and accordingly they can refuse them nothing. For this reason, we must also lobby energetically, defending ourselves against the eventuality of the government pushing us into the arms of the Magyars.

Another difficulty arising from the preservation of the Austrian Empire is that the Germans gathering in Frankfurt wish to coax Austria to their side. Should this happen, we would have the Germans on one side, and the Magyars on the other. The Germans nurture an ancient antipathy toward us, and for this reason they are inclined to be overfamiliar with the Hungarians. Now, should they unite and create such a position of dominance in Austria, what will become of us? Up to this very day, we have had no autonomous

Slavic commonwealth within the borders of Austria. Let us express ourselves as follows: *We wish to remain in the Austrian Empire as autonomous Slavic commonwealths.* Let us neither say that we desire the preservation of Austria, nor that we wish to create an Austro-Slavic realm. Such a statement would deprive us of the sympathy of the European nations. Let us rather say that, as autonomous Slavic commonwealths, we wish to remain under the Austrian sceptre. In this way, we shall place the accent on the Slavs — and consequently, the Austrian government will find itself able to live with us, on this basis.

For this reason, we must crush the power of the Magyars. As long as the Magyars are in the ascendant, and the Czechs are paralysed, all attempts at inducing the Austrian cabinet to busy itself with Slavic politics will be vain.

I suggest:

1. That we desire the creation of autonomous, united Slavic commonwealths within the bounds of Austria.

2. Immediately thereafter, that we impel the Austrian government to move to shatter Magyar dominance.

[*Speaking after Štúr, Michal Miloslav Hodža, like Štúr a Slovak and a Lutheran pastor, suggested that the matter of Slavic unity be achieved in parliamentary fashion, by presenting it to the Czech, Croatian, and Polish [Galician] regional diets*].

Hodža has contested my speech, suggesting that we ought to have recourse to the regional diets. Good — let's do so. But our resolutions made here will also possess a moral force, upon which we must rely even more than upon the diets. To speak of Vienna, that land does not belong to us, historically. It is a land that we ploughed, and the Germans devoured.[108] From the very beginning of Vienna's reign, you Czechs have had no history of your own. You have only chronicles speaking of when this or that king's coronation took place — that's where all of our deeds are buried — everything there goes right into German rubrics. It was us that defeated the Turks, but the Germans ascribe that to themselves, and so we have no reason to speak of Vienna as historically a Slavic land.

You demand that we present our petitions to the Emperor or the Ministry. Such a thing is unnecessary. We must first get our own house in order;

---

[108] In the original Slovak, this line rhymes: *Je to zem, na ktorej my sme orali, a Nemci žrali.*

the government can help us in nothing. Today, the government is even unable of governing! Ban Jelačić had been confirmed in Vienna by the Emperor himself, and now he's given over into the power of the Hungarian ministry. The government is submitting its will to Frankfurt and if the determinations of the Frankfurt diet are fulfilled, Austria will be destroyed. The government is impotent now, an obsolete formula. As for me, I'm even against the very name Austria — it has a bloody curse upon it. Our one and only aim is the creation of autonomous, free and united Slavic commonwealths within the Austrian realm. It won't suffice for all the regions merely to have equal political rights, they need to be autonomous. First, the Magyar must be destroyed, and then, let the Danube unite our regions. We want to govern ourselves. The rest will be self-evident. You want equal rights for the minority along with the majority — but that's just not possible. If the Czech does not prevail in the Czech lands, the truly Slavic life[109] will not take root here. And if the Magyar is not destroyed, then we'll merely be talking about a Czech culture, for we would have lost the organ which unites us with the Yugoslavs.[110] The Danube is a Slavic river. We must become masters of the Danube, which would provide us with a road to the south of Europe. I repeat: we don't merely desire the preservation of Austria, so as not to deprive ourselves of the sympathy of all free nations. What is Austria? Austria is the quintessence of servility, denunciation and suchlike criminality. What has Austria made of you, you Czechs? She sent you off into Poland, as tools of the most shameful government.[111] What has she turned you into, you, about whom history testifies that never was there a more noble and heroic nation? And now you have become the shameful tools of servility? And what are the Germans up to now? Now they are blaming all the misfortunes of Galicia[112] on you. Now, all of their shame is falling on you — let's not mince words here!

Let's not whitewash anything! This is the most laughable thing of all, that we, indeed, should seek the preservation of the Austrian Empire. If

---

[109] *Pravoslovanský život*, which has a mystical, quasi religious ring to it (cf. *pravoslávny*, 'Orthodox', in Slovak.

[110] Štúr is arguing on behalf of all Slavic minorities in Hungary, here. The idea is, even if the Czechs were strong enough to assert their autonomy, and even if they were able to unite with the Slovaks, the Serbs, Croats and Slovenes would be left hanging, at the mercy of nationalising Magyars, if the Magyar dominance was not done away with.

[111] A good portion of the Austrian civil service in Galicia was made up of German-speaking Czechs.

[112] *Translator's note*: Here and later, Galicia is a historical and geographic region at the crossroad of Central and Eastern Europe, not Spanish Galicia.

that's what we desire, we'll shortly be on the march against the Italians and against the Poles — and perhaps against our very own selves. Let us declare that we desire nothing other than the establishment of autonomous Slavic commonwealths in the Austrian Empire, and afterwards, the destruction of Magyar dominance. In this respect, Havlíček's suggestion is an excellent one, for regiments of volunteers to gather without delay.[113]

If we wish to commence our political life, we dare not be satisfied with the usual tearful petitions. In moving forward, we are providing the other Slavs with an impulse of sorts. Let us act — who knows when we shall meet again like this! War is looming in Hungary. Frankfurt might lead the Czechs into some dangerous intrigues; set yourselves therefore to the task of calling Slavic commonwealths into existence, and not merely the securing of their nationality.[114]

---

[113] Czech poet and publicist Karel Havlíček-Borovský enunciated a call to arms in that revolutionary year of 1848, with the aim of 'paralysing' German and Magyar dominance in the empire.

[114] In other words, Štúr will not be satisfied with cultural autonomy, respect for the ethnic traditions of the non-German and non-Magyar nations — he is after political independence.

Speech at the Slavic Linden

Friends and Brothers!

I bring you greetings from the Slovak lands beyond the Danube, greetings and sincere best wishes for the success of the undertakings which have brought you all together here, united in this numerous assembly. In the lands from which I hail such a noble enterprise also once arose, in Great Moravia, at the time of Rastislav and Svätopluk, who wished to unite all the tribes of Slavdom in one commonwealth, one family. Now, although Great Moravia has passed away, these ideas did not perish. For both your Břetislav and Bolesław Chrobry, King of Poland, attempted to realise them, though without success. And thus, as our forefathers were separated one from another, so were our powers diminished, our ancient commonwealths dispersed, and thus our great misfortune. For, one after another, we all fell into bondage, losing our independence, being reduced to slavery, upon which a whole range of other misfortunes poured down upon us. Great Moravia fell, Velehrad crumbed into ruins, you[115] lost your independence, as did the Croatians, the Serbs, the other South Slavs, and at length, even the Poles.

Behold — the Slavic world — our great family — and that world, our family, has sunk into servitude, and all because our forefathers were divided amongst themselves, splintered into small fragments. Need I describe that misfortune to you? Need I describe that wretchedness to you, which pressed in on us from all sides? Need I describe to you the shame which descended upon us? Look — there — White Mountain[116] — O, that Slavic eye had never looked upon it, upon that sarcophagus in which the bones of your heroes moulder into dust,

---

[115] Speaking in Prague, when Štúr uses the direct address in the second person, it is the Czechs he has in mind.

[116] Bílá hora — a mountain near Prague, which gave its name to a battle fought there (8 November 1620) — traditionally considered as the stifling of Hussitism and the independence of the Czech lands from the Holy Roman Empire.

in which your glory lies broken… Gaze upon it, I say, and in that one glance at that mountain, cursed to Slavic memory, call to mind all of the catastrophes which, following that fateful battle, descended upon you, blind-sided you! Pillaged and destroyed was your desolate clan. Foreigners became the lords of your Motherland, a land of hard Czech travail, a land imbued with Czech blood, a land made famous by the Czech name! Strangers have taken their seat at your table, feasting, while you have stood at their back, to serve them. Your mores and customs evaporated, your language disappeared — your speech was lost! Your speech — your word — your *Slovo*;[117] and the word *Slovo* also means 'song' in our Slavic tongue — gone! So, hey — where have they fled to, those songs of yours? Where is that 'Arise my brothers! / Arise my brothers, and let us boldly go, / In arms against the wolfish foe! / Brothers, to battle let us go!'?[118] Where have they gone, the other songs of your nation? That have all gone silent — dumb!

Such catastrophes dashed against our other tribes, for this reason to: that we did not aid one another. Thus were we ever splintered in the face of the united power of the foreigners. And so — alas! — on one side, we were repressed by the German, on the other by the Magyar, on the third by the Turk, on the fourth by the Italian, and on the fifth by the Tatar…[119] Everywhere, the foreigner became our lord, and we his servants! Our fragmentation was

---

[117] *Slovo* is a word common to all Slavic languages. Meaning 'word,' the Slavs derive their general name (cf. Polish *Słowianie*, Slovak *Slovania*) from it. This indeed may be because of the very close relationship between the Slavic languages, which to a great degree are mutually intelligible. The word for 'German' in the Slavic tongues is some variant of *Niemiec* (Polish; *Nemec*, Slovak) — which is similar to the word for 'dumb, without speech' — (cf. Polish *niemy*, Slovak *nemý*) — and thus perhaps derives from the description of 'a person who cannot speak our tongue.'

[118] *Vzhůru, bratři, pojďme směle na dravého nepřítele! Vzhůru, bratři! Do boje!* A song from the Hussite years (and thus dear to the hearts of Czechs and Slovaks — especially Protestants — who have tended to idealise the Hussite rebellion as a national resistance to the invading (Catholic) Habsburgs. The song is included in a collection of songs edited by the Czechoslovak poet Jan Kollár. Štúr has modified the opening lines somewhat, which in the original read: *Vzhůru, Češi! Poďme směle na hrdého nepřítele, vzhůru, bratři, do boje!* ('Arise, *Czechs*, and let us boldly go, against the *proud* enemy…')

[119] Like all Pan-Slavs, Štúr conveniently passes over the 'repression' that Poles experienced, from a 'sixth' side, i.e. the partitioning of Poland by the Russians — as if only the Prussians and Austrians were to blame for the demise of the Polish Commonwealth. Similarly, the great Russian poet Alexander Pushkin bristled at Western support for the Poles during the November 1830 uprising against Russia, saying that the French and the British have no right to meddle in 'family squabbles.' Štúr is likewise silent on the matter of the treatment of Ukrainian peasants at the hands of their Polish (and Russian) landlords — those Slavs also might have something to say about 'repression' at the hands of their 'brothers'…

our weakness, our weakness was the strength of our enemies. And when we began to sense that weakness of ours, when we began to approach one another with open arms, our oppressors impeded us, or forbade us to do so. O, with what sour pusses did they look upon us then! Surely you are aware of the fact that when we spoke of our fraternal, Slavic ties, they said: 'Das sieht gefährlich aus, das reicht nach Panslawismus,'[120] etc? Surely you have heard them say, 'We have no need of Slavs, but rather loyal Czechs, loyal Croatians,' and so forth, and so on? Yes, let us repeat it once more: Our coming together is our strength, and our strength is our enemies' weakness. We need only unite, to no longer be the servants of Germans, Magyars, Turks, Tatars, and Italians; we shall then be what we wish ourselves to be: we shall be free. And now is the time for us to be ourselves, for up until now we have been everything except that. Up until now we have been Germans and Magyars and Turks and Italians, but not Slavs. The Croatians have even come up with an ironic song. Poking fun at themselves, they sing: 'We have been rather Italians / Germans, Gipsies, and Hungarians.'[121] But we shall not be Italians or Germans or Hungarians when we become Slavs. And when we have become Slavs, then shall we truly become Czechs and Poles, Croatians, Serbs, and so on.

And so I bless your good intentions, I bless this association of yours, the aim of which is the unification of the fragmented tribes of Slavdom; your association, which has come into existence to repair what long ages have ruptured. But you have this obligation too, as the first to have fought your way ashore following our shipwreck, to life and freedom. He who has first rescued himself, let him make ready a boat and send it forth to deliver safely to shore his brothers still struggling in the billows of the uncertain and dangerous sea of life. In the Middle Ages, my brother Czechs, you, with your culture and science and your university, were a lamp brightly shining in the North of Europe. Be such again, today, in your enterprises and Slavic achievements: a northern light to all of Slavdom!

---

[120] German: 'That's dangerous! That smells like Panslavism!'
[121] *Bili smo već Taliani, Nemci, Ugri i Cigani.*

A Glance at Current Events in Slavdom, 1848

Let us have a look at the world so dear to our hearts — the Slavic world. Who looks forward to better times more anxiously than our nation? And who has more cause to so anticipate their arrival than we? For so many ages now, the Slavic world has been in decline, and except for the heroic liberation of the Serbian nation from beneath the atrocious Turkish yoke,[122] there has been no event to gladden the yearning Slavic soul. Torn asunder and suppressed, yet offering our talents, our strength, and all other of our means in sacrifice on behalf of others, but achieving nothing for ourselves in return save oppression at home and contempt in the eyes of the wider world, our nation has lived, as the poet says, like a puddle in the darkness.[123]

The advent of this new age was greeted with rejoicing by Slavic hearts, but our tribes, burdened with heavy yokes, dispersed, still not fully awakened and still only weakly united to one another, have not yet learnt how to make use of these present days, so that Sláva's sons might emerge from that puddle, that darkness. Meanwhile, certain branches of our nation, more developed and self-aware than others, particularly the Czechs, have risen to the occasion and taken advantage of the exceptional times. They have acquired some more extensive political rights in Vienna, yet up until now, more in promise than in reality. The other branches of Slavdom in Austria have arrived at the same rights without the effort and endeavour. Thus, the Poles in Galicia, the Slovenes in Styria, Krajina and Carinthia enjoy similar rights. The Croats as well, united to the Magyar crown, arrived at what they desired. But such demands as the Croats, Poles and Slovenes particularly sought, have not been fulfilled, but entirely repudiated, with the one exception of the Croats, who obtained as Ban a son of their own nation.[124]

---

[122] In 1835.

[123] *Jako kaluž ve tmách.* From Jan Kollár's *Slávy dcera* [The Daughter of Sláva, 1832] Sonnet 325.

[124] For historical regions (for example, the Polish regions of Galicia were annexed to the

On the other hand, the other branches of the Slavic family were so neglected still, so set at odds through foreign influence, that they allowed themselves to be led to a clear-cut suppression of their national life — indeed, in their blindness, they scrambled toward it themselves. For example: the Moravians, the Poles in Silesia, and a portion of the Slovenes too, elected representatives to the German diet in Frankfurt, submitting thus to the arbitrary will of the Germans. The German carpetbaggers in Moravia and Silesia unfurled the tricolour banner of Germany on our lands, persuading the blind among the folk there to join up with Frankfurt. Those adroit repressors of ours tore the Moravians away from the Czechs, the Silesians away from the Poles, by every possible means at their disposal. By similar chicaneries Dalmatia allowed herself to be blinded, and still has not joined hands with her sister Croatia. Bravely and nobly, the Czechs repulsed the German attacks, spurning all the directives of the German government in the matter of electing representatives to Frankfurt. Further, they manfully shattered all the German machinations that had spread about the land. In this way, they became a thorn in the side of the Germans, who wished to appropriate this beautiful country, this cradle of heroes. But the genius of Sláva joyfully looked down upon this land, which despite long ages of permeation by German influence, has still manfully preserved its Slavic character.

Our fragmentation is our enemies' strength and our grave. Our confederation is their bane and our salvation. Even the Poles in Poznań leapt to their feet when the other nations arose. At that time, constrained by the urgent matter of the revolution in Berlin, the King of Prussia granted the Poles a new constitution for the Polish province, though, it is true, still under his sceptre.

With joy the Poles set themselves to work. Yet no sooner had they begun when, lo, the Prussian army arrived, shooting, burning, hacking apart everything possessed of a Polish character, and rousing up all possible elements

---

Habsburg crown only recently, toward the end of the XVIII c.) certain areas of the Austrian empire enjoyed more nominal autonomy than others. The Czech regions were highly germanised by the time in which Štúr was writing, more highly developed industrially, and had a harder row to hoe to convince Vienna that recognition of their autonomy did not constitute secession from the empire per se. The Slovaks in the Kingdom of Hungary faced mounting pressure from the Magyars, ironically, during the latter nation's own push to emphasise their own ethnic identity. Any hopes the Slovaks had of Vienna coming to their aid in the revolutions of 1848 were disappointed, as the Austrians were more concerned with appeasing the powerful Magyars and retaining Hungary for the Habsburg crown than the rights of the ethnic minorities there. As for Croatia, as a result of the Spring of the Peoples in 1848, Josip Jelačić was appointed *Ban* of the Croatian regions of the Hungarian kingdom. Štúr was often critical of Jelačić for his subservience to the Emperor.

against the Poles. We must recall that the Germans had already usurped a portion of the province of Poznań, which they proceeded to germanify, promising to leave the remainder to the Poles themselves. But what a cruel lie that was! As soon as they had the chance to, they fell upon the Poles like wolves, setting fire to everything, pummelling and hacking. Against the potency of the regular army, even the spirit of a Mierosławski could not hold out. The Poles lost, and the land was taken over by the Germans. The Germans committed — in these modern days of ours! — unheard-of cruelties in Poznań: many of the captured Poles had their foreheads branded. There's German culture for you!

This opened the eyes of the Poles to just what sort of sympathy the Germans have for them. When they wished to exploit the Poles as a weapon against their kindred tribe of Great Russians, for whom the Germans have so-called *Respekt,* German mouths overflowed with words of sympathy for Poland. But from the moment that the Poles gave evident proof that a German yoke lies no less heavily upon their necks, and wished to cast it off, well, the Germans branded their foreheads! The gullible Poles, convinced now of the quality of German sympathy, and having lost faith in the French, have now turned their gaze toward their brother Slavs, from whom they had kept their distance — not from any ignorance of the sacred bonds of brotherhood that unite them, but from some sort of deference to the nations of Europe, from their selfish and intrinsic particularism, from their fear of the Russians. And in the midst of all this comes the Slavic Congress in Prague. With hope and heartfelt emotions, Slavs from the north and the south, from the east and the west, gathered in this city, the mother of Western Slavdom.

Never before had there been such an assembly; never yet, from the time of their ancient division from one another, did the sons of Sláva so embrace one another. Much had they lost since the days of their separation. Some of them had fallen under foreign yokes, as slaves to foreign masters; others received serious wounds in battles which took a long, long time to heal; others partially rescued themselves from mortal danger, while still others completely perished, becoming dead to their brothers — these last adopting foreign manners so, that they hardly recognised their own names any more. What joy then, what ecstasy reigned at that reconciliation after a thousand years of mutual ignorance, after so many dangers! The event was phenomenally great, a poetic ravishment, and this Prague of ours was the rally-point and tribune for that pageant. Every Slavic guest was greeted with joy and fêted with dignity during those days in Prague. The opening spectacle made an indelible impression on every Slav: all of our brethren marching together, beneath all the banners of Slavdom, their lungs pouring out the strains of ancient Czech heroic song.

It seemed as if the ancient walls of Prague had come alive and were whispering to us of our history. Following this phenomenon of universal exaltation, the members of the Congress got down to work. Our people wished to make their minds known to Europe and to remember themselves to their Slavic brethren; to continue to make their pleasure known to the Austrian government, and, at last, to conclude an association of the branches of Slavdom. Such were the deliberations of the Congress. But our old enemy, the German, turned a spiteful eye upon the activity of those he had previously held in subjugation, who had now determined to consider something different to the German demands of servitude. To this ancient enemy the obscurantist, backward-scuttling Crab Party[125] joined forces, enraged at the Slavs, of whom nothing but humility and servitude were required, for raising their voices in a spirit of freedom, and thus displaying themselves to the eyes of the world. And so they determined to disperse the gathering, which aim — egged on by the Magyars as well — they encompassed.

In this business Windischgrätz became a weapon in the hands of our ancient enemy. He was assisted by persons who at other times had been friendly toward us — but only for show — especially Count Leo Thun. And so the Slavic Congress was dispersed. But not, as the Germans had wished, without having achieved anything. Indeed, although nothing positive in a concrete sense came of it, an ineffable moral victory was won. All of the participants came to know one another's heart and mind; they also came to understand the true nature of those whom, in their gullibility and blindness, they had taken to be their friends and supposed to be a powerful refuge for at least one portion of Slavdom. This united them, and thus, their enemy was seen to have somewhat over-calculated. But meanwhile, the Congress fell under the pressure, as did our brother Czechs, at whose newly-achieved liberties the blow had really been aimed. Of these liberties they were deprived, and others that remained were only temporarily left in place, to be taken away too at the next best opportunity.[126] But all the same the spirit of the Czech nation was not throttled by this attack, for, as can be clearly seen, it has indeed arisen all the more valiant and noble.

....

[125] *Strana račia* — since crabs are supposed to walk backwards, the 'Crab Party' is the opposite of progressivism.

[126] The dispersal of the Slavic Congress resulted in the June Uprising (12 – 17 1848), after which martial law was enacted in Prague.

In these days, when nearly all the nations of Europe are acquiring their liberty, when equality and fraternity are being promised to all, the Slavs subject to the crown of Hungary are also yearning to cast off the ancient and unfair Magyar yoke. But that the Magyars, fellow-countrymen of the Mongols, comprehended the spirit of this age, can be seen from the fact that, not only did they not concede anything to the nations inhabiting Hungary in respect to their ethnic nationality, but, what is more, they began repressing them more than ever before and imprisoned all who dared speak of the sacred rights of their nation. And because the Magyars value no one higher more than themselves, the shadow of the gallows looms over the heads of all other nations in Hungary. In the spirit of the ages of barbarism, they have determined to rule forever and ever and dispose of the other nations as they please. Unfair to the Slavs is that Magyar yoke, and very harmful; unfair, because it is set upon their necks by the fellow-countrymen of the Mongols, who exist by grace of our wisdom, our strength — as the entire history of Hungary testifies, as well as the history of our own day and age; harmful, because the Magyars stand in the way of the great association of the Slavic tribes. Now is high time for this yoke to be cast off, when the Magyars have torn themselves loose from Austria and have become their own masters; when, as a result of the recent steps they've taken, they have fallen among serious difficulties. The present state and order of things has seen the Croatian branch of our people take the first step in this struggle, but it doesn't seem as if they have comprehended the historical significance of their calling. The Croatians form one of the most distinguished tribes of Slavdom, but they know of Slavdom only in its corporate sense, not its spirit. That time has not yet arrived at full maturity among them. A provincial spirit still pervades their thinking, and such a spirit does not incite one to action; one doesn't make history with such an attitude. For this reason, the Croats allowed the Serbs to overtake them in the struggle. Fiery and full of feeling, strong and possessed of a rich historical treasury in their songs, the Serbs have been the first among all the Slavs to rise to their feet against our ancient and unfair enemies. They are the bonfire around which all the Slavic tribes gather. God is with them, as is victory, as is the world's blessing. We shall soon see how they will acquit the hopes of all Slavdom and how others, especially the Croats, will aid them in their patriotic endeavour, which the Slavic world is following with the greatest interest. Their liberation from the Magyars would result in the bestirring of the Slavs who have been groaning for ages beneath the Turkish yoke. Incline your ear but once to the yearning voices and moaning of these Slavic brethren of ours! Though no one else hear them, hear them ye, who are closest to them in speech and in blood.

The Contributions of the Slavs to European Civilisation

Lately, some people have tried to prove that the Slavs have never played a fundamental role in the shaping of the spiritual life of Europe. That Slavdom hasn't even factored into the vitality and humanity of Europe, for such merit, and that all praise therefore, belongs solely to the Romance and Germanic nations, to whom the Slavs, they assert, are but some simple, incidental element following in their footsteps. That such and other similar expressions have no basis in fact, is, I believe, completely clear to anyone who should inspect the course of European history with objective, non-partisan eye. Now, facts speak louder than such words, which we, relying on historical truth, boldly call blatant inventions. The aim of this present essay is to highlight, effectively and briefly, the pertinent facts that will allow us to assess the role played by the Slavs in the life of Europe up till now.

Not only spiritual, but also physical might was indispensable to the foundation and consolidation of European civilisation. This was particularly true in such times when it was most threatened with extinction. Whereas the West provided the spiritual energy requisite to its founding and establishment, the latter, physical vigour, was provided by the East. Due to the varied qualities of the nations of which the continents are made up, and especially the reciprocally inimical religious paths of each, Europe and Asia entered into a conflict that could not be settled by rational conciliation, but only by the sword. As if in anticipation of the looming danger it faced, Europe attempted to stifle the hostile element on its own ground. Here we find the reason behind the expeditions to Asia undertaken by the Crusaders. Indeed, their repeated efforts succeeded in reining in the malignant element for a while, and in establishing the Kingdom of Jerusalem. However, that state was not long-lived; it disappeared quite quickly, leaving the enemy of Europe even stronger than before, invigorated now with a consciousness of its own might. Having overcome the western powers in Asia, Islam, the eternal enemy of Christianity, was not satisfied with just that victory. Having acquired so much territory there, it swarmed onward in an attempt to do what the West had accomplished earlier against it, that is, invading Europe in turn, in order to destroy Christianity on its own home ground. The Turks established a firm base in Europe, and prepared to spread their rule farther.

It was then that the Slavs came to recognise their vocation, namely, as a civilisational offshoot of the Christian West, which should serve as a bulwark breasting the tide of Eastern barbarism. Since that time, even up until today, the Slavs have fought, without respite, bloody wars against the arch-enemy of Christianity. The Serbs, that famed branch of the Slavic tribe of the Illyrians, was the first to come to grips with them. After having inflicted grievous wounds upon their enemies, after a long and heroic resistance, in 1389 they succumbed at last to his overwhelming numbers on the battlefield of Kosovo. The Eastern Roman Empire, the capital of which was blockaded, surrounded, and besieged, fell to the clutches of the Mohammedan conquerors,[127] which opened the way for their expeditions of plunder and subjugation against Christendom. And here we find that it was the Slavs indeed who, undaunted, set themselves in firm opposition to the fanatic hordes, risking their very existence in long years of war in defence of the freedom of Europe and Christendom. Many a blow did they exchange on behalf of their brothers in this so exhausting, and therefore all the more heroic service. Here we see that at different times, varied Slavic nations led the resistance against the arch-enemy. They were supported in this endeavour by the Magyars, who in this case can be termed their allies. The grand Suleiman I had sworn the destruction of Christianity entire. Yet his pride was harshly chastened by that Slavic Leonidas, Šubíc Zrínsky and his Croatian heroes. Innumerable regiments of Turkish brutes found their unlooked-for graves in the fosses of Szigetvár. Amurat penetrated all but to the heart of Europe, laying siege to Vienna. The starving city was hardly able to hold out, and had the Turkish chief overwhelmed the imperial capital at one fell swoop, he would have proceeded to fall with his frenzied regiments upon the disunited and exhausted Germans.

Who can imagine all the cruelties, who can describe all of the horrible, terrifying scenes that would have played out there, in consequence? Islam would have been forcibly spread throughout the German lands; the noble cathedrals of Vienna, Köln and Strasbourg would have been turned into mosques, and on the battlements and crenellations of the ancient imperial cities of Cách (Aachen) and Frankobrod (Frankfurt am Main), from

---

[127] In 1453.

which the German emperors once dictated laws to the descendants of the world-ruling Romans, the Ottomans would have fixed their crescent moon and horsehair *bunchuk*. The towers, from which the elevated human soul, gazing up at the endless swarms of stars sailing along the roads of Heaven, admired the omnipotence of God, would be changed into minarets, from which a melancholy wailing would call forth the faithful Muslims to prayer, and the German nation would obediently turn their faces in the direction of Mecca — invoking Allah and his great prophet. Thus German culture and scholarship would have met their end, along with German philosophy. Hundreds of thousands would go to their death in fetters, far away from their fatherland. Somewhere in Asia, or in the desert sands of Africa, would they find their graves, or, as janissaries they would fall, in shameful battle against the faith and freedom of Europe, to the accompaniment of the curses and anathemas of their unknown relatives. But who should limn out these pictures to the full? All Europe sensed the fateful moment approaching, and all were atremble in anxious trepidation, expecting to hear of the fall of Vienna. But then there appeared a chivalrous angel of salvation in the person of king and hero Jan Sobieski, who with his 40,000 Poles scattered the innumerable hordes of the Mohammedan destroyers of humanity — and all of Europe was liberated.

The Magyars, led by the heroic János Hunyadi, also fought successfully against the Turks. Nor was his son, that glorious star of the heavens above Hungary, Matej Korvín, less fortunate in his battles against them, in which the Slavs eagerly participated, fighting by his side. The fortunately chosen leader Pavol Brankovič (from whose ancient Slavic title *kinisi* the word *kňaz* derives) and his victorious Black Legion, achieved the most excellent victory over the Turks; Brankovič was a Serb, and the Black Legion, made up of Czechs and Slavs of the Tatras, was particularly dear to the foresightful king's heart, due to their valour.

In more contemporary days, the Russians have distinguished themselves in their wars against the Turks. Their victorious regiments have crossed the Balkans, entered Adrianople, and, along with the British, inflicted a deep wound upon the Turkish power, upon Islam, from which they shall find it difficult to recover. One consequence of these victories, this ominous catastrophe for the Turks, is the liberation of several Christian nations from the shameful Mohammedan yoke, under which they groaned for long centuries on account of the name of Christ. Because of the meagre forces at their disposal in comparison to those of the Turks, they were unable to cast off this burden by themselves, their strength unaided.

Moreover, during the age of the Crusades, the Mongol horde swarmed over Central Europe. Sent forth by the horrid Genghis Khan for the despoiling and subjugation of Europe, it numbered some half a million men. In pursuit of their aim, they battered and murdered everyone they came across. No one escaped the sharp blade of the savage, bloodthirsty Asiatics. The Hungarian peoples dared set themselves up in opposition to those horrid barbarians, but their army of one hundred thousand men, led by King Bela IV in person, was completely routed at the River Sava, so that the king himself had a difficult time of it escaping death and making his way back to the Tatras. Then too did the all-throttling, all-destroying horde spread out over nearly the entire face of the earth. What pen is able to fully describe the wretchedness of those days? All around, everything was laid waste, toppled into the dust. The smouldering cities and villages splashed with human blood — such were the scenes that met men's eyes in Hungary. Thus emboldened, Batu Khan, the commander in chief of this savage horde sent half of his troops onward, farther west, in order to spread the terror of his sword yet wider. But after making their way to Olomouc, that mob was met by the combined forces of the Moravians and Czechs led by the great Jaroslav of Šternberk. After a long, bloody battle, the Mongols were routed. No sooner had news of this catastrophic defeat reached the ears of Batu Khan, than he immediately set out on his return journey, escaping with the remnants of his horde to Asia in order to save them, and himself, from complete annihilation.

From these facts, it is easy to judge what sort of role in the development of European culture fell to the Slavs. Howbeit the West laboured for its establishment and its spread, the Slavs had to work hard so that it should take hold, and be able to shed its beneficent light on all hands. Without the Slavs, without their physical valour, which was indispensable in the face of the savage might of the barbarians, the development of European culture would certainly have been retarded by many years, if not stifled entirely. And thus that Providence, which rules all of humanity — and who would dare refuse to bow down before its wise decrees? — destined for the Slavs a role different to that of their neighbours. Europe has an obligation to the Slavs, in that the Islamic enemy can no longer seriously consider subjugating us and, in place of our Christian faith, without which no civilised nation can exist, set up their saecular creed which appeals but to the senses and throttles true civilisation.

And so, the Slavs fulfilled the task set before them in glorious fashion, something that is acknowledged by all Non-Slavs who do not begin their considerations from some narrow-minded position, but look upon history with impartial eye, as one coherent whole. And so it is no invention, as a certain German writer once commented so broadly in an article dealing with the Slavic Empire, to proclaim Slavdom as the third factor in European might and culture. As the aforementioned facts clearly show, Slavdom is a true shaper of today's way of life in Europe, with this one distinction to the Western formative powers: in that our contribution was of a different sort, requiring different sacrifices. This also sufficiently explains why the Slavs lagged behind other European nations, such as the French and the Germans, in the field of higher culture; for we were waging almost constant war. This often led to the impoverishment of the entire Slavic nation while our neighbouring nations, enjoying the gratifying blessings of peace, were free to develop their spiritual life.

By the same token, we are not of such a mind as to deny the fact of the Slavs' active participation in the establishment of the present life of Europe, or — as it has become the fashion to say — to deny them their just share in the great European capital of education, civilisation and authority as far as Christianity, politics, scholarship and enterprise are concerned. For here they too have done their utmost, as far as circumstances permitted, which shall be sufficiently proved by the facts I am about to present.

Here we find ourselves somewhat at a loss, faced with an *embarras de richesses*, as to what we should mention first to those who would completely deny us our share of that great capital. We do not intend here to go into the question whether it be ignorance, or conscious unwillingness to acknowledge Slavic history, which is the root cause of such an attitude. Research into the most ancient culture of the Slavs, preceding the advent of Christianity, touching upon the first periods of their history as Christian nations, has not yet been fully developed. But a consideration of the diligence and ambition in learning that has motivated the Slavs during periods of lasting peace and prosperity — which at last they have had the occasion to enjoy — and how this same has opened up new vistas before them, is convincing proof of the fact that, even in those far-off ages, the Slavs were never such barbarians as some would gladly make them out to have been.

Above all, proof sufficient of this is offered by the Old Church Slavonic language, into which SS Cyril and Methodius translated Holy Scripture. They must have seen this language as a cultured tongue already — for such verbal culture cannot be simply conjured up at once out of thin air. 'Of all the modern tongues,' adjudges the great historian and linguist Schlözer (Nestor III, 224), 'the Slavonic (Old Church Slavonic) is the most cultured,' and further: 'Among all languages, the Slavonic is again first as far as culture and development are concerned. How do the German, French and English tongues, among others, compare to it in the XIII and XIV centuries? The reason for this success was indeed a confluence of fortunate circumstances. Translation from learned Greek was carried on here constantly, for centuries, and the divine services were celebrated in the tongue of the people. All chronicles, charters, deeds and suchlike documents were prepared in the national tongue, and not in Latin, as was the case in the rest of Europe. Just how much we Germans especially were set back by this (for in reality, only for the past seventy years have we been writing in cultured German, at which we have mostly arrived through translations from the French and the English), I sense very strongly whenever I read a Russian legend from the XIV century, let us say, and then turn my attention to a German postil printed in 1674. There I find order in the delivery, closed periods, dependent clauses linked by abundant participles, along with powerful and magnificent expressions, etc. Here, in contrast, I find the script of a poor German homilist, whose style does not surpass that of a Regensburg scribe!'

Alongside such learned works, priceless documents of Old Slavic poetry that have come down to us, also give the lie to the supposed roughness of the Slavs. For example we can point to the Czech poems in the *Manuscript of Dvůr Králové* published by Hanka,[128] on behalf of which Goethe, already in his advanced age, learned Czech so that — as he put it — he might 'become inebriated with the gracefulness of the *Manuscript of Dvůr Králové*.' Today, these poems have been translated into just about all of the languages of Europe, including the German, and their worth has been universally recognised by judicious persons. We are not over-stressing their worth at all when, on account of their natural, fully blossomed poetic power, their strength of expressiveness, their boldness of thought, their breathtaking heroism and indeed their ancient origin, we speak of them as 'our Homer.' Here too belongs that most beautiful *Lay* of the Russian Igor, which was discovered in 1790 by Count M. Pushkin, a poem no less excellent in its soaring poetic élan in thought and expression. It describes Igor's campaign against

---

[128] In Czech, the *Rukopis královédvorský*, and a second manuscript, the *Rukopis zelenohorský* or *Green Mountain Manuscript*. These are poetic works written in an archaic form of Czech; published in 1817 and 1819, they were lauded at the time as authentic early mediaeval texts proving the antiquity of Slavic letters. Most linguists — including Josef Dobrovský — considered them forgeries, most likely by the hand of Václav Hanka, a student of Dobrovský's, who based his judgement on a familiar pattern of linguistic errors, characteristic of a student of his (whom he did not name). Despite that, some scholars still today consider the works genuine.

the Polovtsians.[129] Nor can we pass over in silence the ancient Russian law code known as the *Russkaya Pravda*, which Yaroslav had published around the year 1018 in gratitude to the towns which had supported him in trying times, and which later came into general use. All of the examples introduced above, which testify without question to the Slavs' cultural capabilities, appear to indicate a bright day, a brilliant age, enjoyed in the distant past by the Slavs. But then the incessant storms, which thundered over all the regions of Slavdom for so long, made them detour from this progress in beauty so far commenced, in order to labour on different fields, and give other obligations their due. These storms were harmful to the Slavs only insofar as they aborted their further progress in cultural development, retarding the same, so much so that the spiritual fruit they had up till then acquired had been almost completely consumed by the ravages of time, destroyed. What treasures of intellectual accomplishment dating from those early ages might we now display before the eyes of the world, had not the Mongols swept through Rus and Poland; had not in later times the hatred of severe Italian and German clergymen for what they considered a barbarian language — although they understood it not — shamefully destroyed the documented monuments of Slavdom, despite the hospitality shown them by the Slavs? For these tribes, especially the Czechs, who had suffered less at the hands of the invading barbarians, amassed a wealth of veritable literary treasures by the XIV century. But even these treasures, unfortunately, suffered the same destructive fate in later ages.

From all of the above, it is abundantly clear that the Slavs made the greatest possible effort toward cultural development, depositing in their own tongue the acquirements of other nations. However, they were held back from this by unpropitious circumstances. And yet we can still point out individual examples of high culture amongst the Slavs such as have escaped the ravages of time, and shine before our eyes even today, deserving of universal praise.

There is no historian alive today to whom the *Chronicle of Nestor*, composed in Old Church Slavonic by a monk of the Pechersky monastery in Kiev, is unknown. This chronicle was translated into German and outfitted with a historico-literary commentary by Schlözer for the benefit of non-Slav-

---

[129] Although the original manuscript of the *Lay of Igor's Campaign* perished in the great fire of Moscow in 1812, causing some to doubt the authenticity of the text as presented by Prince Aleksei Musin-Pushkin, most philologists accept it as an authentic text composed in the XIII century.

ic historians. Its importance to research in the history of the Middle Ages is universally acknowledged. All historians have made use of it, and they continue to do so — whoever aims at an elucidation of mediaeval times and the tangled history of the migration of the nations, which is generously treated therein. — At the request of the Czech estates, Karol IV established the higher schools of Prague after the pattern of such institutions in Paris and Bologna, which, despite their later alienation, we can consider ultimately Slavic. At the time, they constituted a sun of intellectual enlightenment for an entire half of Europe: Czechs, Poles, Moravians, Russians, Hungarians, Swedes and Germans all studied here. The University of Prague, established in 1348, then became a model for the German universities founded later: Vienna (1365), Heidelberg (1386),[130] Leipzig (1409) and so on. Accordingly, who should wish to deny its influence on the galvanisation of science in Germany itself? — Who is unaware of the fact that, before the XV century, nearly the entire world believed that the world stood still and the sun revolved around it? And who does not know that, today, everyone understands the contrary to be sufficiently proven as true? But they do not know, or they do not wish to acknowledge the fact that the world learned this truth from a Slav, who, endowed with immeasurable perspicacity, recognised the doubtfulness, indeed the falsity, of the Ptolemaic system, and extrapolated another, more accurate theory, the truth of which, I reckon, no one will ever overturn. Although in these modern days there have been attempts to shake it, none have succeeded in the very least. Kopernik is the name of that great man, and it is great praise to him and his fellow countrymen that the undisputed modern conception of our solar system is known as the Copernican system. He was born in Toruń (Thorn) in western Poland on 19 February 1473; thus, he was a Pole, a Slav, and it is only envy that has sought to appropriate him from the Slavs, to whom he belongs both body and soul. In a certain German script we read, 'The fame of Kopernik shall shine brilliantly as long as the sun continues to shed its rays.' We are proud of the fact that the fame of our great man is prophesied to have the same longevity as the sun that warms and nourishes us; such fame is truly unassailable and, I reckon, eternal.

Who might then dare to state that we've constructed no system whatever, in any field of science? Would such a thing not be a pure contradiction of

---

[130] Štúr got two dates wrong in his list: he originally had Heidelberg founded in 1387, and in the case of Vienna, transposed the last two numbers as 1356. We give the actual dates in our translation. For some reason, he overlooks the establishment of another mediaeval university on Slavic soil: the University of Kraków was founded in 1364 as the second university north of the Alps; it precedes Vienna by a year.

the historical record? Zalužanský, the renowned natural scientist, was of the Czech nation. He wrote of the gender and fertilisation of plants a full century and a half before the great Linneus, decidedly and clearly pronouncing on the subject in his work *Methodus rei herbariae* [The Botanical Method]. Our intention here is not to prove that Linneus drew upon his work, although this cannot be completely denied; we merely wish to show that the Slavs are not lacking in men with ability enough to discover and prove new, excellent systems in the sciences. But their efforts are often hampered by the obstacles set in their way, which have a detrimental effect upon their work, but which in any event have less to do with their nationality than the circumstances attending their labours.

Komenský, a native of Komna in Moravia, that educator of great merit, that reformer of the educational systems of the greater part of Europe, was also a Slav. In 1632 he was ordained bishop of the Czech and Moravian Brethren, and from 1648 he was presiding bishop of that entire denomination in Poland. Because of his learning and elevated moral nature, that sage and industrious man was also summoned to many another land for his expertise in educational administration. Thus was he summoned, in 1641, to England, Sweden, Prussia, Transylvania and Hungary, and he fulfilled the important tasks set before him magnificently. The merits that, as a paedagogue, he accumulated due to his work on behalf of the development of education in his century, are of worldwide historical significance, no less than are his writings, which remain in print to this very day. Let that author, in his *Augsburg Universal News*, list some works that would equal, in number of translations into the languages of Europe and Asia, and also continuity and number of print runs, Komenský's *Orbis pictus* [The World in Pictures], *Janua linguarum reserata* [The Door to Languages Spread Wide], and so on. We very much doubt that anywhere are there to be found writings more widely disseminated than those of this Slavic scholar.

Furthermore, we are simply unable to comprehend how the author in question might contrive to argue that the Slavs never accomplished anything of brilliance in the military sphere. For all the world well knows how the heroic Hussite leader Žižka overcame all of his enemies, above all in the field of strategy, employing against them his own unique manner of waging war, which he himself invented. (Needless to say, his skill as a commander was combined with the valiant ability of his heroic army). What we are speaking of here are his wagons, arranged in different ranks and tightly bound together, forming a defensive enclosure impregnable to all enemies. Against this redoubt, against the heroism of the Czechs, unconquerable in those days, all of the enemy regiments who inundated the Czech lands like floodwaters, beat in vain.

In these latter days the ardour of knowledge has again awakened in Slavdom, and such men have arisen there as have drawn the greatest attention to their writings in those branches of the arts and sciences to which they dedicate themselves — works of truly epochal significance. Amongst such we might make mention of the profound linguistic studies of Dobrovský, Shishkov, and the sublimely polished works of Katančić, whose assiduous labours have borne fruit in works such as *De Istro ejusque accolis* [The Danube and Those who Inhabit its Banks], *Orbis antiquus* [The Ancient World], and so on, books that are in constant use by both native and foreign writers. And what might be said, after all, concerning the admirable writings of Šafárik, whose most recent work, *Slavic Antiquities*, characterised by such critical profundity, is of such importance, not only to research in Slavic history, but to the history of Europe as a whole in ages long past? In the fields of historical research, along with Šafárik, the indefatigable Polish historian Lelewel has distinguished himself by his admirable abilities, united to an almost iron industry and dedication — which the Germans themselves have been moved to acknowledge and praise. It is he, who as even the Germans dare not deny, has succeeded in unravelling the most difficult riddles presented by the study of ancient history, and in pouring new light upon many an obscure corner of the ancient world. To these two exacting Slavic historians it is fitting and proper to add Palacký, to whom all of Slavdom owes a debt of gratitude on account of his many deep writings, especially those dealing with Czech history. Nor should we overlook here the names of Naruszewicz, Kucharski, Maciejowski, Karamzin, Ustryalov, Pogodin — amongst others worthy of mention in this context.

But that which to this day has most happily blossomed amongst the Slavs is poetry — the natural consequence of the richness of imagination and amplitude of feeling characteristic of our nation. The rare ability of the Slavs in the composition of poetry is nowhere more essentially exemplified than in their pure,[131] melodious, witty songs, which here treat of love, there of misfortune, here again of the heroism and great deeds of their forefathers. To the great value of these songs, the sublime Goethe himself, and the admirable Madame Talvj, in her translations of Serbian folk songs and elsewhere, have so beautifully borne witness. Knowing this field well, and taking into consideration the fact that such songs have naturally arisen in all the nations

---

[131] Štúr uses the adjective *nevinný*, which can also be translated 'innocent.'

of Slavdom, we are well within our rights to call the Slavic nation herself a great poet. From amongst the many noteworthy Slavic poets, some of whom have already achieved a pan-European reputation, their works being translated into foreign tongues, may we be permitted to introduce the names of some of the greatest, such as the Poles: Czajkowski, Goszczyński, Krasiński, Krasicki, Mickiewicz, Malczewski, Kraszewski, Magnuszewski, Zaleski, etc.; the Russians: Delvig, Gogol, Kozlov, Marlinsky, Pushkin, Podolinsky, Zhukovsky, Zagoskin, etc.; the Little Russians: Kotlyaryevsky, Padurra; the Czechoslovaks: Čelakovský, Hollý, Kollár, Klicpera, Mácha, Polák, Turinský, Tyl, Tupý, Vocel, etc.; the Illyrians: Demeter, Gundulić, Milutinović, Mušicki, Palmota, Prešeren, Stanko Vraz, Vukotinović, etc. We look upon all these with pride and pleasure, with true joy. All of this gives the lie to the statement that it is a vain thing to learn a Slavic tongue, because — according to the opinion of such people — the small number of significantly original, first-rate works in Slavic does not yet warrant the time and labour required to read them. In no way do we insist that foreign nations should learn our speech, thereby flattering, as it were, our national pride; we merely express here our bitterness at the manner in which our spiritual fruit is held in such disrespect, as it is by the author of the aforementioned article, and as is often the case in the scribblings of other journalistic hacks.

Well, just as it is well worth the effort to learn Spanish for the sake of reading but one novel of Cervantes, the deservedly renowned *Don Quixote*, why should it be that one should not acquire facility in the Slavic tongue, which would place in one's hand the key to much greater treasures?

In this brief account of ours, we have been forced to restrain ourselves to merely point out the merits of the Slavs as touch upon the life of Europe, a subject which might be treated fully only in a much more detailed and lengthy work. Such an enterprise, God willing, we shall attempt at another time. For after all, we should not wish to expend a lot of useless words on the assessment of the great future that lies before the Slavs, of whom, however, with conviction, we may publicly state our belief that their future, ever more active participation in history cannot be to their disadvantage, or that of Europe as a whole, but rather will result in no small benefits to both. For humanity, in its progress, can simply never retrogress.

Pan-Slavism and our Country

All of Europe has been snapping and shrieking about Pan-Slavism. The word has been bandied about, and spoken of in fear, in nearly all of the nations of Europe; hundreds of periodicals have written about it; it has been spoken of in social circles; indeed, even in diets and parliaments it has been the target of fiery speech. We too, wherever we have turned, have had the word Pan-Slavism shrieked into our ears. Whenever we have appeared at any sort of national event — everywhere and always, these events were classified as Pan-Slavist, and, wherever they might, the powers that be have impeded such gatherings, setting up obstacles in their way, bringing them to nought. So what is this wondrous thing, this word 'Pan-Slavism'? What sort of miraculous power does it possess, that so many men are seized with terror at its mere mention, and filled with anger and bile toward all that is Slavic? A person might think that, perhaps, behind the slogan Pan-Slavism there lurks some sort of crusade[132] about to be unleashed against the nations of Europe. Indeed, things much worse than a mere crusade they sense behind the word Pan-Slavism. Nothing less than all (Pan) the Slavic nations (Slavi) under the leadership of Russia, they think, are to rush upon Europe in the manner of the Attilas and other such terrible warriors of the past, to lay waste to Europe, and to enslave the European nations. This is what they think! In Pan-Slavism, then, Attila and his rapacious, greedy hordes is to be reborn, to twist a new scourge of God, with which to flog the Europeans. This is the picture that, here and there, the word Pan-Slavism still conjures up in people's

---

[132] In Slovak, *križacke ťaženie* — which in a Slavic context conjures up images of the Teutonic Knights of the Cross. This militant religious order, mostly made up of German nationals, was the instrument of German expansion in the north-east of the continent. At the XV century Council of Constance, the Polish theologian Paweł Włodkowic argued against their policy of enforced conversion of pagans in Lithuania. Defeated at the battle of Grunwald by a combined Balto-Slavic army led by Polish King Władysław Jagiełło, the order was reduced to a Polish fiefdom at the outset of the Renaissance. The term thus has a very biting irony to it.

minds. But mostly among such people as are far removed from today's generally accepted currents of thought.

Without a wind nary a grass blade bends, as the Slavic saying goes, and so there must be something behind this all, something that engendered such a vision of horror that was seen to wander through all the nations of Europe. Since so many people were able to bring forth such a terrible image before the mind's eye, there must be some good reason behind these European imaginings. We do not hide the fact that, at times, such conceptions may have had a basis in reality. But it is no less certain that, in the European imagination, the soft whisper of a breeze seemed to roar like the report of massed cannonry, and the soft lament of a nation fallen so low boomed in their ears like the rumbling of a distant volcano. This bears some discussion.

If there be any nation that has been left behind in human development, that nation was and certainly is the Slavic nation. The cause of their retardation is neither bad will nor their incapacity to develop. For even in its decline, it has provided beautiful testimony to its good will, its abilities, and its moral and intellectual strengths. Rather, geography and all the historical consequences arising therefrom, are to blame for the situation in which the Slavs find themselves. It's well and good for the Germans, the French, and other western nations to speak with pride of their culture. But if the Slavs enjoyed the same geographical placement as these, they would have achieved just as much as, if not more than, the Germans, the French, and so on. The Germans, the French, and their other neighbour nations border upon the ancient cradle and homeland of human enlightenment and culture. The areas they came to occupy lie close to those, enriched by the ebb and flow of Italy; the areas they occupied are not far distant from the classical lands of Hellas. And hence everything which had cultural and educational value in the Greek and Roman worlds arrived at their settlements simply and directly. Because of this proximity, all they needed to do was to stretch out their hands in order to gather the gleanings of the excellent, renowned ancient world, with which to sow and make fertile their own fields.

The fate of the Slavic nation was different. For, separated from the ancient classical nodus of Greek and Roman culture, set on the eastern and northern marches of the European continent, between Asia and Europe, and thus exposed to all the attacks and onsets of the atrocious Asian peoples, who were continually rolling in waves toward Europe, the Slavs were in no condition to be guided by the lights of the ancient world to a higher human existence. They simply could not take advantage of it. In this respect, the Slavs were much less fortunate than the Germans, the French, and other western European nations, who not only came to sip at the very fountainheads of ancient culture, but entered into direct intercourse with the cultivated ancient world, and this continually affected and moulded them. Who would dare contest these facts? The constant contact of a rawer person with someone who is more cultivated is for the former a true education, and the Greeks and the Romans provided just such a school for the western European nations. In contrast to them, the Slavs had as neighbours the as yet crude Germans on the one side, and the wild nations of Asia on the other. Thus, they had no real opportunity to acquire a more elevated humanism. Instead, they were continually obliged to fight, and that ferociously, against the wild nations pressing in droves toward Europe, who regularly renewed their incursions, pillaging the continent from the IV century AD until the XV. In these wars, nearly all of the Slavic nations were engaged, the Russians as well as the Poles, the Czechs, Slovaks, Croats, Serbs and Bulgarians. Slavdom was obliged to battle against the Huns, the Khazars, the Avars, the Pechenegs, the Kumans, the Mongols, Tatars, and Turks. In these wars, the Slavs gloriously and victoriously accomplished their tasks, breaking the wild power of these nations, and protecting the cradle of ancient culture from the danger, with which it was threatened. At the same time, their cultural refinement was greatly delayed, and the fact that much of the Asiatic brutality, with which they had to deal, adhered to the tribes of Slavdom, everyone sees and admits. In Russia, for example, such an intrenched tradition as serfdom would never have arisen; man would never have defaced himself so, with such severe corporal punishments, had the Russians not become accustomed to such beneath the heavy Mongol yoke. No — such savagery and slavery combined have no claim, at bottom, to the open Slavic soul, which is humane at its core.

So, on the one hand, Asian savagery fell upon the Slavs, halting them in their development, and on the other, the Slavs were separated from the classical regions of culture by a large band of nations. From this alone it should be clear to all that the Slavs found themselves in a very inconvenient situation in regard to educational development and the acquisition of high culture. Even the very word of God, the Christian faith, arrived among the Slavs at a much later date than it did amongst the other western European nations. It had a much longer road to travel. The Germans and Franks received the word of God as early as the III, IV, V, VI, and VII centuries after the days when Christ walked the earth, whereas in contrast, only in the IX and X centuries did those sacred teachings spread generally among the Slavs. Such was the natural course of events, at any rate. From Italy, and specifically from Rome, the Christian faith could not arrive among the Slavs before first coming to the Germans and the Franks, whose settlements bordered on Italy. It might only take root in the Slavic lands and inspire their peoples to a more elevated life only after having first passed through the neighbouring lands.

Likewise, commonwealths were founded amongst the Slavs much later than they were in the Germanic nations or amongst the Franks, and it is only then, when a nation has established a real political community that a more vigorous, more ordered and lawful common life may begin. The Germanic nations and the Franks outpaced the Slavs in the commencement of communal life, that is to say, a more settled, lawfully regulated and safer life, by whole ages, because they founded their commonwealths whole ages before them. Only in the IX and X centuries were the Slavs ready to organise a more vibrant public life, as Great Moravia, Bohemia, Poland, Rus and other Slavic commonwealths bear witness. And thus from the foregoing everyone must admit that the Slavs simply had to remain far behind the Germans and the French as far as culture is concerned — but the blame for this lies with their geographical setting and the history contingent upon it. One may laugh and mock the Slavs and cast open aspersion at their backwardness, but such mockery is entirely unreasonable and unconsidered. It reveals an ignorance of history, a lack of historical research; it is a frivolous judgement, historically speaking. Had the Slavs settled those lands and regions which the Germans, the French, and the other western European nations occupied, they would certainly have achieved as much, if not more, than those aforementioned peoples. But even so, well and good — for, such being the case, so much greater is the future that lies before them.

Now, even at such a distance, and in those far off days of the Slavs' disadvantageous situation in respect to ancient culture, they proved themselves to be admirably industrious in learning, producing beautiful fruits of their richly endowed spirit, displaying to the world pleasing invention in the intellectual spheres of learning and science. In those active ages of the XIV and XV centuries, the Czechs mounted great heights in learning and seemed poised to assume pride of place amongst all the nations of Europe. During the reign of the Zygmunts, in that golden age, Polish literature also proved itself capable of soaring to sublime heights among the nations of Europe. And what is more, to whom belongs the glory of discovering the eternal harmony of the cosmos, so characteristic of Slavic thought, if not to Kopernik, and through him, to the Slavs? To whom the glory of discovering the eternal and immutable order that regulates nature if not Zalužanský, and, through him, his nation? We shall refrain from mentioning others here, as it is enough for now to call to mind these two Slavic stars that gleam in the firmament. Yet all of this was attenuated, as new storms gathered on the Slavic horizon, and these first buds and blossoms were assailed by new tempests and hail; the skies grew dark above Slavdom, and, in sorrow, the Slavic spirit withdrew once more from the world's stage.

Yes, long ago the Slavic nations remained in such a condition, until those great changes occurred in the western world that gave a new impulse to such human events. Ancient learning, which earlier had been confined to Greece and Italy, slowly began to spread and take root amongst the French and German nations. And thus it came into close proximity to the Slavs, and soon began to spread among them as well. As time went by, the intercourse between the Slavs, the French and the Germans became more frequent and meaningful, and through their attention to the western European manner of life, their ever closer commerce with those political, ecclesiastical and scientific systems, it was simply inevitable, obviously, for this to have great implications for the Slavic tribes.

It would be worth the effort should one trace all of the transmissions of western European enlightenment to the Slavs and describe its effects on them; however, such a task is beyond the scope of the present essay. But suddenly, the thunder of the French Revolution resounded throughout Europe, shaking nearly all of the tribes of Slavdom most strongly. The sons of Sláva, too, rushed to the armed camps — some to that of the French, and others to those opposing her, and so the Slavs did battle with the world, and one another. But whatever was the outcome of those terrible wars, the result of these events upon the Slavs was gigantic. Through these wars, the Slavs came to know the more developed, more perfect, style of life in Western Europe in every respect, while at the same time coming to recognise the depths in which they found themselves in respect to the other nations of Europe. In these battles they became more familiar with the ideas born of the French Revolution, which later matured into that colossus of a man, Napoléon. He, standing at the forefront of the French forces, opened with his sword a road to the dissemination of those ideas throughout the world. So too did they reach the Slavs, where all the more briskly they nourished and inspired their spirit. Now did the Slavs come to know how lowly, how far beneath the other nations of Europe they did lie, and how unable they were to compare themselves to them on an equal footing. Meanwhile, after the French wars, the life of the European nations, particularly that of the French and the Germans, the neighbours of the Slavs, continued to develop and progress. Ever more swiftly and freshly, one followed hard upon the other: the public life of these nations, under the aegis of newly developing legislation, resulted in ever greater liberty. Social life became more pleasant, through the slow equalisation of former class divisions. Science and learning slowly descended from their tower to mingle amongst the people, becoming part of their everyday life. The heretofore low standards of living began to rise as these benefits began to percolate even to the lower classes. Consequently all this had a powerful effect on the motivation of the heretofore petrified Slavic tribes, who ever more surely began to navigate the twists and turns of Western European life.

If up until now the Slavic tribes had been snoring, deep asleep, from those days forward they could slumber no more. They have been awakened — and this has been followed by great commotion and unrest among them all — a few years earlier in some, a few years later in others, but all of the tribes of Slavdom have experienced it. This commotion in a heretofore dormant nation, the most broadly spread throughout Europe — but, all the same, dead, so to speak, unnoticed — could not but have a wondrous effect upon the nations of Europe, indeed. It was as if some miraculous phenomenon had suddenly materialised in their midst, to rattle the foundations of the continent. It really was like the advent of some wonderful, heretofore unknown thing, this bestirring of the Slavic tribes; it elicited a yelp from the nations of Europe — shock, and fright! But when people come to know the natural causes behind any extraordinary phenomenon, it ceases to be looked upon as miraculous, and no longer rattles them. So indeed shall it be with this sudden awakening of the Slavic tribes. When the European nations come to understand whence it naturally arises, it will cease to appear to them to be such an alien thing, and they will no longer fear it. On the contrary, as they wish well to others, they will be pleased at the fact of so many people demanding a better and freer life for themselves.

So, it was this sudden bestirring of the Slavic nation, having been held so long as nought or as comatose in a spiritual sense, which gave the first real impulse to the terrible rumours concerning so-called Pan-Slavism, and, as a consequence, the hateful obloquy, calumnies and finally persecution of all things considered to be manifestations of Pan-Slavism. But the intelligent and unprejudiced onlooker will assess the matter quite differently. The nations of Europe considered what had spontaneously arisen in the lives of the Slavic tribes as something the Slavs had conspired toward, interpreting what was a necessary and inevitable result of the current of European affairs as a dangerous Slavic threat to all other nations. They took the movement not as a sign indicating a better and freer life for a people heretofore downtrodden but as a rebellion and a subversive grasp for power that would violently undermine the status quo and elevate the Slavs to a more exalted position among the European nations — especially taking into consideration their might. But from all the foregoing, it is obvious that these apprehensions and notions concerning the Slavs were utterly crooked and mistaken.

The real truth of the matter is that the Slavs suddenly arose and began to stir themselves, not because they had earlier conspired to do so, but rather because they had all been asleep, shuffling somnabulistically, in a slavish existence until events in Europe took a sudden turn and awoke them. The real truth of the matter is that all the Slavic tribes experienced a sudden upsurge of the will to better their lives — not at the cost of others, to pull others down — but rather to raise themselves up to the level of the other European nations, after having lagged so far behind for so long. Having taken note of the development and liberty of others, they wished the same for themselves. The truth of the matter is that all of the Slavs began to refer to their ethnic nationality — not to employ this in some threatening fashion — but rather because every nation that wishes to progress must begin here: with a consciousness of what constitutes the foundation of its existence, and that is its national essence.

And so we see how it came about that Pan-Slavism acquired the reputation that it is still tainted with here and there, but that the truth of the matter, and the direction of the movement itself, is something completely different, something that, from all the foregoing, must be the conviction of anyone who considers the matter without prejudice. The Slavs, it is true, have been far behind. Yet it is also true that every nation, including that of the Slavs, must progress. It is not sensible or wise to seek to impede or stifle something that is absolutely necessary, for nothing will come of that but violent explosions. On the other hand, it is sensible and wise to support the development of something which is natural and necessary. Decency and justice demand the same for the Slavs. As we say above, the progress of the Slavic tribes can be aided in good conscience, and in this way, everything will be resolved in a natural and peaceful manner.

While this hue and cry about Pan-Slavism pervaded many places, nowhere was this more so than in our country. Newspapers and periodicals were full of it, as was our daily life itself. The smallest steps taken toward the betterment of our educational system, of the standard of living or the civil rights of the Slavic nation, were decried as Pan-Slavism. So far was this phobia of Pan-Slavism carried in our country, that, as the Magyar demagogues following Camille Desmoulins during the French revolution put it, it was identified with insubordination to the government and treason to both State and Liberty. Should someone or other retire from public to private life, they cried: Suspicious! What's he conspiring? Should someone else emerge from private to active public life: Suspicious! He's looking to work up a cult of the individual and undermine liberty! That fellow there is a poor man: Suspicious! He'll sell his services to those who would fight against liberty! That other fellow is wealthy: Suspicious! He'll be using his money to assemble hirelings for the fight against liberty! This one's like that, that one's like this — to the guillotine! Off with his head! Such was the situation to which the frenzy around Pan-Slavism arrived in our own country. Someone wanted to reform our wretched Slavic schools — Pan-Slavist! Someone published a book for our neglected nation: Pan-Slavist! Someone founded a charitable association — Pan-Slavist! That's a conspiracy of Pan-Slavists! Someone's arranged a Slovak entertainment for us Slovaks: Pan-Slavist! Voices were raised in pain at the injustices done to our nation: Pan-Slavists! In the end, anyone who dared say any word about the Slovak nation was already called a Pan-Slavist.

Today, thank God, the universal uproar around Pan-Slavism has died down, receding to dark corners and back alleys, as the more sensible folk come to understand that it all was much ado about nothing, and even the more skittish ceased to tremble, once those invasions of Attila failed to materialise. Now, we have seen where the truth lies in all this cried-up Pan-Slavism. We have seen that the bestirring of the Slavic tribes did not arise from conspiracy, but because the Slavic nations had lagged so far behind the others for so long. This movement, far from being threatening and dangerous, was noble — all the more so as it concerned what is noblest in humanity: enlightenment and liberty. He who is enlightened is able to recognise the yearning after enlightenment in others. He who truly longs for the liberation of all men is gladdened when liberty blossoms among others.

If anyone ought to desire the enlightenment and liberty of the Slavs — we state this with the utmost conviction — that will certainly be the nations of Europe, and the Magyars. For then, the Slavs will never allow themselves to be used as a tool to keep others in darkness and servitude. This is a matter of great import for us, which any sensible and unprejudiced man will properly recognise. But let us be clear about one thing: Magyar liberalism, which by its own definition sets itself to the task of establishing enlightenment and liberty in Hungary, has suffered up to this very moment from one great wound — a wound which from its very inception was fatal, and made of it a laughing-stock in the eyes of the world and suspicious and hated in the eyes of the Slavs. And that wound is this: the enlightenment and liberty for which the Magyars profess to be fighting is intended for the Magyar nation alone. Magyar liberalism is, therefore, to the highest degree, nothing but egoism and tyranny.

The Slavs want no part of such enlightenment and liberty as is found beneath the banner of Magyar liberalism. Quite naturally: for should the Slavs accept such a thing, they would be turning a weapon against themselves.

There is no need to pile up mounds of evidence for proof of what we say. Let us introduce here only one proof, but that a very telling one, touching upon the freedom of the press. Much has been said and shouted about it, and in the very seat of government it was determined that, yes, the freedom of the press shall be established in our land. But only for books in Magyar. This one example, we reckon, will be convincing enough to everyone concerning the truth of Magyar liberalism. And against whom did that Magyar liberalism come out so strongly? Against whom did it so fulminate? Whom did it wish to stifle, to destroy practically at one blow? Truly — one would hardly believe it — the Slavs!! The oldest, most ancient, most faithful companions of the Magyars. Their neighbours to the west and to the north, to the east and the south. The constant companions, surrounding neighbours, and friends of the Magyar nation from the very first days of their appearance in Europe, and throughout history. Those, who earnestly aided them to establish their commonwealth, who led them into the Christian Church, who taught them agriculture and the crafts; their instructors in the basics of education and enlightenment. This liberalism of theirs seeks the destruction of a good nation, an adventurous nation, a nation of comely men and women, full of ability; a nation upon whose wisdom and freedom, should they reflect a just a little, and weigh with honesty, certainly the Magyars, if anyone, should find that they infinitely depend.

But a hue and cry against the Slavs reverberated throughout Europe, raised first by the Germans, and soon augmented with the voices of the Magyars. Some joined in the chorus because they assumed that what they were doing was right; others — the majority — out of mere custom and fashion. We are not surprised at the Germans, the ancient and obdurate enemies of the Slavs from time immemorial, who have constantly aimed at undermining the Slavic tongue whenever they had the chance — but we are surprised at the Magyars, our old companions, earlier our good friends. Magyar liberalism hastened to emancipate the Jews — that wandering tribe of immigrants — while at the same time rushing to eradicate the Slavs, to cast them into darkness and still greater servitude. Oh, those plunderers of our Motherland! To treat thus the first craftsmen and industrialists in Hungary, her first and most ancient citizens, the people who distinguished the Hungarian land in every respect, laving it with their blood and covering themselves with fame on account of all their merits in her regard. And so, behold, it has come to pass: they aid and exalt villainy, while harrying and cudgelling the good. In the end, our firm belief is that when the Magyars progress further in education and culture; when, as a consequence, they become more thoughtful and just, when they reflect more closely upon their state, their situation, and understand it better, more than one of them will shake off his bias and seek enlightenment and liberty not only for himself, but for others, especially the Slavs. What is more, not only will they wish it for the Slavs, they will actively engage in aiding them to its acquisition, not as now in the case of their adoption of the cause of Jewish emancipation, out of current vogue, but from good will, true conviction, and, let us still add — from prudence. We firmly believe that this will come to pass, we say, and, further, we believe also that we shall see the days when each oppression, indeed every incitement to oppression of the Slavs, will meet with round rejection and condemnation, while the more sublime amongst the Magyars will aid the Slavs to greater development and liberty, working toward these goals and publicly encouraging them.

In regard to our written tongue as well, we have 'naturalised' ourselves as citizens of our own country. Before, in this matter, we stood side by side with the Czechs, making use of their speech in our written works, but we have severed that long-lasting bond as well — and that with pain — only in order so that in this case too we should be entirely at home in our land.[133] Let no one suppose that we took this step lightly, or to please anyone — no, we have not fallen so low as to be so dazzled by what others think of us that we should decide on something so important to our national affairs for such a petty reason. We took that step out of concern for ourselves alone, for our

---

[133] Czech and Slovak, and the varieties of Czech spoken in Moravia, are mutually understandable to such a degree that some linguists consider them to be dialects of one tongue, rather than separate languages. The history of the establishment of Slovak in its own right is complicated, with many Catholics, such as Anton Bernolák, favouring its codification separately from the Czech, others (mainly Protestants) advocating Czech as a literary language for the Slovaks, to which they had become used through centuries of ecclesiastical usage, and others still, like the poet Jan Kollár, advocating the development of a general 'Czechoslovak' language based on both dialects. In his age of intensifying national / ethnic consciousness in the multinational Hungarian kingdom, Štúr was also motivated in his advocacy for Slovak by politics: to deprive the Magyars of the possibility of repressing the speech of the Slovaks as a foreign import (Czech), not native to the region, and imposing Magyar upon them all the more strongly as a result.

national life, our unity. There are of course among us still those who do not want to understand our behaviour in this affair, and who are still drawn toward the use of Czech. In what concerns Slovak life, however, such people live in books alone, in literature, and care little for other aspects of our national existence, indeed understanding them even less — such as civic matters, for example. But such people cannot contribute anything of their own to our national affairs, which are spreading ever more broadly and demanding even more attention, while their number is paltry now, and growing ever smaller. These men can set up no barrier whatsoever to the vital current of our nation, and the work that we have begun we shall conduct to its successful completion. One might already consider the matter as having been brought to a successful conclusion, and as such, we find ourselves, at once, at home in our land and in our ethnic nationhood. Enough then: we are here, and here we wish to be at home.

We shall see, however, whether or not the others, and especially our fellow-countrymen the Magyars, will welcome us as natives, at home; we shall see if they will treat us as native sons or, all the more, continue to consider us foreigners. They shall do the latter if they continually impose their language upon us, introducing it into our schools, expelling our tongue from our churches as an alien speech, prying it, as they have been doing up to the present day, from our social and civic spheres. They will continue to consider us foreigners if they continue to berate us for God knows what reason, persecuting us with repression at the least national striving of ours, condemning us for our love of our nation, shunting us aside, whenever possible, from contact with the friends of our nation, forbidding us that noblest thing of all, friendship. But we say to them beforehand, and such is both our conviction and the spirit and will of the times in which we live, that they will not stifle us or our nationality. In the place of one man so stifled, ten more will arise, as has ever been the case, and all of their efforts, strive they never so hard, will be in vain.

RUSSIA

Pushkin. A Lament

The Russians

Slavdom and the World of the Future

Pushkin. A Lament[134]

You shed, O graceful sun, upon the Black Sea range
Of hills the blessings of a splendid spring — for what?
You cease, greedy north wind, to rage, ceding your place
To zephyrs wafting fragrance instead of sleet — why?
Caucasian vales, O hide your charms now from the world!
For whom now do your blossoms burst into bloom? What use?
He is no more, who so lovingly described
The beauties of your magnificent springtimes.
Beneath the soil he moulders now. It is fitting
For you to cast off joyful garments for sackcloth,
And from the cloudy skies above the icy Volga
Once more, O spring, to veil your cheeks in shadows dark.
Restrain the charming trillings of your harbingers
Beyond the sea; and in your depths remain, O sweet
Maiden of the Volga. Look! See you not the mound
Topped by a white stone? Know you not what it contains?
Peace abandons my heart when I think how many years
He might have flourished yet in his homeland — buried now!
He was the flower of one day, her greatest son;
The summer fields now bring her only bitterness.

---

[134] First printed in the Czech journal *Květy*, in 1837, the year of Pushkin's death (1799 – 1837). Pushkin was killed in a duel by Georges-Charles de Heeckeren d'Anthès (1812 - 1895), a French Royalist serving in the Tsarist Army (hence the references to strangers and refugees in the poem). The duel was over Pushkin's wife Natalia, with whom d'Anthès seems to have been obsessed to the point of marrying her sister in order to have an excuse to be near her. Some rumours suggest that the duel was provoked in service to Pushkin's enemies, who wanted him dead ('Moscow's Ivan'). The 'pogrom of blooms' destroying 'another and another' seems to refer to the Decembrist conspirators, many of whom were put to death in 1826, while many others were sent off into Siberian exile. Among their number were some poets and writers, including the poet Kondraty Ryleyev (1795 – 1826). Although the Decembrists were inspired by his poetry, Pushkin himself seems not to have been let in on the conspiracy.

How my heart rages with tempests when I recall
The earth was torn for that grave by a violent hand!
The savage Mongol raged along those banks, pillaging
Too often, murdering the children of the land;
Now soaring fortresses of stone repulse such hordes,
But this dark stranger entered through a gate spread wide:
In flattering disguise he stole within, awaiting
His hour — for which the son of Russia now looks in vain.
Another and another is lost; a pogrom
Of blooms that shakes the wide-spreading Slavic motherland!
Who now shall summon you, O Maiden of the Volga,
Upon the stage in comely costume of homespun?
You shall remain now, far away in cottage hidden,
For Moscow's Ivan has roared Pushkin into his grave.
And if another were to summon you before us,
Surely he'd trick you out in borrowed foreign rags;
Not to his taste, your homespun, although your beauty
Shines best in your native fabric, like the chaste moon.
Who now shall steer thy gaily flower-bedecked barge
To Moscow, to Petrograd and one hundred cities more?
Who shall transmit the thunderous voice of Tsar Pyotr
To the world, that mighty voice creative — 'Arise!' —
Which called Russia to life? Now Sláva trains her eyes
In sadness and in ire upon the grave, in which
The one who had such love for all her children rests.
Too briefly, his countrymen along the Váh riverbanks
Had commerce with Pushkin, emulating his songs
Enraptured; now laments are what Sláva has them sing!
But though Pushkin has died, his spirit shall ever soar
Above the lands of Slavdom, alive in his great lyre —
Enthroned he is atop the highest Slavic summit,
While from the vales below, holocausts of praise arise!

The Russians

Sharp eyes are trained on the Slavic north — on 'Svataya Rus' — amidst these new developments in Europe. The nations of Europe had been expecting, and the Germans particularly hoping for, news of unrest in Russia, but as yet they have been disappointed. There is not the same sort of discord between ruler and people in Russia as there is elsewhere. In this respect, there one finds more concord than perhaps anywhere else in Europe. The Russian nation is engaged in a great undertaking: the gigantic task of self-development, and, accordingly, the people willingly follow the lead of their government, which anticipates them in the task. This national instinct for the unification of government with nation cannot be disrupted by any European considerations. One thought courses throughout Europe today: will the Russians join in our present labours, or not? Whatever the case may be, one thing is certain: Russia is proceeding, with slow, but well-considered, steps. When the time will come for action, the Russians will not be able to avoid it, as is frequently the case among the other Slavs, from frivolity or insufficiency of vigour. And when the Slavic north puts its shoulder to the wheel, a great deed, a gigantic work, will be the result. Such deeds one finds inscribed on every page of Russian history. All of the other Slavs lost their independence, their national authority, and to this day have not regained them, but the Russians have accomplished great things therewith, and have preserved them in glorious fashion. Wherever the Slavs have met up against the Germans, says Kohl, they have been defeated and lost their independence, and, thereafter, upon their ruins the German oak has taken root. One day more and all of the Slavs would have been subjugated by the Germans — but that day was determined otherwise, miraculously — I am speaking of Poltava. On that day, Pyotr the Great defeated Charles XII — the greatest hero of the age. And a second such victory, in an even more enormous battle, was gloriously won by the Russians at Borodino! All of Europe, led by that great soul Napoléon, fell upon Russia, desiring her destruction. But the Russians, the sons of Sláva, performed wonders in that battle, and were victorious. Hundreds and hundreds of thundering, death-dealing cannon were unable to make the Russians retreat an inch. To them are due the thanks and profound respect of all Slavdom! Let the Slavic spirit spread even wider throughout Russia; let the progress of freedom appear there as well, and that land will accomplish great and important things for Slavdom, significant and decisive things for the world entire.

When we examine current events in Europe, it is easy to see in these movements a certain grass-roots, national engagement directed toward an independent, free and fraternal, reciprocal association. All of the nations are arising and, within the borders of their ethnic nationalities, striving to bring order to their houses and unite their common strengths. It is enough to turn one's eye to the Germans, the Italians, the Gauls (the Irish). God grant them all success! For only then, when they, and others too, bring this task to its accomplishment, will the dawn of the long yearned-for, long demanded age of humanity at last appear on the horizon. In place of the old congresses there shall be congresses of the nations, determining international affairs. Such a thought was first expressed by the Slavic Congress — and even German cannonry, indeed, was unable to stifle it. At the moment, we may still be fettered, but all the same we find ourselves, in Europe, at the very beginning of a drama, which is soon to develop. Doubtlessly, the Crab Party of the so-called reaction will employ all of the means available to it and exert all of its strength in order — as much as such a thing will be possible — to reestablish the old status quo. However, such attempts, although they may succeed for some time, cannot be long-lasting, and the means they employ, according to universal opinion, will but prepare their own grave, after striking one last blow. But may the Slavs be watched over by the benign spirit of the world, the spirit of history, so that we may not seek our own salvation indeed, by such means, so often used in similar circumstances!

Turning our gaze before us then, in good hope, we bring these thoughts to an end with the words of a young, currently imprisoned Slavic poet:[135]

We await the dawning of the sun divine!

---

[135] Janko Kráľ.

Slavdom and the World of the Future

1. THE SLAVS IN THE PAST
WHAT THEY LACKED AND WHERE THEY EXCELLED
THE QUESTION OF THEIR MISSION IN HISTORY

The time has truly arrived, my brothers, for us to come to an understanding. These sad days are calling to us from on high, summoning us directly, with sonorous voice, to deeds, and for that we need, above all, accord.

Give ear, therefore, to these words, the aim of which is concord among us all, brothers; give ear to them, all of you — you who find yourselves at the distant, powerful north-east, you there in the enslaved south, and you too, beleaguered, in foreign service to the tyrants of the west; give ear to them all of you, in all regions and hamlets, wherever the Slavic tongue resounds, in whatever dialect, and bear them in turn, like heralds, to everyone capable of understanding them; everyone who senses within him the strength to bring them into action. Know you all, that from our first coming into existence here, we have never yet come to an understanding between us; we have never achieved anything together, and yet we are born brothers, pressed by the same fate, heirs to the same future.

Candid, direct, well-considered and manly these words are to be, which gush forth from the breast of a man whose soul, from his very earliest years, has been brimming with care for the destiny of our tribe.[136] These eyes have passed over the pages of our past, full of suffering, in sadness, but they have also flashed with joy at the longed-for, great, sublime future awaiting us that has been revealed to them. The man who speaks to you has accomplished many sorts of things on behalf of our tribe, suffering much. He is a man

---

[136] Most often, Štúr uses the word 'tribe' in reference to the particular branches of the Slavic family (Poles, Czechs, Slovaks, etc.) while reserving 'nation' for the Slavic conglomerate as a whole. It is rare when he uses the word *kmeň*, tribe, in the singular, as here, in reference to all Slavs.

immune to any sort of external pressure. But he asks you to lend him your ears not for himself, but for his message, his mission.

Let there be no mistake about it: we are speaking here of the Slavic idea with unprecedented sincerity, in all candour, and as never before. Let the shrinking souls among us, those of little faith, not be flustered at the directness of our speech. For if it is unity we desire, and action, we must clearly set forth our common aim. Then will our might grow, day by day, while the might of our enraged enemies will weaken and decrease. If only we take the courage necessary to act, certain victory awaits us, while they are doomed to inexorable defeat. No might, not even that of governments, is able to crush our life, which bears inside it the idea of the future. Both good fortune and adversity will aid it; whether the sun shine or the rain fall, in thunder and lightning it shall grow. Such are the very cycles of nature! Disaster, pressure, exploitation and oppression of any sort merely prove our strength as a touchstone, urging and scourging our spirit, strengthening and steeling our will. And for the great work that stands before us we need strength, as well as an aggressive, enterprising and bold spirit, a fire-proven and indomitable will. Hey, let us speak our minds openly and in manly wise, my brothers!

Which one of you, led by a spirit more sublime, has risen above the tribulations of everyday life and allowed his eyes to wander the great expanse of our world; who among you, I ask, has not sent forth a groan from the depths of his soul over the fate of our nation, widely-spreading on all hands, and the millennium of misfortune, with which it is oppressed, or the burden that weighs it down, the ignominy, with which it is covered? Hey, unspeakably great is the misfortune of our nation! And should an onlooker, deeply moved at the sight, pose the question, how might this have come to be, how might it all have come to this? Instead of offering an answer, our nation is struck dumb from its great pain.

Indeed, it is a heartbreaking spectacle to look upon, this nation, the most numerous in all of Europe, shattered, divided; as in its atomisation it groans here beneath the Turkish yoke, there in long ages of servitude to the Germans: first to the Holy Roman Empire, and now to the Austrians, Prussians and Saxons. And there, she is engulfed and enslaved by Italian or Magyar. Everywhere she is dragged in triumph, bound to the chariot of foreigners. She toils to raise comfortable constructions for others, receiving in return nothing but the abasement poured upon her, the disgrace hurled at her; O, what a sorrow to behold, how the greater part of the nation inhabiting the banks of the Laba and Odra and along the Pomeranian sea-coast has already gone extinct in German slavery of the most severe type. How those to the north of Italy have also been absorbed into a foreign nationality; how in Turkey they have fallen away from the faith of their fathers and become abettors of the oppressors of their own brothers — all of this, as we have already said, is for the awakened Slavic soul a spectacle just as depressing as all the graves and ruins of her nation, her world, might set before her. Many of us indeed have felt a deep pain at these things and have given vent to our sorrow in mournful plaints. Let one speak for the many: the talented Niccolò Tomasseo, who having been in the service of strangers, still did not forget his nation. From foreign lands he gazed in sadness upon the Slavic world and gave voice to his feelings in his sublime *Sparks*. The seventieth spark reads thus:

> Thy limbs have been torn asunder, O dear Slavic nation, and yet they are animated still with the fulness of life, and day by day Thy blood seethes and courses through them, ever livelier. A long winter it has been, cold and stormy, but now the days of spring break over Thee as well, and flowers nourished by so many of Thy tears begin to bloom. A great significance hath this Thy renaissance: just as sister resembles sister, so do Thy tribes resemble one another, my dear Nation; Thy dialects give proof to their sacred and immortal brotherhood. A great import hath this Thy renaissance, but mountain summits and wide, unwelcoming barren wastes, like a sea, separate brother from brother, and the wretched son cannot recognise the offspring of his own mother. Wretched are we, amongst whom hatred swells easier than love; who are more ready to separate than congregate; whose hands are quicker to strike than to embrace. We have done too little up until now, as evidenced, to come to know one another, to extend a hand in fraternal greeting, to take one another in our embrace. We have permitted misfortune to scatter us as the wind scatters straw. Everything among us is equivocal, indeterminate: our pronunciation, our orthography, our wisdom, our laws, our customs. All of this must be renewed. A great labour this, but for all that, our joy will be all the greater once our task is brought to completion. Let us bow before the noble, the exquisite destiny that awaits us. Let us arm ourselves in mighty patience, in magnanimous humility. Now is not the time to speak of the great deeds of our past. Just as a man bearing a great burden groans and sighs, so we, burdened, must labour, and through our painful efforts we shall win the heavy crown of our salvific liberty.

It is not enough that the great part of the Slavic world lies in ruins as a consequence of these far from trivial divisions and splinterings, above which the genius of Slavdom broods sadly, for ages now, weeping like Isis over the dismembered limbs of Osiris. Above and beyond this horrid dissection, to add to their misfortune, the Slavs themselves, as Tomasseo justly notes, have forgotten their common generation, and as a consequence, have allowed all the ties of their common blood, their fraternal unity, to sink into the dark night of oblivion. Now, in this lonely night, in this barren, sad time for the Slavs, when their body lies as if without sense or feeling and foreigners all the more rend and tear at the ligatures that bind their limbs together, drawing ever closer to the beating heart of Slavdom, not one single tribe has given thought to the sufferings of another, but rather, crammed into alien slops and tied to leads in the grip of alien proprietors, they have been made to serve the comfort of their lords, like instruments for the oppression and further enslavement of their own brothers.

In this dark night, when all of us have forgotten one another, from time to time a voice resounds amongst the sleepers, reminding us of our common origin — now louder, now softer, according to the greater or lesser might and abilities of the one issuing that summons, seeking to rouse the deeply slumbering Slavic world — and such are the only voices that carry, more or less, the Slavic spirit to the ears of snoring humanity. Voices reminding the dismembered Slavic tribes of their common generation and the unity lost have echoed in the Slavic world since the days of SS Cyril and Methodius, Nestor, St Prokop, Dalimil, Piasecki and others, binding, as do ancient tales, all of our tribes in a sense of our congeneric origin, a sense which stretches through the ages and has not completely disappeared even today. And these tales often speak, directly and clearly, of the common origin of our tribes, such as the story of the wandering of the three brothers Lech, Czech, and Rus from their original hearth; or the ancient folk allegory of the quarrelling brothers who set out from their father's house because of their envy of their eldest brother. They went off to enter into the service of foreigners only to return home after bitter experiences, to live once more in reciprocal harmony and peace. Yet not a single action has been undertaken by the individual Slavic tribes to prepare themselves, to develop their strengths, for the realisation of the above-mentioned, still unclear consciousness of this unity. And thus in the mighty Hussite movement — concerning which we are in complete agreement with the Russian Yelagin as opposed to Palacký — we see a revival of the memory of the Greco-Slavic origins of the Church of our forefathers, which is in some way common to all of our tribes. For example, the Hussites negotiated with the Patriarch of Tsarigrad[137] concerning the intercommunion of their assemblies with that Church. And various mighty Slavic princess — such as Samo, the Great Moravians Rastislav and Svätopluk, the Croat Ljutovid, the Serb Dušan, the Czech Břetislav and the Pole Bolesław Chrobry — similarly strove to unify all the circumjacent, related tribes within their empires. But all of these efforts were merely half-measures, and ran aground in the shallows of our tribes' unawakened national consciousness.

Let us therefore overcome our pain as befits men and, having regard for the organisation of a better future for our tribes, let us proceed to a consideration of how it might have come about that the Slavic world declined into such an unparalleled calamity, to the great advantage, for the most part, of aliens.

Above all, the Slavs are grounded in the life of the family. They are gladdened by the good fortune of those who belong to their family, considering others' happiness their own. Nowhere else does the term family — *rodina* — have such a glowing significance as among the Slavs; nowhere else are people as viscerally involved in its life as among them. When a Pole speaks of his *ojczyzna* — his Fatherland — he is thinking, above all, about his near and dear, and those who are near and dear to them, who in this way constitute the *naród* — the nation — in its broadest sense. No other nation celebrates its familial anniversaries with such warmth, poetry and magnificence as the Slavs — nor, at the departure of those who exit the family circle forever, those, of whom it is said, 'go off to their forefathers,' experiences this parting more deeply, nor mourns the deceased more sincerely, bewailing them as much as they. Life, for the Slavs, is a wheel in the midst of which he lives and moves with the greatest delight, at which he both gazes with melancholy, and contemplates with deep pleasure. No nation besides the Slavs possesses such poetry praising and glorifying life. The commonwealth, for the Slavs, is a broad extension of the family. This is both a strength and weakness that the Slav truly sees things in this way. Adequate testimony to this fact can be gathered from the form it takes among all our tribes. In the old days, the local commonwealth was the guarantor of the welfare of all its members. Beggars were not tolerated, but all who were ill, or were seen to be in need, were taken care of, as if it were not a question of citizens, but family members, as if immovable property belonged not to the individual, but to the people as a whole. This last, truly Slavic institution has continued to this very

---

[137] That is, Constantinople. Štúr uses the Slavic name of the ancient capital of the Eastern Empire. Not only Pan-Slavs used it; the word appears in Adam Mickiewicz's *Crimean Sonnets* too.

day in Russia, as it has in other Slavic lands, which have not completely lost their Slavic soul, where Slavic customs have been preserved more or less down to our own day and age.

To this very day there pertains the custom in Slavic villages, according to which all regulations and instructions coming from the government, such as the collection of taxes, the summoning of recruits, etc., are carried out not by governmental officials, but rather by the town elders, who, just as their own fathers had done before them, carry them into effect after careful consideration and according to their best lights, apportioning the burdens among individuals and gathering recruits, etc., with justice.

Such a very important broadened local community in the Slavic world is the župa, or county. Just as the affairs of the village are seen to by the town elders, the heads of individual families, the affairs of the entire county (župa, województwo) are determined in concert at gatherings (in Poland: *wiece, sejmiki*; in the Czech lands *sněmy; kongregácia* in Hungary and *skupštine* among the Southern Slavs). All freeholders resident in the county have equal rights of participation in all the deliberations of their land. Originally, these were all heads of families (*vladykové*, or squires, from whom the earliest aristocracy developed). In Russia such assemblies could not develop the importance they have, for example, in Poland, in Hungary, etc., as there the highest authority acts as a brake. But even in Russia to this very day the nobility possesses the right to hold independent assemblies, to elect their own marshals and judges of the first instances, as well as certain officials of the administration.

From the county level we proceed to that of the state, as the supreme power, to which all of the counties are subject and which maintains the unity of all. Yet such a powerful state was unknown to the Slavs, or, we might even say, the Slavs did not wish to call to life and establish a power appropriate to their calling. At the level of the village and the county, the assemblies must, as far as this is possible, take into account the views, demands and interests of all, with respect. Those who take part in the deliberations of these assemblies are those directly concerned with the matters under discussion. Besides this, they consider themselves members of one family, equal brothers (*równi bracia*). With the state, it is a different matter altogether. The function of the state, in both internal and external policies, is the security of the whole. The state is almost entirely intent upon universals rather than particulars, and needn't take into account the opinions, demands and interests of every single person. Much more frequently, the state finds itself faced with the necessity of enacting what it has determined to be the best course of action, even over the objections of individuals; what is more, it is compelled to exploit the mental and physical powers of the individuals subject to it. This sort of self-denial, this subjection of the individual to the universal, in service of such a whole that a man can comprehend only as an idea, rather than a concrete object; this frequent denial of the organic life of the family and the village, so dear to the Slav, is repugnant to Slavic nature. For this reason, our tribes, everywhere and with all their strength, have opposed the creation of a strong government, an organic state, and never allowed for a great statal unity to develop from our individual tribes. The larger unified state cannot take the individual much into consideration, as it demands more self-sacrifice, more self-denial, and the sort of solidarity it seeks can only be achieved by recourse to greater force — and this is something to which all of our tribes are opposed. A cursory glance at Slavic history suffices to bear out the truth of the foregoing statements. If ever the Slavs had reason enough to create firm, powerful states, that was surely in those places where they bordered upon alien nations — on the banks of the Laba, the Odra, the lower Danube — and nevertheless it is there where we find the contrary. Nowhere else can there be found such atomisation and splintering; nowhere is there more disunity and quarrelling than here. Is it any wonder that here, everyone ended up as the prey of foreigners? Let us but consider how this came to be.

On the banks of the Laba and the Odra, which is to say there, where the germanising pressure was the greatest, we see the Slavs divided into three groups: The Bodriči, The Lutici and the Sorbs, which groups fragmented still further into countless splinters and tiny shards, all of which had their own particular bonds, their own petty princes. There was no question of any significant unification amongst them, not even when faced with obvious threats. Indeed, on the contrary, we observe them engaged in nearly endless quarrels, and should one ever dare reach out his hand toward the other, to drag him by force, if need be, if not to his benefit, at least to common action, these gather, out of spite to the whole, under the protection of German kings, as often was the case amongst the Bodriči and the Sorbs, if only to preserve, as long as possible, their individual, distinct situation. We observe these Slavs, unmindful of their origins, as they battle almost constantly, and indeed boldly, alongside the Germans, although, after the victory has been won, they search about themselves for a friend, in vain. Instead of this, constantly, more and more, they fall into a state of enslavement to the Germans, in which they perish, disappearing in death after a horrific struggle, until nothing is left of them but some insignificant remnants of the Sorbs in both

Upper and Lower Lusatia. And there they remain to this very day, so that, in the name of that extinct Slavic world there — and now in the name of the Slavic world being reborn — they should greet the new dawn.

On another border-line of the Slavic world, later, the Czechs arose, and the Great Moravian Empire; further to the south Croatia and Carinthia came into being; to the southeast: Serbia, Bosnia, Bulgaria, lands that were later enriched with the addition of new regions such as Kraina, Istria, Dalmatia, Slovenia, Herzegovina, and so forth. These regions sprung up just like mushrooms after a rainfall. And just as mushrooms were once much sought-after delicacies on the boards of the mighty, so these additions of ours have been to the taste of our patrons, who control us, as we can see in the newest crown lands of Austria — as they enjoy her 'special attention, care, and benevolent favour.' Not a single one of them may be touched with impunity, nor — God forbid — may one set their foot upon their soil; all of them are to exist in their strength and blossom according to the once and for all accepted principle of co-equality.[138] Besides the fact that all these statal associations, which appeared on our borders, were too small and weak to withstand for long the foreigners who trickled into our lands from all sides, the stewardship they submitted to was just as noisome as that which fell to the lot of the Slavs on the Laba.

Amongst all these associations, the most significant was undoubtedly the Great Moravian Empire, which united our tribes far and wide into one whole. Convinced of the fact that it was necessary to establish a strong Slavic state in Central Europe, they actively welcomed the missionaries who arrived amongst the Slavs and proclaimed the gospel in their midst, in their own tongue. And yet as soon as that state reached such heights as to be able to plan far into the future, this came to the notice of its foes — namely, its most natural enemy, the German Reich — which began its attempts to cross its intentions, arming itself against it both openly, and in secret. At this time the Czech princes, Spytihněv and Vratislav, seceded from the Great Moravian union into which their father Bořivoj had entered, placing themselves under the protection of the German Reich, so as to satisfy their own particular interests as instruments in alien hands against Slavic unity. In this way, Great Moravia lost one of its strongest supports. It found itself exposed on that side, and this damaged its links with the Slavic tribes grouped beyond the Czechs — and so was pushed into the maw of its enemies by the hand of

---

[138] Štúr bitterly speaks of the Austrian principle of 'co-equality,' which he sees as no equality at all, but rather a policy favouring German settlement of newly-annexed Slavic territories.

a brother. There is no denying the fact that, on this side, the Czechs resisted German blows for the longest time, for centuries mounting the most heroic resistance to all attacks aimed against their independence, constituting on this upper frontier the last outpost of Slavdom slowly receding in the struggle against the German element. But it sealed the fate of Great Moravia, or at least hastened its end, and this was to affect the Czechs later, too, if not immediately. Their decline was hastened as well until the Czechs were also made to thrust their heads beneath the German yoke just like their brothers neighbouring them.

On the aforementioned borderline they fared no better than the other Slavic political unions which arose among us. Croatia, which foundered in incessant quarrels with its counts fighting to maintain their particular positions, presently had to reconcile with the Magyars, since it could not enforce internal unity, and recognise Kálmán as lord. Carinthia more or less attached itself to the Reich; in the same way, Serbia fell in bloody quarrels amongst its counts and, although the state was preserved for a while, although it pursued far-reaching plans, for all that it presently fell prey to foreign barbarians, meeting the same fate as Bosnia striving for apparent autonomy in the Slavic sense, and as Bulgaria still earlier. With the fall of Serbia on the southern boundary, all the perspectives of the south Slavic tribes were buried for several centuries. And so it happened that all the Slavs who appeared at that borderline immediately fell into slavery, and into indescribable poverty and abasement.

The manner in which the Slavic tribes conceive of a unified state is most clearly seen in the practice of the Polish state. There, an individual was to receive satisfaction not only at the village level, but, according to Polish custom, their squires and rulers had to consider and appease him even at general assemblies and in the deliberations of the state as a whole. As we have seen, the nobility developed from the heads of families acting as village elders. At general deliberations, the views, demands and interests of each and every one of them not only had to be discussed, but accepted and gratified in such a comprehensive manner that, if a certain motion was not met with universal approbation, even on the account of just one uneasy, dissenting voice amongst all those present, the entire matter was declared totally null and void. Thus appeared in practice the co-equality of the Poles. In regard to the whole, one single person enjoyed the fulness of rights; he was as it were on the same level as the whole, which, being a universal, the will of all manifested in public deliberation, still had no rights vis-à-vis the individual. And thus, the welfare of the state entire was placed at the feet of each individual. In this manner, the state actually became dependent on the individual will, and thus the perspective of arbitrariness was spread wide open, setting the state at the mercy of corruption of any and all sorts, which is basically what led to the total destruction of that state. And thus occurred what was clearly foreseen to be in the offing: Poland fell on account of her dreadful *nie pozwalam,* on account of her proverbial 'Polish housekeeping,' on account of her 'rightfully understood' Polish freedom.[139] May the Lord God preserve us from such freedom! For there are always more than enough Slavic sons led astray and all but destroyed by their ideals, who are still ever carping about 'democrats' and 'democracy,' while what they have in mind is nothing more than their own 'ego,' their own 'aye,' the conceited ones, concerned only with their own claims. What good ground for an equally good Western European democracy!

The statal associations of the Slavs arise in a totally different manner from the statal unions of their neighbouring nations, concretely: the Germans. The statal association of the Germans, who are animated by an inner drive to conquer, is, as it were, determined by applied force. At the head of his armies stands the Heriro or Schora (Sire) who evolves into a prince, and military discipline becomes societal, governmental order, and thus the army and the county administrations are headed by the king's servants, the so-called Grafs. In addition to this, the king does not rule his realm arbitrarily, but is bound by decisions that possess a universal application, by the *placite regia,* by the counsel of the leaders, while his servants consider it their absolute, unconditional duty to show the prince the allegiance that even in the olden times was truly alive in their hearts. From all this it is clear to see that here

---

[139] Štúr is correct. The 'noble democracy' of the old Polish republic was such that no motion, no matter how crucial, could be enacted unless there was absolute agreement. All it took was one noble to rise and cry out *Nie pozwalam*; 'I don't permit it,' and the whole matter had to be rehashed until the recalcitrant noble was convinced. This was the so-called 'golden freedom' or *liberum veto* which could be, and was, exploited by the neighbouring empires of Russia and Prussia. To control what was happening in the Polish *Sejm* — all they needed do was buy the vote of one corrupt representative. The widespread democracy of the Polish republic, which enfranchised some 10% of the male population — a large number, given the percentages in Western Europe, which were below 5% even in the United Kingdom — hovered near anarchy, something that some Poles held up as a political virtue: *Polska nierządem stoi* — 'Poland stands through lawlessness,' was a phrase often invoked by supporters of the 'golden freedom' and bitterly fought against by those who sought stable policy. Although the Constitution of May 3, 1791 (the first modern constitution in Europe) formally abolished the 'golden freedom,' the reaction from hegemonic Russia was too strong for the weakened Polish kingdom, which shortly disappeared from the political map of Europe due to three progressive partitions in the late eighteenth century.

we have to deal with a firmly apportioned state unity, such as creates the necessary conditions for the healthy development of the whole and is capable of supporting grand enterprises. It is quite a different matter amongst the Slavs. At one time, the Slavs existed in entirely patriarchal conditions; they were divided into many tribes and gave no thought to grand enterprises or wider unity. This opinion of ours is given credence by the testimony of Procopius, according to whom the Slavs are not governed by one man, but live in a democracy. Now there are some — and amongst them, some of the wisest — who explicate this testimony as a celebration of the ancient Slavs. They would like to see in this 'democracy', I reckon, something akin to the Greek republics. But as we see it, Procopius' words must be understood in quite a different way. Influenced by the Byzantine imperial idea, Procopius considers it something fundamental that the Slavs have no single ruler over all; the democracy that he alludes to can in reality be understood as the patriarchy of smaller groups in which the Slavs lived. Now, what this life of theirs looked like at the time is shown us by Maurice, who supplements Procopius. He states that the Slavic tribes would never suffer any one man among them telling them what to do. There was also hatred among the tribes as well as among their leaders (*reguli*), that is, the tribal elders, the patriarchs. If such were not the case that they lived in such free, loosely reciprocal units, feuding amongst themselves, how could it have happened later that each and every barbarian cohort, passing on to Europe from Asia, be they Huns or Avars, Khazars or Pechenegs, passed through them so easily, without encountering almost any resistance from them, carrying them along in their wake and treating them in the most base fashion? How else might it have happened that the Magyars could cross right through the midst of the Slavic nations, which were as if in the deepest slumber, to take possession of their most beautiful plains, in the very heart of Slavdom?

O model democracy of our forefathers! To allow itself to be dragged about and torn apart without a whimper of protest! To tamely bend its neck beneath the yoke and bind its descendants in the fetters of a millennium of slavery! O cut it out already, with those paeans sung of the democracy of the ancient Slavs! Stop shedding those tears over the sufferings that our nation underwent at the hands of the barbarian Asian hordes and express, rather, a righteous repulsion to the weakness, the recklessness and the helplessness of our nation! The democracy of the ancient Slavs, as recalled by Procopius, was nothing more than the initial, undeveloped state of our nation's childhood, but we did not remain children, after all. Although the Slavs were oppressed and ground underfoot on all sides, and their neighbours all around them threatened to swallow their existing, or newly arising states, they gathered together from their loose groupings and, at last, even they arrived at the establishment of states. However, wherever they continued to hold on to their village and county structures, which originally served as the foundations of the tribe, they were not able to coalesce into a unified state. In such cases, the state emerges from negative, rather than positive ideas; from existential impulses, such as the need to coexist, and the need for common defence. Here there is no question of a strong impulse such as we find, for example, among the Germans, and consequently the emergence of a state does not signify the realisation of something sound and strong. It is not the mighty, brave, enterprising individual that emerges as the head of the state, but the simple, peace-loving farmer, such as Piast among the Poles and Přemysl among the Czechs. In Carinthia, the prince, newly summoned to the throne, had to appear in the simple garb of a farmer before the nation assembled at his coronation.

The Serbs are an exception. Stronger than our other tribes, as soon as Stefan Nemanja attained supreme power, he subjected not only the other counts, but also neighbouring tribes to has rule. The Russians are a total exception, as their state was not founded by the Slavs. It was not they who united the scattered elements there, from the very start, into a grand whole, but the alien, Germanic Normans. Their strength, grafted onto the Russian nation, became the motive power of the capable Russian state, particularly of those who wielded supreme power. This, basically, is what enabled the Russian state not only to outlive all of the other Slavic states, but also to acquire such a character that today it stands firm in its majestic greatness and constitutes the unique, mightiest bulwark against further incursions of alien elements into our world. Indeed, Russia has put an end to that infiltration in all cases. All of our other tribes have succumbed to that seepage, which comes to a halt at the wide borders of Russia, where foreign elements themselves enter into the service of the Russian state.

As we have said, while it is true that states have emerged among the Slavs, they have never been so successful as to secure such a peaceful existence for our tribes as would allow them to fulfil a higher purpose. This is because of the emotions that are introduced into government, which are, rather, proper to the family and the citizen's immediate community. And when emotion is introduced with equal intensity there, where reason must rule, this is the cause of much evil and misfortune. This has occurred in our states whenever rulers tightened the bridle of power in the belief that in this way they could revive the unity indispensable to the state. What actually happens is that their intentions are opposed by those who are not at peace with them, or the dissatisfied; the princes in question fall to quarrelling and, in the end, are banished by those who doggedly oppose them. According to the testimony of the Metropolitan Yevgeny, over the space of one hundred years, the people of Novgorod shunted aside or banished more than thirty of their princes, and today the Serbs are emulating our forefathers with gusto in this matter of expelling their princes from their land. Everyone who thinks he has the slightest right, or pretension to rule, even if it be pure fabrication; whoever yearns for accolades, power, or even the most supreme sovereignty — and most of us think that we have matured to it — but at the same time does not obtain his goal; everyone, whose claims are beneath being taken into account, whose views and opinions are not considered authoritative, becomes agitated, burning with a thirst for vengeance. And if the one who incites his dissatisfaction is he who wields supreme power, in his ferocity he will cease making distinctions between the man himself and his function as head of the whole, preferring to nourish evil in his soul and, at the first opportunity, topple his opponent into destruction. Our history is filled with such shameful deeds. In the Czech lands, when, on the occasion of the legal quarrel between the Klenovičovci brothers, wise Libuše ruled, according to the customs of the land, that both brothers were to receive an equal share of their paternal inheritance, the elder of the two fell into a rage and demanded — according to German custom — the rights to a majority portion on account of primogeniture. At this, Libuše expressed her displeasure with the words 'Go then and summon unto you a man who will decide your case with iron in his hands.' Thus Gostimysl, the last prince of Novgorod, who renounced his princely authority due to the incessant quarrelling and strife among his subjects, advised them to call to the throne such a prince who would rule with a weapon in his hand. And just such a prince appeared in reality: in the person of the Norman Rurik.

Even the Great Moravian Svätopluk, longing for supreme power, betrayed his lord — who had also been his benefactor, his own uncle, the wise and mighty Rastislav. Handing him over to his bitter mortal enemies the Germans, he plunged the state into the greatest peril, from which, however, it is true, he rescued it, bitterly regretting his deed. He dealt the Germans some awful defeats and extended his sway so far and wide that the Carolinians and their reich were made to tremble. But once again it happened that two of his sons, for the same reason as their father, rebelled against their elder brother, and, summoning allied troops into the country from Germany to further their evil designs, caused the weakened empire, already tottering at the edge of the abyss, to fall into final catastrophe. Even the gallant Serbian prince Štefan Dušan, full of grand projects, committed a heavy crime on account of his precipitous, bold desire for power, which he only partially redeemed by his subsequent great deeds, which were to bring blessings to his nation. From dirty, greedy motivations, Tugumír of Brandenburg betrayed the Polabian Slavs at the very moment when they had successfully formed a coalition with the neighbouring tribes and, with ultimate exertion, cast off the German yoke and manfully arose in rebellion. Thus too acted Milotu out of petty vengeance directed at his heroic king Otakar, and right at the decisive moment of his warring, when the heroic king had all but added some new provinces to his Czech kingdom and become the terror of the Germans. So did the power-hungry Brankovič betray his prince Lazar and the Serbs to the Turks on that fateful Kosovan field, thrusting his nation at the same time into centuries of shameful slavery and debasement. Yes, the names of these three wretches, Tugumír, Milota and Brankovič, who later hadn't time enough to redeem the shameful results of their deeds, ought to be nailed to the pillar of shame, as the names of the most perverted criminals, wherever the Slavic tongue resounds! And for what reason must the Serbian princes of today flee their country again and again? Because certain magnates, possessed by the evil demon of ambition, nourish in their hearts secret desires and hunger for supreme power. For this reason, the mighty, though not entirely sinless, Miloš had to leave the land; for this reason even his well-disposed son, the noble Mihailo, had to depart! And how does the matter stand amongst the Poles? At the partitioning of that unfortunate land, it was teeming with actual traitors, who — fortunately — were in the service of a more capable fraternal tribe, better suited to rule.[140] There, a countless number of presumed 'traitors' were uncovered. For the Poles, more than anyone else, are stubborn and egoistic, and anyone who does not share the views and opinions of him who they consider the greatest patriot, or who is not a supporter their faction (of which there are many in Poland) they call a traitor. And thus in our own day and age even such men as Chłopicki and Skrzynecki have been branded traitors!

---

[140] *Translator's note:* Štúr may be right about not all Poles being angels at the time of the Partitions, and some working actively to further the plans of the partitioning powers at the cost of their own country. But the manner in which he phrases this treason, excusing, or at least mitigating, its shame on account of 'service' to a 'fraternal' tribe 'more capable and better suited to rule' (the Russians) must rankle the Polish eye. It is this kind of attitude that goes furthest toward explaining why there were so few Pan-Slavs in Poland.

Disaffected men and impatient sons of kings are not lacking in other nations, in Germany, for example. For their margraves have stormed off in anger many a time, even unto the princes of our nation, begging their protection. But their desire for vengeance never so rages, their actions are never so motivated by fury as is often the case with our rulers, and it always happens that, before the situation worsens beyond repair, they become reconciled to one another and set aside their disputes. Indeed, it even happens that they who had earlier fallen out join forces in armed league against the former protector of the disaffected party! There can be no question of evil intentions aimed at the Reich itself; such disaffection is brief and directed only at individuals. The Treaty of Verdun was conditioned and made possible by three distinct groups, three nations: the German, the Italian and the French. Nothing was dismantled on account of this treaty except that which did not further the organic whole.

On the other hand, the situation of our principalities is not much better than that of the nation. Our princes treat their states as a sort of family inheritance and accordingly often divide it amongst their sons. Providing the younger with a large share, the eldest is set over them as an apparent superior. The civil law of the Slavs does not recognise primogeniture at all. That Germanic tradition is maintained by an abstract conception of family, which is satisfied with the mere continuation of the family line, and has little, if any, concern for the earthly lot of all the members of the family. Now the Slavs and their institutions are greatly concerned with all family members, and for this reason guarantee an equal distribution of the paternal inheritance, with special provision made for the youngest. Such an establishment is the diametrical opposite of primogeniture. In their states, Slavic princes continue to act according to these traditions, and their nations suffer this. And so the Great Moravian leader Svätopluk divided his empire amongst his three sons, although with obvious trepidation, already on his deathbed, and fostered thus the fall of his own state, which he had defended and made sound with the greatest effort and ultimate, self-sacrificial exertion. In exactly the same way did the Polish king Bolesław III divide Poland amongst his four sons, whereby his empire did not only become the scene of many an internal struggle and subversion, but also indicated the path which would lead to the complete loss of Silesia to the Germans. Even that descendant of the Normans in Russia, Vladimir the Great, had become so Slavicised at least in this, that he committed the error of dividing his empire amongst his twelve sons. This led to nothing less than the crushing defeat of the many divided Russian princes at the hands of the Mongols at the River Kalke, the direct result of which was the enthralment of Russia to the Mongols, an event deeply lamentable to all Slavs, which was to last a full two hundred and twenty six years. And to how many divisions were the Czech lands subjected during the reign of the Přemislids!? Very little was lacking for their empire to disappear entirely as a result of the strife and disruption that arose therefrom. The fact that all of the princely sons were compelled to acknowledge the dominion of the eldest was of little worth, whether it be the Polish brothers submitting to the Grand Prince at Kraków or the Russians to him enthroned in Kiev; this neither stopped nor even retarded the misfortunes brought about by the divisions of the country in question.

What a dark and sad prospect does this world present to the eyes of any friend of Slavdom! The sight of a world which, by its own fault, ended up crumbled into ruins, will provide little consolation to the eye that lingers upon it. That which cannot maintain itself will fall to pieces; that which contains no vital vigour is moribund — the same is true of entire nations. If they are not capable of enduring, of government and administration, for whatever reason, or if they do not set all they have to the task of maintaining their own existence and independence, they simply must enter into the service of others, and be completely swallowed by them in the end. This frequently occurred among the Gauls, and similarly, among the Slavs in the north-east of Germany. The ruins, which meet the eye of the observer, are truly not a sight to offer any consolation.

On the other hand, some comfort can be derived from the past, from history, and the very spirit. Just as a man, who is not bound in his life to any special labour, who does not allow himself to be transported, inspired in spirit, kept vibrantly alive by a mature thought, often falls prey to himself, as it were, tumbling into a whirlpool from which no power can extract him, so have we witnessed the same in the case of the aristocracy, which has become derailed. The same is true even in the case of a large segment of the Catholic clergy. And the same can be said of entire nations — history provides us with multiple examples. The Hebrew nation, once mighty and united thanks to its faith in the one God, fell into impotence when some men of that nation began merely to feign the faith inherited from their fathers, and with appearances obscured the loss of substance, while others gave up the faith entirely, looking upon it as something ridiculous. Others still, escaping from such a decline, walled themselves up in distressful meditations, finding consolation in lonely contemplation. In a word, there, where the Hebrew nation fell apart into sects of Pharisee, Sadducee and Essene, the bonds that held them together were ruptured. The Hebrew nation splintered further into more factions, until it was battered prone and hurled into the vacuum. It had to subject itself to Roman rule, falling for all time with the destruction of Jerusalem.

The Hellenes were great, not in the number of their citizens, but in their strength and sublimity — as long as beauty existed amongst them not in the mind only, but in piety, in the state, and in their social life. But as soon as the Greek turned his eye from the ideal, which he had earlier held in homage, and sacrilegiously turned his hand to works of pure art in place of those dedicated to the gods; as soon as he began to ridicule his own religion and abandon his earlier state traditions — it was all up for Hellenism and Hellenic freedom. In place of earlier beauty we find in Greece only the atrocious Peloponnesian War, in which Greek rages against Greek without any moral checks whatsoever, just as if the various parties of the individual city-states were competing with one another to see which could most quickly bury its own world, its own freedom. There, where at one time a mere few thousand men sufficed to defeat countless hordes of Persians crashing down upon Greece, even the eloquence of a Demosthenes was unable to fire the quarrelsome Greeks to a successful defence of their own liberty. And so they had to bow down before the power of Philip, only, before long, and together with these same Macedonians, to submit to the rule of Rome.

The Romans themselves became great, free and mighty; indeed, they began to rule the entire world thanks to their most exacting, and yet voluntary subjection of the self to the interests of the fatherland. Yet no sooner had they departed from that voluntary obligation, giving themselves up to a hedonistic lifestyle, allowing others to perish on their behalf, than — as we have seen — they fell victim, at first to many powerful adversaries, and at last, to only one, who had annihilated all the rest. And thus at his feet the Roman world sank into an obscure, desolate existence, which we find abominable in each and every way. And it foundered on — deeper and deeper. The power, which had held everything together, grew weaker and paler; the praetorians, with their imperial candidates at their head, tore at one another over the Empire; the provinces grew distant; in the end, there was nothing more to do than to leave the Empire, along with what remained of the Roman world, to the uncultivated, but more powerful and driven Germans.

But although we see the Western Empire decline in lamentation and wretchedness, it is another matter entirely in the East. There, the historically traditional ideal of the *dominium* did not so endure or reproduce itself as it did in the West. Christianity was unable to enliven that over-ripe world, which had completely fallen into corporal hedonism, and although it was externally accepted just as it was in the West, it never penetrated deeply into these nations. Instead of an invigorating force, Christianity served the over-ripe eastern nations as an occasion for the most varied and acrimonious quarrels, the result of which set apposing parties to battle one another over the merest trifles, murdering thousands on both sides for nothing at all.

In ages not so distant from our own, and even today, the Papacy has suffered a bitter fate. As it carries out its mission among the nations, it not only becomes disunited in its own self in that pope and anti-pope face off against each other, excommunicating one another and waging atrocious battles against each other, but losing ever more the support of the nations and growing weaker with each passing year. The Reformation marks a complete refusal of obedience to Rome, when entire nations were pulled away from the Roman Church. Under its influence and operations, the Papacy, as an institution, once so deeply rooted in the life of the nations, was deprived of the last glimmer of its beauty. Neither excommunication nor league were anything worth; in vain did the terror-inciting Spanish Inquisition torture hundreds of thousands of people; in vain did the Jesuits employ their myriad pranks to help the Papacy reclaim its saecular authority. Today there is no more breeding ground for the Papacy among the nations, which is kept alive in its miserable, lowly state merely by the grace of some mighty powers.

When a person gives up the ghost, nothing remains of him but a corpse. In the same way each and every phenomenon ends its life, every establishment, as soon as it abdicates its mission. Even when they continue to endure some short while — this is nothing more than a physical existence, just like a corpse which has not yet decomposed.

Our tribes have been completely lacking in any sort of unifying and elevating ideal. A common origin is no such ideal. It cannot even bring about a turning away from disunity and a discontinuation of inter-tribal quarrels. For it can certainly come about that brothers inhabiting the same house can fall to quarrelling; how much more frequently does this happen amongst tribes who, over the course of time and due to physical separation, become ever more alienated one from another in customs, speech, and much of their establishments. The Normans of Scandinavia waged frequent wars against the Germans, with whom they are related through a common origin, while in Britain they conquered their kindred Angles and Saxons. As we have said, blood relationships between our tribes cannot form adequate bonds linking us one to another. They cannot act so invigoratingly in order for us to successfully, and for an extended period, stand toe to toe with our chief, bitter enemies the Germans, our neighbours along the entire extent of our western boundary, who, in contrast to us, have pursued spectacular ideas resulting in the creation of capable institutions. These are the same Germans who gradually brought the Roman Empire to the edge of the abyss, though the latter was considered at the time to be the *imperium orbis*, and in so doing, acquiring the right to set forth their claims to the empire, and keep it in existence.

This imperial idea, with the passage of time and the growth of Papal power, became even more established and took on sharper contours. For the Bishop of Rome understood himself to be not only the successor and representative of St Peter, and, in consequence, the *primus inter pares*, but also the person to whom, in the light of that succession, the Lord entrusted apostolic power over all of Christianity, being the defender of the Saviour's flock. These attempts at obtaining sovereignty and dominion, at first only in the spiritual realm, were propped up in every possible way by the see of the Bishop of Rome and the city of Rome itself, with which the *imperium orbis* was identified in the eyes of the world. Since the Frankish kings more than once protected the Bishop of Rome from dangers that threatened him, aiding him even in saecular matters and in the maintenance of his political independence, the so-called *Patrimonium Petri*, the successive bishops not only participated personally in their coronations, they uneven anointed and crowned them Emperors in Rome. They began to understand the power that they thus conferred upon them, or even recognised them as possessing, as proceeding directly from the Vicar of Christ on earth, of which only the successor of Peter was entitled to be considered. From this time forward it was accepted that the reputed successor of St Peter was to have supreme governance over all spiritual matters on earth, just as he who was his representative in saecular matters was to have in the worldly sphere. Chosen and anointed by the Pope, the Emperor — all the more so considering the prevailing ideas of the time — was to continue the work of the world-encompassing Roman Empire. Thus the Frankish realm continued to be known as the Holy Roman Empire, and its emperors were taken to be the only chosen plenipotentiaries empowered to rule by the grace of God. Immediately, we witness the supposed Roman Emperors laying claim to the control of all lands bordering on their realm, which claim they derive from their right of executing supreme power under the law. They lay claim not only to such tribes as had not yet sufficiently matured to the establishment of their own states, but also to all neighbouring countries and empires, such as the Czech lands, Hungary and Poland. They bestowed crowns upon their princes, demanding in return that these accept the rule of their lands back again as fiefs granted them by the Emperor, in regards to whom they would be in a feudal relationship, as his vassals. Such an ambition is not peculiar to the Carolinians; it also marks the rulers of the following dynasties: the Saxons Heinrich and Otto, and the Weibling Hohenstaufens. Insofar as spiritual motivations entered into the thinking of these latter-mentioned kings, one sees that several of the Hohenstaufens, namely Konrad III and Friedrich II, even determined upon crusades in the East. Besides the fact that these endeavours, as great as they were in and of themselves, essentially and considerably fostered the unification and structuring of their empire, enlivening also the idea of chivalry with its rich concepts of fidelity and honour, all of this was a motivating factor to the Reich, not only in its external affairs, but also in that it had a retroactive influence on its consolidation and its strict, tight unity. How could our tribes oppose this unified empire, saturated with and upheld by a knightly caste, which continued to spread the Christian idea and the authority of the Church, setting a claim to world rule? With our paganism, our paltry chiefs and our communities in disunion? In such a situation, the victory was never in doubt, and indeed it was not long in coming.

But the fact that this happened at all was due to the situation of both nations in the world. The Germans pressed south until they bordered upon Italy, as in the case of the Germanised and Romanised Gauls. Italy was the last repository of ancient culture; here, finally, was concentrated not only all that the Romans had created, but all that they had received from the Greeks. Moreover, Italy was the first country where Christianity spread far and wide, thus gaining the first major state to its side. It was in the order of things that the Germans, having arrived at the cradle of culture and the Christian faith, should receive the bases of that ancient culture along with Christianity, and in consequence be elevated to a higher level. Our tribes came along in the train of the Germans. They were more distantly located from the nexus of ancient culture and were fated to rely on their distant and infertile steppes. A long period of time is required for a nation such as the Germans, themselves naturally rough, to internalise all the wisdom of the world, process it, enrich it, and hand it on further to its neighbours. And thus the Slavs came to world culture only through intermediaries such as the Germans and their neighbours farther afield, the Gauls.

The conclusion that arises from all this is as follows. Our tribes did not fall into a decline of their own fault. Their life was a weaker one, less equipped and less capable where they came into direct contact with a nation of a more developed life, containing within itself a mission to which they had no choice but to adapt and submit. In a word, back then, our time had not yet come. In nature, not everything grows at the same speed, nor blooms at the same time. Each nation has its own time beneath the sun that the Lord sends beaming down upon the earth, — the linden is just beginning to bloom when the oak has already shed its blossoms!

But does there exist such an idea as would aid the Slavic tribes to arise from their fall? Have these tribes, in their history, in their humanity, their own higher calling? Or are they fated to a subservient position, to the common service of others? Have these many stirrings, which have recently emerged amongst the Slavic tribes, everywhere at once, so to speak: in literature, in social life, politics, indeed even in the latest tempests — in the war against their oppressors, the Magyars — any meaning, any significance? Any goal, even if such were not always clearly defined? Or is this all but a vain imitation of the West? Are we witnessing the final convulsions of a moribund world on its way to disappearing, or — as our enemies like to express it — just the galvanic experiments of Slavdom? Have they any content, any vital strength, or have our tribes so submitted themselves to alien influences that they no longer know who they are, no longer recognise themselves and are no longer in a position to free themselves from the ruins in which they lie buried? It is obvious that these questions are of prime importance to the Slavs, and upon their fundamental solution depends the 'to be nor not to be' of our future life. So let us begin considering them without prejudice or preconception, and with a soul that longs for the truth!

[PART TWO: 'WEST AND EAST: A COMPARISON' IS OMITTED HERE]

3. A THREEFOLD PROGRAMME FOR THE POLITICAL LIBERATION OF THE SLAVS

Speaking of states with a federal form of government, which can only, it seems, be realised in the form of republics, here we must immediately exclude Russia and all of our tribes which are either part of her, or under her internationally recognised protection, or are to such an extent subject to her sway as to be unable politically or naturally to become disentangled from her. Such is the case of the larger part of Poland — the so-called Kingdom of Poland — the Serbian principality, all of the Slavic tribes that find themselves in Turkey, the Bulgars, and the Slavs in Bosnia, Herzegovina, Albania and Montenegro. Only a fool could believe that a republican form of government might take hold in Russia and develop there. In the case of the states in her sphere of influence, Russia will fight tooth and nail against anything she does not, nor ever could, allow within her own proper borders. If then we set aside Russia and the countries in her sphere of influence, what remains us are the Czech lands, Moravia, Lusatia, Silesia, Poznań, Slovakia, Galicja, and the Slavic tribes in Krajina, Carinthia, Styria and Istria, further: Croatia, Slovenia and Dalmatia, the so-called Militärgrenz along the southern borders of Austria and Hungary, and Serbian Vojvodina. Moreover, in each of these cases, social conditions must be taken into account, as well as these lands' mutual relations and their situation as regards other neighbouring nations.

Politically speaking, not a single one of these tribes or lands is autonomous. Thus, they must all first struggle to wrest independence for themselves, and this consideration leads us to the clear fact of their being divided within, by enemy elements, into hostile camps. This paralyses their strength. As far as their continued existence is concerned, it makes their situation a precarious one. In the Czech lands there are three million Czechs to over one million Germans. In Moravia, there are more than two million Slavs and somewhat over 500,000 Germans. In both parts of Lusatia there are only 142,000 citizens of Slavic ethnicity; all the rest have been germanised. In both Prussian and Austrian Silesia there are 2,500,000 citizens, of whom 1,500,000 are Slavs. Among a million Slavs in Poznań there reside many Germans and Jews. Slovakia is, as a whole, homogeneous, although that unity is weakened by the external influence of Magyars, and many renegade Slavs who have become magyarised. The Slavic population of Galicja consists of approximately five and one half million citizens divided into two inimical factions of Ruthenes and Poles.[141] Now, following the late catastrophe in that province, there exists absolutely no chance of their merging together. Besides that, Galicja has lately become inundated with many Germans, as it had been earlier by the Jews, and thus Slavic activity is almost completely paralysed.

The Slavic tribes in Krajina, Carinthia, Styria and Istria, consisting of more than a million citizens, are spread far and wide and mixed in among

---

[141] Galicia, or Halicz, was that part of Poland that fell to Austria during the partitions. Stretching from areas neighbouring Moravia and Slovakia in the west into a large portion of today's Ukraine, the major cities were Lwów and Kraków. The relationship between Poles and Ukrainians has always been a complicated one, exacerbated in the XIX century by the Polish nobility's often harsh treatment of peasants, many of whom were Ruthenes (Ukrainians) in eastern Galicia. Here, Štúr may be referring to the so-called *Rabacja* or 'Galician Slaughter' of 1846, a bloody peasant uprising against the (mainly Polish) aristocracy, or the demands of Ukrainian representatives to the Slavic Congress in 1848 for the ethnic division of Galicia — something diametrically opposed to what the Pan-Slavs were trying to achieve — or both. These events were fresh in the minds of all in 1853, when *Slavdom and the World of the Future* was first published.

Germans and Italians. The number of Slavic citizens of Croatia and Slovenia does not extend to more than a million, and the Slavs who dwell in the cities, especially, are subjected to German and Magyar influences. Amongst its 300,000 inhabitants, Dalmatia counts many Italians, especially in the cities, and there are many Germans and Romanians among the 1,000,000 inhabitants of the Militärgrenz. In Serbian Vojvodina, itself a product of tender Austrian care and the ideal of equal rights before the law, this latter principle resulted in an influx of Germans as well as Magyars and Romanians. While we are speaking of this, we must not overlook the fact that the largest cities of these aforementioned lands, in which the strengths of civic consciousness ought to be concentrated, are in the main populated by foreigners, even if it be true that this is not entirely the case everywhere. Here above all we are speaking of Moravia, the largest cities of which — Olomouc and Brno — are almost entirely German. Further, we have in mind Lusatia and Silesia, where the cities are entirely inhabited by Germans, and then Carinthia, Styria and Istria, as mentioned above, as well as Dalmatia and Prague — the main city of the Czech regions — all of which are thickly populated by Germans. In the capital of Poznań their number grows daily, due to the efforts of the Prussian government, and German levels are fast-fixed as well in the cities of Slovakia, as in those of Galicja, Krajina, Croatia, Slovenia and Vojvodina.

These foreign hosts completely retard the development of our national life and activity, not only through a conscious opposition to our efforts, but also passively — something that we sense the more keenly, the greater are their attempts at withholding from us the material resources accumulated in our lands by the aliens. During the revolution, the Germans in the Czech lands made a pretext of wishing to associate themselves with Frankfurt. This kept the Prague Germans on a short leash for a tiny spell during the June uprising,[142] but they contributed nothing to that senseless and unnecessary rising and, wherever and whenever they could, they came out against it. Germans from Moravia, Silesia, Krajina, Carinthia, Styria and even some from the Czech regions sent representatives to the Frankfurt Parliament in an attempt to set our tribes beneath German rule. The Moravian and Silesian Germans persecuted all and sundry, whomever sympathised with the Slavic idea. The Lusatian Sorbs have already capitulated entirely to the Germans; the Germans in Poznań strove to undermine all Polish movements there, maltreating and even martyring the Poles they took into captivity. In Galicja, the Germans incited the Ruthenes against the Poles who had risen

---

[142] Of 1848, with which the Slavic Congress in Prague came to an end.

up,[143] provoking the common people against the nobility, and giving rise in this way to a horrendous bloodletting. In Slovenia and Vojvodina, the Germans held with the Magyars. They did the same in Slovakia during the late uprisings there, and in Croatia held the Slavs in a lethargic inertia, while in Dalmatia the Italians fought tenaciously against the accession of the region to Croatia. What is the reason for this, that the latest stirrings in these lands took such an irregular course? Why did they meet with such a sad end, such little success? Part of the blame must be ascribed to the immaturity of our tribes, but most of it must be lain at the feet of the foreigners, particularly the Germans, who erode our national existence.

In the same way we cannot overlook the confessional differences that exist amongst the above-mentioned Slavic tribes. Although our tribes, overall, ascribe to Catholicism, Protestantism is also represented in some of them, and there are many adherents to the Orthodox Church as well. This variety acts as a brake, and, to a large extent, is a cause of dissension among individual tribes. In the Czech lands, it is as if the old Hussite movement were spreading again under the guise of Protestantism. Although up till now it has not acted as a retarding factor on Czech national aspirations, in Slovakia, the purblind Catholic masses have allowed themselves to be fanaticised and set up by Magyar agitators against the Slovak national movement, which has spread amongst the Protestants. As for the Ruthenes, even though they acceded to the Union,[144] they are not pure Catholics, and this seemingly unimportant ecclesiastical variance also played its role in the hostility of the Ruthenes toward the Poles and the horrific scenes that unfolded in recent days. Amongst the Serbs, where confessional differences play an important societal role, all of the Bunjevci or Šokci — that is to say, Catholic Serbs — are seen as renegades and apostates. In the most recent Serbian uprisings, which were the most powerful among all the Slavic stirrings, we witnessed how the Catholic Serbs, as auxiliaries of the Magyars, either fought actively against their own people, or looked upon the national uprising with passivity.

Besides this, one has to take into account the fact that the level of spiritual development is not the same across all the tribes, and that some of them are

---

[143] The afore-mentioned *Rabacja*, which many suggest was fomented by the Austrian authorities in order to put down a conspiracy of Polish nobles, centred in Kraków.

[144] The Union of Brześć (1595) united Orthodox dioceses in Poland with the Roman Catholic Church. While retaining their own liturgical traditions, including the right of priests to marry, the *Unici* or "Uniates" recognise the supremacy of the Pope. The church exists to this day and is often referred to as the "Greek Catholic Church." It remains a bone of contention in Ukraine and Russia.

not capable of developing into such a federal political constellation as we describe; these have more vital matters to deal with, such as mere survival.

Among the stirrings of our tribes, the national movement of the Czechs has been the most successful. Yet the Czech nobility — with a few praiseworthy exceptions — has displayed an unfriendly attitude toward the life of the nation, having succumbed to alien influences and become an aristocracy in the western sense of the word. Betraying our family of nations, they have degenerated into a low, extreme sort of egoism despised by the people. What have they done lately for the cause of their nation? Whereas the Magyar nobility endured sacrifices on behalf of theirs, the Czech aristocracy, wealthy enough and not lacking in western education, felt that it was enough to toss some alms the nation's way and the matter would be settled.

In Poznań, great spiritual activity was developing, and at quite a pace, before the attempted uprising. But now after its suppression, and the further setbacks of the movement, it seems as if everything had fallen into a coma. The germanisation of the province proceeds by leaps and bounds as the Prussian government floods the region with German officials and colonists. Germans wishing to settle there receive financial support from the government, and the province is being germanised through the instrument of a citizen's militia as well as quite all of the resources at the government's disposal.

After the bloodshed in Galicja, any sort of national activity there has been undermined (which activity, it is true, never blossomed before, God only knows why). Because of the rivalry between the two hostile tribes, the Austrian régime, its bureaucracy and police, neither the Ruthenes nor the Poles will achieve anything worthy of mention. The Ruthenes are hampered by the spirit of Austrian bureaucracy, and the Poles by their recklessness and their separatist tendencies. One might say, in general, that the outlook presented by this land is pathetic indeed.

Because of obscurantist Catholicism, the Slavic element in Croatia has sunk into an apathetic languidness. Profoundly demoralised, it proceeds no further than mere initial attempts, is successful at nothing, and, such being the case, even the outstanding men of the nation flag in spirit. In the end, along with all the rest, they sink into the morass of despair, apathy, and surrender themselves to the prosaic joys of everyday life. Even though demonstrations are daily occurrences there, as well as torchlight parades and balls, and societies are founded and buildings purchased for the purposes of the nation, there's nothing serious about it all. Slavonia has even a much slighter significance than her sister-region Croatia. There is no tribe there to assume leadership over the others, and for that reason there is no decided direction or effort — one shuffles about aimlessly, in place, without any display of vigour.

In the borderlands of the Militärgrenze, Austrian military discipline and order will allow for no spiritual activity. Strength, courage and a spirit of self-sacrifice are not lacking there, for sure, but the Austrian government, through its educational system, its bureaucracy, and the paternalistic German establishment, sees to it that this might is kept well under control.

Just as in the borderlands, there are powerful and capable Serbs in Vojvodina. But the individual men that this nation has produced are unable to disentangle themselves from the swaddling clothes of selfish and partisan interests. Although they have some sort of a grasp of universal goals concerning their society as a whole, up until the present moment they have lacked the strength needed to boldly realise them.

Slovakia is in a very bad way indeed. As a result of their magyarisation, the Slovak nobles have turned their back on their own nation, and furiously combat any sort of expression of national aspiration, committing crime after crime upon their own people. In the tribe itself, there is freshness enough; its friends are talented and capable; what is lacking is resources, and that is the case everywhere. Moravia is even worse off. There, the nation is restrained from developing by an extreme form of Catholicism and the aliens who have settled in the cities. Behind Moravia hobbles Dalmatia as far as national stirrings go. There, Italian influences dominate and, because of its cities, the little country is in tow to Italy. Because of German sway in Silesia, national activity there is at its last gasp. Things are no better in Krajina, Carinthia, Styria or Istria, where there is but a handful of Slavs (although they are not lacking in zeal, firmness and talent) surrounded by Germans, who are decaying them from within. The few Slavs in Lusatia are abandoned to an insignificant literary dilettantism, which is praiseworthy, but all the same will be unable to produce anything grand until the sun of Slavdom bursts forth at morning.

In the majority of the above-mentioned tribes, aspirations as yet are focussed on the purely national question, because what our tribes need above all is security for their existence, although in some of these countries — particularly in those that border upon the West, concretely: the Czech lands, these efforts take on a political colouration. This results in the creation of parties. There can be no mention of real need here; the parties arise out of haste, braggadocio and a race to imitate the West, the constitutions and constitutional escapades of which are so pleasing to the Czechs. In this way the words 'constitution' and 'reaction' have become slogans of the day, which the nimble-witted and giddy Havlíček has begun to spread. In the Czech lands, radicalism as well as republicanism, and even communism, have quickly found adherents; some broadcast these western ideas, while others repeat them like parrots without even comprehending an iota of their meaning. In this way, the Czech lands grow more and more alienated from us through Western ideas (in which Rieger abides and with which Havlíček seeks to make a career for himself), growing distant from Slavdom and hampering our development. This is how older, wise, serious and experienced leaders of a purely national inclination lose their significance, abandoned by the masses in their rising, as they set out on the path of their own impulses, or gather round some irresponsible leaders. To speak frankly, we would expect some more prudence and tact from the Czechs. Their well-balanced character had permitted us to hope for such, until the events of these latter days, which have brought us disappointment. And in this their claim to hegemony over the rest of the Slavic tribes falls away. In Poznań and Galicja the so-called aristocrats and democrats are fighting in turn, which only unnecessarily increases the misfortune of the Poles. Elsewhere, fortunately, these western products have not penetrated, and it seems that there they would find no fertile ground.

Common, successful action in the reciprocal relations of these lands and tribes is met with insurmountable obstacles. The first of these is the very separation of the individual tribes, each of which fosters its own dialect and its own literature. The tribes we find in this complex of countries are the following: Poles in Poznań, Silesia and Galicja, Sorbs[145] in Lusatia, Czechs in Moravia and Bohemia, Slovaks in Slovakia, Ruthenes in Galicja and Hungary, Slovenes in Krajina, Carinthia, Styria and Istria, Croats in Croatia, Slavonia, Dalmatia and the Miltärgrenze, southern Serbs in Vojvodina, Slavonia, the Militärgrenze and in Dalmatia. Thus, there exist eight tribes and myriad dialects and literatures. While some scholars seek to derive these dialects — with the exception of the Russian[146] — from three fundamental

---

[145] Perhaps in an effort to underscore the ethnic unity of the Slavs, Štúr uses the term 'western Serbs' here, as he uses 'southern Serbs' later on to speak of the Serbs proper. He was not the only one to do so; until very recently, the Slavs inhabiting Lusatia were spoken of as 'Lusatian Serbs,' although the term 'Sorbs' has now come into general use.

[146] It is possible that Štúr means Ukrainian here, the language of the Ruthenes. He would not be far wrong; all of the other languages (or 'dialects' as he would put it) belong either to the West Slavic or South Slavic subgroups; Ukrainian, like Russian and Belorussian, belong to the East Slavic tongues. It is the only such language in former Austria-Hungary.

ones, this does nothing to correct the bad present situation; it does not take into account the development of particular tribes and progressively paves the way to even greater misfortune. For according to this way of thinking, the present state of our tribes can only be a temporary one. And if these tribes were to merge into some larger groups, some would still stubbornly stand by their particularism and be even more reluctant to join together in one whole. A perfect example of this is provided by the Poles, who, second only to Russia, constitute the mightiest Slavic tribe and possess — again excepting Russia — the richest literature and history. And yet, more than any other tribe, they are resistant to the great goal of Slavic unity and cleave to the West. Now, to keep the whole, and not the individual, before one's eyes, to come out against a particularism that seeks to expand itself at the expense of the whole — this is the most sacred duty of each and every Slav. Because each individual gains life through the agency of the whole, and thanks to it enters upon the happier future, so yearned after through long centuries.

It's only natural that a perfect conformity among eight tribes and their literatures cannot be accomplished, and thus it's no wonder that despite all our praiseworthy efforts, the unity we aim at has not yet met with much success, nor, as things stand today, does that desirable unity appear to be within reach. The chances for this happening will be all the less, the more that the individual tribes will be led by their own unique historical precedences, intent upon their present development, which lead to a separate existence; the more that they will strive to break loose from the whole, while others, more conscious of their Slavic nature, even if weaker they are as tribes, resist this tendency. As we see it, this sort of antagonism is at the core of the strife between the Serbs and Croats, or rather the so-called Illyrians, between the Ruthenes and the Poles, and in the matter of language and literature, between the Czechs and the Slovaks. The experiences gained in the school of life teaches us that such separatist ambitions are deserving of condemnation, and that all protests against them are to be applauded. A further circumstance that occasions difficulty in reciprocal accord and societal progress is presented by the geographical situations of the various tribes and the distance between them. Poznań lies far away from Bohemia and Moravia, and even farther from the lands inhabited by the Slovaks and Ruthenes, to say nothing of the Serbs and Croats. Even the Czechs are far distant from the lands of the Ruthenes, and even farther from the southern Slavs. Between them, a German and Magyar wedge has been driven. Have these tribes enough strength, then, to overcome these accumulated difficulties? Hardly. How might they join together in a federation if these obstacles are not first removed?

Nor dare we overlook the religious divisions, which constitute an abyss between individual tribes. We have spoken of these divisions in reference to the Ruthenes and Poles — they are even more striking in connection with the Serbs and Croats. The former cling tightly to the Orthodox Church, while the latter are strict Catholics. During the last uprisings, the Croats did not keep their pledged word to the Serbs. They supported them only tepidly and weakly; they even stood in their way on account of petty differences. The scandals occasioned by Bishop Haulik, the Catholic bishop of Zagreb, that faithful servant of Catholic Austria, are well known to all. How could he allow himself to act in such a way toward a sincerely Slavic-minded tribe, favourably disposed toward its brethren? Even the clear-thinking, though weak, Ban Jelačić but folded his hands upon his heart, remaining silent, and doing practically nothing when he ought to have supported the Serbs with all the means at his disposal. The result of such indolence and equivocation was, on the part of the Croats, the friction that arose between two fraternal tribes, by which Vojvodina grew even more distant from Banovina, which, by the way, was of no profit to Slavdom at all.

The external conditions of these tribes entirely prevent the practical realisation of a federation, even though Austria would not constitute any particular obstacle to this, as she is old and weak and merely awaits future developments in trepidation. The real obstacles are, on the one side, the Germans, on the other the Italians, with the Magyars in the centre. Can the federalists be so absolutely naive as to imagine that all of these nations will just look on calmly, awaiting the completion of their theoretical construction? In the meantime, will the Germans not fall upon the Slavs in Bohemia, Moravia, Krajina, Carinthia, Styria and Istria, those Germans belonging to the German Confederation? Will they not fall upon Poznań, too, while they're at it? Will the Magyars not attack Slovakia, Croatia, Slavonia and isolated Vojvodina? Will the Italians not lay claim to Dalmatia and the rest of the coast? Are these tribes strong enough to hurl such claims crashing to the ground? How large are they, number-wise? They are not more than nineteen million altogether. Yet in their fragmentation, can they imagine that they will be strong enough to affirm and defend their independence against German, Magyar and Italian? And if they are not strong enough to assert themselves and win their liberty, what then will remain of the idea of a federation of their states? Absolutely nothing, except a theory rattling around some learned heads. Did these aforementioned nations not keep a firm grip on the Slavic lands during the recent disturbances, or, at least, did they not attempt to conquer them? If such was not the case, why did these lands begin to cling frantically to Austria as if to a life preserver in a tempest at sea? Let us assume that these tribes, by some miracle, actually succeeded in overcoming all of the above-cited difficulties. How then would Russia react to the appearance of a federation of Slavic states? Above all, out of principle, and with all her might, she would fight against the rise of such an independent Slavic state; she would not allow it to happen, for one simple reason: every non-Russian Slavic state would inevitably set itself up in opposition to her, and would either seek to influence her, in principle, or would have to fight against her, with the aid of western ideas and western nations. Russia is well aware of this. Only thus can we explain why she has up till now so little supported Slavic tendencies. It is quite possible that this is also the reason behind her approval of the demands of the old Hungarian conservatives:[147] so that she might in this way prevent the theoretical emergence of a so-called Austro-Slavic state. And Russia is powerful; immensely powerful, and she has, along with her power, a mission and a right to pulverise all separatist Slavic tendencies and claim for herself hegemony over the entire family of Slavic nations.

But if you all wish to liberate us from our yoke and establish states, where is your strength, your indomitable will, your creative power? Where is your centre of operations, where is the capital necessary for the foundation and maintenance of your state? And finally, where is the unbreakable unity of the people's will? With a heart filled with pain, we must openly confess that our might has been broken by foreign domination. With the sweat of our brow and our very lives we nourish and maintain the foreigners who yield us but meagre means for our own development, if they don't deny us them entirely. Our lands are nothing more than the ruins of a nation, which can be revived into a unified whole only by a homogeneous, benign, energetic force. We may be able to clear away putrefaction here and there, but we are simply not capable of reviving and maintaining ourselves by our own strength. Away then with utopias, and let us set ourselves rather to work with knowledge of the conditions and course of history. The task before our tribes is not the establishment of states, but unwavering, continuous laying of the groundwork for the creation of a great work, the vivification and preparation of that sort of national life, which will enkindle the inspiration and consciousness of all for the advent of the great day of Slavdom, firing them to tasks such as will be needed for the attainment of our long-awaited salvation. And

---

[147] Acceding to their pleas for military aid against the rebellious masses during the Spring of the Peoples.

so, let not a single day pass without you, O Slavs, sons of the Slavic tribes, accomplishing some good work on behalf of your nation. Defend her right, dedicate yourself to her service and never become the servants of her alien masters. For too long now, your tribes have lived in bondage; for far too long they have dragged along the triumphant chariots of foreigners, bearing their invective and insult in return.

The idea of creating a federation of states is rooted in the fact that the aforementioned lands once did constitute politically autonomous wholes, something of which the majority of them may justly brag. But such a principle is now but a dream. Nothing in history repeats itself in the same guise. The world has changed completely since those days; nations progressively and continually join together into larger groupings and the Slavic tribes have already shown what they can effect in the world when they are isolated one from another. In our consideration of this affair we have arrived at the conviction that federal states fall apart and nothing remains of them because the Slavic tribes are weak in the number of their citizens; they are surrounded by foreign elements who also cause them to decompose from within, and in the main, they are under the control of foreign metropolises, which strip them of the resources indispensable to their development. These tribes are often backward, in many things internally divided, and separated from one another by great distances, their strength broken by foreign might. In their separatism, which is moreover threatened by both foreigner and Russian, it is simply impossible for them to capably establish their own states. At the very least, no reasonable man can believe it possible.

As we have noted above, it would be nonsense to assume that Russia would accede to such a union. Now, we wish to briefly touch upon the question of such a general project of a federation of the Slavic states as the Russians Pestel, Muraviev, Ryleyev, Bestuzhev, Kakhovsky and others attempted to realise. The unsettled post-Napoleonic period is what influenced their plans. That it was nothing more than a chimera is best proven by the disorder which followed the uprising[148] provoked by this plan. The uprising was quashed in but a few hours. The units that took part in it only did so after having been convinced by their officers' fabricated report of Constantine's forced abdication. But following the energetic initiative of the Tsar, they stood down immediately, and even their leaders weren't completely aware of the course and range of the rebellion. And thus was brought to an end something which could not be realised, at the cost of the lives of such

---

[148] That of the Decembrists.

men whose bravery, sang-froid and strength might serve us for an example, and who deserved a better fate. Such men could only have arisen from the Russian tribe! To establish republics in these areas, considering the natural traits of our tribes, would be tantamount to total anarchy and a complete overthrow of all order.

The second version, according to which the Slavs are to become independent, is based on the idea that Austria is to become the centre of all the southern and western tribes, by virtue of which they are to have a fundamental influence on her continued existence. Before we even begin, we must confess that this theory is even more nonsensical and worse than the first, since it would set our tribes on an inadequate, and what is more, exhausted and unsound base. By having our tribes supported by something 'positive,'[149] it covers them in apparent success. And yet the efforts and the strength of the tribes are directed in such a way that will hitch them to an idea that will wear them down. Thus, they will never become capable of achieving their goal, but will fall into a lethargic state. Let us examine the matter closely! The task of Austria, or the Eastern March, which originally was the easternmost German outpost of the Carolinian Reich, was the germanisation of Slavdom. Throughout all of her existence, Austria has conscientiously fulfilled that calling, and so she shall, until her last breath. She arose from German soil, was founded by Germans, and the function, with which she was entrusted answered the interests of the Germans. She rested upon a German ruling dynasty that always thought in German categories, and although her positive strength did not flow from the German Reich, its significance did, as well as its moral support. Austria lives upon German historical reminiscences and, due to the fact that it has already fulfilled the larger part of its calling, it cannot give over its Germanness without giving over its very essence. To exist and remain German, or to cast away its Germanness and cease to exist, means one and the same thing for Austria. Has Austria indeed not expended all her efforts to broaden the reach of the German spirit in all of the lands subject to her influence? Has she not, I say, driven all of the nations whom she has attached to herself into the German sheep-fold? What has she effected in Krajina, Carinthia, Kärnten, Styria and Istria, if not indeed the complete germanisation of all the Slavic tribes found there, breaking them down through the introduction of the German element? What has she accomplished in Bohemia, Moravia, Silesia — especially in Bohemia — with unheard-of cru-

---

[149] I.e. Austria, or the Habsburgs, — an existing and thus 'positive' nucleus around which to develop Slavic autonomy, rather than creating a new Slavic federation *ex nihilo*, as it were.

elty? And is she not doing the same thing today in Galicia? Has the Austrian bureaucracy in that land not unleashed the cruelest oppression upon the citizenry there, opening the country, subsequently, to foreigners on all sides? At whose encouragement, and under whose protection, did foreign hosts settle all of the Austrian lands? Does Austria not support today, as she once did, the *Drang nach Osten*? Whose idea is it today to send colonists into Slavonia, Vojvodina, Banat, etc.? And what is the point of all this? Is it not that they may thus 'educate the rough nations in the ways of German customs and culture?' With Slavic forces — Serbs, Croats, Czechs and others, but with Russians above all — the Austrians recently crushed the Magyars, Italians, and even their own Germans.[150] Thanks to the influence of the Slavs they were compelled to declare the equality of all the nations before the law, and equality in questions touching upon the use of languages. And where did that equality, promised so many hundreds of times, lead? To the self-serving German bosom, because German was declared the administrative language everywhere that such a statute did not yet exist, and where it did, they left it so. In the higher schools, German became a compulsory subject for students of all nations, and even where, from time to time, instruction in the local language was permitted by way of exception in this subject or that, it was only allowed so that the nation in question would not cause a fuss. According to the regulations, a knowledge of German is required of all state functionaries — down to the lowest night watchman on the village roads. And still Austria was not satisfied with this. Her present guardians and architects — Schwarzenberg and Bach — have decided to formally subordinate us to German law, in order to get the nations completely under their control, associating the entirety of Austria with the German Confederation. They determined to herd into the German pincers all of the Slavic, Magyar, and Italian national groups without consulting their will in the slightest, or their historical and national circumstances, or their deserts — particularly the merits of the Italians. And all of this in the name of widely-proclaimed equal rights and benevolence toward all nations! Woe to you, Slavs, woe to thee, Slavic Austria! Can there be found anyone among you still so daft, so blind, after all of our historical experience with Austria, and after the obvious proofs of our own day and age, after so many cruel disappointments, who still believes in a Slavic Austria, or an Austria of equal rights for all? On what

---

[150] A reference to the putting down of the revolts in the 1848 Spring of the Peoples. The Russians aided the Austrians in dealing with the nationalist rebels in Hungary, which most concerns Štúr the Slovak.

foundations can a Slavic life be built, if we are to have Austria as our support? Anyone with eyes to see, anyone who wishes to see clearly, will make it out as if it were resting on the palm of his hand.

Since the foundation is so powdery and rotten, it will not bear the weight of any new structure. Here lies the non-productivity, indeed the danger, of all attempts at transforming Austria into a Slavic empire. Austria's historical mission was to unite into one, greater — Central European — state all the tribes and nations separated from their previous wholes, and to create from these torn-away parts one wide-spreading new whole, in which the individual nations, after the removal of all earlier frictions and quarrels, would develop peacefully alongside one another, able to successfully repulse the barbarian incursions of the Turks. But circumstances changed with time; Austria lost her calling, having played her role to the end, for today hardly anyone in Europe fears the Turks. Another power — Slavic, moreover — has deprived the Ottoman Empire of its military hankerings and each day keeps it under close observation, to see if the time has not yet arrived for a Caesarian section.

The nations grouped with Austria, the Slavs above all, have awakened to a spiritual life, and have begun to sense an ineffable desire for expansion. That said, they feel no need for anyone to keep leading them along, like a dog on a leash; they wish to act, independently and in their own name. This is the reason why they are constantly ready to break away from Austria and join up with their national group. The Germans in Austria feel a kinship with Germany and look toward Frankfurt. The Italians are filled with yearning to belong to a united Italy. Romanians turn their gaze toward Romania; the Magyars feel strong enough to constitute an independent state by themselves, and the Slavs wish to join in spirit with Russia, the only independent, organised Slavic state, and their global representative. We may now state this openly: that following our most recent negative experiences, the harsh disappointments of these latter days, our hearts have opened wide to Russia.

What then will remain of Austria? Neither beautiful Vienna, nor its once obedient nation, well-trained in dressage. Everything is in a state of total decomposition. And since there is no life in decay, even that corpse which is Austria must inevitably succumb, after a short time, to the universal fate of all beings and states deprived of their spirit and reason to be. The majority of the nations in Austria are turning away from that state, and although during the latest revolutionary stirrings nearly all of the Slavic nations stood at Austria's side, she was not able to face the growing storm on her own. She had to appeal to foreigners for rescue, and only thus was she able to survive those difficult times. It is as clear as day that if the majority of her nations, the Slavs among them, were to turn against her, it would no longer be possible for her to resist them, and Austria would disappear from the face of the earth. Then no power on earth would be capable, however mighty it be, of gluing back together the parts of Austria dismembered. They would no longer belong together, and no spirit of life could then be breathed into her nostrils. Whatever has run through the course of its life and lost its significance and meaning — and such is the case of Austria — must vanish. Austria lost her own independence during the late unrest, being unable to help herself and, of necessity, having to turn to others to beg their aid. Now it is impossible for her to evade Russian influence, and if similar, if not (what is probable) still greater, aftershocks were to occur, Austria would most definitely lose her life in them, that is, the apparent life she currently leads. What sort of 'first-class power' or 'first-class state' is it, which can't even come to terms with its own subjects? Is it capable of acting freely, externally and within? All signs point to the fact that the Slavic tribes will no longer aid Austria; most likely, they will do precisely the opposite. For certainly they would be out of their senses if, in aiding Austria, they were to forge their own fetters with their own hands, and hurl themselves once more into bondage — voluntarily submitting themselves to germanisation and permitting themselves to be locked in a German dungeon, maintaining that which cannot be preserved, and calling down upon their own heads the opprobrium of all nations on account of those 'benefits' and 'advantages.' For them, to support the Austrians presents itself as a danger, and signifies their own ignominy. While we are here, we would draw the reader's attention to the fact that following each unsuccessful attempt of that sort, their motive strength has grown weak, unable to rouse them, and again and again they have fallen into apathy. With great sadness, the friend of the Slavs witnesses how the spirit of the Slavic tribes falls into helpless impotence upon such failures as it has suffered in Austria these days.

Should these tribes refuse to aid Austria, or should they even turn against her — and nothing other that that can be expected of them — it would be extremely difficult, if not impossible, for Austria to turn to Russia for help. Because, before the face of its own people, the Russian government will neither wish, nor be in a position to, take upon itself the heavy moral responsibility resulting from a support of Germans turning against kindred Slavic tribes.

As is well known, the Russians were not merely actuated by a desire to help Austria during the recent troubles, but also came to the aid of their brothers, the Slavs, against their Magyar oppressors. But when at length, as the events unfolded, they came to know Austrian perfidy — that all the Austrians were concerned with was themselves, and how the Austrians looked down upon them with barely-concealed contempt, as nothing but auxiliary cannon-fodder, the Russians began to feel some sympathy for the Magyars, as people oppressed by the Austrians. And so they withdrew, with barely suppressed distaste, their hatred of Germans doubled.

By all accounts, after the manner in which Austria led them by the nose and deeply disappointed their expectations, the Slavic tribes have become entirely alienated from that country. After their occupation and subsequent ill-treatment, a savage hatred amongst other nations was aroused by Austria on account of the countless solemn vows she proclaimed, which later were never fulfilled. Besides this, another aggravating circumstance was the increase of existing taxes, and the introduction of new, burdensome ones, collected with no respect for the private property of individuals. And yet Austria's national debt continues steadily to rise, with quarterly increases, in the face of a lack of government credit — all these deficits despite the swelling taxes.

Spies, and an army of police agents both public and secret, decimate the nations, whose life is burdened by a hated bureaucracy and the policy of germanisation. This keeps them at a constant boil and in lasting protest, if silent, against Austria.

The end can easily be foretold. Austria no longer has a nation of its own. They are neither Germans nor Italians nor Magyars nor Poles; neither the rest of the Slavs, nor the Romanians constitute such a nation. Amongst these peoples there is not a single caste sympathetic to her. With the exception of some Magyar, Italian, Austrian and particularly Czech nobles, the Italian, Magyar and Polish nobility are exceptionally antipathetic to her. The same is true of the clergy, whether Catholic, Greek, or Protestant — with the exception of the loyal Catholic bishops — although even these participated in the recent stirrings against Austria. The Catholic clergy for this reason — that they would abolish the rule of celibacy and do not wish to submit to the strict discipline of the bishops, but at the same time do not expect any change to their sorry position under the Austrian régime. The bourgeois of the cities, like the common people, are just as adversely disposed toward Austria. This is partially from political reasons and on account of taxes, but also because of their convictions. Where then can we find support for this Austria of today, which once in the bliss of beery intoxication the Austrians, with good cheer, were wont to call the 'heavenly empire'? There is no such thing upon the earth any more. Austria is nothing but a geographical term. Its soul has ascended into that heavenly empire, leaving behind a galvanised corpse, which will shatter into small pieces at the first strong blow. The saddest thing in all of Austria is the fact that there will be no one, I reckon, who will shed a single tear at her graveside.

Could a country such as Austria have found itself on the very edge of the abyss after only a half year of war, if it had within itself the merest spark of vital strength? Just what Austria's attitude to its nations is can be seen from the fact that she holds the majority of them — as one might say — in a continual state of occupation — which is tantamount to her considering 'her nations' as her mortal enemies. Everything said or promised by the government is received by the nations, quite simply, as empty words. Anyone who still tries to believe in such things is either laughed to scorn, or suspected of being a 'loyalist' — in other words, an agent in the government's pay. So far has Austria progressed with her security and political faith! The inertia of Austrian life can best be seen by a consideration of her own servants — those in the military and those in the civil administration. After all these many events and troubles, the good old military convictions have given place to new notions; the loyal officers indeed try to inspire one another reciprocally by frequently invoking the Emperor, but it is obvious by looking at them that they are forcing themselves to the effort, which actually leaves them cold. It is a beautiful thing to honour, and to have always before one's eyes, Him who evokes the idea of the whole. But such a person must at the same time truly represent that whole. The Emperor must figure forth the Empire — its magnificent mission, its grandeur and power, which elevates each and every individual subject. And yet Austria represents nothing of the sort. Behind it stand at most: bayonets, a few constables, the revenue office and police stool pigeons. Nor must it be forgotten that a sizeable contingent of soldiers in the revolutionary troops was made up of those who had first served beneath the government's colours.

Turning to Austrian officials, we must say that they have a peculiar trait: they work, and yet despite that they get nothing done, or they do everything wrong way round. This is because they confine themselves to working only on that which is unavoidable. They labour without enthusiasm, except when they are to arouse unfavourable attitudes toward the government among the people by the measures they introduce. This is the reason why so many Austrian civil servants resign from their positions, and why there are so few 'loyalists' among them.

The government gropes about as if in the dark: Schwarzenberg along with Bach, an aristocrat to the very marrow of his bones with a man of the barricades, who once rushed the palace on a charger, and now, with his lack of principles, plays lackey to Schwarzenberg, who thinks himself to be Cardinal Richelieu, or Metternich. Bach makes believe that he's Colbert, at least, and meanwhile all government policy, foreign and domestic, is worth nothing, mediocre. In foreign policy Austria must obey the will of others, while at home, all of her attempts at organisation and order come to shipwreck, and this despite all regulatory and organisational projects. Old and new, regulation and abrogation, fresh provisions and their abolition — everything is at cross purposes here, where a horrid chaos reigns. Whoever thinks that the civil service is truly a governmental thing would be gravely mistaken — *non lucus a lucendo* — it's just the opposite: different cliques are formed about the ministries: on the one side we have the ladies of the court, on the other the base aristocratic coterie, who, as soon as they sniffed danger in the air, crawled off to whatever spa was within reach — and next time they'll crawl right back. And then the Council of State with its special powers. Who knows who's in charge there!

It seems as if Europe does not recognise the necessity of Austria even existing. During the recent uprisings, England left Austria high and dry; indeed, she even supported the rebels. Carefree France, apparently, didn't bother her head overmuch wondering whether Austria would continue to exist or not. Germany was delighted at the danger facing Austria, while Prussia washed her hands of it all. And now, the Russians too are deeply insulted and filled with a profound hatred of Austria and her 'white caftans.' *Ja nie tvoj bruder*,[151] one Russian officer replied to a certain Austrian military chief, when parting from him in Lwów, at the latter's extending his hand and calling him 'brother.' Perhaps in this we can see the final farewell of the Russians to the Austrians. With their well-known gratitude, perhaps the Austrians will be able to sidle up to a few Serbs — although even here that's far from certain — or Czechs, or Romanians, or Slovaks — but the Russians, they know how to give them what for!

With their aristocracy and Catholicism, the main supports of Austria, they won't get far either. Neither the one nor the other has much of a future, as the nations have ceased believing in them. Nor are the clients of Austria worth much — let the dead bury their own dead.[152]

The idea of making Austria over into a foundation for the Slavic tribes of Central Europe was born in the heads of the Czechs. It is a product of

---

[151] Russian and German: 'I am not your brother.'
[152] Matthew 8:22.

that truly accomplished and sober — and yet despite it all, thoughtless and shortsighted — Czech historian Palacký, whose idea, at its creation, got into the wake of the Czech aristocracy dependent on Austria. Thus were opened to the Czechs the perspectives of gaining hegemony over the other Slavic tribes inhabiting Austria — indeed, the perspective of transforming Austria according to their conceptions. Of necessity, this denoted the relinquishing of power into their hands — hence the joy, with which they greeted this idea, all the more so since because of their Catholicism they inclined to Austria anyway. They made every effort to impose this idea upon the Slavs. Indeed, they were successful in obtaining the so-called Illyrians to their side. It is true that Illyrism proceeded from other ideas, but when it came up against the strong resistance of the Serbs, which was quite disillusioning, it lost its assertiveness amongst the Croats. Because some of the Illyrist leaders had been bribed by Metternich or otherwise 'processed,' the movement allowed itself to be coopted to the Austro-Slav project, which was lying in wait for it in the Czech lands. It was all the more easy for this ascription to the new direction to take place as there are quite a few points where the Croats line up nicely with Austria — for example, in their ossified aristocracy clinging to its privileges, and their Catholicism. In this way then did the Austro-Slav alliance come into being, supported by the aristocracy and Catholicism, to which Austria acceded in the hope that this would come in handy from time to time in support of her continued existence and the solution of her own important ontological dilemmas. The Slavs adhered to it because it enkindled their hopes of bettering their living conditions with the aid of Austria. The thing was — who would turn out to be stronger and more capable? Into his lap, naturally, would fall the fruit borne by the alliance.

When the most recent troubles began, the first opportunity to show what the alliance was capable of occurred. So the Czechs quickly summoned the Slavic Congress to Prague, about which so much had been said, which had been so often discussed. They figured that all the other Slavs would be convinced into following their lead. During the Congress the Czechs were very engaged in the promotion of their maxim, pressing it, so to speak, upon their brother tribes. Still there were many who didn't grasp the correctness of such a procedure, but they couldn't agree to the dissolving of the Congress before the bombardment of the city by Windischgrätz. Under the duress of the circumstances, they gave their agreement — almost without a word — to the Czech desiderata, and by these the majority were governed during the uprising, which broke out shortly thereafter. Everyone knows how that ended, and who it was that reaped the harvest. Hopes were dashed,

Austro-Slavic hearts broken, and the begetter of that policy, Palacký, was declared a radical by the Austrians, labelled an enemy of the government, which he more than anyone else helped out of the emergency.

Ban Jelačić, the most vigorous advocate of these plans, who had been carried onto the stage of action on people's shoulders, to the cheering of hundreds of thousands, was transformed into a feeble man, a mere shadow. What has become of your leaders, your *bans*, O Croats? What has become of your mighty military slogan, *Vivat banus cum Croatis*?[153] Your *ban* has been shrunken into an Austrian bureaucrat, who already lacks even so much vinegar as to shout down a wretched constable, for fear of endangering his cushy position. Your song has grown silent! But what's there to sing about, anyway? For you are just like all the rest, in the hands of bureaucrats and police toadies who rob you blind and eavesdrop on your every word. That's how the stab at Austro-Slav politics turned out! O, that every separatist effort in the future should meet with similar shame and punishment!

How did the Austrian government show her gratitude to the Slavic tribes? How did she respond to their efforts? How did she react to the thousands who sacrificed their lives, falling for the continued existence of Austria? By setting the yoke of a ruthless bureaucracy upon the necks of independently functioning nations. Every manifestation of their once free and unfettered life was followed by thousands of intently pricked policemen's ears. The government introduced German amongst those tribes in which that language had not been used before, and maintained it there, where they had previously imposed it by force. Their answer consisted of German bureaucracy and Magyar officials, who everywhere oppressed and crushed Slavic life. The Austrian government made a direct assault on Slavic aspirations, and because that government was in debt, impoverished, and lacking in credit, it took the nations in hand and raised taxes — the people were made to suffer on account of food taxes, a tobacco monopoly, stamp fees and so on. In the borderlands, where, according to press reports, 24,000 wives had become widows when their husbands fell as soldiers in the service of Austria — no one says a word about the orphans — the government went ahead and raised the price of salt on the poor women. Their response to the sacrifice of the Slavs — concretely, the Serbs — is, ultimately, the attempted annexation of their lands.

Austria responded to the Czech designs that saved her with the terrible verdicts handed down in Prague on those who were perhaps too light-mind-

---

[153] 'Long live the ban and the Croats, together united.'

ed, but almost exclusively young, immature boys. There's that legendary Austrian gratitude for you! Now, the Magyars had risen up in rebellion against Austria, seeking her complete overthrow, cursing her ruling dynasty and covering both it and Austria entire with shame and opprobrium, and just look! Their trials were completed nearly a year before those of the flighty youths of Prague, who were merely charged with *wanting* to do something! Yes, the Magyars were the junior partner in the association for the oppression of the Slavs, and that's the reason behind the care and charity shown them in this regard! In the Council of State it was decided that, in the future, only German and Magyar would be considered administrative tongues, on the level of diplomatic languages. All the rest of the languages — concretely, that of the Slavs — had that privilege taken away from them, although there are 16 million speakers of the Slavic tongue in Austria.

In their dealings with the Slavs, the Austrians merely sought to pull the wool over their eyes and use them as a bugbear against the Magyars. But their alliance with the Magyars did not work out, because the latter, dazzled by the possibilities of unmolested hegemony, fell upon the Austrians and brought their friendship to an end forever. It's really a shame that that nation, which from time immemorial belonged to the Slavic circle, sharing their outlook and living in good neighbourly relations with the Slavs, went so far in the blindness of their self-conceit as to turn their anger upon the Slavs! In this they displayed a total lapse of reason, not having matured to a recognition of the fact that a brighter future for them can only be achieved in common with their old neighbours! Now is there anyone among the Slavs so blind, or so blighted, as to allow himself to be deceived by the prospect of a Slavic Austria, an Austria of equal rights? It's clear to everyone what happened to the Slavic idea of equal rights in the hands of those people, but come, let them be — let them finish with shame what they began with evil intentions!

We are convinced of the fact that the very pioneers of Austo-Slavism among the Czechs: Palacký, Havlíček, and others — have now changed their tunes. Both of these men have fallen into disfavour. In Prague, Palacký, embittered, declined to sign a letter of gratitude addressed to the Austrian government, reasoning that to do such a thing would be a display of servility. He declined in his own name, and in those of like-minded people. As for Havlíček, he expressed this harshest truth brutally, and eye to eye with that evil government. Earlier on, by the way, Palacký published an academic theory of an Austrian federated state, which might extend the life of Austria for a few months more, a few years, at the outside. But Palacký's federation would have fallen to pieces very quickly, and Metternich knew exactly what he was doing when, by holding the nations on a short lead, he let them vegetate — except for the Magyars, whom he was unable to tame. Slavic Austria must be left to a few Czech aristocrats, some Czech bishops, and their venal slaves!

In particular, the Czechs have no reason to squire the Austrians. Have they really forgotten the horrible, bloody scenes that played out in the Staroměstské náměstí in Prague? Have they forgotten that, after the Battle of Bílá Hora they lost 2,400,000 of their citizens to martyrdom at the hands of the Austrians, banishment, and war itself? Do they no longer see with the eyes of the soul those horribly bloody scenes? Can they no longer hear the groans of the tortured and the exiled? Have they forgotten the words of warning enunciated by that noble old man, Kaplíř ze Sulevic, who addressed his descendants before his execution: 'Let none of you serve those good-for-nothing Austrians'? Ah no — these words are still very much alive, keenly felt by every Czech soul, in which hatred of Austria is deeply rooted. So what good then are these unnatural feelings and associations, from which sooner or later the whole nation will turn away? Not the existence, but the disappearance of Austria and Turkey, that other prison of the Slavs, is necessary for the blossoming, once and for all, of that better future, so long desired. Then Slavic life will be able to develop freely on the wide, beautiful plains stretching from the Krušné Hory to the Bosphorus:

> From Mount Ararat to the Dvina's banks,
> From the Ore Mountains to the Bering Sea,
> The Slavic chorus, linked in joyful ranks
> Shall lift their voice in song, exultantly.

Such is the conviction of the Russians. One successful blow against the Turks, and the final bell shall toll for both Slavic prisons.

Since neither the first, nor the second of these options is practical, since the Slavs cannot organise themselves into a federation of states, independently or under the aegis of Austria, there remains only the third option: that of annexation to Russia. Only this project is reasonable; only it has a future. Come, my brothers, rest your hands on your hearts and admit it: Was it not Russia, indeed, that, throughout the sad ages of our past, shone like a beacon in the dark night of our existence? Was it not Russia that enlivened our hope, sparked our courage, revivified our will to live when it was all but extinguished? Was it not Russia who came to the aid of our individual tribes, like the Serbs, for example, when they were struggling to cast the unbearable foreign yoke from their necks? Or the several fraternal tribes who were grappling in these recent days with the Magyars, the oppressors of our nation? Was it not the Russians, even if in the guise of Austrian allies? Was it not Russia who, by her strong words, expressly contributed to the recognition and internal autonomy of the Serbian principality, and who, thanks to her great influence in the world, continues to defend our other enslaved brother nations — the Bulgars, the Serbs in Bosnia, Herzegovina, Albania, and elsewhere, making lighter their heavy lot and meeting their needs in other matters, too? Is it not Russia, being a great power, who forces our enemies to make our lives at least a little more secure? Let us candidly admit it: given the boundless antipathy of the foreigners, to whom we had already once fallen subject, and who wish to continue to extend their power over us, would our national ambitions have any sense and significance, if not for the Russians? Would they have any future at all? Would the Turks, even in their weakened state, not fall once more upon the Serbs? Would not the Germans, in concert with the Magyars and Italians, crush us, due to their numerical superiority and their many other advantages, as we have already shown in our discussions of the idea of a federation of states? Would we not be left at their mercy, prey to eternal bondage and a slow death? Even there, where Russia has not actively advocated for Slavdom, she has rendered us important vital services. Thus, since our national awakening has found its *point d'appui* in Russia, who has ever stepped forth to meet our needs and continues to do so, as our very existence, all our existential questions, are bound up with her, why on earth should we defy her? Why, in our short-sightedness, should we oppose her in word and deed, up in arms, insanely full of bile?

We have shown how all of those Western ideas are worth nothing to that nation, and can merely lead it to the edge of the abyss. Why then should we introduce such ruin into our own lives? Why must we be the enemies of Russia, tossing away our one opportunity to flourish? We have learned much from the West, truly much. But we cannot begin with something that is near its own end; we must build, rather, on that which has become great and mighty. As far as the state is concerned, the West can teach us a strict subordination to the state's interests through a removal of arbitrariness and unfounded individual claims, without surrendering ourselves. We can learn from the West many practical establishments in the state. Their former self-discipline can serve us as an example; we can draw many extraordinarily beautiful things from the store of Western scientific knowledge. We must allow ourselves to be ushered into the cathedral of learning so that we might ascend the summits of human perfection, and attain the application and realisation of universal human ideals. We can also learn from the experience of the progressive decline of the West, by familiarising ourselves with its causes and learning what to avoid. We have already described these causes elsewhere.[154]

If we wish to free our life from the ruins in which it lies buried, to preserve it and develop it, above all, we must be Slavs. This is the main condition of everything, and for this reason it is necessary to discard all separatist tendencies and the particular interests of the individual tribes. We must put what is to the advantage of the living whole before that which benefits some, while not being in the interest of others; for that which benefits this whole, for which we all yearn, and in which each individual will be able to realise himself. There has been more than enough separatism, and tears on account of it, amongst ourselves, chiefly. Do we really wish to vegetate as miserably as the Germans?

It is obvious from these few sketches that the motive force, the *choragos* of our entire national chorus is Russia. So let us join ourselves to her, let us entirely enter into the spirit of our nation, submitting to the leadership of the tribal elder given us by history.

As it is, Russia already encompasses nearly six-eighths of our nation, the entire population of which has climbed to 80 million. From among 79 million Slavs, roughly 54 million live within the borders of Russia. She protects six million Slavs in the Serbian principality, as well as in Turkey, either directly, or by holding over them the protective arm of her potential might and irresistible influence. On their part, these tribes are frankly devoted to Russia, partially from gratitude, but above all on account of their common Orthodox faith,[155] while the Slavs enslaved in Turkey gaze toward Russia as their defence and only saviour. A few years ago, these tribes welcomed, with deep emotion, the Grand Duke Constantine, son of the Tsar, on his travels from Tsarigrad. The carriage that bore him was accompanied all along its route by such great, joyful crowds that the press of people practically prevented its progress. Except for a few of their compatriots educated in Paris, the Serbs — although enjoying internal independence — would never raise

---

[154] Mostly in Part II, which we omit here. Among other causes of the progressive fall of the West are a decline in morality, and an abandonment of Christianity, which Štúr blames on the influence of Marxism.

[155] Rather confusingly, Štúr uses the term 'Greek Catholic' here.

arms against Russia. Miloš, on the other hand, along with other mistakes committed during his reign, turned away from Russia to rely on England and France. This policy of his, at odds with his own nation, made him unpopular with his people, and fundamentally contributed to his fall, which removal from power was also supported by Russia.

The remainder of the Slavs belong to Austria and Prussia, with a small number of them also inhabiting Saxony. The Austrian Slavs number some 16 million, while something over two million live in Prussia. As far as the Austrians are concerned, it is important to note that a small portion of them adheres to the Orthodox Church while a further significant number of them, thanks to the wheeling and dealing and shepherding of the Austrian government, have entered into a union with the Catholic Church — although they too feel the irresistible attraction of the church of their fathers.

Following the bloodshed in Galicja, the Poles living there also feel a new attraction to Russia, despite their universal antipathy to the Russians. It is less obvious why the remainder of the Slavs are drawn to her, but this is partially from recognisable motives, such as the antipathy they feel toward Austria due to their most recent disappointments. The Orthodox Slavs are bitter about the concealed attempts of the Austrian government to annex them to the Catholic Church — all the more so at the government's retention of valuable relics which had been sent by the Russians for the restoration of Serbian churches devastated by the Magyars. Thus Austria rushes headlong to her destruction.

The Prussian Slavs are constituted by Poles living in the Poznań region and in Silesia, as well as a few Sorbs in Lusatia. The strongest of these groups are the Poles inhabiting Poznań and its environs. Even though the Poles feel a deep repugnance toward Russia, it cannot be overlooked that the Germans dealt very harshly with them during the most recent uprising there, martyring many. The liberal Frankfurt parliament expressed its desire to co-opt Poznań into a united, Greater Germany. The alliance of these Poles with foreigners availed them nothing. At length, they merely fell more deeply under the control of Prussia, or whatever other German alliance there may be, from which nothing can be looked for except certain germanisation. Now, due to their Slavic constitution, however, their resistance to the Germans exceeds their aversion to the Russians. But Prussia herself is none too steady on her own legs, and so if the Poles wish to preserve their ethnic nationality, there is but one route open to them — to annex themselves to Russia. The Poles in Silesia feel no animosity toward the Russians; indeed, they have no reason to. They have been trod underfoot by aliens for whole centuries, without any basis of hope that Poland would be renewed. Above all, they feel the need to escape the German prison as soon as possible, be the turnkeys Austrian or Prussian, exchanging it for a safe and secure Slavic sanctuary.

Thus, the clamouring of the Slavic tribes for Russia is universal. With some it arises from interior longings of the heart, while with others it issues from circumstantial inevitability, the object of which is the preservation of their life. Now, who can reject such an insistent inner voice? Individuals here and there may raise a fuss, but they will achieve nothing through their resistance, overwhelmed as they shall be by the pressure of events. The theories of the West find here no appropriate, fertile soil in which they might take root. They lead to nothing, after all, nor can they. Follow then, O brothers, that voice you hear, summoning you along the proper route to such a goal as we have never before achieved!

The only Slavs who bear malice toward Russia, and who would come out against her at the first opportunity, are the Poles. But their audacity is on the wane already too, since, after all, their efforts have not been crowned with success. In addition to this, the Poles' ethnic identity is threatened by foreign domination; yet the foreigners have deceived them in promising them aid and disappointing them, while the Poles themselves, due to their reckless and never successful actions, as well as their affiliation with foreigners, have lost much of their reputation amongst their brother tribes, as well as much of their affection. Their entire history shows them to be always attempting something, always creating something, but never being able to lead the Slavic tribes. A short overview of their history will confirm this.

After the extinction of the Past dynasty, which had produced several strong kings, their empire was considerably weakened by its division amongst several royal sons. Then, the still mighty clan of the Jagiellons ascended the throne. Yet the last few rulers of that dynasty proved too weak to keep a firm hold on the reins of the expansive and power-hungry nobles. When at last this dynasty too was extinguished, and the Poles elected a king, the imperiousness of the nobles knew no bounds. Before his coronation, the Poles deprived each newly-elected king of more and more of his rights,[156]

---

[156] While it is true that historians often point to the democratic excesses of the Polish nobility, and the lack of a strong central authority, not to say an absolutist monarch, as one of the contributing factors in the decline and eventual disappearance of Poland from the map of Europe, methinks that Štúr doth here protest too much. The first king elected after the extinction of the Jagiellonian dynasty at the death of Zygmunt II August in 1572, was the French prince Henri Valois (1551 – 1589, known in Poland as Henryk Walezy). Poland, famed during the Reformation as the 'paradisus hereticorum' on account of its broad tolerance of Protestants

and even through they were voting on behalf of the nation, they imagined that they could do whatever they pleased, as if the whole country belonged to them alone and existed only to serve their well-being. The result of it all was, giving no consideration to the state's authority, indeed even with its acquiescence, they cast the entire nation into the deepest bondage. Partaking of western mores and luxury, they imposed slavery upon the people. There was no power by which the kings might intervene and bring the nobility to heel. For this reason, Poland was cut off from the sea, which then impeded the development of her trade — and the development of her cities, which would have been the firmest support of the royal power. The ever more callous nobility now freed itself from any sort of restraint and reasonableness, and on the basis of a wrongly understood principle of equality, made it so that every nobleman must give his assent to public resolutions, and, conversely, the only way of objecting to them is by causing their complete annulment, vetoing them.

Every nobleman regarded the country as his own landed property. He acted as a steward on his own land, doing with it as he pleased. So-called *zajazdy*[157] came into fashion, and these forays were endless; the spirit of sacrifice and the eagerness to fight for one's country were drowned in luxury and hedonism; the free Cossacks, whom the noblemen had wished to enslave and expose to the mercy of the Jews, rose up against them, seceding at last from Poland and seeking the protection of Russia.

While the nation thus groaned under such a burden, Poland's neighbours consolidated their monarchies — especially Russia, where the nation was strong enough to submit to a unified statal power. The Polish state was shaken, and rotten on all hands. It wasn't difficult to find a pretext to poke

---

dissenting from the Catholic faith, sent a delegation to Paris before Henri's formal accession to the throne in order to have him swear, before the altar in Notre Dame, to uphold the Warsaw Confederation, which guaranteed freedom of religion in Poland. It was important to have the king take this oath because, as was well known, Henri was one of the motive forces behind the slaughter of French Huguenots known as the 'St Bartholomew's Day Massacre' in 1572. When the prince attempted to demur, Hetman Jan Zborowski of the Polish delegation stepped forth with the words *Si non iurabis, non regnabis!* ['If you don't so swear, you shall not rule!'] One would think that the Lutheran Štúr, who argues against religious intolerance in so many of his works, including the present one, would at least be able to appreciate this constriction of the king's 'rights.'

[157] In the old Polish Republic, the *zajazd* was an execution of a nobleman's rights by armed force — which could be seen as a strong man taking the law into his own hands, with no-one to oversee or prevent his actions. The Polish national epic, *Pan Tadeusz*, composed by Adam Mickiewicz in the early 1830s, has just such a *zajazd* as one of its leitmotifs, hence the subtitle, *Ostatni zajazd na Litwie* ['the last foray in (the Polish province of) Lithuania'].

into her business; it was even easier to strike and divide a tottering state, in which the king had no power and no one heeded his commands; where the pampered nobility had forgotten its martial mettle and was easy to procure — and where the people were sunk deep in abjection and misery. Who bears the blame, then, for the partitioning of Poland? The Poles themselves! The nation that allows its own state to fall cannot be called upon to organise other peoples. As the Slavs say, we'd be clothing ourselves in tatters indeed if we allowed the Poles to dress us. They want no part of entrusting themselves into the hands of such a hegemon. For how can they help others who are not able to help themselves, even in their time of greatest need? The repeated attempts at reuniting the country after her partitioning have all come to ruin, chiefly on account of the Poles themselves, who are divided. In some cases, it was senseless experiments and political associations established by the Poles in foreign lands that were at the bottom of it all. These were supposed to engineer a renaissance of the Polish state, and, however many such plans there were — and there were more than a few — they all evaporated thanks to the malignant Polish spirit, arbitrariness, and the division that resulted because of it. The choice of means: their enlistment in the service of foreign powers, which they sought to exploit for the reconstitution of their state, does not offer much positive testimony to their judgement. They expected much of Napoléon, who actually exploited them, imagining that they would be satisfied with a crumb of Poland.[158] When he later came to understand their makeup, he completely excluded them from his political plottings. Just what his opinion of them was can be seen from the following words, which hit the nail right on the head: 'Anyway, the Poles seemed little suited to the fulfilment of my aims. They are a passionate and frothy people. Everything they do is promoted by fantasy, not a system. Their enthusiasm is violent, but they know neither how to govern nor sustain it. That nation carries its ruin in its own character.'[159] The Poles also cast their eyes toward Germany. They aided in the establishment of the secret societies Arminia and Germania, even cementing their friendship with the Germans in anticipation of their salvation arriving at the hands of the German liberals. And yet, when these liberals took their seats in St Paul's Church,[160] they had no more

....

[158] The Grand Duchy of Warsaw (1807 – 1815).

[159] *D'ailleurs les Polonais m'ont paru peu propres à remplir mes vues. C'est un peuple passioné et léger. Tout se fait chez eux par fantaisie et rien par système. Leur enthusiasme est violent, mais ils ne savent ni le régler ni le prepétuer. Cette nation porte sa ruine dans son caractère.*

[160] Where the Frankfurt Parliament held its deliberations.

urgent business than the annexation of the Poznań region to their united greater Germany! The Poles waited in vain for French assistance during the uprising in Warsaw, and today they are being exploited by the Magyars,[161] who enkindled new hope in them, and who achieved most of their victories thanks to their bravery and military talent. And yet they too in the depths of their soul took them to be a lightheaded people, deceiving them, treating them badly and finally breaking with them in a bad way.

The Poles fought on all the barricades of Europe, but this brought them neither glory nor benefit. Do the Poles not know that it is impossible to draw vital strength and freedom from others? Will they not, finally, learn from all their cruel disappointments and set off along the path that has been marked out to us all? They've already tried their luck everywhere (at the present moment, they might still give it a whirl in Turkey) but without success.[162] They've allied themselves to everyone except their own brother tribes, on whom they've turned their backs. And meanwhile they, like all the rest, can find salvation only in a pan-Slavic life! Such a great shame it is, O brothers, that you cast away your talents so, and so vainly squander your courage! You deserve a better fate!

You complain of the hardness of the Russians, but just remember how much evil you have caused them! During the days of your alliance with the Cossacks, did you not aim at casting them into slavery? Did you not wish to hand them over into the filthy clutches of the Jews? And what did you do in the western Russian provinces, when they were under your control? How much evil have you wrought through the Union of Brest-Litovsk with the Catholic Church? Did you not convert Orthodox churches into stables for your nobility's horses, or hand them over to the Jews to rent them out? Was the wretched Orthodox deacon not obliged to rent — for a huge fee — the keys to the church doors from the Jew each time he wished to serve the Mass? And were those who resisted the Union not martyred in frightful ways? Every crime will meet with its punishment, even by the hand of one's brother. You must bear the strictness of the Russians since you take every opportunity to harm them.

---

[161] An allusion to the Polish general József Bem (1794 – 1850), who fought for the Magyars during the 1848 Revolution. Somewhat of a renegade, he later fled to the Ottoman Empire and embraced Islam, after being appointed Governor of Aleppo.

[162] Again, Bem springs to mind here, as does Adam Mickiewicz, who died in Turkey, attempting to raise a Polish legion to fight on the Ottoman side against the Russians during the Crimean War.

We have mentioned your uprisings, your foreign alliances, which in the end and as a matter of course are aimed at the Russians, your fighting on the barricades of Europe — now, who has spread the thickest, most shameful untruths about Russia amongst the nations of the world? Your never-ending war against the Russians was, at bottom, a struggle over hegemony in Slavdom. This was to decide which of you was the more capable and destined to rule, but it was you who grabbed the short end of the stick in those struggles, and thus you fell under Russian domination. Beautiful and true are the words of the great Pushkin concerning the Polish-Russian fight, in his poem directed against the calumniators of Russia:

> This is a quarrel, not of enemies,
> But kindred tribes, within one Slavic state;
> A civil war, deciding destinies
> Between brothers long struggling with hate.
> The lightning battered both sides with its might:
> Sometimes they fell, and sometimes it was us.
> Who shall prevail in the uneven fight —
> The arrogant Lach, or the faithful Rus?
> All Slavic brooks flow to the Russian sea,
> Leaving behind... a desert? Where? We'll see...

As we see it, it was a great good fortune for the Slavic family of tribes, following a millennium filled with tribulations, that this struggle ended the way it did. For what would have happened had the victory gone to the Poles? Russia would have been shunted off the European stage; the Poles, in the end, would have been unable to consolidate their power on account of their inner weakness and fractionalism; sooner or later they would have succumbed to great foreign pressure, and this would have sealed the fate of all the other tribes who lie farther to the west and bear a foreign yoke.

Russia has not just triumphed over you, but over Europe entire. Her mission and her miraculous strength have been confirmed in all things — she now reaches deep into Europe, bordering upon all of our tribes, who so need her aid. Can it be that you wish to deny the will of Providence in all this? Would you maledict the dawn that is breaking in our heavens, the shining daystar of our era? All of your resistance, all of your plots and anger will shatter against her iron might, her felicity and Slavic mission. But if despite it all you do not come to your senses, but will continue to struggle against and hinder the common destiny of our family of nations, we may not be able to achieve our goal together with you, but indeed we shall, without you, and even against you!

Nor have the Czechs treated the Russians in a very brotherly manner of late, and what is truly regrettable is the manner in which hatred, among other things, has begun to steal into their writings. In the days of the first stirrings of the Czech national revival, the age of Nejedlý, Puchmajer, Rautenkranz, Sedláček, Hněvkovský, and the venerable Jungmann, Russia was always spoken of in their circles with awe, and their longing gaze was frequently turned in her direction. But as soon as some of the younger literary dilettantes thought up the theory of a federation of Slavic states, as soon as some snobbish gentlemen under the influence of aristocratic ideals entered the game with their incongruous, inconsistent projects for a Slavic Austria, the journals were crammed with mean invective directed at Russia, such as particularly the young German Slavs of Austria allowed themselves to hurl. In Germany, a shower of abuse was poured upon the central power of the Slavs, on hated Russia, and in the Czech lands it was also felt to be in the interest of Austria to pile on. What is more, these fellows were certain that they would be praised by the Austrian government for such ardent service. Some heads were even haunted by the idea of unification with Germany in support of Czech nationalism, which felt threatened by Russia. The events of these latter days have shut the mouths of such idiots, and we are convinced that such wretched opinions will soon give way to a completely different point of view, because the Czech nation is reasonable, and in the depths of its heart decidedly sympathises with Russia. All the more so, the less they skip to the Austrian tune these days, in this period of prosaic living conditions, and they find the other Slavs more attractive.

Literature is certainly being cultivated here, but in the sciences of the spirit, philosophy, history and the like, nothing worth noting can be found apart from Palacký's *Czech History*, and in art and poetry, excepting Mácha, the Czechs have no creative genius of whom to boast.

The development of the technical sciences enjoys greater success, for the idol worshipped is wealth, for which the nation so yearns that, being out of reach for many in the fatherland, it becomes a great spur to emigration. All of this, of course, is of no service to the Czechs at all, insofar as their influence upon the rest of the Slavs is concerned. Their scope of possible operations is too small, their nation is crammed into too narrow bounds, though the demands of the spirit are great and far-reaching. The Czechs must accede to a greater whole, for in isolation they cannot maintain themselves, let alone create anything great.

After the Austrians deceived them and the Czechs worked over the so-called Illyrians, these same Catholic Croats took voice against the Russians in that bought-and-sold newspaper of Gaj's,[163] but that squawking too has quieted down. The Croats may be slow, but they are not lame, and will come to be kindled with the Slavic ideal and begin to be led by it, just as soon as they mature to a proper understanding thereof.

As we have said, the attraction of Russia for the Slavs is irresistible. Now, this sympathetic disposition has one other cause. Amongst all the Slavs, the Russians are the only nation to have preserved their independence, and in doing so they have redeemed the honour of the Slavic name. As the traveller Kohl wrote in the *Augsburger Allgemeine Zeitung*, all the Slavs succumbed to the Germans wherever they came into contact with them; on their ruins the mighty German oak has taken root and flourished, beneath which they are now at rest. Just one day more, and it would have been all over for the entire Slavic world. But that was the day on which the Battle of Poltava took place! There, Peter the Great and his Russians won for the Slavs a battle that will be remembered for all time, since everything had pointed to a Swedish victory.

But the Russians also had their stormy days to weather. Once, at the River Kalka, they were defeated by the Mongols, which led to two hundred years of suffering under Asian rule. But even then they continued to develop, with courage and unprecedented strength. The Swedes, in alliance with the Poles and the Turks, had their designs on subjecting them, but the Russians shattered them and, as punitive reparations, tore a large tract of their land from one of these nations; others they incorporated into their state, leaving to foreigners the remnant of their land, while to the last they administered a lesson not to be forgotten, taming them and depriving them of a large part of their realm.

Later, all of Europe fell upon the borders of Russia under the leadership of a great military genius. She was able to shatter even that colossal power, and the star of Napoléon was extinguished on Russian soil.

Today, Russia stands before us in all her sublime beauty, and, what is more, youthful vigour. Before much longer, Russia will become a first-class nation, if not first above all others in the world. For what other state has such boundless strength and such resources at its disposal? The people and the Tsar are united in Russia — and in this lies the main strength of the coun-

---

[163] Ljudevit Gaj (1809 – 1872), Croatian publicist, publisher of the *Novine Horvatzke* [Croatian News].

try. Her nobles are selfless even if they do not enjoy political freedoms. This can be seen from the gigantic sums of money donated by them to public institutions during the reign of Tsar Nikolai.

The cities are inhabited by nationally-minded citizens. During the French invasion of Russia, the merchant class set half — ha! *three quarters* of their wealth at the disposal of Tsar Alexander.

The scholars of Russia are hard-working, and they open great perspectives before the country; the clergy is pious and passionate about the Russian religion. The common people are good and, what is more, strong, obedient and selfless, talented, and of a strong nature.

Russia is an immense landmass. It comprises 375,000 square miles. Turkey could fit inside its borders nine times. It is 28 times greater than Scandinavia, 29 times Austria, 30 times Germany, 36 times France, and so on. It stretches from the north-eastern corner of Asia from lonely Kamchatka all the way to the upper west of America, and from the north of Europe almost to the Carpathians, the Danube, the Black Sea, south nearly all the way to Mount Ararat.

The population of Russian subjects has risen to 63 million, the great majority of whom being Great and Little Russians. There is an average of 165 people per square mile — 605 in the European part of Russia, and only 48 souls per square mile in Asia. This is not the best proof of the relative strength of Russia, but it certainly offers good testimony of its further expansion and strengthening, and its means for averting pauperisation. 79% of the people live from tilling the soil, which has set the national economy on the safest basis. The granary bands of Russia are found in its central regions, while the steppes are extraordinarily suited to pastureland for the raising of stock, and the endless forests provide an abundance, indeed even a superabundance, of lumber for the construction of ships, and the bowels of the earth, especially in the Asiatic regions, are blessed with a wealth of minerals, gold, platinum, silver and iron besides — three million hundredweight of which are processed every year. The annual yield of gold here reaches 12,250 pounds per annum.

Manufactured goods are on the increase annually, which was particularly the case during the reign of Tsar Nikolai. As we have shown, the roads of trade are open to Russian business in all directions, and this too increases with each passing year. Average imports for the years 1824 – 1833 amounted to 90 million guilders, and exports — 106 million.

Even if cultural conditions in Russia have not attained the level of the other states of Europe, the government pays careful attention to the development of education, and Orthodox Russia has not closed herself off in so *a priori* a manner to the sciences as is the case of strictly Catholic countries.

Russia's scientific accomplishments, her admirably edited journals, in all fields, such as the *Moskovitianin*, for example, her learned men and the poets of whom she may justly boast — Karamzin, Dierzhavin, Pushkin, Gogol, Shevirev — would be the pride of any nation.

The might of the Russian state is in a healthy ratio to its total power. It possesses extensive property, and its peacetime army counts more than 700,000 men — though some estimate the number to be one million.

At the time of writing, the Russian Navy consisted of 36 warships, 32 frigates, 27 corvettes and brigs, 82 smaller vessels, 25 floating batteries and 128 cannon-boats with some 6000 cannon and a sufficient number of matelots and marines.

The exchequer is well organised. Revenue far exceeds expenditure; the national debt is relatively insignificant and the nation's credit is high. The foreign influence of Russia, a country based on such might, serves as a model for other states. In European relations, Russia carries a lot of weight, which can be judged from the fact that in Europe Russian diplomacy enjoys a reputation for great adroitness and an almost miraculous strength, which yet does not intervene everywhere that Russian influence can be sensed. For Russian diplomacy is both clever and calculating. Russian diplomats know how to control themselves; they are well acquainted with circumstances. No other Slavic tribe possesses such a diplomatic corps — although not all Russian successes are due to diplomacy alone.

That power, which arises from inexhaustible springs and animates a united, selfless, youthful and mighty nation, has created immense works, subjected many to its influence, and is the chief cause of the aforementioned successes. Everything furthers Russia's advancement: both friend and enemy, war and revolution as well as stable conditions, Schwarzenberg and Bach, Manteuffel and Radowitz, the same as Kossuth and Szemere, Herwegh and Ruge, Turk and Greek, German and Slav. Or perhaps it is otherwise? Did Russia not drive Europe before her, repulsing troops led by Napoléon himself? Did she not shatter his dominions and aid paralysed nations to their liberation? Was it not her word at the Congress of Vienna that was most important? Does Austria not remain in existence solely by the grace of Russia? Does Prussia dare extricate herself from her influence? Was it not she who had the decisive voice in German affairs, and if Turkey still exists, does she not merely at the pleasure of Russia? The consciousness of Russia's strength is expressed by the Russians thus:

> Russia had but burst her fetters, free, joyful, mighty and proud,
> In her, the Slavic soul reborn, and although soon bolts
> > from the clouds
> Rained down upon her in torrents, unbent she stood all the same;
> Mongol, Tatar, Persian, Arab, French and German met with shame,
> All beaten back from her firm borders, wave after haughty wave;
> Today the Ottoman kneels before her, Russia's abject slave.

And just how threatening Russia's attitude can be, Napoléon himself can testify! With one arm she embraces Asia, the other stretches toward America. She is unapproachable from the direction of Europe; her back is safe and before her there is but Austria in decay and the carrion of Turkey! On this grand canvas great merges with small, diversity with unity; between her two outermost boundaries are found Christianity and paganism and Islam, the miraculous with the prosaic, the legend with the reality. This is the image that lives in the soul of each Russian. One hundred different nations unite themselves to the great Russian tribe; one hundred tribes are motivated by one united will. The shaman is neighbour to the dervish; minarets rise next to Byzantine cupolas. The Arctic Sea merges with the Pontus, Kamchatka with Wilia, ancient Colchis follows upon the Baltic; the mountain upon which, according to ancient legend, the cradle of humanity was located, gazes at its reflection in the River Don. The tropics of Crimea are here wedded to polar nights that last half a year. Asia meets Europe, morning with eve; the sun never sets on this empire! It offers ingenuity such a scope for labour and creative power — how the fantasy is irresistibly captivated by the possibilities she offers! It was no coincidence that Napoléon paused a moment, motionless, upon first catching sight of Moscow, that splendid image of Russia in miniature! He was ravished by its sublimity and majesty!

Now, despite the fact that her power has reached such heights, it is not chiefly on account of this that the Slavs ought to join themselves to Russia. The chief reason, rather, rests in the creative might of the Russian nation, and their ability to maintain all that they have achieved. Besides the fact that the Slavic spirit is best preserved in the Russian character, and in the Russian civic system, in Russian customs strength is wedded to humility and good-heartedness. The Russian state has avoided the greatest errors of Slavic nation-building and has proven itself capable of establishing a strong, united realm.

Only in that — Russian — state can Slavic life find a firm foundation for its development. Only creative and conservative Russian might is capable of resurrecting our nationality from its ruins. The Russian character is very attractive to all of our tribes who have not become alienated from their nature.

When we but consider how the Russian state began and developed, how it grew, consequently, step by step, and yet, despite all this progress, how it could still remain so benign; how it never succumbed to invasions, never lost what once it gained or fought for, why, that might, that consequentiality, cannot but inspire us, even if against our will!

In most cases, we have attested the virtue of Slavic customs through examples from Russian life and Russian history, and this has been for one simple reason: that nation is a faithful image of our soul, and has had the most opportunity to reveal its inner nature on the great stage of history. The Slavic tribes can trust such a hegemon without fear, because the Russians are mighty and don't impede the peaceful commerce and development of foreign nations. They will welcome their long lost brothers in one state union on brotherly terms.

The foreigners are ever claiming that Russia will not be able to maintain her greatness and is doomed to disintegrate. *Disintegrate* is a horrible word, but is such a thing possible? That, which we desire and hope for, shall be fulfilled! But — praise God — there can be no question at all of her falling apart. For is Russia not based, after all, on a unified nation? Is not the Great Russian tribe itself, which forms the core of the state, mighty enough to bind all the others together? And is Russia not united under one church? Does not each Russian bear deep in his heart the unity and immensity of his motherland, which cannot be separated from his existence, with which he identifies that existence? But perhaps the unity of the Russian motherland has been shaken by some instances of unrest, which, appearing here in insignificant numbers, have still left behind some deeper traces? This consciousness of unity is so deeply rooted in the Russian nation that even those Russian conspirators — such as Pestel, Muraviev and others — who came to terms with the Poles, refused to surrender even a fragment of their Polish territory. The simple Russian people believe that there is no end whatsoever to their boundless homeland. Should anyone wish to divide this unified whole, and thus provoked to common action the might and self-sacrificial will of the Russian nation, one can be quite certain what the outcome would be. Why is it that the Russians are so fond of great deeds? Why is everything that they accomplish so imposing? For one reason, and one reason only: because such colossal works testify to their might and remind them of the extent of their homeland.

Now the Slavs complain that the Russian government is not favourably disposed toward progress. Such a pronouncement predicates a division of the government from the people, and in making such a distinction, they make it appear as if they were standing up for the latter. They don't respect the government; they are uneasy with Russia's consistent association of herself with foreign powers (which results in the avoidance of conflicts, which might bring liberation to the Slavs). At first glance, it might seem as if these charges were well-founded. However, upon closer inspection, one sees that they are baseless.

The Russian government supports progress in all areas, and with all the resources at its command: in science, in industry, in the societal sphere, in all of these it is vigorously active. Can we find any other such example in all of history, of any country overcoming its crude circumstances and getting so far in such a short time? As we have mentioned above, does the Russian government not support the liberation of the common people from indecent servitude? Does it not, I say, hold everything in its own hands, awaiting the successful maturation of every such work? When was serfdom abolished in the other lands of Europe? Were these countries not closer to the cradle of humanistic culture, and yet did they not think themselves enlightened, while yet it existed among them?

If we're speaking of training, here the Russian state is extraordinarily active and agile. Every year brings a perceptible rise in the number of schools for the education of the common people, as well as educational establishments of all sorts. The fact that the educational level in Russia is so uneven is the curse of serfdom, which will not last long in Russia anyway.

Scholarly associations — Statistical, Geographical and Archeological Societies — are all coming to life, and the government supports them with a liberal hand. From what one can see in Russia today, the nation is preparing itself for a great work, which will be accomplished in the near future. Literary and scholarly journals discuss scientific questions a good deal more openly than was the case in the Austria of Metternich, and — we hasten to add — even today. As far as industry is concerned, the Russian progress here has outstripped all expectations. The British, those lords of industry, know this well enough. Above all, one must consider that the very idea of progress needs a lot of time to arrive, and take root in such a huge country as Russia. Great things sprout and develop slowly, while those that burst forth and blossom quickly wither just as fast. The Magyars hastened the growth of European culture in a hothouse — and the experts know what sort of quality fruit that produced; the whole world sees what sort of harvest the Magyars reaped. The Russian government does not allow many western products into the country, which are abhorrent to the people — and both the people and the government are quite within their rights to do so.

As we have shown, it is entirely senseless to separate the people from the government — for many reasons. The French succeeded in bringing about such a division, even though in the end this effected a mere replacement of the exiled Bourbons with Louis-Philippe, and later, the latter's own replacement by Louis Napoléon.

Every government answers to the particular situation, convictions, needs, degree of development, and customs of its people, although the western nations often forget about this. Not only governments can be bad; peoples as well can be blighted, and their governments merely reflect this quality. Why is it that the British government, and even that of the Prussians, are more above-board than the other western governments? Is the reason for this not to be found in the people themselves? All the less can the government be separated from the people in the Slavic lands. This is partially because of the completely different moral level here than in the West, and partially because an unlooked-for misfortune would result if such a thing were to take place. As long as the government is of one mind with the great whole of the state, the people will trust it, even if it be strict, or altogether harsh. They will submit to it and heed it, and on its part, as long as the people so allow, the government will strive to guide them as best it can. Trust begets trust, distrust is the cause of reciprocal hatred and oppression. If the bonds between government and people are ruptured, the government will strive to repress the people, and the people to harm the government. O Slavs, preserve your unity! It is your treasure, and with it your states will flourish!

The Russian nation has reason enough to trust its rulers — have not all of them striven to do what's best? Has not each of them been a true aggrandiser of the realm, and not just in name only? Pavel was a bit muddled in his soul, but he was still a man capable of sublime inspiration and grandiose plans. Alexander wished to achieve the very best for his people, and that which he was able to do must be valued in every aspect. Nikolai, a strict and consistent man, had a good understanding of the state and comprehended its greatness. During the French invasion, Tsar Alexander stated that he would rather become a monk than sign a peace treaty dishonourable to Russia, and *gosudar* Nikolai would rush joyfully into the embrace of death, if it were for the good of his empire and his homeland. O, you Romanovs, whom the West curses so, hating you and heaping abuse upon you because you are the rulers of the Slavs, of a Slavic state; you hope of all the tribes of Slavdom, you are worthy of a better fate! You have accomplished great things — a greater deed yet awaits you. Will you accomplish it?

Attentively, the Slavic world has listened to the tales of the tsareviches.[164] You too, O Obrenović clan, enjoy the trust of the Slavic world. You have been unjustly deprived of the Serbian throne, and this at the instigation of our evil spirit! O you, who led the Serbian nation during its times of the greatest danger and never abandoned that unfortunate land! And of you, Petar Petrovič, *vladika* of Montenegro, lord of the mountains, hero, the same holds true.

We have seen why it is that the Russian government has concluded pacts with foreign powers — so that this might put an end to western revolutions and block their expansion. But on this account, doubts arise in our souls. We have no view into cabinet secrets, it is true, but, all the same, when the Russian tsars in Europe were accustomed to act boldly and freely, all of the western nations took them for free persons and held them in high regard. Now, it seems to us that ever since they began negotiating such unnatural alliances, the respect has been somewhat diminished.

In our judgement, Russia has a different mission than that of standing guard for those who are unable to maintain their own power, and are in decline. What is more, it seems to us that these alliances have a bad effect on the tsars themselves. For by them they are moving closer to foreign regents, who themselves have poor relationships with their peoples. Although Tsar Alexander was the author of the Holy Alliance, and that alliance was a good idea in and of itself, as we see it, it had a bad influence on him. It would be a great mistake if the tsars took western rulers for their models, because, along with their nation, they are progressing along a path different from that of the western nations, and it would be bad if this led to artificially created conflicts. Nevertheless, the Slavs should not fear that it should never arrive at a collision between Russia and the foreign powers, to which they are subject, and that they should not be liberated thereby. The immense might of Russia is ever pressing ahead. It cannot be stopped; it is constantly in search of new arenas of action. The Slavic consciousness is quickly awakening in Russia; it is seizing the country more and more — and this alone is reason enough for the Slavic tribes to trust that they will not be long made to remain in bondage and abasement. The states that are situated more deeply inside Europe, far from Russia (chiefly Turkey and Austria) are untenable. They will disintegrate by themselves, and Russia will be obliged to step in there out of concern for her own security. The Russian eagle will ascend the summits of the sky; it will soar high above our world, and the eagle of the

---

[164] It seems that in using this word, Štúr is not referring to the sons of the Tsar, but the 'little tsars' of the other autonomous realms he admires: Serbia and Montenegro.

north will be recognised by its brothers. To rely upon the Slavic tribes, to rely upon Slavdom as a whole, this, as we see it, is the only natural politics adequate to Russia. If the Slavic tribes who, up until now, find themselves outside of the Russian state, merely unite with her in one whole, she will richly reward them for the foreign allies they lose. Be patient then, O Slavs; our day will arrive — it is already dawning in the southeast. Who then will be able to successfully withstand our united strength? Who then would dare to deny us our right to life? It is now time, high time, for Russia to recognise her mission and become conscious of the Slavic idea. For further hesitation, as we see it, can only lead to unpropitious results.

Now, in order for Russia to expand by annexing other Slavic lands, and in order for Slavdom to awaken and become a reality, she must organise herself as the spirit of Slavdom requires, as well as the current state of her development and situation of the world. From our considerations, we may draw the following conclusions:

In ancient days, our land was the inheritance of our ever-mobile tribes, who tilled and defended it. It was not a property seized, a conquest, and thus no one could present it to anyone else in gift. This is why slavery and dependence of any sort is seen by us today to be a serious sin committed against our nation; a crime against the spirit of our nation. The land, as we see it, can only belong to freeholders. In Russia, servitude is considered the greatest evil. We have witnessed the noble efforts of both individuals and the Russian government to put an end to it. But even so these actions have been insufficient up till now, and the gravity of the matter demands a much greater enthusiasm in order for such an evil finally to disappear. It is not our intention to force anyone to hasty action, for severe wounds do not heal at once; but now is the time to set our shoulders to the wheel. Christianity itself urges us to the task, for it condemns all slavery and all exploitation of men.

In this way, all the heads of all families will become free landowners and acquire human dignity. But this doesn't mean that they can do whatever they please with their landholdings. For this concerns not only themselves, but all the many who belong to them, and all who will come after them. The land belongs to the commonwealth and is the property of each individual. The jurisdiction of the Slavic commonwealth — and we still find these in their pure form in Russia, Montenegro, Bulgaria and elsewhere — should enact a law concerning this, that all adult individuals should receive an equal allotment of the land, which after their death would be taken back from them. In those places where the Slavic commonwealth has vanished, it must be renewed. Where this will prove impossible, the indivisibility of land ownership must be decreed, so that each family should have enough to support themselves as a whole. The division of land must be forbidden by law. In this way, pauperisation can be forestalled, and many members of human society rescued from their undignified lot. The West gave liberty to the individual, and then left him to his own devices. This merely led back to the lack of freedom, and misery. It is our duty to care for each individual in the interest of preserving the whole.

As can be seen, the preservation of the whole in our commonwealth is realised through the protection of each individual. Should anyone be visited by misfortune of which he was not himself the cause, the good spirit of our nation will provide him with sufficient aid. Indeed that same spirit, after a certain time, will even show mercy unto the wretch who finds himself in misery of his own making. This spirit, peculiar to our nation, is preserved in all of our establishments. Even with the best of intentions, the commonwealth cannot prevent all instances of misfortune from arising; even an entire commonwealth can be beset with misfortune. Therefore, the singular, helpless local community must be aided by the county (župa, okruh, województwo, okruží, or whatever it may be known as) which, as a collection of many such local communities, is bound to bring sufficient aid in all cases of such misfortune that befall both individuals and entire villages. In the same manner the counties aid each other in instances of great catastrophes. Large municipal communities are also organised along this principle, while the smaller ones are components of counties. According to the founding idea of our nation, the village or local community is an extended family, the county an extension of the local community, and the state a union of all the counties. And thus the practical maintenance and realisation of this principle entirely fits the spirit of our nation, which only waits for the right time to reawaken — there is no need to establish it by decree. This principle will begin to assert itself accordingly as life itself develops.

Great labour associations exist in the cities of Russia — cooperatives, the elected leaders of which, at the discretion of all, distribute the profits of their labour amongst all the membership. In this way, they imitate the rural commonwealth. The social questions, which they in the West struggle to deal with in vain, are solved among us by these two establishments. They arise from practical commandments, the blessings of Christianity, and the soul of our nation. Due to their lack of active charity, western institutions and associations for the eradication of misery and misfortune have become but modest answers to the real demands, and what is more, they have degraded into monetary speculation. And this, in cases of misfortune!

In all of our tribes, the local community manages its own affairs. It is all the more entitled to do so, as it consists of free landowners. This right to self-administration is a most reasonable, and genuinely sacred thing. In this way, nothing is imposed upon the nation; it can continue to practise its particular customs, while nothing impedes the development and enjoyment of life to the fullest. By the self-government of the commonwealth we mean that it protects the common property, administers the common treasury, elects its own council of elders, sees to its own security, settles minor disputes between private individuals, and enjoys the right of adjudicating lesser criminal cases. It executes the requirements of the government, such as tax collection, the raising of levies for the defence of the motherland — these things belong to the responsibility of the entire community in respect to the general government. It investigates instances of misfortune befalling individuals and ensures the necessary assistance; it deliberates upon common affairs, summons the elders, is empowered to gather freely to debate further actions, and when it confirms that a breach of order has occurred, it duly informs the plenipotentiary of the general government.

Now since, according to our customs, the family is represented by its eldest member, and only through his mediation may the family access communal property, the law allows only the fathers of the families — that is, adult persons known to the community — to govern by acting in the name of all. As we see it, this Slavic approach to such matters is the most sensible, the most reasonable, for the individual here is not representing himself alone; he is no egoist, but represents others as well. And this condition obliges him to circumspection, probity and ardour. In such a representative system we differ from the West, which empowers all people of a certain age (with certain small exceptions, such as beggars) with the right to vote, and in this way seeks to circumscribe and indeed already has partially succeeded in circumscribing, personal representation. In Russia and in Serbia, the local commonwealths enjoy complete self-administration, and this we consider to be the greatest blessing enjoyed by these countries.

In the Slavic understanding of the term, the county (župa, okruh, okruží, województwo, and so on), possessing all the rights of the commonwealth, also must enjoy self-government. And so the county will take care of its own security, constitute the first and second instances of the judicial system, inform the local communities of the government's by-laws, distribute among them the established tax quota, determine the contingent of the levy, work to ensure the well-being of all local communities, and come to the aid of those touched with misfortune, through none of their own doing, when the local communities are unable to do so. Through the apportionment of common funds, to which all must contribute according to the county's determination, arrived at after a consideration of their financial circumstances, the county supports its hospitals and similar charitable institutions. As previously mentioned, the county supports other individuals who find themselves in difficulties not of their own making, and provides commensurate support to local communities when disaster strikes and the communities themselves are in no position to compensate for the damages on their own. In such cases in which a county is unable to aid its citizens by itself, it will approach other counties for help, or, as the case may be, the state itself.

The county controls the collection of taxes from the local communities by state officials, preventing deceit and seeing to the smooth functioning of the collection process. It is the county that selects its own administrative officials and those of the county court, convening free assemblies for their control, matters pertaining to election and for the consultation of affairs that touch upon all. The individual members of the commonwealth participate in these assemblies through the mediation of their representatives, but no one has any right to intervene here personally, on his own behalf. At these gatherings, the government is limited to the identification and elimination of potential unrest.

In such a way, the spread of the unbearable rashes of western bureaucracy is forestalled. Instead of the deathly silence of bureaucratic inanition, here we have positive bustle; the administration itself is not overly costly, and those whom the nation has entrusted with their offices are dignitaries who feel more honoured by their selection than they would have been, had they been mere officials paid for their service. This can lead to lower taxes and the economies of all estates can be managed more efficiently.

In Russia, the nobility of each *guberniya* has the right of free association. They elect their own marshals (i.e. župans, county administrators), the judges of the first and second instance, the presidents of these courts, and in the districts: the administrative cadre and the police officials. In addition to this, they control the financial affairs of the appointed governors.

The people themselves share in these rights, although to a lesser extent. And so, the principle of our ancient counties is still alive and well in Russia, but it must be applied to the local communities too, in accord with the spirit of our nation and the idea of a purposefully reasonable statal system. Naturally, the aristocracy would need to relinquish its unilateral privileges and transfer these to the nation as a whole, as a right to which it is entitled, since clannish privilege is foreign to the spirit of our nation and Christianity teaches us that both divine and human rights belong to everyone without exception.

As we have said, the Slavs never proceeded to taking the successful step from county unit to state. Such a step consists of unconditionally entrusting the state with all governmental power, an adequate existence ensuring its elevated, grand mission. Accordingly, all law that exceeds the ambit of the counties would belong to the state, particularly in the active sphere of municipal societies, and thus: legislative power, higher administrative and judicial powers, from which the state derives a force commensurate to its role, a power of uniting all the counties in one whole.

Its mission then is to do everything in its power to create inner unity in the state, a whole, which consists of varied forces in cooperation, and activities ensuring the state's independence from outside influence, while representing it abroad among other independent states.

Such is a monarchy, which in the West they term absolutist. Indeed, because of the errors which our tribes have committed in their attempts at the establishment of states, we have need of just such a monarchy — taking into account the immensity and the variety of our tribes, the conception of our nation concerning the monarchic idea, as well as the needs of the age, our growing activity and place in the world. Such a monarchy exists in Russia. All that is needed now is to reconcile it with the above-mentioned democratic institutions adapted to the spirit of our nation. With this the question of the necessity of further state development would be solved completely and all unnecessary revolutions would come to an end.

The government possessed of such a power cannot be separated from the people, hovering above them in the sky. It must walk alongside them, hand in hand, allowing their spirit to support it, and holding to them according to their customs and the needs of their calling. For this reason it must be accompanied on all hands by the hosts of its counties, which aid it in everything, supporting it with their counsel and acting as intermediaries between the government and the nation in vital, reciprocal contact. Thus the institution of the senate,[165] which has always existed and still does exist in all of our states — up until today in Russia, Serbia and Montenegro, in the last mentioned two countries representing the counties before the central government.

It would be extraordinarily harmful if the senate was to become a mere shadow of itself. For then the government would lose that living contact with

---

[165] Štúr employs this term in its original sense — a collection of elders, from the Latin *senex*.

the nation, and both would become gradually alienated from one another, which misfortune would lead to unforeseeable consequences. And these consequences would appear immediately upon the split, even if they would not be immediately apparent.

In the case of state matters of grave importance, such as in instances where the government is unable to venture something on its own, lift something by its own strength, when it is not certain what the nation's opinion might be in reference to a given measure that is to be implemented, then the plan in question would be entrusted to the counties' deliberations. Or — and this is still more in keeping with the Slavic character — the government would summon representatives from the best, most experienced and most esteemed of the counties, not so that they should dictate legislation and quibble, engaging in legislative playacting, but to counsel it with their advice as the elders of the people. If the government has a genuine vital contact with the people, and if the people trust it, and it them as well, then the government will take absolute cognisance of the people's advice and will be ruled by it, according to its best lights. In all of our states the national assemblies were originally of this character, and such we recognise in the contemporary *skupština* in Serbia and Montenegro. Even Tsar Alexander summoned just such an assembly shortly before the French invasion of Russia, and — as it turns out — this assembly accomplished its task with dignity.

Between a people and a government that has such an attitude toward the nation no foreign element, such as a secret police eating away at reciprocal trust will ever come to be, to incite mistrust on both sides, and elicit an artificial scissure and the demoralisation of the nation. O, that each and every Slavic government would take this to heart! Bad intentions are not always lurking behind every free expression, nor does every free movement signify a coup in the offing! Should hotheads and traitors plot and forge something, the municipal authorities will inform the government, which will then put a timely end to it all. The great Petrovsky beseeched Russia to remove the unnecessary and notorious secret police, but unfortunately without success. However, its continued existence can be attributed to the fact that the well-intentioned *gosudar* Nikolai had been surprised — right at his ascension to the throne — by the Pestel plot.

In foreign affairs, as we see it, an end ought to be put to all of those political alliances, the sole intent of which was to maintain tottering thrones and impotent dynasties, for that, which is already moribund, can be preserved in life by no earthly power whatsoever. The Slavic government is based on completely different foundations, supported by an entirely different nation.

By identifying itself at times with untenable governments in mortal decline, such as have lost faith in themselves, all it wins is the hatred of the nations, while losing the respect of its own people. By neglecting to do what it ought to be doing, it loses the trust of the other tribes as well. In our opinion, the effectiveness of such alliances could be sufficiently compensated for by the Slavic tribes who still live beyond the borders of Russia. If only the Russian government would realise its great mission on the stage of world history, and be governed by the Slavic idea — of relying on Slavdom. Only then will the Slavic tribes feel ready to annex themselves to Russia.

There is no need, and such would be superfluous, to speak in advance of the methods by which this annexation would take place, or of the subsequent relationship of the Slavic tribes to the country of Russia. This will occur according to the conditions prevalent at the time. Above all, we desire the preservation of Serbia and her independent internal administration. The Serbs are devoted to Russia; they share their Orthodox faith; they are a bold, wise nation who also have a real poetic vein. They are a nation that has preserved a pure Slavic establishment, some aspects of which have not survived even among the Russians. Only in respect to the Russians are the Serbs, as a whole, in second place among the Slavic states. We consider the preservation of Serbia a reasonable and politically advisable policy. While they do not constitute a large nation, the Serbs are courageous, energetic, capable of exaltation and can conduct their enterprises more easily than the Russians, who must take an array of European relations into account. Besides this, the Serbs find themselves under the protection of Russia. Finally, it must not be forgotten that the Serbs have drawn the attention of all the southern Slavs to themselves, and have won among them a well-deserved preeminence.

It is very true that in a Slavic state, everything must have the blessing of the Church. She is the Alpha and the Omega. The real Slav will not commence anything without first begging the assistance of God, and he completes each task with prayers of gratitude and thanksgiving. This principle is preservative of both individual men and their states, and cannot disappear from the Slavic state; it must remain unspoiled, living, and sacred. What might serve as the fountainhead of our activity if not the divine afflatus? 'Seek ye therefore first the kingdom of God [...] and all these things shall be added unto you.'[166] All of history confirms the eternal validity and truth

---

[166] Matthew 6:23, Luke 12:31. The entire quote reads 'Seek ye therefore first the kingdom of God and His justice, and all these things shall be added unto you.'

of these words. Nations that cast away the Kingdom of God, along with righteousness and truly human behaviour, forgetting about God and striving only after 'all these things,' that is, the things of earth, fall — again and again we see it happen — and that assertion will be proven true in the future as well. Boldly then, fellow Slavs! These words pertain to our lives — let us bear them in our hearts. Our Church must constantly remind our tribes and the world entire of these words, and our states must cling to them.

That Church has ever had its vital calling before her eyes, being in an appropriate relationship with the state, which is capable of protecting her. She is not about creating her own spiritual kingdom; she does not elevate herself above the state, nor is she subject to it; rather, she progresses along at its side, hand in hand. She is united to it, and there were times when she was strong enough to step out in front with the Patriarch at her head, cross in hand, to castigate those Russian leaders who forgot their sublime calling and sought to oppress the nation, recalling them to their duty. May this Church of ours always remember that; may she never seek to grasp saecular power; may she never allow herself to be abased or diverted from her elevated position.

We do not consider it necessary to enter into details in the course of these reflections, as everything becomes evident of itself from a consideration of these chief historical moments. It is not for the Slavs to plan, delineate and prescribe details in statal terms and legislation; let us leave such petty officialdom to the bureaucrats, so distasteful to our tribes. Amongst us is the fulness of our tribal customs, to which code and regulation are unnecessary. All of this flows directly from our moral state, and these are obvious to all of us at first glance. That which is the consequence of our moral nature is so much more valuable than all of your bylaws and regulations, paragraphs and measures, letters patent and resolutions of your bureaucrats, your Germans! The German carries everything about in his head. Everything arranges itself into ideas, conceptions, from which paragraphs arise, and even if nothing of this can be put into any human tongue, at least it can be made public to all on paper! Their spokesmen cite their utterances as professors do their lectures. The Slav, on the contrary, carries everything within his heart and soul, and is capable of expressing it all by the power of speech. All of our tribes have a great oratorical talent, and there, where this has been lost — among the Czechs, for example — such has come about as a result of bureaucracy, pressure from above, and the consequent silence that falls thereafter.

Above, we have outlined what sort of expectations we have in regard to the Slavic state; now it is proper that we remind the tribes of Slavdom of their duty and show them the path they must follow, according to our views, if they desire to attain their noble goal of living a Slavic life and attaining unity.

And here, in the first place, we have the Orthodox Church. The distinction between the western and eastern portions of the Church catholic does not lie — as is generally assumed — in the fact that one recognises the Pope and the other does not, or does not permit the meaningless word *kai* (*et*, that is, 'and') in the dogma of the Holy Trinity, and suchlike external issues. The distinction is substantial, and touches upon the whole. The Orthodox Church never raised a *one and only spiritual kingdom,* and thus, logically, never needed a Pope for its preservation and administration. She never permitted herself to be governed by a priestly caste; she was satisfied with the organic improvement of the Church alone. Of course, the clergy, which no church can do without, has its place in her. However, the clergy was entrusted only with the higher calling of the Church, as we have already explained. That mission consists of sacerdotal obligations: to proclaim the Gospel to all successive generations, and to nourish those who have already accepted those immortal teachings, constantly and continuously expounding them, helping those who have fallen to rise, strengthening the weak, humbling the mighty, exalting the humble, comforting those in misfortune, warning the self-complacent and bringing all into a sincere relationship with Christianity through the holy sacraments. The Orthodox Church has remained true to this, claiming nothing more. As we have just said, the clergy took this elevated mission in hand, and, even if it established no sort of kingdom of its own, neither had it any need of any administrators. Although she called to life a priestly estate entrusted with the mission of the Church, she did not make rulers of her representatives, as is the case in the Roman Catholic Church, with the nations as their subjects. She did not restrict education to the clergy; she did not set them up as the unique gatekeepers to the Kingdom of God. She merely entrusted them with the leadership of the people — not separating the one from the other, not enjoining the unnatural state of celibacy upon them, on the contrary: she allowed them to enter into matrimony. She did not forbid the common people the comprehension of her teachings and liturgy by setting them in a foreign language. Rather, she introduced the mother tongue of the people to the Holy Scripture and to the Church itself. She did not establish, as did the Roman Catholic Church, that only the fulfilment of acts prescribed by the priests leads to eternal life. In short, she did not impose upon the people a mechanical, thoughtless drill and other so-called good works, the reception of surfaces rather than fundamentals, external appearances rather than inner values. And so she never enslaved the people, dulling them and herding them into bigotry.

The Orthodox nations are justly pious in all their lands, but nowhere so blind or bigoted as Catholic nations. With this is closely allied the fact that ritual did not become the chief aspect of divine service, but has its own, certain place alongside preaching. There, where this differs, it is an exception, perhaps an error, such as arises through the inevitable formation of the clergy. Further, this is united to the fact that the Orthodox Church has never, even for a moment, forgotten Christ in the veneration of the Virgin Mary; that the images upon which the Orthodox people gaze in their churches, are, as we know, purely spiritual visualisations of beings completely deprived of all sensualism. People do not pray to these images the way that Catholics do, and although they visit monasteries where the greater part of the relics of the historical past are preserved, these have not become places of pilgrimage, the moral sense of which would have been completely lost today, as in the case of the Catholics. Here we find none of that audacity, imperiousness, enslavement and shallowness of the Catholic Church, and yet here too is a clergy, though of a different sort, and likewise a knowledge of the Sacrificial Liturgy, and that a breathtaking liturgy.

On the other hand, she is not lacking in ecclesiastical organisation such as we find among the Protestants. Unlike them, the Orthodox Church possesses unity, and the Sacrifice, although similarly to them it exhibits a like fervour, scholarship and accomplishments, or at least leaves the door open to such. In such ways Orthodoxy rises above both Catholicism and Protestantism, correcting their shortcomings and one-sidedness. That Church never sought an earthly realm through spiritual imperiousness as did the Catholic Church. She never lowered herself to exploit the most holy religion as a means to attaining worldly, often repugnant, aims. She never sullied her hands with crime, never had anything to do with the unchristian, diabolical work of an Inquisition, or the Jesuits, and others like them, but always clove unto the state and aided it. When the state malfunctioned, she knew how to bring that to its attention. O, that the Orthodox Church should never lose sight of her magnificent calling! In Russia, the ruler of the nation is simultaneously the external representative of the Church. May the spirit of Slavdom aid him always in the fulfilment of that exalted role!

Besides this, one mustn't forget that the Orthodox Church has never ossified as has the Catholic Church; it never expressed itself in an unfriendly manner toward the Protestants. The result of this has allowed for a deepening of faith, a greater ardour, a closer understanding and more precise grasp of Church teaching — the while Catholicism hurled eternal curses upon the Protestants, branding them heretics, without in the least striving to develop itself, as if there were no need of such a thing. However, the progressive development referred to above must not degenerate into one-sidedness, or the splintered nature of the Protestant confessions, but must be a constituent part of the Church. As we see it, there is no cause to fear a one-sided development such as we see among the Protestants, because the Slavs are not governed by reason in such things as are the Germans, but by the heart and the soul. Besides that, the Orthodox Church never persecuted those who thought differently than she, but rather dealt with them in the spirit of the Christian commandments. The Russian nation never fell to hating and oppressing other nations only because they confessed to another religion. This is quite the opposite of Catholicism and Catholic governments, who have particularly persecuted those who held different opinions in religion, if only they had the power to do so. The excesses in Spain, France, and Austria are known to all. What is currently going on in Poland, whatever the Russian government is doing there, however harshly, is politically motivated, not directed at Catholicism in any fundamental sense.

When we gather together all that we have said concerning the Orthodox Church, we arrive at the inevitable conclusion that she is the church of Slavdom, and the future.

O holy Church of our fathers, who first blessed our tribes with Christianity from the summits of Nitra, Velehrad and Vyšehrad! Who was once set to unite in spirit the entire family of our nations! O, return Thou to us! Lift up our hearts toward the Eternal and nourish our soul, so that it might realise its magnificent calling. Nearly all of our tribes, the Czechs as well as the Slovaks, the Poles and the Croats, once rested upon Thy bosom, O Thou mother of the Slavs! Only when the foreigners irrupted into our lands to rule over us wert Thou banished and the Catholic Church introduced, which solidified foreign overlordship over our tribes and set us at the mercy of aliens! The rule of foreigners undermines Thee yet today, wherever it has Thee within its reach — but this shall fall long before Thou shalt. To Thee the gates of the future open wide; 'tis Thou shalt lead forth a nation capable of life, in which soul and mission are in accord! When the hated occupation of the foreigners shall fall and shatter to pieces, the hearts of those near to Thee shall greet Thee, flying to Thee spontaneously, O Thou blessed one!

It is customary for foreigners to charge this Church with stagnation. But when we have a closer look, we see that a church which has maintained a nation in the fear and respect of God, preserving its might and freshness, its purity of heart — such a church is not stagnant, but, on the contrary: it must be full of vital strength. The fate that has befallen Orthodoxy is the same as befalls anyone who does not push to the front, but prefers to remain where he is, amongst his own people, dedicated to his calling. Later on, of such a person it is often said that he was not made for this life, and men pay little attention to him. Well, but all things have their proper times. Up until now, the Orthodox Church has remained amongst her own, fulfilling her role. But the day will come in the course of her history when she will enter onto the wide arena of action. And then she will develop in the fulness of life.

Can anyone name a church that could fully act if not in concert with a nation possessed of a world-encompassing mission? Up until now, the Slavs have remained in the background of history, and their Church has remained there with them.

Let no one charge us with advising the Slavs to exploit their Church as a means of political unification. Nevertheless, it is clear what we wish to accomplish by the means of Slavdom — and only that Church is in accord with that mission. Slavdom will never be associated with Roman Catholicism, while the eastern Church was once common to nearly all of our tribes, their true treasure. We are only drawing their attention to what already belongs to them.

The other thing that the Slavs must develop is a common written tongue. For who will not admit that the variety of literatures sets up extraordinary obstacles on the path to common understanding, spiritual development and social action? The Slavs have many literatures, but as small as they are, will they be able to respond to the grand call of human development? And how, pray, will they more and more enter upon the stage of world history? In comparison with the western literatures, German, French and English, all of them, with the significant exception of the literature of Russia, are small and by a long shot insufficient — not excepting the Czech — in their splintered state, incapable of effecting anything of import. What sort of intellectual impulse, what means have they, what deeds can they hope to accomplish on the little fields they occupy — so distant from the possibility of contributing to the development of humanity as a whole? Reciprocity amongst the Slavs is indeed deserving of our respect and praise; however, it is a poor substitute for what we need in our present calamity, and can never spread totally through the life of all of our tribes. For the Slavs to betake themselves to one literature, they have every reason and occasion, and indeed the obligation to do so; indeed, they are bound to do so, from human, political and historical perspectives. There can be no doubt about why we should desire such a literature, if we wish to accomplish anything in this regard more than the threshing of straw. All of the Slavic literatures, save the Russian, are confined to smaller particular tribes and thus restricted to small areas, geographically speaking. And thus the choice of a universal Slavic tongue would boil down to such an option: Old Church Slavic or Russian. Now, Old Church Slavic, as such, has disappeared; it is practically a dead language, and no longer has the elasticity and panache of a living tongue. And it is the vibrant, living word that we need; therefore, all that remains is the Russian. Only Russian fits the bill, as it is the language of the largest, independent and most widely-spread tribe, which governs large areas of the world and to whom hegemony in the family of Slavic nations is due anyhow. Besides this, it is the richest of all the Slavic languages, the most active, effective and most sonorous, marked by power. As far as these categories are concerned, only Serbian runs a close second.

In saying this, I do not mean to imply that, when Russian becomes the universal literary language of Slavdom, writing in the literatures of the particular Slavic tribes should cease — not at all, especially in the case of poetry, etc. But we cannot stubbornly stand by our particular literatures. For an analogous example, how can Danish literature hope to complete alongside German? Russian literature is also proposed as a universal literary vehicle for the Slavs for this reason: because it possesses a precise alphabet, capable of perfectly expressing the spoken language in written form, without any sort of makeshift means as are necessary for all the other Slavic tongues, besides Serbian, who must shabbily aid the Latin alphabet they have adopted. Now, given human selfishness, one cannot expect of all of our tribes a voluntary accession to such a great step toward uniformity. And in such circumstances, when they find themselves under foreign dominance, it cannot be in any way enforced. Such a great work for the welfare of the Slavs can only come about under the pressure of compelling political events. For now, it is good to arouse interest in the matter, to speak of it and to prepare ourselves for it in spirit.

In Nature, autumn follows every summer before giving way to winter, and such a process can also be found in world history. Nations exhaust themselves in fervent activity to gradually withdraw from the arena, after which they enter upon a period of lethargy — a spiritual winter, with which the cycle of their life comes to its completion. The fulness of Greek life is followed by a vexatious period; the blossoming of the Roman Republic gives way to the repellant period of Empire, and to us it seems as if such a time of civilisational fainting were now upon Europe. And yet the development of humanity never ceases; eternal truths never perish; indeed, on the contrary: just as Nature awakens to a new, flourishing life with the coming spring, reprising its activity with freshly-renewed strength, the same thing applies to human life. What fulness of life, what strength developed among the Germanic and Romance nations upon the fall of the Roman Empire!

One other peculiar phenomenon characterises the activity of historically great nations — namely, that after attaining the summit of their might and asserting spiritual dominance over other peoples, they strive to set the seal of their own spirit upon them. Thus we see Alexander the Great race over the face of the earth with his Greeks in an ardent desire to inundate the world with Hellenic culture. In the same manner, the Romans struggled after the attainment of the *imperium orbis*. Thus were the Germans animated by the concept of a universal Christian empire. The last Western attempt at something like this was the pursuit of the Roman way by Napoléon, that man of destiny. Of course, all of these attempts ran aground, as they must, for they are unrealisable. But just as, with his sword, Caesar opened the road of history to Gaul, where it soon took root, so did Napoléon clear the path for history to the land of the Slavs, dragging the Slavic world onto the brightly-lit stage of history by violence.

As if in gratitude to this extraordinary man, whom the French on the one hand hated, and on the other adored, and the Germans hated, having suffered at his hands, it was the Slavs who, in the forefront of the evenly-matched fight overcame him, yet still esteem him and appreciate him best. The most excellent Slavic spirits, 'be it Pushkin, be it Mickiewicz,' describe him most truthfully, and now, the Russian Demidov, has established a museum dedicated to Napoléon on Elba. This man had only a murky premonition of what the future held, which he confided to his friends in conversations on the island of St Helena. He did not come to know Slavdom, only Russia, on the plains of which his star fell, in the depths of which his broken magic sceptre lies buried.

Humanity is in decline, so it would seem. And yet it cannot be untruthful to itself for long, betraying its essential nature — especially given the progress of the new age that is upon us. Humanity is ever on the move, forward, and where it will eventually end up, no one can foresee. It can get worse only for a little while.

Lift up, then, O Slavs, your long despondent hearts, and with the help of God, set yourselves to your tasks! All nationalistic vanity is an empty thing — a seed which can bring forth no strong fruit. It's all about humanity, in the end, of which we are an organic part just like all other nations.

Such then is our message! May it be welcomed in the spirit in which it was intended.

GLOSSARY

Alexander, Tsar (Alexander Romanov, 1777 – r. 1801 – 1825). Tsar of Russia during the Napoléonic period. His political profile in this regard is more complicated than Štúr describes it, shifting as the winds blew between opposing Napoléon and allying himself with him. Although commencing his reign with liberal leanings, he became increasingly more conservative. He was the architect of the Holy Alliance, following the fall of Napoléon, to combat revolutionary movements in Europe. At the fall of Napoléon he was crowned 'King of Poland' and 'Grand Duke of Finland.'

Amurat (Murad I, 1326 – r. 1362 – 1389). Ottoman Sultan, who expanded Turkish influence in the Slavic Balkans. It was he who fought — and died — at the Battle of Kosovo (15 June 1389) which brought to an end the independence of the remaining Serbian principalities not yet subject to the Ottomans.

Bach, Alexander von (1813 – 1893). Austrian jurist civil servant. Originally a radical in his political views, his service in the government of the conservative Minister-President Prince Felix Schwarzenberg was, as Štúr mentions, something of a political sea-change. Whether from practical considerations or the unscrupulousness he is often charged with, Bach was transformed from a liberal into a rigid conservative during his time in office as Minister of the Interior (1849 – 1859), supporting policies that many considered oppressive, including the muzzling of the press.

Béla IV (1206 – r. 1235 – 1270). King of Hungary. Routed by the Mongols under Batu Khan at the Sajó River, he fled Hungary for Dalmatia. The Mongols practically razed the entire country, occupying it for a year. Upon Béla's return, he proceeded to fortify the country, relying on the quasi-independent counts, and waged several wars to re-constitute the country, which had been preyed upon by neighbouring European states. He is known by the Magyars as *második honalapító*, or 'the second founder of the state.' A pious Catholic, three of his children were deemed worthy of veneration by the Church, especially St Margaret of Hungary (canonised in 1943).

Bernolák, Anton (1762 – 1813). Slovak Catholic priest and linguist. His proposal for the codification of Slovak was based on the western regions of Slovakia, around Trnava. It was Štúr's proposal for the central Slovak dialects that eventually carried the day, but Bernolák's contributions were nonetheless important for the official distinction of Slovak from Czech.

Bestuzhev, Alexander Alexandrovich (1797 – 1837). Russian Romantic poet and soldier. Exiled to the Caucasus for his part in the Decembrist Uprising. He wrote under the pen-name of Marlinsky, by which Štúr refers to him.

Bestuzhev-Ryumin, Mikhail (1801 – 1826). Russian military officer executed for his role in the Decembrist plot.

Bolesław Chrobry ('the Brave,' 966 – r. 992 – 1025). First king of Poland, who expanded his realm westward to encompass Pomerania, Lusatia, and Bohemia, and eastward to Kiev. Ally of Emperor Otto III, yet Poland remained independent of the Holy Roman Empire. Bolesław Chrobry also established a Polish episcopal hierarchy independent of German influence.

Bolesław III Krzywousty ('the Wrymouthed,' 1086 – r. 1107 – 1138). King of Poland. His division of the Kingdom of Poland, described by Štúr, is known in Poland as the *rozbicie dzielnicowe* or 'district breakdown.'

Bořivoj (c. 852 – c. 890). Historical protoplast of the Přemislid dynasty in the Czech lands. A thane of Great Moravian ruler Svätopluk, he was baptised, along with his wife St Ludmila, by St Methodius.

Břetislav (c. 1002 – 1055). Illegitimate son of Oldřich, Přemislid duke of Bohemia, he successfully opposed Stephen of Hungary's territorial incursions into the Czech lands, and re-took Moravia from the Poles.

Charles IV of Luxembourg (1316 – 1378). Holy Roman Emperor, who made Prague the capital of the empire. He is famed for many improvements to the city, including the Charles Bridge, which is named for him, and the foundation of the University of Prague (1348), which also bears his name.

Chłopicki, Józef (1771 – 1854). Served in the Polish army before the Partitions, and then with the Napoléon, with distinction, eventually rising to the rank of General. He was awarded the Legion of Honour. During the 1830 uprising against Russia, he was in command of all insurrectionary troops for little over a month. His policy of negotiating with the Russians is seen by some as pragmatic, by others as defeatist.

Colbert, Jean-Baptiste (1619 – 1683). French statesman; Secretary of the Navy and Comptroller General under Louis XIV. Credited with making France a dominant European power.

Constantine (Constantine Pavlovich Romanov, 1779 – 1831). Russian Grand Duke. Viceroy of the 'Kingdom of Poland' created after the Congress of Vienna and annexed to the Russian Empire. An enigmatic figure, he ruled Poland harshly, yet sympathised with the Polish drive for autonomy. The November Uprising of 1830 drove him from power.

SS Cyril and Methodius (c. 827 – 869; c. 815 – 884). Brothers, the Thessalonian Apostles to the Slavs. Cyril taught at the Patriarchal Academy in Constantinople, Methodius was the Abbot of a monastery. They were called to Moravia by Rastislav (Rostislav), and proceeded to evangelise the Slavic areas now contained by Slovakia, the Czech lands, and southern Poland. With the Pope's permission, they translated the liturgy into what is now known as Old Church Slavonic, inventing the Glagolitic alphabet for the purpose — a variation of the Greek alphabet, which eventually developed into the Cyrillic alphabet in use in Russia and other Orthodox lands. The use of Slavic in the liturgy was opposed by German clergy, but ratified by Pope

Adrian II, until Pope Stephen V imposed the universal use of Latin on the Slavic areas as well as the rest of Western Europe. With their translations and writings, SS Cyril and Methodius set the foundation for all the Slavic literatures. Their feast day is 14 February in the West, and 11 May in the East.

Czajkowski, Michał (1804 – 1886). Polish soldier and poet. After serving as a cavalry officer in a Cossack regiment during the November Uprising of 1830, he emigrated: first to France, and later to Turkey, where he agitated on behalf of his country against Russia. He converted to Islam in order to serve in the Sultan's armies fighting against Russia in the Crimean War, but later returned to Europe where he re-converted to Orthodox Christianity. One of the few Polish Pan-Slavists, he advocated the accession of all Slavic lands to Russia.

Čelakovský, František Ladislav (1799 – 1852). Czech poet and translator of the *národní obrození* ['national revival'] period. He is most famed for his recreations of Russian and Czech traditional poetry in the *Ohlas písní ruských* [Echo of Russian Song, 1829] and *Ohlas písní českých* [Echo of Czech Song, 1839].

Dalimil (fl. XIII c.). Purported author of the early Czech chronicle in verse known as the *Dalimilova kronika* or the *Kronika boleslavská*. The attribution to 'Dalimil' was made only in the XVII century.

Delvig, Anton (1798 – 1831). Russian neoclassical poet of German ancestry. A friend of Pushkin's, with whom he co-edited the *Literary Gazette* (1830 – 1831).

Demeter, Dimitrija (1811 – 1872). Croatian poet and dramatist of Greek ancestry, one of the founders of the Croatian National Theatre.

Derzhavin, Gavrila Romanovich (1743 – 1816). Russian neoclassical poet, generally considered the most important poet of the Russian XVIII century.

Dobrovský, Josef (1753 – 1829). Czech philologist, Catholic priest, founder of comparative Slavic philology and one of the most important Slavic philologists. Among his seminal works are the *Geschichte der böh-*

mischen Sprache und Literatur [History of the Czech Language and Czech Literature, 1792], *Lehrgebäude der böhmischen Sprache* [Method for the Acquisition of the Czech Language, 1809], an important work for the codification of modern Czech, and the *Institutiones linguae slavicae dialecti veteris* [Principles of the Old Slavic Language, 1822], an important study of Old Church Slavonic.

Domaschko, Michael (Michał Domaško, 1820 – 1897). Lusatian Lutheran pastor, devotional poet, editor of an anthology of Lusatian Sorb poetry; one of the founders of the Sorbian Society, with which Štúr came into contact during his trip to Lusatia.

Dušan, Stefan (Stefan Uroš IV, 1308 – r. 1331 – 1355). King of Serbia, from 1346 Emperor of the Serbs, Greeks, and Albanians. Military leader, who significantly extended the territory of his kingdom, at one time waging war against the Byzantine Empire (although being the Emperor's son-in-law), annexing portions of the empire to his realm. He established a code of law that long remained in use.

Emmerich, Georg (1422 – 1507). He founded the replica of Christ's Tomb constructed in Görlitz (between 1481 and 1504) following his pilgrimage to the Holy Land in 1465. Besides the Tomb of Christ (*Das heilige Grab*), the complex also contains the Adam Chapel (*Adamskapelle*) and *Golgothakapelle* (Golgotha Chapel).

Friedrich II Hohenstaufen (1194 – r. 1220 – 1250). Holy Roman Emperor. Cultured ruler, whose court in Sicily is noted for its multinational culture and significance for the development of poetry in the Italian vernacular. Excommunicated thrice.

Géza (c. 940 – r. c. 970 – 997). Grand Prince of the Hungarians. Father of St Stephen, the first King of Hungary.

Gogol, Nikolai Vasilievich (1809 – 1852). Ukrainian-Russian humorist and dramatist. His writings had a great influence on modern Russian literature, from Realism to the quasi-Kafkaesque absurd. His unfinished novel Мёртвые души [Dead Souls, 1842] is his most well-known work in prose, whereas Ревизор [The Government Inspector, 1836], a satirical drama, is one of the classics of the Russian stage.

Gostimysl (Gostomysl, fl. X c.) Grand Prince of the Obrodites, father of St Ivan, first hermit of Bohemia.

Goszczyński, Seweryn (1801 – 1876). Polish soldier and poet. He took part in the November 1830 Uprising. His most famous work is the Gothic narrative poem *Zamek Kaniowski* [The Kaniów Castle, 1828].

Gundulić, Ivan (1589 – 1638). Croatian poet. Author of the epic *Osman* (composed 1651) celebrating the Polish victory over the Turks at the Battle of Chocim.

Hanka Václav (1791 – 1861). Czech poet and literary scholar, most well-known for his 'discovery' of the *Rukopis královédvorský* and *Rukopis zelenohorský* [The Králový Dvůr and Zelená hora Manuscripts, 1817, 1818], purporting to be mediaeval Czech poetry. Most scholars, beginning with Josef Dobrovský, considered them forgeries, although they caused a great furore among nationally-minded Czechs and Slovaks such as Štúr, who considered them to be evidence of the antiquity of Czech literature.

Haulik, Bishop Juraj (Juraj Haulik Váralyai, 1788 – 1869). Slovak-born first Cardinal Archbishop of Zagreb. Despite Štúr's reservations, Haulik, who twice served as *ban* of Croatia, was a tireless supporter of Croatian identity, especially as regards official respect for the Croatian language.

Haupt, Joachim Leopold (1797 – 1883). Lusatian Lutheran pastor. With Jan Arnošt Smoler, editor of the anthology *Pěsnički hornich a delnich Łužiskich Serbow* [Songs of the Sorbs of Upper and Lower Lusatia, 1841, 1843].

Heinrich (der Vogler, i.e. 'the Fowler,' 876 – r. 919 – 936). Son of Otto the Illustrious, founder of the Ottonian dynasty of Holy Roman Emperors. He expanded his realm by victorious military campaigns against the Danes and the Czechs.

Herder, Johann Gottfried von (1744 – 1803). German Lutheran pastor, precursor of the *Sturm und Drang* and Romantic movements. His theories concerning language and the sense of history had an influence on the development of ideas of ethnic nationality attractive to thinkers like Štúr.

Herwegh, Georg (1815 – 1875). German poet and socialist revolutionary; he took part in the 1848 uprising against the government in Baden, at the head of a large contingent of German and French workers.

Hněvkovský, Šebestián (1770 – 1847). Czech poet associated with the National Revival movement of Czech Romanticism. During a time when the modern Czech language and literary traditions were just forming, he sought patterns for his original verse not in translations from foreign works, but in folk literature.

Hollý, Ján (1785 – 1849). Slovak Catholic priest, poet and translator — the first great poet writing in the Slovak tongue as codified by Bernolák — which has earned him the somewhat overblown title of the 'Slovak Homer.' His most significant works are three epics, all dealing with the legends and ancient history of the Great Moravian Empire: *Svätopluk* (1833), *Cyrillo-Methodiada* (1835) and *Slav* (1839). He also translated Virgil's *Aeneid* into Slovak (1828), as well as composing devotional poetry.

Hraběta, Jan (1796 – 1859). Czech clergyman, chaplain at the Saxon court in Dresden, educator and classical scholar. He taught Czech to Prince Johann of Saxony (later King of Saxony, 1801 – r. 1854 – 1873).

Hunyadi, János (c. 1407 – 1456). Hungarian general, governor of Hungary (1446 – 1452); earlier military governor of Severin (in present-day Romania), governor of Transylvania. He waged war against the Ottoman Empire; like Cromwell in England, he is known for creating an early modern-type regular army (of multinational character), counting some 30,000 men, who successfully repulsed the Turks from many of the Slavic areas of the Balkans in 1444, forcing the Sultan to sue for a ten-year peace. King Władysław Jagiełło acceded to the Hungarian throne with Hunyadi's support in 1439, to die five years later fighting the Turks in Varna (for which he is known in Poland as 'Władysław Warneńczyk.') In 1456, he achieved a signal victory over the Turks besieging Belgrade, with an army of untrained commoners.

Immisch, Friedrich (Jaroměr Hendrich Imiš, 1819 – 1898). Lusatian Lutheran pastor, and Pan-Slavist, one of the founders of the Sorbian Society, with which Štúr came into contact during his trip to Lusatia.

Jaroslav of Šternberk (1220? – 1287?). Legendary Moravian warrior, who is said to have won a signal victory over the Mongols (Tatars) at Olomouc in the mid-XIII century. He is first mentioned in the 1541 *Kronice české* [Czech Chronicle) of Václav Hájek z Libočan.

Jelačić, Josip (1801 – 1859). Croatian soldier and governmental figure, serving as *ban* of Croatia from 1848. Štúr describes him as somewhat of a Hamletish figure for his timidity in furthering Croatian independence, while remaining loyal to Vienna.

Jiskra z Brandýsa, Jan (c. 1400 – c. 1469). Moravian warrior, who spent most of his active life in Slovakia. He fought in the Hussite wars in Moravia, and against both Turks and Hungarians in Slovakia, where he created a de facto independent realm that lasted some twenty years. Although a good portion of his military force consisted of former Hussites, he was a Catholic.

Jungmann, Josef (1773 – 1847). Czech philologist, translator, and poet of the National Revival period, whose lexicological and literary-historical work was of great significance for the development of the modern Czech literary idiom. Among his other writings, his translation of Milton's *Paradise Lost* is greatly valued as evidence of the suppleness and expressiveness of Czech.

Kakhovsky, Pyotr Grigoryevich (1799 – 1826). Russian military officer, executed for his part in the Decembrist uprising.

Kálmán (1070 – r. 1095 – 1116). Learned king of Hungary, who ascended the throne at the death of his childless uncle, St László I. Croatia was annexed to Hungary during his reign.

Kaplíř ze Sulevic, Kašpar (1525 – 1621). Czech nobleman, Imperial counsellor and Austrian general. Executed for his role in the 'Bohemian Revolt' of Czech Protestants during the Thirty Years' War.

Karamzin, Nikolai Mikhailovich (1766 – 1826). Russian poet and historian of anti-Polish convictions.

Katančić, Matija Petar (1750 – 1825). Croatian Franciscan. Poet, translator of the Bible into Croatian, promoter of Croatian literature.

Klicpera, Václav Kliment (1792 – 1859). Czech dramatist of the National Revival period, also a gymnasium professor. Amongst his students were the future writers Karol Jaromír Urban and Jan Neruda.

Klin, Bjedrich Adolf (1792 – 1855). Lusatian Sorb activist, jurist, representative to the Saxon diet, who saw to the passage of the law allowing the use of the Sorb language in schools.

Kollár, Ján (1793 – 1852). Czechoslovak poet, Evangelical minister, promoter of Slavic cultural 'reciprocity,' which did not suppose any political union between Slavic 'tribes.' His most influential work is *Slávy dcera* [Sláva's Daughter, 1824, 1832], a Dantesque journey through Slavdom, which had a great impact on the development of Pan-Slavist thought. He also published significant collections of Slovak folksong.

Komenský, Jan Amos (1592 – 1670). Moravian writer, minister of the Moravian church, widely respected in Europe as an educational reformer (Poland, Great Britain, Sweden, Hungary, Netherlands).

Konrad III Hohenstaufen (c. 1093 – r. 1138 – 1152). King of Germany (King of the Romans). First king of the Hohenstaufen dynasty, crusader.

Kopernik, Mikołaj (Copernicus, 1473 – 1543). Polish priest and astronomer of partial German descent, whose work *De revolutionibus orbium coelestium libri vi* (1543) set forth the heliocentric theory.

Korvin Matej (1443 – r. 1458 – 1490). King of Hungary and Croatia, pretender to the Czech crown, populariser of Renaissance culture north of the Alps.

Kossuth, Lajos (1802 – 1894). Hungarian politician and revolutionary of Slovak extraction, although he considered himself a Magyar and promoted the magyarisation of the Hungarian state. Elected governor of

Hungary by the Hungarian Diet in revolt against Vienna in 1848, he fled the country in 1849 upon the entry of Russian troops at the request of Austria, and spent the remainder of his life abroad — including stays in Great Britain and the United States.

Kościuszko, Tadeusz (1746 – 1817). Polish general and revolutionary of Belarusian heritage. Kościuszko fought on the Colonial side during the American War of Independence, returning to Poland to take part in the military actions against Russia during the period that led to the partitions of the country. His last struggles, in 1794, when he assumed command of all the insurrectionary forces, ended in defeat after some initial successes, and this led to the complete disappearance of Poland from the map of Europe. This last campaign is popularly known as the Kościuszko Uprising. He refused repeated requests of Napoléon to command portions of his army, due to Napoléon's equivocating policies concerning Polish independence. His body rests in the royal necropolis in the crypts of Wawel Cathedral in Kraków.

Kotlyaryevsky, Ivan (1769 – 1838). Ukrainian poet and dramatist, hailed as the father of modern Ukrainian literature. His *Eneida* (1798) is a farcical transmutation of Virgil's epic amongst the Cossacks, and is the first work written entirely in Ukrainian.

Kozlov, Ivan Ivanovich (1779 – 1840). Russian romantic poet and translator from the English.

Kráľ, Janko (1822 – 1876). Slovak romantic poet and revolutionary who took part in the 1848 uprising against the Magyars.

Krasicki, Ignacy (1735 – 1801). Polish priest and Neoclassical poet. Bishop of Warmia, eventually Archbishop of Gniezno (Primate of Poland). As a writer, he excelled in all genres of Neoclassical literature, from the fable to the picaresque novel. Of special interest are his mock epics, such as *Myszeis* [The Mouseiad, 1775].

Krasiński, Zygmunt (1812 – 1859). Polish dramatist, often grouped with Mickiewicz and Słowacki as one of the national bards of Poland. He is most noteworthy for his somewhat Byronic closet drama *Nieboska*

Komedia [The Undivine Comedy, 1835], which is both a critique of Romantic poetry as an escapist worldview, and a treatment of the class struggles, which he foresaw as an insoluble threat to the European social fabric.

Kraszewski, Józef Ignacy (1812 – 1887). Polish Romantic author, the chief prose writer of the period. He authored over 600 works, mostly novels based on Polish history and legend. Arguably the most popular of these remains *Stara baśń* [An Ancient Tale, 1876], which deals with an idealised pre-Christian past.

Krušwica, Jan (1811 – 1880). Lusatian Lutheran pastor and devotional author; one of the founders of the Sorbian Society, with which Štúr came into contact during his trip to Lusatia. His son Jan Bjarnat Krušwica (1845 – 1919) continued his father's activities in the fields of Sorb literature and culture.

Kucharski, Andrzej (1795 – 1862). Polish Slavist, who travelled among the Lusatian Sorbs, and in Slovakia. His most noteworthy work is the *Najdawniejsze pomniki prawodawstwa słowiańskiego* [Earliest monuments of Slavic lawmaking, 1838].

Kunhuta (Kateřina z Poděbrad, 1449 – 1464). First wife of Matej Korvin. Betrothed to him at the age of eleven, the marriage was consummated only in 1463. She died in childbirth at age fourteen.

Kupa. Legendary rebel, who is said to have risen against King St Stephen in 998.

Kuzmány, Karol (1806 – 1866). Slovak Lutheran pastor, poet, editor of the literary periodical *Hronka*, officer of the Matica slovenská.

Lazar, Stefan (Hrebeljanovič, c. 1329 – 1389). Serbian ruler, executed by the Turks after the catastrophic defeat of Serbian forces on the Kosovan Field.

Lehmann, Johann (Jan Wićaz, c. 1820 – 1866). Lusatian Lutheran pastor and devotional poet; one of the founders of the Sorbian Society, with which Štúr came into contact during his trip to Lusatia.

Lelewel, Joachim (1786 – 1861). Polish historian of German descent, professor and friend of Adam Mickiewicz. As a scholar, he was mainly interested in the Middle Ages, composing works on mediaeval numismatics, geography, and the early history of Poland.

Libuše. Legendary daughter of Prince Krok, wife of Přemysl Oráč, the legendary first ruler of the Czech lands. Prophetess, founder of the city of Prague. The story of her judgement may be found in the purportedly mediaeval *Manuscript of Zelená hora* of Václav Hanka.

Ljutovid (fl. XI c.). Serbian ruler of territories presently in western Herzegovina and Croatia.

Lubjenski, Handrij (1790 – 1840). Lusatian Lutheran minister, Lusatian activist, collector of Sorb folksong and legend.

Mácha, Karel Hynek (1810 – 1836). Czech Romantic poet, the national bard of the Czech nation. His Byronic narrative poem *Máj* (1836 – 1836) is the most important text of the National Revival period. An actor during his student years in Prague, his life was cut short after ingesting cholera-infected water while helping out on a bucket-brigade during a fire at Litoměřice. Influenced by Walter Scott and Adam Mickiewicz as well as Byron, he left behind fragments of historical novels, plays, and lyric poetry in both Czech and German, as well as a journal that was only fully published in the 1990s.

Maciejowski, Franciszek (1793 – 1883). Polish historian; author of a four-volume work on Slavic jurisprudence.

Magnuszewski, Dominik (1809 – 1845). Polish actor and playwright, whose works are mostly derived from Polish history.

Malczewski, Antoni (1793 – 1826). Polish Romantic poet, mainly known for his Byronic narrative poem *Marya* (1825). A mountain climber, he was the first Pole to conquer the summit of Mont Blanc.

Manteuffel, Otto Theodor (1805 – 1882). German politician, Prime Minister of Prussia during the constitutional discussions following the unrest of 1848.

Matúš z Trenčína (Matúš Čák, Csák Maté, c. 1260 – 1321). Slovak palatine of Hungarian descent, claimed by both nations as a symbol of the struggle for independence. In his poem, not only does Štúr seek to emphasise Matúš as a Slavic patriot, by shrouding his birth in mystery, but he also plays fast and loose with historical fact. He clothes his hero's forceful acquisition of territories as a patriotic endeavour to re-establish the Great Moravian Empire, and also greatly simplifies his relations with the Czech King Václav.

Maurice (539 – r. 582 – 602). Byzantine emperor and solider, author of the *Strategikon* or Military Manual, in book nine of which, as Štúr notes, he describes the Slavs against whom he has fought.

Metternich, Klemens von (1773 – 1859). Austrian statesman, originally from the Rhineland. Foreign Minister of the Austrian Empire from 1809 until 1848. He was an architect of Europe redrawn at the Congress of Vienna in 1815, which had wide-ranging ramifications for Poland and the nations of Central Europe.

Mihailo, Prince of Serbia (Mihailo Obrenovič, c. 1780 – r. 1815-1839 – 1860). Serbian monarch, participant of First and Second Serbian Uprisings, and architect of Serbia's autonomy from the Ottoman Empire.

Mickiewicz, Adam (1798 – 1855). Poland's greatest poet. His literary output includes important works in all genres, save prose fiction — unless we include here his *Księgi narodu polskiego i pielgrzymstwa polskiego* [Books of the Polish Nation and Polish Pilgrimage, 1832], which inspired Štúr's own pseudo-biblical 'The Slovaks in Ancient Days, and Now.' *Pan Tadeusz* (1835) is the national epic of Poland, though it is more of a rustic idyll than a truly Vergilian epic. *Dziady* [Forefathers' Eve, 1823, 1832], perhaps his most important work, initiates the Polish Monumental stage, and his *Sonnets* (1826), contain both the finest descriptive sonnets ever written (his Crimean cycle) and a Petrarchan cycle of erotic sonnets that follow the progress of a relationship from initial enthusiasm through cynical disillusionment. Mickiewicz died in Turkey, attempting to form a Polish Legion to wage war against the Russian Empire during the Crimean War.

Mierosławski, Ludwik (1814 – 1878). Polish general, who took part in all the major uprisings of the Poles, from that of November 1830 through the January Insurrection of 1863, of which he was elected the first dictator. He was involved in the Polish uprisings in the Poznań region against Prussia, for which he is mentioned by Štúr.

Miloš, Prince of Serbia (Miloš Obrenovič, 1821 – r. 1840-1842, 1860 – 1868). Serbian monarch, advocate of Balkan unity in the face of the Ottoman threat. He was deposed as a young man, then regained his throne only to be assassinated eight years later.

Milota z Dědic (fl. XIII c.) Styrian nobleman, accused (perhaps unjustly) of betraying Czech king Přemysl Otakar II at the Moravian battle of 1278. The manner in which the legendary Milota withdraws his men from the field at the crucial point in the battle is similar to the treason described by Štúr in *Matúš of Trenčín*.

Milutinović (Sima Milutinović Sarajlija, 1791 – 1847). Serbian poet, who fought in the uprisings against the Turks.

Mojmír II (c. 870 – r. 894 – 906). Last ruler of the Great Moravian Empire. Internal conflicts with his brother Svätopluk II, the ruler of Nitra, and external pressure from Arnulf, the eastern Frankish king, led to the fall of the Great Moravian Empire. His brother Svatoboj is a legendary figure, as is the story of Svätopluk's conspiracy with the Magyars against him. (Mojmír himself settled the Magyars along the Tisa, after their appearance in his realm, and used them at least once as allies in his struggle against Arnulf in Pannonia).

Mosik z Aehrenfeldu, August (Korla Avgust Mósak Kłosopólski 1820 – 1898). Lusatian lawyer and translator, one of the founders of the Sorbian Society, with which Štúr came into contact during his trip to Lusatia, in fact, its first president. He translated Šafárik's *Slovanské starožitnosti* [Slavic Antiquities] into German.

Muraviev-Apostol, Sergei Ivanovich (1796 – 1826). Russian military officer, anti-serfdom agitator and republican theorist, executed for his role in the Decembrist plot.

Musin-Pushkin, Alexei Ivanovich (1744 – 1817). Russian historian and antiquarian. He is most remembered for discovering the manuscript of the *Lay of Igor's Campaign*, which was lost in the conflagration that consumed his entire library during Napoléon's firing of Moscow in 1812.

Mušicki, Lukijan (1777 – 1837). Serbian poet and classicist, translator of Horace and Ovid.

Naruszewicz, Adam (1733 – 1796). Polish poet and historian, Jesuit priest, titular Bishop of Smoleńsk.

Nejedlý, Vojtěch (1772 – 1844). Czech priest, poet and translator of the National Revival period. He is most well known for his epic poems concerning Czech history, such as *Přemysl Otakar v Prusích* [Přemysl Otakar in Prussia, 1832] and *Karel Čtvrtý* [Charles IV, 1835].

Nemanja, Stefan (1113 – r. 1166-1196 – 1199). Grand Prince of Serbia, who waged war against Byzantium during the stormy years of the reigns of the Comnenus Emperors. Later, he renounced his throne in favour of his son to become a monk, taking the name Simeon. He was canonised by the Serbian Orthodox Church in 1200; his feast day is 26 February.

Nikolai, Tsar (Nikolai Romanov, 1796 – r. 1825 – 1855). Tsar of Russia, whose reign commenced with the Decembrist Revolt against him. A staunch conservative, he centralised the government, dealt strictly with all dissent, and presided over the industrial and economic development of his realm.

Otakar (Ottokar I, 1155 – r. 1192 – 1230). Duke, later King of Bohemia, during whose reign the Czech lands saw a large influx of German settlers.

Otto (Otto III, 980 – r. 996 – 1002). Holy Roman Emperor. He furthered Christianity in the east by establishing ecclesiastical structures in Poland independent of German jurisdiction, and acknowledging the independence of the Polish kingdom in the person of King Bolesław Chrobry. He also established the future St Stephen as the first King of Hungary.

Padurra, Tymko (Tomasz, 1801 – 1871). Poet and musician, creative in both Polish and Ukrainian.

Palacký, František (1798 – 1876). Czech historian, politician and activist. His main work is the five-volume *Dějiny národu českého v Čechách a v Moravě* [History of the Czech Nation in Bohemia and Moravia], 1836 – 1867; he also wrote in German.

Pavel, Tsar (1754 – r. 1796 – 1801). Son of Catherine the Great, Tsar of Russia. By turns autocratic and liberal (he forbade corporal punishment of free men, and strove to ameliorate the condition of the serfs), he was assassinated by disgruntled officers.

Pestel, Pavel Ivanovich (1793 – 1826). Russian military officer, republican revolutionary theorist, executed for his role in the Decembrist plot.

Pešina, Tomáš Jan (1629 – 1680). Catholic bishop, historian of Moravia, among whose works are the three volume *Prodromus Moravographiae* (1663) and *Mars moravicus* (1677), a military history of the region.

Petaw, Karl (Korla Moric Pjetawa, 1811 – 1880). One of the founders of the Sorbian Society, with which Štúr came into contact during his trip to Lusatia. He became a teacher in Luppa.

Petrovič-Njegoš, Petar, or Petar II (1813 – 1851). Vladika (i.e. Prince-Bishop) of Montenegro. He sought to modernise the Montenegrin state by centralising power, but his taxation politics caused serious dissent among the people. He was an early proponent of unity with the Serbian state, and is credited as being one of the early architects of South Slavic unity — something which obviously held great appeal for Štúr. Petrovič-Njegoš is also considered an important Serbian poet.

Piasecki, Paweł (1579 – 1649). Catholic bishop, Royal Secretary to King Zygmunt III Vasa, author of a chronicle of Poland.

Piast (fl. X c.). Piast Kołodziej (the Wheelwright) is the legendary founder of the Piast dynasty of kings. His miraculous ascension to the premier place in the Polanie tribe — which was to form the core of the Polish kingdom — plays into the popular legend of the Polish monarchy arising from the people. The most noteworthy ruler of the Piast dynasty was King Kazimierz III, 'the Great' (c. 1310 – r. 1333 – 1370), founder of the Akademia Krakowska (later, Jagiellonian University).

Poděbrad (Jiří z Kunštát a Poděbrad, 1420 – r. 1458 – 1471). The 'Hussite King,' the only Czech ruler to be elected to his throne by the Czech aristocracy, and the last King of Bohemia of Czech blood. He is noteworthy for his concept, worked out in concert with his advisor Antonio Marini of Grenoble, of a peaceful federation of European states, which would respect the inner policies of each member, and refer disputes to an international tribunal.

Pogodin, Mikhail Petrovich (1800 – 1875). Russian historian, devoted disciple of the mediaeval chronicler Nestor and proponent of the Norman extraction of Rurik.

Pohlenz, Bruno (fl. XIX c.). One of the founders of the Sorbian Society, with which Štúr came into contact during his trip to Lusatia.

Polák, Milota Zdirad (1788 – 1856). Czech soldier and poet. His *Vznešenost přírody* [Sublimity of Nature, 1813], inspired in part by James Thompson's *Seasons*, had an influence on the development of the modern poetic idiom in Czech during the National Revival period.

Poniatowski, Józef (1763 – 1813). Polish military hero, nephew of Stanisław Poniatowski, the last King of Poland, Marshal of France who died at the Elster while covering the French retreat at Leipzig.

Prešeren, France (1800 – 1849). National poet of Slovenia.

Procopius of Caesarea (c. 500 – 560). Late Byzantine historian. He speaks of the Slavs and their traditions of government in book seven of his *History of the Wars*.

Přemyslav (Nošák, c. 1332 – 1410). Duke of Cieszyn, Governor of Kraków, Governor of Bohemia. A skilled diplomat, whose power and influence was felt in both Poland and Bohemia.

Přemyslids. Czech royal dynasty, which ruled from the IX to the early XIV century.

Puchmajer, Antonín Jaroslav (1769 – 1820). Catholic priest, poet and translator, one of the moving lights behind the National Revival of Czech as a literary language in the late XVIII – early XIX century.

Pushkin, Alexander Sergeyevich (1799 – 1837). The greatest poet of Russia, and one of the greatest in the entire history of world literature. Among his works are the 'novel in verse' *Eugene Onegin* (1825 – 1832), which destroys the myth of the Byronic hero, *Boris Godunov* (1825), perhaps the most successful Shakespearean tragedy of the Romantic period, and numerous other important works in prose and verse, such as the narrative poem 'The Bronze Horseman,' which he composed as a reply to a portion of his friend Adam Mickiewicz's *Forefathers' Eve*. He died at age 37 as the result of a duel with his brother-in-law Georges d'Anthès, a guards officer, which tragedy was the inspiration for Štúr's lament 'Pushkin.' It is unclear whether or not d'Anthès' unhealthy fascination with Pushkin's wife Natalia was the efficient cause of the duel, or whether it was orchestrated by Pushkin's enemies in Russia.

Radowitz, Joseph von (1797 – 1853). Prussian diplomat, advocate of German unification at the Frankfurt Congress.

Rastislav (r. 846 – 870). Second ruler of the Great Moravian Empire. It was he who effected the Christianisation of the Western Slavs, by inviting SS Cyril and Methodius to evangelise his realm. In 1994 he was canonised a saint by the Orthodox Church in the Czech lands and Slovakia.

Rentsch, Karl (Jan Korla Rjenč, fl. XIX c.). One of the founders of the Sorbian Society, with which Štúr came into contact during his trip to Lusatia; later, a Lutheran clergyman.

Rurik (c. 830 – 879). Founder of Novgorod, Kievan Rus, and thus Russia; a Viking.

Ryleyev, Kondraty Fyodorovich (1795 – 1826). Russian military officer, Romantic poet, executed for his role in the Decembrist plot.

Samo (fl. 600 – 660). Eastern Frankish king who established the first Slavic state, extending from Slovakia through Bohemia, north into the territory of the Sorbs, and south into the territory of the Slovenes.

Sauer Karl (Korla Bohuměr Sauer, 1820 – 1844). One of the founders of the Sorbian Society, with which Štúr came into contact during his trip to Lusatia; he died while studying for the Lutheran ministry.

Schlözer, August Ludwig von (1735 – 1809). German historian of Russia. As a linguist, he is famous for coining the term 'Semitic languages.'

Schulze, Adolph (Adolf Šolta, fl. XIX c.). One of the founders of the Sorbian Society, with which Štúr came into contact during his trip to Lusatia.

Schwarzenberg, Felix (1800 – 1852). Prime minister of Austria following the 1848 revolutions; creator of the centralised Austrian Empire, opponent of German consolidation.

Sedláček, Josef Vojtěch (1785 – 1836). Czech priest, mathematician. His contribution to the National Revival was in the invention of mathematical terms for the resuscitated Czech language.

Shevirev, Stepan Petrovich (1806 – 1864). Russian poet, critic and historian of literature.

Shishkov, Alexander Semyonovich (1754 – 1841). Slavophile Russian Admiral and linguist; author of a trilingual Russian-French-English naval dictionary, president of the Russian Academy of Literature.

Skrzynecki, Jan Zygmunt (1787 – 1860). Polish general. He fought with Napoléon and as supreme commander of the Polish insurrectionary forces during the 1830 November Uprising against Russia. Lampooned by Juliusz Słowacki in *Kordian* for timidity and his desire to negotiate with the Russians, rather than fighting.

Smoleŕ, Jan Arnošt (1816 – 1884). Lusatian Slavist and translator. Founder of the Towaŕstwo za łužiske rěče a stawizny [Society for the Propagation of the Languages and History of Lusatia]. Collector of Lusatian Sorb folksong, his *Pjesnički hornych a deľnych Łužiskich Serbow* [Folksongs of the Upper and Lower Lusatian Sorbs] were published in 1841 and 1843.

Sobieski, Jan III (1629 – r. 1674 – 1696). King of Poland and military hero, who fought in many of Poland's wars. His most famous victory was the lifting of the siege of Vienna by the Turks in 1683. Educated at Jagiellonian University, Sobieski is also important to the Baroque literature of Poland as a stylist, for his love-letters written to his wife Marysia over the years 1665 – 1683.

Spytihněv I (c. 875 – r. 894 – 915). Czech prince, who impelled the nascent Czech state away from the Great Moravian Empire, orienting Bohemia toward Bavaria.

Stephen, St (István, c. 975 – r. c. 1000 –1038). Grand Prince of the Hungarians, subsequently first King of the Hungarians. Accepting Christianity, and later propagating the faith in the territories under his sceptre, Stephen is credited as the establishing monarch of the Kingdom of Hungary. He did battle against both pagan Magyars and the German troops of the Holy Roman Empire. He was canonised a saint of the Catholic Church in 1083; his feast day is 16 August (20 August and 30 May in Hungary); he is especially venerated in Hungary and Slovakia.

Stillbrich, Friedrich (fl. XIX c.) One of the founders of the Sorbian Society, with which Štúr came into contact during his trip to Lusatia.

Suleiman I ('the Magnificent,' 1494 – r. 1520 – 1566). Turkish sultan, whose incursions into Europe led to the taking of Belgrade in 1521 and the ravaging of Hungary shortly thereafter. He too laid siege to Vienna in 1529, unsuccessfully.

Svätopluk (Czech: Svatopluk, Polish: Świętopełk, c. 840 – r. c. 867 – 894). Svätopluk I, Prince of Nitra, Duke of Moravia, King of the Great Moravian Empire, which experienced its greatest expansion under his rule, after his deposing of his uncle Rastislav. His younger son Svätopluk II (c. 884 – 899) rebelled against his older brother Mojmír, which initiated the decline and eventual fall of the Great Moravian Empire.

Szemere, Bertelan (1812 – 1869). Magyar poet and Prime Minister of the temporarily independent Hungary during the rebellion against Vienna in 1848.

Šafárik, Pavol Josef (Czech: Pavel Josef Šafařík, 1795 – 1861). Slovak poet, Slavist and philologist, mainly creative in Czech. His noteworthy works include: *Geschichte der slawischen Sprache und Literatur nach allen Mundarten* [The History of the Slavic Language and Literature in all its Dialects, 1826] and *Slovanské starožitnosti* [Slavic Antiquities, 1837, 1865]. Among his poetry, *Tatranská múza s lýrou slovanskou* [The Tatra Muse with the Slavic Lyre, 1814] is an important pleromatic work in Czech.

Talvj (Therese Albertine Luise von Jakob Robinson, 1797 – 1870). German linguist and translator, especially of Serbian folksongs, which found approbation in Goethe's eyes. She studied Native American languages after moving to the United States with her American husband Edward Robinson, and in 1840 published a literary exposé of the Ossian poems as forgeries.

Thun, Leo (1811 – 1888). Austrian count native to Bohemia, proponent of Austrian federalism.

Tomasseo, Niccolò (1802 – 1874). Italian Catholic linguist and poet; despite his interest in Serbo-Croatian and identification with 'our nation,' more of a cosmopolitan than the Slav that Štúr paints him to be. His *Iskrice* [Sparks] cited by Štúr were published in 1842.

Tugumír (fl. 900 – 950). Polabian Slav leader.

Tupý, Karel (1813 – 1881). Catholic priest, poet of the Czech national revival period; his pen-name was Boleslav Jablonský.

Turinský, František (1797 – 1852). Czech poet and dramatist of the Czech national revival period.

Tyl, Josef Kajetán (1808 – 1856). Czech dramatist and actor of the national revival period; arguably the most important Czech romantic apart from Karel Hynek Mácha. Among his noteworthy plays is the *Strakonický dudák aneb Hody divých žen* [The Bagpiper from Strakonice, or the Feast of Wild Women, 1847], as well as historical dramas from the Hussite past, such as *Jan Hus* and *Žižka z Trocnova* [Žižka of Trocnov]. He is also the author of the Czech national anthem, 'Kde domov můj' [Where my Homeland is]. For a short time, he was a Czech representative to the Austrian diet following the 1848 Revolution.

Ustryalov, Nikolai Gerasimovich (1805 – 1870). Russian historian, proponent of royal absolutism and the russification of non-Russian nations of the empire.

Vinařický, Karel Alois (1803 – 1869). Catholic priest, classicising poet, but propagator of the Czech National Revival. He is also important to the movement as a proponent of children's literature in Czech.

Vladimir Sviatoslavich ('The Great,' c. 958 – r. 969 – 1015). Prince of Novgorod, Grand Prince of Kiev of the Rurik dynasty. He is noteworthy for expanding the extent and power of the nascent state of Kieven Rus. A pagan for much of his adult life, he converted to Christianity and subsequently Christianised Rus; as St Vladimir of Kiev he is venerated in both Catholic and Orthodox Churches (his feast day is 15 July).

Vocel, Jan Erazim (1802 –1871). Czech poet and dramatist of the National Revival period; father of Czech archeology, envoy to the Austrian diet following the 1848 Revolution.

Vratislav I (888 – r. 915 – 921). Czech prince, brother of Spytihněv I (c. 875 – r. 894 – 915) who preceded him on the throne after the Czech lands' separation from the Great Moravian Empire.

Vraz, Stanko (Jakob Frass, 1810 –1851). Croatian poet, translator, collector of folksongs, Illyrist.

Vukotinović, Ljudevit (1813 – 1893). Croatian poet, Illyrist, revolutionary during the Spring of the Peoples in 1848; botanist.

Wanak, Jurij Ernst (1817 – 1887). Lutheran clergyman, Lusatian Sorb activist.

Windischgrätz, Alfred (Windisch-Grätz, 1787 – 1862). Austrian Field Marshal, who served in the wars against Napoléon, but is most remembered for suppressing the uprising in Prague following the Slavic Congress in 1848, suppressing a revolt in Vienna in the same year by laying siege to the capital city, and leading Austrian troops against the rebellious Magyars.

Yaroslav ('the Wise', c. 978 – r. 1010 – 1054). Prince of Novgorod, Grand Prince of Kiev, son of St Vladimir. He promulgated the legal code subsequently known as the Russkaya Pravda.

Yelagin, Ivan Perfilievich (1725 – 1794). Russian historian, poet, translator, director of court theatres under Catherine the Great.

Yevgeny (Metropolitan Yevgeny Bolkhovitinov, 1767 – 1837). Orthodox Metropolitan of Kiev and Galicia from 1822. A respected antiquary, friend of the poet Derzhavin.

Zaleski, Józef Bohdan (1802 – 1886). Polish Romantic poet of the so-called 'Ukrainian School'.

Zalužanský, Adam (1558 – 1613). Czech classicist and botanist.

Zejleŕ, Handrij (1804 – 1872). Lusatian poet and Lutheran pastor. His Sorbian Grammar was published in 1830, which was epochal in its codification of the Sorbian language, reforming its orthography on Czech and Polish models.

Zhukovsky, Vasily Andreyevich (1783 – 1852). Russian Romantic poet, translator from German and English.

Zrínski, Nikola Šubíc (c. 1507 – 1566). Croatian Ban, soldier. Defeating the Turks at Szigetvár, he halted Ottoman advances into Europe, a victory in many ways as significant as Jan III Sobieski's lifting of the Siege of Vienna in 1683.

Zygmunt II August (1520 – r. 1548 – 1572). Polish king, who waged successful wars against Muscovy, adding the territories of present-day Estonia and Latvia to the Polish kingdom. He united Poland and Lithuania into the 'Kingdom of Both Nations' with the Union of Lublin in 1569.

Zygmunt I Stary ('the Old,' 1467 – r. 1506 – 1548). Polish king, to whom Prussia submitted in formal homage in 1525. Patron of the arts, propagator of the Italian Renaissance north of the Alps.

Žižka, Jan (c. 1316 – 1424). Czech general, follower of Jan Hus, participant in the Battle of Grunwald (15 July 1410) during which a multinational army under King Władysław Jagiełło defeated the German Knights of the Cross, thus attaching Pomerania to the Polish Crown. Žižka is credited with inventing field artillery by affixing cannon to wagons, and also for the strategy of drawing wagons into a defensive circle.

BIBLIOGRAPHY

SOURCE TEXTS:

ŠTÚR, Ľudovít. *Dielo w piatich zväzkoch*, ed. Jozef Ambruš. Bratislava: Vzdavateľstvo Slovenskej Akadémie Vied, 1954.

ŠTÚR, Ľudovít. *Starý a nový věk Slovaků*, ed. Josef Jirásek. Bratislava: Nákladem Učené Společnosti Šafaříkovy v Bratislavě, 1935.

ŠTÚR, Ľudovít. *Spevy a piesne*. Bratislava: v tlačiarni predtým Schmidovej, 1853.

SECONDARY SOURCES:

BRÜCKNER, Aleksander. *Mitologia słowiańska i polska*. Warsaw: PWN, 1985.

FROMKIN, David. *Europe's Last Summer: Who Started the Great War in 1917?* New York: Vintage, 2007.

HURBAN, Josef Miloslav. *Slovenskje Pohladi*. 1851:I.5 (25 June): 198.

HURBAN VAYANSKÝ, Svetozar. *Sobrané diela*, Vol. IV, *Tatry a more*. Trnava: G. Bežu, 1924.

JANASZEK-IVANIČKOVÁ, Halina, ed. Ľudovít Štúr, *Wybór pism*. Wrocław: Ossolineum, 1983.

JESENSKÝ, Janko. *Cestou k slobode, 1914-1918*. Turčiansky svätý Martin: Matica Slovenská, 1933.

KOLLÁR, Jan. *O literní vzájemnosti mezi rozličnými kmeny a nářečími slovanského národu*. Prague: Jan S. Tomíček, 1853.

KOLLÁR, Jan. *Prózy*. Prague: Knihovna Klasiků, 1956.

LENDVAI, Paul. *Total Blindness: The Hungarian Sense of Mission and the Nationalities*. New Brunswick: Princeton University Press, 2003.

LUCIANI, Georges. 'Du Congrès de Prague (1848) au Congrès de Moscou (1867),' in *Revue des études slaves*, 47 (1968): 85-93.

ŁOMIAŃSKI, Henryk. *Religia Słowian i jej upadek*. Warsaw: PWN, 1985.

MAXWELL, Alexander. 'Walerian Krasiński's *Panslavism and Germanism* (1848): Polish Goals in a Pan-Slav Context,' in *The New Zealand Slavonic Journal*, 42 (2008): 101-120.

MAGOCSI, Robert. *With their Backs to the Mountains: A History of Carpathian Rus' and Carpatho-Rusyns*. Budapest and New York: Central European University Press, 2015.

MÉSÁROŠ, Július. 'Magyaren und Slowaken. Zur Frage des Panslawismus in der Vormärzzeit,' in Ľudovít Holotík, ed. *Ľudovít Štúr und die slawische Wechselseitigkeit*. Bratislava: Slovak Academy of Arts and Sciences, 1969.

SEKANINA, František. 'O našem Karlu Havlíčkovi Borovském,' in Karel Havlíček-Borovský, *Životní Dílo*. Prague: Věčné prameny, 1940.

ODDO, Gilbert L. *Slovakia and its People*. New York: Robert Speller and Sons, 1960.

OSUSKÝ, Samuel Štefan. *Šturova filozofia*. Bratislava: Slovenská liga, 1936.

PREISNER, Rio. *Až na konec Česka*. London: Rozmluvy, 1987.

ŠPIESZ, Anton. *Ilustrované dejiny Slovenska: na ceste k sebauvedomiu*. Bratislava: Perfekt, 1992.

(UNATTRIBUTED) 'Die Ungarn.' *Archäologie in Deutschland*, Sonderheft, 2008: 75-108.

VLČEK, Jaroslav. *Dejiny literatúry slovenskej*. Turčiansky sv. Martin: Matica slovenská, 1923.

ABOUT THE AUTHOR

Ľudovít Štúr (1815 – 1856) is arguably the most influential author in Slovak literature. Entirely devoted to the cause of the Slovak people's independence, there is hardly a work of his, whether in prose or verse, that is not conceived with his great mission in mind: the establishment of a proud, autonomous, Slovak nation, in brotherly concord, if not outright political union, with all the other 'tribes' of Slavdom. Fluent in Magyar and German, as well as all of the Slavic tongues, Štúr came to understand his nature as a Slovak, and a Slav, while a young boy sent to a distant Hungarian boarding school in the town of Győr. Following his brother Karol to the Slovak lyceum in Bratislava, he threw himself into activity on behalf of the Slovak nation and Slavic culture, even as a student himself lecturing the lower classes on Slavic languages and literatures, inculcating in them a love for their nation, and Slavdom as a whole. His two years spent at the University of Halle introduced him to both a deeper understanding of Hegel's philosophy of history — which, as he saw it, guaranteed a bright future for the Slavs — and Herder's idea of the *Volk*, which sharpened his perception of the traits and nature of the Slavic peoples, in the past and in the present. Upon returning to Hungary from his studies, he undertook agitation as a publicist — especially after being deprived of his position at the Bratislava Lyceum for his opposition to the Hungarian Kingdom's policies of magyarisation. He defended Slovak rights in the Hungarian parliament, to which he was elected in the fateful years 1847 – 1849. The outbreak of the Spring of the Peoples saw him in Prague, as one of the chief organisers of the Slavic Congress. When this was disrupted by the cannon of General Windischgrätz, Štúr took to the barricades during the Czech June Uprising, and later played an active role in organising armed resistance to the Magyars, on behalf of Slovak independence, at a time when the Magyars themselves were in open revolt against Vienna. The quelling of these rebellions by the Austrians, aided by the Russians, put an end to his political activity — consigning him to what amounted to a house arrest in the village of Modra — and disabusing him of any illusions he may have had about the possibilities of a union of the Slavs under the Habsburg sceptre. Štúr died at the young age of 41 from complications arising from a hunting accident. Although his tireless polemics on behalf of his Slavic and Slovak ideals are his most noteworthy writings, he was an accomplished poet as well. His two great narrative poems, *Svatoboj* and *Matúš of Trenčín* are among the treasures of Slovak poetry.

ABOUT THE TRANSLATOR

Charles S. Kraszewski is a poet and translator, creative in both English and Polish. He is the author of three volumes of original verse in English (*Diet of Nails; Beast; Chanameed*); and one in Polish: *Hallo, Sztokholm*. He translates from Polish, Czech and Slovak into English, and from English and Spanish into Polish. Recently, his English version of Jan Kochanowski's *Dismissal of the Grecian Envoys* was produced at Shakespeare's Globe Theatre in London. He is a member of the Union of Polish Writers Abroad (London) and of the Association of Polish Writers (SPP, Kraków).

Forefathers' Eve
by Adam Mickiewicz

Forefathers' Eve [*Dziady*] is a four-part dramatic work begun circa 1820 and completed in 1832 – with Part I published only after the poet's death, in 1860. The drama's title refers to *Dziady*, an ancient Slavic and Lithuanian feast commemorating the dead. This is the grand work of Polish literature, and it is one that elevates Mickiewicz to a position among the "great Europeans" such as Dante and Goethe.

With its Christian background of the Communion of the Saints, revenant spirits, and the interpenetration of the worlds of time and eternity, *Forefathers' Eve* speaks to men and women of all times and places. While it is a truly Polish work – Polish actors covet the role of Gustaw/Konrad in the same way that Anglophone actors covet that of Hamlet – it is one of the most universal works of literature written during the nineteenth century. It has been compared to Goethe's Faust – and rightfully so...

Buy it > www.glagoslav.com

Four Plays:
Mary Stuart, Kordian, Balladyna, Horsztyński

The dramas in Glagoslav's edition of *Four Plays* include some of the poet's greatest dramatic works, all written before age twenty-five: *Mary Stuart, Balladyna* and *Horsztyński* weave carefully crafted motifs from *King Lear, Macbeth, Hamlet* and *A Midsummer Night's Dream* in astoundingly original works, and *Kordian* — Słowacki's riposte to Mickiewicz's *Forefathers' Eve*, constitutes the final word in the revolutionary period of Polish Romanticism.

Translated into English by Charles S. Kraszewski, the *Four Plays* of Juliusz Słowacki will be of interest to aficionados of Polish Romanticism, Shakespeare, and theatre in general.

Buy it > www.glagoslav.com

The Sonnets
by Adam Mickiewicz

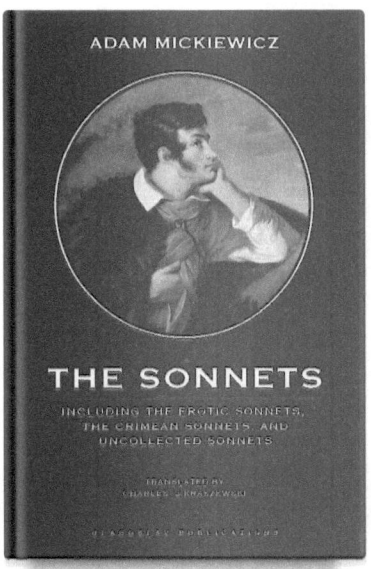

Because the poetry of Adam Mickiewicz is so closely identified with the history of the Polish nation, one often reads him as an institution, rather than a real person. In the *Crimean and Erotic Sonnets* of the national bard, we are presented with the fresh, real, and striking poetry of a living, breathing man of flesh and blood. Mickiewicz proved to be a master of Petrarchan form. His *Erotic Sonnets* chronicle the development of a love affair from its first stirrings to its disillusioning denouement, at times in a bitingly sardonic tone. *The Crimean Sonnets*, a verse account of his journeys through the beautiful Crimean Peninsula, constitute the most perfect cycle of descriptive sonnets since du Bellay. *The Sonnets* of Adam Mickiewicz are given in the original Polish, in facing-page format, with English verse translations by Charles S. Kraszewski. Along with the entirety of the Crimean and Erotic Sonnets, other "loose" sonnets by Mickiewicz are included, which provide the reader with the most comprehensive collection to date of Mickiewicz's sonneteering. Fronted with a critical introduction, *The Sonnets* of Adam Mickiewicz also contain generous textual notes by the poet and the translator.

Buy it > www.glagoslav.com

The Mouseiad and other Mock Epics
by Ignacy Krasicki

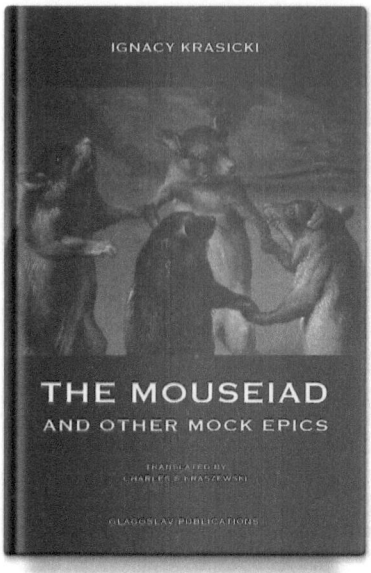

International brigades of mice and rats join forces to defend the rodents of Poland, threatened with extermination at the paws of cats favoured by the ancient ruler King Popiel, a sybaritic, cowardly ruler… The Hag of Discord incites a vicious rivalry between monastic orders, which only the good monks' common devotion to… fortified spirits… is able to allay… The present translation of the mock epics of Poland's greatest figure of the Enlightenment, Ignacy Krasicki, brings together the Mouseiad, the Monachomachia, and the Anti-monachomachia — a tongue-in-cheek 'retraction' of the former work by the author, criticised for so roundly (and effectively) satirising the faults of the Church, of which he himself was a prince. Krasicki towers over all forms of eighteenth-century literature in Poland like Voltaire, Swift, Pope, and LaFontaine all rolled into one. While his fables constitute his most well-known works of poetry, in the words of American comparatist Harold Segel, 'the good bishop's mock-epic poems […] are the most impressive examples of his literary gifts.' This English translation by Charles S. Kraszewski is rounded off by one of Krasicki's lesser-known works, The Chocim War, the poet's only foray into the genre of the serious, Vergilian epic.

Buy it > www.glagoslav.com

A Burglar of the Better Sort
by Tytus Czyżewski

The history of Poland, since the eighteenth century, has been marked by an almost unending struggle for survival. From 1795 through 1945, she was partitioned four times by her stronger neighbours, most of whom were intent on suppressing if not eradicating Polish culture. It is not surprising, then, that much of the great literature written in modern Poland has been politically and patriotically engaged. Yet there is a second current as well, that of authors devoted above all to the craft of literary expression, creating 'art for art's sake,' and not as a didactic national service. Such a poet is Tytus Czyżewski, one of the chief, and most interesting, literary figures of the twentieth century. Growing to maturity in the benign Austrian partition of Poland, and creating most of his works in the twenty-year window of authentic Polish independence stretching between the two world wars, Czyżewski is an avant-garde poet, dramatist and painter who popularised the new approach to poetry established in France by Guillaume Apollinaire, and was to exert a marked influence on such multi-faceted artists as Tadeusz Kantor.

Buy it > www.glagoslav.com

Dear Reader,

Thank you for purchasing this book.

We at Glagoslav Publications are glad to welcome you, and hope that you find our books to be a source of knowledge and inspiration.

We want to show the beauty and depth of the Slavic region to everyone looking to expand their horizon and learn something new about different cultures, different people, and we believe that with this book we have managed to do just that.

Now that you've got to know us, we want to get to know you. We value communication with our readers and want to hear from you! We offer several options:

– Join our Book Club on Goodreads, Library Thing and Shelfari, and receive special offers and information about our giveaways;

– Share your opinion about our books on Amazon, Barnes & Noble, Waterstones and other bookstores;

– Join us on Facebook and Twitter for updates on our publications and news about our authors;

– Visit our site www.glagoslav.com to check out our Catalogue and subscribe to our Newsletter.

Glagoslav Publications is getting ready to release a new collection and planning some interesting surprises — stay with us to find out!

Glagoslav Publications
Email: contact@glagoslav.com

Glagoslav Publications Catalogue

- *The Time of Women* by Elena Chizhova
- *Andrei Tarkovsky: The Collector of Dreams* by Layla Alexander-Garrett
- *Andrei Tarkovsky - A Life on the Cross* by Lyudmila Boyadzhieva
- *Sin* by Zakhar Prilepin
- *Hardly Ever Otherwise* by Maria Matios
- *Khatyn* by Ales Adamovich
- *The Lost Button* by Irene Rozdobudko
- *Christened with Crosses* by Eduard Kochergin
- *The Vital Needs of the Dead* by Igor Sakhnovsky
- *The Sarabande of Sara's Band* by Larysa Denysenko
- *A Poet and Bin Laden* by Hamid Ismailov
- *Watching The Russians (Dutch Edition)* by Maria Konyukova
- *Kobzar* by Taras Shevchenko
- *The Stone Bridge* by Alexander Terekhov
- *Moryak* by Lee Mandel
- *King Stakh's Wild Hunt* by Uladzimir Karatkevich
- *The Hawks of Peace* by Dmitry Rogozin
- *Harlequin's Costume* by Leonid Yuzefovich
- *Depeche Mode* by Serhii Zhadan
- *The Grand Slam and other stories (Dutch Edition)* by Leonid Andreev
- *METRO 2033 (Dutch Edition)* by Dmitry Glukhovsky
- *METRO 2034 (Dutch Edition)* by Dmitry Glukhovsky
- *A Russian Story* by Eugenia Kononenko
- *Herstories, An Anthology of New Ukrainian Women Prose Writers*
- *The Battle of the Sexes Russian Style* by Nadezhda Ptushkina
- *A Book Without Photographs* by Sergey Shargunov
- *Down Among The Fishes* by Natalka Babina
- *disUNITY* by Anatoly Kudryavitsky
- *Sankya* by Zakhar Prilepin
- *Wolf Messing* by Tatiana Lungin
- *Good Stalin* by Victor Erofeyev
- *Solar Plexus* by Rustam Ibragimbekov

- *Don't Call me a Victim!* by Dina Yafasova
- *Poetin (Dutch Edition)* by Chris Hutchins and Alexander Korobko
- *A History of Belarus* by Lubov Bazan
- *Children's Fashion of the Russian Empire* by Alexander Vasiliev
- *Empire of Corruption - The Russian National Pastime* by Vladimir Soloviev
- *Heroes of the 90s: People and Money. The Modern History of Russian Capitalism*
- *Fifty Highlights from the Russian Literature (Dutch Edition)* by Maarten Tengbergen
- *Bajesvolk (Dutch Edition)* by Mikhail Khodorkovsky
- *Tsarina Alexandra's Diary (Dutch Edition)*
- *Myths about Russia* by Vladimir Medinskiy
- *Boris Yeltsin: The Decade that Shook the World* by Boris Minaev
- *A Man Of Change: A study of the political life of Boris Yeltsin*
- *Sberbank: The Rebirth of Russia's Financial Giant* by Evgeny Karasyuk
- *To Get Ukraine* by Oleksandr Shyshko
- *Asystole* by Oleg Pavlov
- *Gnedich* by Maria Rybakova
- *Marina Tsvetaeva: The Essential Poetry*
- *Multiple Personalities* by Tatyana Shcherbina
- *The Investigator* by Margarita Khemlin
- *The Exile* by Zinaida Tulub
- *Leo Tolstoy: Flight from paradise* by Pavel Basinsky
- *Moscow in the 1930* by Natalia Gromova
- *Laurus (Dutch edition)* by Evgenij Vodolazkin
- *Prisoner* by Anna Nemzer
- *The Crime of Chernobyl: The Nuclear Goulag* by Wladimir Tchertkoff
- *Alpine Ballad* by Vasil Bykau
- *The Complete Correspondence of Hryhory Skovoroda*
- *The Tale of Aypi* by Ak Welsapar
- *Selected Poems* by Lydia Grigorieva
- *The Fantastic Worlds of Yuri Vynnychuk*

- *The Garden of Divine Songs and Collected Poetry of Hryhory Skovoroda*
- *Adventures in the Slavic Kitchen: A Book of Essays with Recipes*
- *Seven Signs of the Lion* by Michael M. Naydan
- *Forefathers' Eve* by Adam Mickiewicz
- *One-Two* by Igor Eliseev
- *Girls, be Good* by Bojan Babić
- *Time of the Octopus* by Anatoly Kucherena
- *The Grand Harmony* by Bohdan Ihor Antonych
- *The Selected Lyric Poetry Of Maksym Rylsky*
- *The Shining Light* by Galymkair Mutanov
- *The Frontier: 28 Contemporary Ukrainian Poets - An Anthology*
- *Acropolis: The Wawel Plays* by Stanisław Wyspiański
- *Contours of the City* by Attyla Mohylny
- *Conversations Before Silence: The Selected Poetry of Oles Ilchenko*
- *The Secret History of my Sojourn in Russia* by Jaroslav Hašek
- *Mirror Sand: An Anthology of Russian Short Poems*
- *Maybe We're Leaving* by Jan Balaban
- *Death of the Snake Catcher* by Ak Welsapar
- *A Brown Man in Russia* by Vijay Menon
- *Hard Times* by Ostap Vyshnia
- *The Flying Dutchman* by Anatoly Kudryavitsky
- *Nikolai Gumilev's Africa* by Nikolai Gumilev
- *Combustions* by Srđan Srdić
- *The Sonnets* by Adam Mickiewicz
- *Dramatic Works* by Zygmunt Krasiński
- *Four Plays* by Juliusz Słowacki
- *Little Zinnobers* by Elena Chizhova
- *We Are Building Capitalism! Moscow in Transition 1992-1997*
- *The Nuremberg Trials* by Alexander Zvyagintsev
- *The Hemingway Game* by Evgeni Grishkovets
- *A Flame Out at Sea* by Dmitry Novikov
- *Jesus' Cat* by Grig
- *Want a Baby and Other Plays* by Sergei Tretyakov
- *I Mikhail Bulgakov: The Life and Times* by Marietta Chudakova
- *Leonardo's Handwriting* by Dina Rubina

- *A Burglar of the Better Sort* by Tytus Czyżewski
- *The Mouseiad and other Mock Epics* by Ignacy Krasicki
- *Ravens before Noah* by Susanna Harutyunyan
- *An English Queen and Stalingrad* by Natalia Kulishenko
- *Point Zero* by Narek Malian
- *Absolute Zero* by Artem Chekh
- *Olanda* by Rafał Wojasiński
- *Robinsons* by Aram Pachyan
- *The Monastery* by Zakhar Prilepin
- *The Selected Poetry of Bohdan Rubchak: Songs of Love, Songs of Death, Songs of the Moon*
- *The Lawyer from Lychakiv Street* by Andriy Kokotiukha
- *Mebet* by Alexander Grigorenko
- *Where Was the Angel Going?* by Jan Balaban
- *The Code of Civilization* by Vyacheslav Nikonov
- *The Orchestra* by Vladimir Gonik
- *Everyday Stories* by Mima Mihajlović
- *Subterranean Fire* by Natalka Bilotserkivets
- *Duel* by Borys Antonenko-Davydovych

More coming soon...

www.ingramcontent.com/pod-product-compliance
Lightning Source LLC
Chambersburg PA
CBHW021428080526
44588CB00009B/459